A FEW

SECONDS

OF PANIC

ALSO BY STEFAN FATSIS

Wild and Outside
Word Freak

A FEW SECONDS OF PANIC

A 5-FOOT-8,

170-POUND,

43-YEAR-OLD

SPORTSWRITER

PLAYS IN THE NFL

STEFAN FATSIS

THE PENGUIN PRESS | NEW YORK | 2008

THE PENGUIN PRESS
Published by the Penguin Group
Penguin Group (USA) Inc., 375 Hudson Street, New York, New York 10014, U.S.A. •
Penguin Group (Canada), 90 Eglinton Avenue East, Suite 700, Toronto, Ontario, Canada
M4P 2Y3 (a division of Pearson Penguin Canada Inc.) • Penguin Books Ltd, 80 Strand,
London WC2R 0RL, England • Penguin Ireland, 25 St. Stephen's Green, Dublin 2, Ireland
(a division of Penguin Books Ltd) • Penguin Books Australia Ltd, 250 Camberwell Road,
Camberwell, Victoria 3124, Australia (a division of Pearson Australia Group Pty Ltd) •
Penguin Books India Pvt Ltd, 11 Community Centre, Panchsheel Park, New Delhi–110 017,
India • Penguin Group (NZ), 67 Apollo Drive, Rosedale, North Shore 0632, New Zealand
(a division of Pearson New Zealand Ltd) • Penguin Books (South Africa) (Pty) Ltd,
24 Sturdee Avenue, Rosebank, Johannesburg 2196, South Africa

Penguin Books Ltd, Registered Offices:
80 Strand, London WC2R 0RL, England

First published in 2008 by The Penguin Press,
a member of Penguin Group (USA) Inc.

1 3 5 7 9 10 8 6 4 2

Copyright © Stefan Fatsis, 2008
All rights reserved

Library of Congress Cataloging-in-Publication Data

Fatsis, Stefan.
A few seconds of panic : a 5-foot-8, 170-pound, 43-year-old sportswriter
plays in the NFL / Stefan Fatsis.
p. cm.
Includes bibliographical references.
ISBN: 978-1-59420-178-3
1. Fatsis, Stefan. 2. Sportswriters—United States—Anecdotes. 3. Football players—
United States—Anecdotes. 4. National Football League. I. Title.
GV742.42.F565A2   2008
070.449796092—dc22
2008002919

Printed in the United States of America
Designed by Stephanie Huntwork

For Melissa and Chloe

CONTENTS

A FEW

SECONDS

OF PANIC

Martin Gramatica's Dad

push through a set of orange double doors. Sunlight pours onto my face. My pupils dilate. The Kentucky bluegrass is gorgeous, not a blade out of place. The yard lines and hash marks are whiter than a sheet of copy paper. Glimmering navy blue helmets dangle from the players' arms like purses. The goalposts stand like fluorescent yellow glow sticks held aloft on a pitch-black night. I've seen perfectly manicured grass and new uniforms and towering uprights before—millions upon millions of frames plastered to my brain during a lifetime of sports watching—but these images are Technicolor, high-def, hyperreal.

I'm playing in the NFL.

It is the last day of May in 2006, and the first day of a three-day "team camp" at the Paul D. Bowlen Memorial Broncos Centre, the suburban compound where the Denver Broncos train. Take away the blue and orange border on the roofline and the place could be mistaken for the headquarters of a biotech company or an aviation parts supplier or any of the other businesses in a bland stretch of office parks not far from where gold was first discovered in Colorado in 1858. I've been invited by team owner Pat Bowlen, son of the building's namesake, to join the Broncos as a kicker.

Spotting me in the locker room earlier, one player had asked another, "Which Gramatica is this one?" I think it was a joke, although it's conceivable I've been mistaken for one of the small, eccentric Gramatica brothers, the modern stereotype of the kicker as someone worthy of disdain, derision, and disgust. As in, "Get the fuck out of my locker, *kicker,*" which is how the Broncos' veteran starting quarterback, Jake Plummer, will greet me, with a smirk, when I sit in his space one day talking to a teammate.

On the field, I stop to greet Plummer and two other quarterbacks. One is the backup, Bradlee Van Pelt, whose New York Giants linebacker father, Brad, I watched as a kid. The other is the fourth-string Preston Parsons, a "camp arm" in NFL parlance, who is needed to help execute the voluminous passes and handoffs required during the summer but who has little chance of making the team. Like most of the players I'm nervously meeting, the quarterbacks, still the cool kids they were in high school, laugh when I tell the story of how I came to be standing on the field with them rather than on the sidelines with the klatch of reporters permitted to observe the first ten minutes of practice. But the quarterbacks also seem to think the presence of a writer—at least one sanctioned by the owner—is kind of cool. Van Pelt, a barrel-chested blond with deep-set eyes, tells me he suspected I wasn't an "actual player."

"Oh, yeah?" I say. "What gave it away?"

Was it my Gramatica height? My sub-Gramatica weight? Or the gray hair mounting a hostile takeover of my temples? Of the ninety or so players attending the camp, not a single one was alive when Cyprus-born Armenian Garo Yepremian helped usher in the era of the weirdo soccer-style kicker with the Detroit Lions in 1966. After converting a meaningless extra point, Yepremian ran off the field with arms raised. When his teammate Alex Karras asked him what the hell he was doing, Yepremian shouted, "I keek a touchdown!" a line that would be used to denigrate a generation of kickers.

The blast of an airhorn sends the players trotting from the full-size field parallel to the main building to an adjacent full-size field. I don't know what the horn signifies, so I do what I'd planned to do: follow the kickers. There are three: punter Paul Ernster, who was drafted by the Broncos a year earlier but tore an ACL during the season; Tyler Fredrickson, a punter and placekicker who graduated from the University of California, Berkeley, in 2004 and was cut by the Broncos last summer; and Jeff Williams, a rookie punter from a small college in Colorado. The incumbent veteran starters, placekicker Jason Elam and punter Todd Sauerbrun, aren't at this camp. They've been excused by head coach Mike Shanahan because they're incumbent veteran starters.

"How many kickers do we need?" one player shouts as we jog past. Another spots me. "It's Martin Gramatica's dad!" he says.

When we arrive on the far field, Tyler Fredrickson helpfully explains that we're assembling to stretch before practice. The players arrange themselves in ten or twelve rows of eight or ten across. The offense, and we kickers, wear white mesh practice jerseys with navy blue numbers trimmed in orange. The defense wears blue jerseys with white numbers trimmed in orange. There seems to be some organization by position: quarterbacks near the front to the left of center, defensive backs by the right sideline, linemen toward the back of the pack. The four kickers cluster on a rear line. Facing the team is number 56, Al Wilson, the captain and starting middle linebacker. The mood is carefree, the background noise light, male chatter and laughter.

"You know they're going to call you up," Tyler says.

Huh? Call me up where?

"Welcome to training camp!" Al Wilson bellows. "Today we have a special guest—Mr. Stefan Fatsis." He says it like I'm the next contestant on *American Idol*. I met Wilson briefly in the locker room this morning, and he pronounces my last name correctly (the way it's spelled) but Europeanizes my first name, saying STEH-fahn instead of STEH-fin. "He's from the *Wall Street Journal*! He's going to write about us! And now he's going to come up here—and break it down!"

I'm going to *what*? I realize that I've been summoned to stand in front of a team of professional football players, but to do what I'm not certain. Tyler nudges me forward. I bow my head to one side and smile, trying to look unflappable, jocklike, as I jog slowly up my row. Ninety heads swivel as one. Rhythmic clapping collapses into applause.

I high-five Wilson and take some initiative, restarting the synchronized clapping. The players join in, whooping and shouting at the rookie writer kicker. They are clearly amused. But clapping is also clearly not all that I'm supposed to do up here.

"Gimme a dance move!" Wilson barks.

Growing up in a predominantly white suburb of New York City in the unhip 1970s, I was a small and insecure kid who would no sooner dance before a crowd than challenge the school bully to fight. As an adult, I graduated from the self- and genre-mocking school of dance. Now, with behemoths lined up before me like troops awaiting orders, I realize that I need to do something with the rest of my body, fast. I perform a few awkward, side-to-side steps. The players eat it up. Plummer stands directly in front of me. I ask him what to do next.

"Give us a move!" he says, his long blond hair bobbing to the beat of the clapping.

For no discernible reason—maybe my body was invaded by aliens—I leap into the air with legs and arms splayed into an X, like a cheerleader, perhaps, or a professional wrestler jumping off the ropes. My first feeling upon landing is relief to not have ruptured a ligament. Then embarrassment over what I have just done. But the performance seems to have worked: a chorus of wild applause, a sea of laughter, with me, at me, whatever. I'm relieved it's over. I high-five Plummer and every player down the line as I return to the womb of my fellow kickers.

"That was awesome," Tyler says when I return. "You're in."

1

I'm No Plimpton

When the writer George Plimpton reported to Detroit Lions training camp in July 1963 to document his experience as a "last-string quarterback," the National Football League consisted of fourteen teams, eleven of them east of the Mississippi River. The league had just awarded its first national television contract, to CBS for $4.65 million a year, and had just formed a licensing division, National Football League Properties. The operational details of professional football were mostly a mystery to the handful of reporters who covered the sport, its local pockets of fans, and the general public.

The modern NFL, by contrast, is a thirty-two-team, more-than-$6-billion-a-year cultural institution. Its TV contracts, with six broadcast, cable, and satellite networks, command more than $3 billion annually. The tiniest details of the league are observed, documented, recorded, deconstructed, and shared with the world around the clock by a boundless assemblage of media and fans.

I was born three months before Plimpton went to camp. The book that resulted from that summer, *Paper Lion,* was a journalistic marker, a work that helped shape how people thought not only about sports but about sportswriting, participatory journalism, and literary journalism. Almost innocently, Plimpton seemed to ask, a few years before his Harvard buddy Bobby Kennedy actually did, "Why not?" and went where most reporters had never imagined possible.

Plimpton's exploits were inspired by Paul Gallico, a sportswriter for

New York's *Daily News* in the 1920s who boxed Jack Dempsey so he could understand what it felt like. By the time Plimpton gained entrée into the NFL, he had started, with friends including the writers William Styron and Peter Matthiessen, the *Paris Review.* For an article in *Sports Illustrated,* he'd had his nose bloodied by light heavyweight champion Archie Moore. He'd pitched in an exhibition of Major League Baseball all-stars and written a book about that. And he would go on to do plenty more, playing goalie for the Boston Bruins, guard for the Boston Celtics, and sleigh bells for the New York Philharmonic during Mahler's Fourth Symphony. In the former tenement on the Upper East Side where he lived for years, Plimpton hosted soirees that cross-pollinated stars of the literary, athletic, political, and social firmaments.

Lord knows I'm no Plimpton. He was the tall, *Mayflower*-descended son of the founder of a white-shoe law firm. I'm the short, first-generation son of a Greek ship captain. By virtue certainly of the privileges he enjoyed but more of the personality that allowed him to capitalize on them, Plimpton was a presence. "He looked for ways in which he could make himself a ridiculous figure, and not only on the football field, but in all walks of life," Matthiessen once said. "That made him a great storyteller."

Still, I doubt that if Plimpton materialized as a young writer today he could pull off what he did in the late 1950s, '60s, and '70s. Those were times when celebrity sportswriters like Plimpton and Dick Schaap could forge deep, personal bonds with a Muhammad Ali or a Joe Namath and enjoy unguarded conversation at the same gatherings. Athletes today are weary of the media invasion, schooled to handle it with bromides and banalities, and generally uncurious about its practices and provenances. Breaching the levee that separates Reporter and Jock is more difficult now.

Plimpton began *Paper Lion* with a declaration: "I decided finally to pack the football." Those seven words quickly established the author's Everymanhood. The message was that the workings of pro football are such a mystery that training camp very well might be BYOB, bring your own ball. "The Detroit Lions officials had not sent me the sort of list one remembered from boys' camp—that one should bring a pillow case, a mattress cover, a flashlight, a laundry bag, etc."

Forty-plus years later, such naïveté isn't plausible. We are routinely escorted inside the locker stalls and medicine cabinets, the Armani-stuffed closets and Bose-loaded Hummers of today's professional athletes. We are fed an endless cycle of sports news and blather, in print, on television, on talk radio, on the Internet. Every fan is a columnist, every columnist an expert, every expert a media star. In NFL equipment rooms, six-packs of official game balls are stacked floor to ceiling like cordwood. I pay $74.99 for one at retail. I won't pack it.

Plimpton didn't prepare to become a football player. His training consisted mainly of flinging a Spalding ball into his couch or tossing it alone in Central Park. He was the curious writer juxtaposing his glorious ineptitude against the profound skills of the pros. As a comic device, this worked well in the 1960s, when little was known about how a sports franchise worked, and when the financial, social, and athletic gap between pros and Joes could still be bridged. Plimpton's Lions were big and strong and fast, but they didn't stand out in a crowd as do today's improbably massive guards and tight ends and linebackers. Hell, those guys had off-season jobs.

Plimpton wrote that he wanted to play "to see how one got along and what happened." We know what would happen today. There are almost no jobs left in sports in which someone with no advanced experience, nothing beyond high school, could make even a marginally credible showing. Baseball? Good luck hitting a back-door slider. Basketball? The pace is too quick. Same for soccer. And we know how a modern Plimpton would get along at quarterback: He would be hurt, possibly badly. In 1963, the average defensive tackle weighed 260 pounds. Today he checks in at 307. Oh, and he runs the 40-yard dash in 4.8 seconds.

So I twist the Plimptonian proposition. Can I learn one very specific athletic skill? Can I overcome obvious shortcomings—body type, musculature, age, the missing thousands of hours of repetition and observation that transform athletes into "experts"—to do well enough to at least blend in? I embrace the idea of dressing up denial in the cloak of work.

Not because I daydream about throwing a game-winning touchdown pass in the Super Bowl but rather because, like millions of men my age and temperament, I daydream about one last moment of glory on a field, any field.

Like Plimpton, I have never played football competitively, excluding a spot on the Prospect Hill Elementary School touch-football team. In the fifth grade, I intercepted a pass and, with nothing but open space between me and the end zone, slipped and fell. I didn't weigh enough to pad up for Pop Warner. But I did play high-school soccer, not badly for 1976 to 1980 but badly enough to recognize that I had no chance of making my Division I college team. I played intramurals instead, and then, in my thirties, picked up the game again in indoor leagues in New York City.

So there is one job for which I figure I am as qualified as any writer: NFL kicker. Today's average placekicker stands six foot two and weighs 200 pounds. Some, like 255-pound Sebastian Janikowski of the Oakland Raiders, are bigger than linemen and linebackers in Plimpton's day. But not all kickers are yes-sir large. In early 2005, when I begin my undertaking, I am, at five foot eight and 160 pounds, as tall as and just ten pounds lighter than the two smallest placekickers in the NFL the previous season, Martin Gramatica, who was with the Tampa Bay Buccaneers and Indianapolis Colts, and Paul Edinger of the Minnesota Vikings. If I make it to a camp that summer, I will be six years older than Plimpton was when he was a Lion but well inside the outer boundaries of the life expectancy of an NFL kicker. I am just one year (and nineteen days) older than the league's oldest placekicker, John Carney of the New Orleans Saints. If Gary Anderson, who has just retired, gets a phone call, I'd be number two by four full years. If his fellow almost-AARP member Morten Andersen straps on a single-bar helmet again, I'd slip to number three.

All of which is to say that I think I can—if I grow my upper body and legs—come close to fitting in on an NFL team. I could lope out to practice with the kickers and, gray hair hidden by a helmet, not immediately be mistaken for a trespasser. When the ball is snapped, strength, speed, technique, and accuracy are what matter—and those attributes can surely be developed. Given my soccer background, I know I won't flip onto my back when approaching the ball, like Charlie Brown. I know I can kick a (soccer) ball a reasonable distance, and rather hard. I know I'm not overweight or athletically inept. I know, in short, that I can learn to become a kicker—not an NFL-caliber kicker, perhaps, but a credible one, as good on my very best day as a pro on a middling one.

To have any chance of tricking a team into letting me do a Plimpton, I need to behave like an undrafted collegian searching desperately for a tryout. I need to flood the market with the journalistic equivalent of a highlight reel and fawning cover letter. Those videotapes and DVDs usually wind up in a box in the corner of some assistant coach's office. But I've got contacts. Writing about the sports industry for the past decade, I've interviewed, pestered, and befriended numerous NFL team owners and executives, plus league honchos from the commissioner, Paul Tagliabue, down. The gadget in my playbook is that I'm a nonsportswriter sportswriter. I'll be telling a goofy and high-minded tale of life inside the modern NFL, not ripping the quarterback for an errant pass on third and 10. I, Kicker will be good for the league.

I'll need the NFL's seal of approval, so I run the idea past Brian McCarthy, the league's business public-relations man. I've known Brian for years. He's slipped me scoops and arranged interviews on multibillion-dollar television contracts and sponsorship deals, on disputes with the players' union and intramural battles over how much revenue teams should share, on Janet Jackson's exposed breast at a Super Bowl halftime show. Brian operates with the sober caution and moral certitude required of successful employees at market-crushing cartels.

Brian knows my work as a reporter and author. But he also knows how old I am, how small I am, and that I've had a little, um, major reconstructive surgery on both knees (torn ACLs, indoor soccer, ages thirty-three and thirty-eight). So when I finish my rambling spiel— "modern Plimpton . . . it's been forty years . . . league has changed so much . . . want to be a kicker . . . you know I played soccer . . . fans would love it . . ."—there's a long silence between my cubicle at the *Journal* a few blocks from the White House and Brian's small office on the seventeenth floor of the NFL's Park Avenue headquarters. No verbal cartwheels tumble down the line, which I chalk up to the sober caution part of Brian's job description rather than disbelief at what I've just requested. Brian promises to run it by his bosses.

A few weeks later, I get my answer. "If you can find a team that'll let you do it," Brian says, "we won't stand in your way." As it happens, I'm scheduled to meet with the president of the New York Jets. After discussing the team's (ultimately failed) effort to build a $2 billion stadium on the west side of Manhattan, I pop the question. Jay Cross says that he, personally, likes the idea. He's also confident that Jets coach Herman Edwards won't. "I already know the first thing he'll ask me," Cross says. "'How does this help us win the Super Bowl?'"

As soon as the words are out of his mouth, I realize that my biggest obstacle won't be my age or my lack of experience. It will be the militaristic culture and win-or-else paranoia that govern every NFL team. Football has managed over time to control its product and its message more tightly than any other sport. Access to players is infrequent and rigorously monitored. During regular-season practices, only a few meaningless minutes of stretching are open to reportorial scrutiny. Locker rooms are off-limits for all but a prescribed handful of minutes per week, and players have the option of vanishing if they choose. All of which helps explain why the NFL is sometimes called the No Fun League— and why no writer since Plimpton has managed to suit up for a team.

So while Cross pledges to ask Edwards, my reporter radar tells me he won't, so ridiculous is the demand not only to be allowed inside but to actually play. Subsequent calls to the Jets go unreturned. I press on, evaluating teams based on media friendliness, franchise appeal—Green Bay Packers, yes; Jacksonville Jaguars, no—and, mostly, how well I know their executives. I contact my hometown Washington Redskins, the Dallas Cowboys, the Pittsburgh Steelers, the New England Patriots, and the Philadelphia Eagles. All of them quickly pass, usually because the head coach doesn't or won't like the idea. The Packers seem like a natural fit. Players riding kids' bicycles during training camp. The legend of Vince Lombardi. Midwestern hospitality. The team's chief operating officer, John Jones, a helpful source on business matters, breaks the news to me: too much potential "intrusion."

Indianapolis Colts president Bill Polian doesn't respond to the snail-mail letter the team's flack has me send. The St. Louis Rams, whom I recently featured in a front-page article about how NFL players don't wear as many pads as they used to, don't get back to me, either. The Chicago Bears have one of the most reclusive ownerships (the family of NFL founding father George Halas) and tightest-lipped front offices in football, but after a string of lousy seasons I figure they might be looking to boost their image. "It's just not who we are," a PR guy says dismissively. Even the Seattle Seahawks turn me down. Because, heaven knows, the Seattle Seahawks just get too much national media.

The brightest hope turns out to be the second closest to home: the Baltimore Ravens. The team and its coach, Brian Billick, are, by NFL standards, media sluts. The summer after winning the Super Bowl in 2001, Billick allowed HBO access to training camp. He let a writer chronicle the 2004 season. Over breakfast at the Ravens' new suburban headquarters, PR chief Kevin Byrne and club president Dick Cass explain that Billick welcomes scrutiny because he believes it's part of the game. They instantly understand what I want to do—not just the embedded journalist aspect, but the midlife kicking crisis part, too. When Billick sits down nearby, Byrne says, "Brian, I want you to meet your next kicker," and I'm ecstatic. But months pass without an invitation to the 2005 training camp. The timing isn't right, Byrne says, but next year could work.

So that fall I attend a Ravens game against the Cleveland Browns and study veteran kicker Matt Stover from afar. I notice that he's on the field before all the other players, ninety minutes before kickoff. I notice that he inspects the field from all angles, gauging wind and distance. I notice that he practices kicks, first with a tripod contraption that keeps the ball upright and then with human snappers and holders, in five-yard intervals from the right hash mark, the left hash mark, and the center of the field, from distances of less than 30 yards to more than 50. I notice that Cleveland kicker Phil Dawson kicks one from the far 45-yard line—that is, a 65-yard field goal—and clears the crossbar with room to spare.

After the game, I find Stover in the locker room. He is a lean, normal-sized human being—five foot eleven, 178 pounds—with the enthusiasm of a motivational speaker and the earnestness of a preacher. As he spritzes deodorant and slips on a pair of jeans, we talk about the psychology of kicking—I ask how he recovered from missing three field goals in the first game of the season—and about the tight fraternity of kickers. He gives me his cell phone number and promises to help me get ready for training camp.

Another kicker, Doug Brien of the Bears, comps me a membership to his kicking Web site, which features training regimens, videotapes, inspirational advice, and a bustling message board. When Chicago visits Washington, I track down Brien in the cramped and overheated visitors' locker room.

"There are probably a hundred guys who physically can do the job," he says, loosely fastening a silvery blue tie on a spread-collar shirt. "But the ones who can make it day in, day out are the ones who can do the job." Brien says he meditates every morning at 6 a.m. He works through a range of concentration drills and relaxation exercises, some of which he has posted online. I'd already printed his "Relaxation Script," which he recommends recording and listening to before bed while lying comfortably on the floor, without a pillow. A climactic excerpt:

> You are totally relaxed. Your leg is twitching—waiting to strike the ball. Your head, though, is perfectly calm. You are perfectly in control. Nothing can make you lose this focus. Anyone trying to make you lose your focus just intensifies it because you know you will make the kick. You run out on the field with total confidence as if you own it. You line up your spot. You take your two or three steps back, two steps over and assume your position. At this point, no matter what

the wind is doing, you feel like it's blowing slightly behind you, always helping your ball. As you approach the ball, your eyes are focused on the exact spot where you want to make contact. Your head is down and torso upright. Your leg and foot are locked and pointed. Your hips will come around, just enough to give you enough power because you never kick the ball short. The ball always goes as far as it needs to go. Your leg will follow through straight down the line helping the ball to go straight down your desired path. The ball will go straight and high.

"Coaches will say, 'Just go out and kick,'" Brien tells me. "But there's a million things going on. You have to learn how to focus down and shut all that out. That's the art of kicking. Once the ball leaves your foot, you don't control it. That's why I read all these Zen books."

"Like what?" I ask.

Brien unzips a black wheelie bag and extracts a copy of *Zen in the Art of Archery,* a slender 1953 volume by Eugen Herrigel, a German philosophy professor who studied with Japanese archery masters for six years as a path to understanding Zen Buddhism. I'll have to develop more than my quads to pull this off.

As players file past us collecting boxed dinners en route to the team bus, I update Brien on my prospects for attending an NFL camp. The Bears' punter, Brad Maynard, has been listening to our conversation from the next locker.

"Dude," he says to me, "I'll give you a thousand dollars if a team lets you go to training camp."

The Ravens finish the 2005 season with a 6-10 record. Dick Cass, the team president, tells me that access and exposure will be reduced the next season. "In that environment, it just wouldn't work," he says of my plan. But Cass gentlemanly offers to help find a replacement. He promises to speak with San Francisco 49ers head coach Mike Nolan, a former assis-

2

Chippin' and Skippin'

Two days later, on a hot and humid, Al-Gore-is-right spring morning, I drive to Edison High School in Alexandria, Virginia, just outside of Washington. I lace up the tatterdemalion Umbro soccer cleats that I've had since college, the right toe unglued from the sole. A high-school track meet is in progress on and around the football field, so Paul Woodside and I walk down a hill to a rutted baseball diamond.

I had begun looking for a kicking coach the previous fall. A Google search for "football kicking camp" yielded 1.1 million hits. I read about the Ray Guy Academy, run by the famed Oakland Raiders punter from the 1970s and '80s. I learned that the Chris Boniol Kicking Camp, whose proprietor placekicked in the NFL for six seasons, is a "God-centered business." I found Doug Brien's kicking.com and a site run by the only kicking coach I'd heard of, Doug Blevins, who from a wheelchair has trained Super Bowl hero Adam Vinatieri of New England. Blevins has cerebral palsy.

But I cared less about pedigree than geography, which led me to 4th Down Sports of Springfield, Virginia, and the voice mail of Paul Woodside, director of high-school kicking and communications. "I love this!" Paul exclaimed when I described my plan to kick in the NFL, and I knew immediately that I had found my coach. The energy and playfulness in Paul's voice told me he wasn't some humorless football robot. He rambled about the loneliness of the long-distance kicker, about why placekicking (field goals and point after touchdowns) is superior to punting (booting the ball to the other team after the offense fails to get a first down), about the thrill of molding young kicking legs and minds. "This is my passion," he said. "I do everything else to pay bills." That everything else is delivering packages for UPS, a job he has held almost since he was one of the last players cut by the Buffalo Bills in 1985.

Paul invited me to a kicking camp in Virginia a few days later. I was older than some of the campers by almost thirty years. There I learned the basics of kicking. Where to position my left, plant foot (about a foot to the left of the ball). How to take a backswing (left knee slightly bent, upper body straight, left arm extended to the side for balance, right heel reaching back to the right buttock, right foot pointed and locked like Baryshnikov's). How to execute a proper downswing (snap the lower leg, keep the right foot locked and perpendicular to the body when striking the ball). How to finish the kick (straight at the goalposts).

I drew back awkwardly. My foot didn't lock. My hips didn't open. I lost my balance and stumbled to the side. Paul wasn't worried. Kicking is a reflex skill, he said. The goal is to learn the motion, repeat it correctly a zillion times, and "drive it into your subconscious." Soon enough, he promised, my plant would generate momentum and power, propelling my body forward. My right foot would explode through the ball. My foot and the ball would rocket upward toward the goalposts.

With the campers, Paul's technique was textbook *Dead Poets Society*: the quirky teacher asking mysterious questions of uncomfortable students who think themselves mute. When we spoke on the phone, Paul had suggested I watch the movie as a representation of the subculture of kicking. Observing him on the field, bopping on his toes, gesticulating wildly, I wondered whether he reached his young kickers the way Robin Williams did his beblazered prep-school students, and whether Paul, like the character played by Williams, was an outcast, too. "You've got to be obsessed with this," he told us. "You've got to have a great imagination. It's great to be a kicker."

At the end of the day, I asked Paul for an assessment of my potential. Even if I had none, I'm sure he wouldn't have said so, certain in a belief that he could mold me into a legitimate kicker. "We'll have you hitting some forties and fifties," Paul said, meaning 40- and 50-yard field goals.

"Really?" I replied in happy disbelief.

"Really."

Over the winter, at a private gym in Georgetown, I continued working with a personal trainer, Steve Kostorowski, who trains NBA and NHL players, as well as Washington lawyers, lobbyists, and stay-at-home moms, and had transformed me from a relatively sedentary desk monkey into someone in the best muscular and cardiovascular condition of his life. I attended a few sessions of an outdoor conditioning camp for kickers run by Paul. I banged my ankles trying to hoist a bent leg, rapidly and nonstop, over three-foot-high hurdles lined up fifteen in a row. Around a snow-covered football field, I dragged metal sideline benches connected to my upper body by a thick rubber harness.

But I have yet to kick a football through a set of goalposts under a coach's supervision. My meeting with Paul at Edison High School is the first time.

Paul's initial task is to convert me from soccer player to football place-kicker. Soccer players often kick on the run, surgically adjusting kicks for power, distance, placement, spin, and purpose: a long ball over the defense, a curving corner kick, a short pass hugging the ground. There's no time or need for a lengthy drawback or an extensive follow-through. Kicking a stationary football, by contrast, requires virtually the same motion every time, with maximum leg speed created by the drawback, downswing, and follow-through.

Paul squats and grabs my right foot. He twists it open, instep facing forward, sole flat on the ground. "This is a soccer pass," he says. To kick a football, my right foot still needs to be perpendicular to the rest of my body. But my toes need to be taut and pointed, my ankle locked with the heel slightly higher than the rest of the foot. In a long, elevated soccer kick, my foot (at a smaller angle to my body at contact than ninety degrees) would roll over to the right, crossing in front of my body. In a football kick, my foot should be almost at a right angle to my body when it alights. A soccer kick moves like a windshield wiper, a football kick like a pendulum.

Paul clusters a few balls, crouches, and grabs one. I place the front of my left foot just ahead of the pointy part of the standing ball and twelve inches to its left. My right toes nestle under the ball. As we did at the one-day camp in the fall, we start with no-steps: left foot planted next to the ball, draw right leg back, bring it down, stop. "Heel to butt, heel to butt, *thwap, thwap, thwap, thwap,*" Paul says, making me repeat the motion deliberately and precisely. Then he lets me kick the ball. The sound on impact is of a softly thrown baseball hitting a glove. The distance traveled is just a few yards.

"Awesome," Paul says. He tells me to make a divot to stand the ball and backs down the left-field foul line. He tells me to punch at the ball gently, then increase my leg speed and follow-through. He tells me to move my left foot forward. He tells me to keep my head behind the ball, rather than hunching over it. That was his problem when he kicked, Paul says. On impact, his body contracted and his momentum stopped, the force of his body driving down into his plant leg. "That's why I've got the limp," he says, explaining that over time, his left thigh bone was pushed about an inch and a half into his hip socket. When my foot strikes the ball, Paul says, my body should rise up, my left heel should lift off the ground, and my left foot should skip through toward the target. "It's just a flow," he says. "Like you're a navy plane on an aircraft carrier. I'll shut up now."

I take two big, mother-may-I steps backward, bringing my feet together after each one, like a toddler ascending stairs. I stop, realign, and move left. Then I realize I've forgotten whether the right foot should be behind the left or the left behind the right to begin the approach toward the ball. Three weeks to my NFL debut and I don't even know where to position my feet. Jesus. Paul pretends I'm not hopeless. "It's going to be left foot forward, right foot back. Right, left, kick," he says. "Some guys take a trigger step or jab step. Left, right, left, kick."

Before we try full-motion kicks, we do one-steps. One step back from the ball, one step to the left. Left foot back a step. Left foot to the plant. Kick.

"Nope. Soccer kick," Paul says when I'm done. "It's fine. It's going to take time. You're training your mind. Same way you did as a student in school. The hardest thing is retraining."

I take another kick and again apply too much crossover. Rather than criticize, though, Paul praises, saying it's clear I had a "wicked" soccer shot. His dime-store psychology works. Already he is the most patient, enthusiastic, and encouraging sports coach I've ever had. Almost everything I've done is, technically, wrong. But Paul doesn't mention the mistakes, only the corrective measures. The logo on his T-shirt reads "World Martial Arts Masters."

I take some swings at an imaginary ball. I exaggerate the drawback (heel to butt), exaggerate the locked ankle and pointed toe, and exaggerate the follow-through, landing authoritatively on my still-open right foot. Paul tinkers some more. I kick one over his head. He hobbles over and high-fives.

"What?" I say.

"You saw the ball?"

"I saw the ball."

We move on to a full, two-step approach and kick, the real thing. The remnants of years of crusty white chalk are visible in the dirt. I search for a patch of even grass. Paul recommends a slightly elevated clump to give the ball a boost. "Chippin' and skippin'," he says.

"Nope," I say after my first kick. The ball hasn't traveled very far, maybe 25 yards. It probably wouldn't have cleared the outstretched arm of a defensive lineman.

"What do you mean, no?" Paul says. "Look! Look! You got end-over-end rotation. And the ball's going right!"

"Which is better than going left," I say, perking up, because it means I didn't kick it soccer style.

"Exactly. Exactly. The hardest part and the most important part of any and every kick is the ball strike. Every time you're doing it you're training your brain. That's what's awesome. You're awesome."

I kick a dozen balls and we analyze each. My foot is still closing. My head is tilted down the right side of my body on impact, which is good, but my shoulders are moving forward with my head, bending my upper body forward, which is not good. My shoulders need to stay erect and level with the ground.

"You see a lot of guys who are right-footed who instead of chippin' and skippin', they dip their right shoulder. Their motto is dippin' and rippin'. From soccer they want to come in and rip the ball, when they don't need to."

I line up again.

Thwack.

"There's the visual and there's the feel, but did you notice the sound? The thud? The sound was nice."

I struck the ball on the right quarter panel, Paul explains with the observational precision of a diamond cutter. My foot was pointed on the downswing. "Your body's working its way up to here," he says, pointing to his head. "But this is awesome. This is awesome. I love your imagination. Because that's what this is. You have to see it before you can do it."

For the next hour, Paul works me hard. I do a long minute's worth of continual no-steps, drawing my foot back to my butt, kicking his hand two feet off the ground, and hopping forward as he backpedals down the field. Paul teaches me to kick off, and I boot one 50 yards. He sets up his video camera on the ground pointed at me. Trying to kick over the baseball backstop, I spray balls into the fence, off my ankle, to the right, into the fence again. Finally I connect on one. "These are thirty-yard field goals," Paul says. "You crushed that ball. That last ball you hit with authority. That was cool. That was awesome."

I notice a flock of geese squawking in a flyby, the whistle of birds hidden in the trees and bushes surrounding the field, the thrum of rush hour on the suburban roads, the public-address announcer calling runners to the starting line at the track meet up the hill. In the blue-gold twilight, sweat pours down my face and through my white shirt. I feel reborn. Not only like a teenager trying to make the team, but like an adult liberated from his daily routine and dropped into a new, demanding, alien one. I feel serious, not ridiculous, as if preparing to play football in the NFL were a perfectly rational undertaking for someone with no history, training, technical education, size, or youth.

I kick another one over the fence. And another. "I got my foot up to my butt!" I announce with pride. Over the fence again. I stop and laugh. As if it was that easy. Paul moves the "spot" back five yards, and I hit a dozen more balls. One resounds with an authoritative *thwack* and sails high and true over the backstop. "Look at that, look at that, look at that!" Paul says.

When darkness falls, we stop. I taste my sweat mixed with the dust of the field and the leather of the footballs. I'm panting. We stuff the balls into Paul's duffel bag. I guzzle a liter of Gatorade and eat a peanut-butter-and-chocolate energy bar. The lights illuminating the track meet blink off. Paul's energy and his goofy, childlike glee don't wane. We walk to the parking lot, but he seems in no hurry to leave.

Paul says that for the next three weeks I should just practice the motion: no-steps, no ball. I don't need to kick a lot. "The pro guys kick twenty balls and go play golf," he says. I need to imprint the reflex, and forget about the goalposts. That I have an interloper's few weeks to prepare instead of an athlete's lifetime is irrelevant. A little bit each day, Paul asserts, and I'll get there. Don't worry.

"You can't perform a subconscious skill like breathing by thinking about it," he says. "The minute you're thinking about it, it becomes a conscious skill. That's why the best practice you'll ever do is without a football. Because as soon as the football is there or an upright is there, there's tension. All of a sudden you lose your true focus for something that shouldn't even be a focus. It's a secondary issue.

"The biggest thing that happened tonight, was you overcoming your fears, overcoming your doubts."

It was a step, I reply. But it wasn't proof that I will kick 40-yard field goals in front of jacked-up teammates and delirious fans in Denver. I ask what makes him so sure.

"Because you did it before," Paul says, referring to my last writerly expedition, into the world of competitive Scrabble, where I did indeed become an expert-level player. "Because you're an athlete."

"Define athlete," I say.

"Somebody that plays out of his comfort zone. You've already mastered that. It's in your mind. It's not in your body. It's in your mind. That's where the power comes from. And when I say power I'm not talking about squatting six hundred pounds. I'm talking about the ability to overcome obstacles. Who kicked down there tonight? That wasn't me. That wasn't me. I have it on tape."

Paul's mind-over-reality optimism is flattering. But I still find it hard to believe that I will be even marginally competent in three weeks. And that's disappointing, because in the three o'clock in the morning of my soul, I don't want to be a writer embedding with the Denver Broncos. I want to be a Denver Bronco.

Paul Woodside was born in 1963 and began kicking footballs five years later. At home in Falls Church, Virginia, he would kick between two oak trees and over a telephone wire. Paul imitated the NFL's early soccer-style kickers: Garo Yepremian, Jan Stenerud of Norway, the Hungary-born Gogolak brothers, Pete and Charlie. He kicked as twilight turned to night, as windshields cracked, as sneakers fell apart.

Paul didn't have many friends. He stuttered badly, unable to talk in class or order a Big Mac. Kicking a football became his escape, and his hope. "I didn't have anything in my life," he tells me. "I would spend eight hours a day kicking." One summer in high school, Paul kicked more than ten thousand balls, or nearly two hundred a day. By graduation, he had kicked a football more than one hundred thousand times, far more "reps"—repetitions—than all but the oldest kickers in the NFL.

At the time, few people were qualified to teach soccer-style kicking, then known as "sidewinding." In 1972, Pete Gogolak wrote a book called *Kicking the Football Soccer Style,* but Paul hadn't read it. Kicking coaches who predated the foreign invasion clung to the belief that the toe was the way to go. One of them was Edward J. Storey, a high-school guidance counselor known as "Doc" because he had a graduate degree in engineering. Storey was one of the first people to study the physics of kicking; he conducted a clinic on the exotic art at the world's fair in New York City in 1940. In 1971—when Garo Yepremian led the NFL in field-goal percentage for a second straight season—Storey wrote in his book *Secrets of Kicking the Football* that, while soccer style had "come into vogue," he was "sure" toe kicking was better.

In the summer of 1976, Paul attended a three-day kicking camp at Widener College near Philadelphia. Paul doesn't remember receiving much technical instruction, only that the campers kicked a lot. He had never heard of Doc Storey, who ran the camp. But he was told that the coach was a kicking genius. While counselors worked with the young kickers, the septuagenarian Storey, hobbled by arthritis, motored around the fields in a golf cart.

On the last day of camp, each kicker received two black-and-white Polaroids of his kicks, eight frames per kick. In them, Paul is a skinny teenager, topless and in short shorts, white tube socks emerging from white cleats and rising to the knees, one thick stripe surrounded by two thin ones—unmistakably 1970s. In the first frame of one picture, Paul's right leg is about two feet behind the ball, on the downward slope to contact. In the second frame, his foot makes contact in a blurry haze, right arm waving behind. His left arm descends in the third frame as the ball rises. It leaves the camera's field of vision in the fifth frame. In the final three frames, Paul's left arm crosses the front of his body and his right leg follows through and climbs above his waist as his plant foot lifts high off the ground. The elapsed time is no more than a second.

Paul stood in line with twenty other sweaty teens waiting for Storey to examine the Polaroids. When he reached the golf cart, Paul handed over the snapshots. Storey gave them a quick glance. "I'm sorry," he said without looking up. "I don't think you can do anything with this. I think you need to find another sport." He didn't deconstruct the form of the five-foot-eight, 130-pound kid. He didn't offer any tips or a few words of encouragement. "He handed the pictures back," Paul says, recalling the day vividly. "On to the next kid."

Paul didn't know whether to be disappointed, demoralized, or devastated. No one could have blamed him had he tossed his cleats in a trash can in the parking lot and taken up tennis. But he was young enough not to care, and he could see that he kicked the ball farther and higher than most of the kids at the camp. "And I just loved doing it," he says.

So he kept kicking. Paul started for his high-school team as a sophomore. He didn't get any college scholarship offers, but figured he could play anywhere. He took a twenty-one-hour bus ride to visit the University of Alabama, which was still coached by Bear Bryant. An assistant coach from West Virginia University, tipped off by a local booster, did visit Paul's home, and then talked the head coach into giving him a tryout if he was accepted.

In August 1981, holding a pair of kicking shoes, Paul walked into the office of the West Virginia football team's recruiting coordinator and handed him a business card. "THE STUTTERER'S CREDO," it read. "If you don't have the patience to listen to what I have to say then you weren't worth my time in the first place." It took Paul about ten minutes to state his name, tell his story, and ask for his tryout. Three days later he was on the team. Then he beat out two scholarship kickers to become the kickoff specialist. By the eighth game of the season, he also won the placekicking job. He received a scholarship and started the rest of his four years.

Paul established himself as the most reliable kicker in West Virginia history, and a frenetic flake. He had a friend paint his kicking shoes in three patterns: zebra stripes, camouflage, black-and-white checkerboard. Paul never measured out his steps. He walked to a spot, took one practice swing facing the wrong direction, and then whaled at the ball. During games, he paced the sidelines maniacally. Friends told him he looked like he needed to pee.

Paul was so odd and so successful that he was off-limits to the coaches. He was a self-motivated loner driven to overcome his speech impediment and show anyone who looked how hard he worked to be good. While the rest of the team practiced, Paul ran. He ran up and down the stairs in sixty-thousand-seat Mountaineer Field three hours at a time. "I just wanted to show them. I can't do what you do. I can't lift what you lift. But I can run. I can do something. I just ran. Like Forrest Gump. Ran and kicked."

Paul much later would understand that running long distances is an aerobic function; kicking a football is anaerobic. Kickers need quickness to the ball and speed through it. Running converts the fast-twitch muscle fibers necessary to the task into slow-twitch fibers. The act of kicking—jamming the plant foot into the ground, jerking the kicking leg downward, slamming the foot into the ball—is extreme and unnatural. Repeating it hundreds of times a week saps leg strength and worsens performance.

But Paul's racing mind overwhelmed his body's inevitable decay. He never missed a game. At the end of his freshman season, in the Peach Bowl against Florida, Paul kicked four field goals and was carried off the field by his teammates. The next fall, he set NCAA records for most field goals in a season (twenty-eight); most games with two or more field goals (ten); and best percentage inside of 40 yards (a perfect 23 for 23). As a junior, he was a first-team All-American. As a senior, Paul made a 55-yarder, still the longest in school history, and a 49-yarder that helped West Virginia beat Penn State for the first time in nearly three decades. For his full college career, Paul was successful on what was at the time an astounding 80 percent of field-goal attempts. More than twenty years after graduating, he still held ten school records.

In his amazing sophomore season, one of Paul's misses was a 52-yard, last-second, game-tying attempt against the University of Pittsburgh that grazed the bottom of the crossbar. A few days later, Paul received a one-page letter addressed to him at West Virginia's football office. "You may recognize my name because I have been teaching and writing about kicking for some forty years," the letter said.

Paul recognized the name for another reason. Dr. Edward J. Storey apparently didn't remember the skinny kid in the white cleats whose form he had judged hopeless. Paul read in astonishment: twenty sentences on why he had missed the kick against Pittsburgh, which Storey had seen on television, and how he might improve. Paul tore the letter into four pieces. Then he changed his mind. He taped it back together and saved it, for motivation.

The childhood encounter with Doc Storey had another meaningful impact on Paul's life, one he would recognize only years later—after he was the 333rd pick of the 1985 NFL draft, after he was cut by the Bills and four more NFL teams, after he took his job with UPS, after he began volunteering to help the kickers at a local high school, after he realized that his failure as a kicker could make him a successful coach.

"I will never, ever, ever tell an athlete you can't do it," Paul says. "You have to work. It's not going to happen by osmosis. But if there's a spark, I'll never throw water on it."

Back at Edison High, a week after our first private session, Paul leads me through two sets of ankle-banging hurdles, after which I double over in agony. Then I perform a half dozen pathetic no-step kicks that skitter along the ground, hook left, or flutter a few yards. Real kickers send no-steps through the uprights from 20 and 30 yards.

"Take off your shoe, no sock," Paul orders.

"Excuse me?"

"This will not hurt. This is a teaching drill," he says with a devious smile.

Barefoot kicking was a fad in the late 1970s and '80s. As long as it didn't hurt, the theory went, kicking sockless and shoeless eliminated the energy-absorbing and -dissipating layers of fabric and leather. And the barefooters said it *didn't* hurt, because they made contact on the hard surface of the instep, about an inch down from where you would tie your shoes. In a 1982 article in the *New Yorker,* Herbert Warren Wind wrote that the right foot of Philadelphia's barefoot kicker, Tony Franklin, "felt lifeless, wooden" with a shoe on it. "He lost the rhythm and power on his kicks—the kind of feeling you get when you hit a 'fat' 8-iron in golf."

I anticipate a contrasting experience.

"This is the kicker's version of *Scared Straight*," Paul says. Kicking without a shoe should quickly force me to kick properly. Yet, kicking no-steps and one-steps and, finally, two-steps down the painted football-field sideline, I baby the ball every time. We move to the middle of the field and set up from 25 yards. I continue to hesitate on contact, my natural and arguably logical disinclination to kick a hard object with a naked foot triumphing over my desire to follow my teacher's instructions. While I'm wimping out because I'm afraid of hurting my foot, Paul says, I'm actually hurting my foot because I'm wimping out.

Finally, I kick a solid ball through the goalposts.

"Even though you bounced left after you kicked it, I don't care," Paul says happily. "You've got to have authority."

I do another one, with requisite authority.

"Excellent! I love the expression on your face."

It is an expression of pain, I say.

"The pain of regret is nowhere near you," Paul retorts. "You're two-thirds of the way done and then you get your shoe back."

"Aaaaww*wwaaaaahhh*!" I scream after the next kick.

"I hope you have a lot of calcium in your diet," Paul says. "Last one." I kick it high and strong with a deep, echoing thud. "Excellent ball rotation. Nice one to finish on. Now you're worthy of your shoe."

I have retired my Umbros for a pair of $90 Adidas Copa Mundials, size 7, one size smaller than I normally wear. Some kickers, Paul says, take a new, too-small kicking shoe, put it on a bare foot, and soak it in the tub to help it form to the foot's natural shape. (I won't do this.) He gives me another kicker tip: Tuck the cleat's long tongue beneath the laces. And tie the laces of the right shoe as far to the right as possible, so the knot won't make contact with, and interfere with the trajectory of, the ball.

On the far sideline now, Paul walks up from the rear of the end zone, dropping a ball every couple of yards. "Ten balls in a row," he says. "Make the kicks." Rapid fire, one after another. No pausing to reflect or analyze. We start with the widest angle, that is, farthest up the field, with the ball on the 10-yard line. Using the Pythagorean theorem, I calculate later that the ball is 33 yards from the center of the goalposts. Paul crouches, holds the ball out and behind him, and makes eye contact with me. When I nod, he barks "Set!" and places the ball down.

I split the uprights.

"Where's Stefan and what have you done with him?" he shouts.

"I'm a quick study," I reply.

The second kick falls short. The third one sails through. Paul reminds me that NFL uprights are 18 feet 6 inches wide, while these are 23 feet 4 inches wide, though from these narrow angles they feel as slim as a supermodel. The fourth ball explodes off my foot. Good. The sound of the fifth kick—we're near the goal line now, 28 yards from the uprights—is flatter, but the ball also gets through. The sixth offers a deep, rich sound. Count it.

"You didn't major in journalism—you majored in engineering!" Paul says. "Look at this!"

Seven: good. "Look! At! This!" Paul starts clapping rhythmically. Clap-clap. Clap-clap. Clap-clap. Eight: good again! Now Paul's laughing.

Overcome with excitement, I rush the penultimate kick, from about halfway deep in the end zone, jamming my right toes painfully into the ground. "You gotta wait till I get my hands down," Paul says. "You gotta remember, you're dealing with these quarterback hands that are worth millions of dollars. Out of your peripheral vision you will see the ball hit his hands."

Ten: From the sharpest angle yet, I hit the near upright.

"Nice set!" Paul says.

The following Saturday, I attend a 4th Down Sports camp. On Monday, I drive to the Ravens' practice facility for a lesson with Matt Stover. On Wednesday, I endure a rush-hour parking lot on Washington's Beltway and meet Paul at Edison High. My ankles are still bruised from last week's high hurdles, as is my right foot, from my bad Tony Franklin impersonation. I'm anxious about the state of my knees, particularly the left one. On days I don't kick, they hurt. I sit on the floor in front of the television, spread my legs like scissors to stretch, and ice both knees. But the pain magically disappears when it's time to kick.

We walk down the football field, across the track, and behind a fence to a steep hill, beyond which lie the baseball fields. Paul announces that I'm doing drills up the hill. The purpose is to get me to lean forward into the ball and push off of my left foot. The grass forms a thick, weedy carpet about three inches high. A blazing sun stares me down. I hop up the hill on my left leg, bringing my right knee to my chest. Then I take full swings up the hill, right foot never touching down.

"Heel to butt. Heel to butt. Toe pointed down. And do it without stopping. This is going to strengthen your left ankle. Don't close your foot. It's all good. Without stopping," Paul commands. "When they carry you off the field on their shoulders, when all the linemen pick you up and you're raising your hand in the air, they're going to see how hard you worked. That you're very serious about this."

Paul empties the duffel bag. He marches up the hill holding my tape recorder. I stand at the bottom kicking the balls up to him, pushing off on my left foot, quadriceps searing. I do six full-steps. Paul retrieves the balls and rolls them back downhill. Five more. Four. "Nobody does it better! That's awesome, that's awesome!" Three. Paul trots down to encourage me. Two. "Attack it! Attack it!" I finish with a weak one. He finds a way to encourage me. "Now your mis-hits are going straight. Your mis-hits have end-over-end rotation."

After the torture of the hill, the flat field should feel effortless. Instead, it's as if I'm kicking footballs filled with sand up Kilimanjaro. Paul says he has fatigued me purposely—I've taken about 250 leg swings and kicked about sixty balls in ninety minutes—to force me to concentrate on technique. But he also says I need to eat a lot more food: six small meals a day, chicken, beans and rice, energy bars, weight-gaining shakes. I've been lifting and exercising constantly for a year, but my weight has peaked at just 164 pounds. Paul wants me to get to at least 170 by the time full training camp begins in two months.

"I know this may seem somewhat depressing to you," Paul says. "But I can assure you it's not. You're the same person who last week was hitting very effectively. I tell all the athletes I work with: I hope it doesn't come easy. I hope it doesn't come fast. That leads to complacency."

Three days later, on Memorial Day, I call Paul. We have talked about meeting for one last session before I leave the next day for my first visit to Denver. It's close to ninety degrees, and oppressively humid. But I'm anxious and insecure, and willing to withstand holiday traffic. Instead, Paul pushes me out of the nest. "You pretty much know the drill," he says. "This is awesome."

3

I Go with 9

Before departing on a Hawaiian vacation, Broncos owner Pat Bowlen neglected to tell the relevant football staff about the new kicker. So until his assistant, Lisa Williams, spread the word the day before my arrival, the only people aware of me were head coach Mike Shanahan, general manager Ted Sundquist, and placekicker Jason Elam, whom Bowlen had told personally. The special-teams coaches to whom I will be reporting, the PR staff that will have to deal with media wondering who the little kicker is, the trainers on whom I will be depending to resuscitate my weary legs, the other players—none of them knew.

Chris Valenti didn't know either. Chris is the Broncos' equipment manager, and my first stop at team headquarters. I arrive at 7 a.m. and am escorted down a hall lined with framed clip-art drawings of team uniforms through time, from the Poupon-and-coffee-colored outfits, accented by vertically striped socks, worn during the Broncos' first seasons as a charter member of the American Football League to today's Nike-designed navy-and-orange duds with a postmodern, slit-eyed, snorting bronco on the helmet. When we meet, Chris says, "You'll probably be in better shape than some of the kickers," proving that it's never too early for a kicker joke.

Chris tells me he joined the Broncos as an intern in 1997 during the first of back-to-back Super Bowl championship seasons. His sprawling operation is a preteen fan's paradise: cabinets stocked floor to ceiling with rib pads and jockstraps and chinstraps and sunflower seeds and toothbrushes; rolling shelves stuffed with game pants, shirts of all sleeve lengths and thicknesses, ankle-, calf-, and knee-high socks, cleats, running shoes, training shoes; clothing racks shimmering with game jerseys, blue for home, white for the road, arranged in numerical order. A life-size cutout of Luke Skywalker dressed in a Jake Plummer jersey leans against one wall. Next to Jake are a dartboard and a bank of hockey sticks. John Elway's square-toed kicking shoe rests on a shelf; the Broncos' Hall of Fame quarterback was an emergency kicker. "We Issue Everything Except *GUTS*," a sign reads. "It should say balls," Chris says. "But, technically, we issue balls."

Our first order of business is a helmet.

"How small do they come?" I ask.

"You're on the small end of a large," Chris says, eyeballing my head before wrapping a tape measure around it. I'm a size 7¼.

"Do you have a chinstrap preference?" Chris says.

This might be the most ridiculous question I've ever been asked.

"I have no idea."

"It's a technicality. You're not going to be buckling it up and banging heads."

"Let's hope not."

Chris removes a shiny dark blue helmet from a box. Without a face-mask or decals, it reminds me that football games once were played by men dressed like Charles Lindbergh. Chris schools me on how to put it on: place the front padding against my forehead and roll the helmet backward, as opposed to pulling the entire contraption straight down.

"How do you get it over the ears?" I ask.

"Just give it a good tug."

Chris screws a hose into the top of the helmet and pumps air, asking when the pressure from the padding feels comfortable. The air lifts the helmet above my eyebrows. He repeats the procedure on the back and sides, and tells me to hold my head still while he twists the helmet from side to side and up and down. For about two decades, Chris explains, football helmets have had air bladders designed to provide custom fit and—as much as possible when humans collide with the force of runaway Volkswagens—safeguard against head and neck injuries. One friend told me I would need to get hit so I could describe "what it feels like." No thanks. I want my helmet to serve cosmetic purposes only.

"Good to go with that," Chris announces.

"Really? Any tricks to getting it off?"

"Just pop it off."

I do, and it doesn't hurt, and I'm surprised, perhaps because the last helmet I wore was a New York Giants model circa 1973.

Chris tells me that about half of the Broncos "play naked," that is, they wear no protection beyond the rulebook minimum: helmet and shoulder pads. No knee pads, no thigh pads, certainly no hopelessly outdated hip or elbow pads—all of which players are convinced slow them down. Only quarterbacks, running backs, offensive linemen, and tight ends routinely wear padding on their legs. Indeed, NFL players today wear less protective equipment than at any time since the early 1900s, when Ivy League students were dying (literally) in primordial gridiron free-for-alls.

In a far-back storage room, ultralight shoulder pads fill a giant ring toss. Boxes of helmets are stacked to the ceiling. Chris pulls out a Riddell Revolution, which has a bigger shell than a standard helmet and an extension down the jawline to protect against concussions. Only about a quarter of the Broncos wear it, he says. Many don't because the oversize dome makes them look like the Great Gazoo. The team's two kickers, Jason Elam and Todd Sauerbrun, wear what Chris considers an especially flimsy helmet made by Bike. "I wouldn't put anyone out there in it, but Todd had to have it when he came here. Then Jason had to have it." He shrugs. *Kickers.* To deter others, Chris displays one in his office that split open like a watermelon during a collision.

I stick with the standard Riddell VSR-4. "How much am I actually going to be wearing it?" I ask.

"Probably not much," Chris says, "especially if you're going to be hanging out with Jason." Never too early for another kicker joke.

I do crave the retro single-bar facemask, the football equivalent of the pocket protector, worn by every kicker when I was a kid. Just two NFL players, both punters, sported the single bar in 2005—thirty-seven-year-old Scott Player of Arizona, who tilts the bar down when he kicks and rotates it up afterward, and forty-four-year-old Sean Landeta of Philadelphia. The Broncos have a couple of the single bars hidden near the top of a cabinet containing two dozen varieties of facemasks. I ask Chris to put it on my helmet, but he refuses. He's afraid a player will then want one. So I choose a Schutt RKOP—Reinforced Kicker Oral Protection—which has a wide viewing window, if not the goofy simplicity of the old single bar.

"We'll detail it up and slap the mask on it and hang it in your locker," Chris says. I tell him I have my own cleats, which is just as well because the team doesn't stock size 7s. "All the clothes are in your locker," Chris says. "Just a rule of thumb. The stuff that's in the laundry bag, put back in the laundry bag when you throw it in the hamper— shorts, T-shirt, socks, jock. That reminds me, are you a jock guy or a compression-short guy?"

I've never been asked to define myself this way. "Compression shorts," I say.

Then Chris remembers one crucial uniform detail: a number.

"We've got two available. The roster is completely full right now. Eight or nine?"

"Wow, tough call," I say.

I pause to ponder this most personal of athletic decisions. I've never worn 8 or 9, in any sport, so I quickly assess my feelings: Never liked 8. Something about its shape, the sideways infinity. Nine looks more graceful. Plus, I can't think of a kicker who wore 8. I'm just grateful the Broncos didn't have time to screw around and give me 0 like Plimpton.

"Nine," I announce. "I'll go with nine."

We exit the equipment room, hang a left, and walk through open double doors etched with the team logo in frosted glass. The locker room is a long, fully carpeted rectangle with deep, tall maple stalls (each equipped with a high-speed Internet connection) on all four sides and more down the center. Flat-screen TVs are mounted to walls and perched atop lockers. R&B is cranking.

Chris stops in front of a locker at the far end of the room. The surrounding players, each a Goliath, slowly realize I'm not just passing through, that I'm the New Guy whose name is printed on the white cardboard strip in the metal slot overhead. Chris hands me a pair of compression shorts, wishes me well, and departs, like the last helicopter from the roof of the American embassy in Saigon.

The physical differences, and the financial and cultural ones, between reporters and athletes are, of course, unmistakable. But being an undersized locker-room supplicant is tolerable because it's temporary. You leave having learned whatever it is you were trying to learn, use the information to articulate some larger idea, and resume a life in which you're not a miniature intruder who can't possibly understand the sophisticated processes around you.

Now, though, I feel exposed. No notebook to hide behind. Surrounded by offensive linemen.

"What's up? What's happening, man?"

I introduce myself.

"P. J. Alexander. Nice to meet you."

P.J. looks to weigh about three hundred pounds. Like many of my new neighbors, he's not exactly cut like Mr. Universe. He has soft eyes, a warm voice, a scraggly beard, and a big smile verging now on delight. A coffee mug on a shelf in his locker is adorned with a photo of a deranged-looking Jake Plummer giving the finger with both hands and a message: GOOD MORNING DOUCHEBAG!

P.J. orders me to sing my college fight song.

"You're kidding," I say.

"No, I'm not kidding," P.J. retorts. "Sing it, man."

It's a meta moment. The singing rookie long ago passed from locker-room rite to locker-room cliché. Plimpton devoted seven pages of *Paper Lion* to college-fight-song singing. But now a modern player is invoking the tradition—with tongue in cheek, I think, because according to the script I should be made to croon during a team meeting or in the lunch-room, not first thing in the morning in a locker room thick with white noise. Blood rushes to my head. I look up at P.J. one more time hoping he'll call it off, but he doesn't. At least no one else seems to have heard his entreaty. So I sit in my stall and sing, in a voice slightly above a whisper:

"Come all ye loyal classmen now,
In hall and campus through.
Lift up your hearts and voices
For the royal Red and Blue.
Fair Harvard has her Crimson,
Old Yale her colors, too.
But for dear Pennsylvania
We wear the Red and Blue."

Five minutes into my NFL experience and I've already betrayed my roots as an Ivy League weenie, as if the players will need more ammunition. I make a command decision to skip the chorus, which requires swinging the right arm open and closed across the chest while singing, "Hurrah, hurrah, Penn-syl-vay, nye-uh."

"All right," P.J. says, offering an outstretched palm. "All right."

First test passed. P.J. laughs with a neighboring lineman, as if I'm invisible. Other players take turns saying hello and listening to my spiel: Writer. Not a beat reporter! Book about life in the NFL. Mr. Bowlen approved it! Should be here all summer. Yes, a kicker. Played soccer in high school!

"Really? That's kind of cool," says Bradlee Van Pelt, the backup quarterback, whose nearby locker is draped in green Christmas tinsel. Bradlee says he played soccer. Until he was old enough to play football.

I see others look at me, turn to a teammate, and knock fists or slap hands. "You know you're a rookie, right?" one says, ominously. As I slip into my white compression shorts bearing the NFL shield, my thighs don't feel nearly as thick as they did in the gym back home. Tan hair curling from beneath a gray skullcap, Matt Lepsis, another offensive tackle, positions himself a few feet away, crosses his arms, and stares down at me like a statue of Lenin. Then he begins chuckling. I try to break the ice.

"Lepsis. You Greek?"

"Lithuanian," he answers, smiling but firm.

"Damn. I thought I'd have an ally."

"We can still be allies." He buries his nose and mouth in his T-shirt as his head bobs with laughter.

To feel more important than I do right now, I remind myself that in pro sports the players are the hired help, temporary and dispensable. In here, the message from the late Harvard Law School dean Erwin Griswold applies. "Look to the right of you, look to the left of you," Griswold purportedly told first-year students. "One of you isn't going to be here by the end of the year." In an NFL locker room, the math is nearly identical but the calendar is just three months long. There are ninety-four players in camp. By the end of August there will be sixty-one, fifty-three on the active roster and eight on a practice squad who will make about a third of the NFL minimum salary of $275,000. Forty-five players will dress for games, forty-six if the team carries a third quarterback, which the Broncos did not do in 2005.

At 7:57—digital LED clocks adorn the walls throughout Broncos headquarters, synchronized, I'm told, per Shanahan's orders—the players begin marching past me and through another set of double doors at the rear of the room. Some grab twelve-ounce bottles of water or Gatorade from a refrigerator before reporting for the first meetings of the day, offense in one conference room, defense in another. At precisely 8:00, it's like a neutron bomb has struck, killing everyone but the kickers.

With one season on an NFL roster, punter Paul Ernster is the veteran of the three actual kickers attending the "team camp." Paul was selected by the Broncos in the seventh and final round of the 2005 NFL draft. He was one of just three punters and two placekickers among the 255 players chosen, compared to fourteen quarterbacks. Paul made the team as a kickoff specialist, and played in the first regular-season game against Miami. But he tore the ACL in his right, kicking knee and spent the rest of the year on the injured list. Four months after the surgery, he was kicking again. His right leg and hip are stronger, he says, but his body feels out of whack. "Kicking is such an explosive movement. It's hard to get everything in balance. If all I had to do is run, I'd be all right."

I ask Jeff Williams, a rookie free-agent punter, where he went to school. "I'm going to throw you for a loop. Adams State. A small Division II school. Twelve hundred students. More guys than girls."

"That means he never got laid," Paul says, before springing off the carpet. "I gotta go lift."

I'm sharing a locker with Tyler Fredrickson, who seems excited to meet me, as if different were interesting. Tyler is boyish-looking and towheaded, with no obvious need for a razor: Ron Howard circa *Happy Days*. He is six foot two and 205 pounds, but slumped shoulders and doe eyes make him less imposing. His voice betrays an earnestness that feels out of place in a business where grade-school standards of initiation, inclusion, and acceptance apply. In terms of outsiderness, Tyler seems like my locker-room doppelgänger, which can't bode well for his football career.

Tyler grills me about whether I have kicked, about journalism, about my previous work, about this book, about whether it will be turned into a movie, about whether he could work on the movie. Tyler studied film at Berkeley and wants to work in Hollywood. For his master's thesis, he made a documentary about Cal's 2003 football season. Parts of it were shown on ESPN, he tells me. Tyler kicked last-second field goals that beat Southern California and, in a bowl game, Virginia Tech, but the movie (a copy of which Tyler gives me later) modestly ignores his own heroics.

Six kickers were drafted in 2004. Tyler wasn't one of them. Market logic argues against drafting placekickers and punters. Most teams employ just one of each, and they know that there's an oversupply of both. They also know that kickers, like certain cheeses, tend to improve with age, so only top prospects get drafted. Paul Ernster was deemed worthy because, as a senior at Northern Arizona University, he led the NCAA's Division I-AA in punting average. Tyler punted three years at Cal to less distinction. As a senior, he placekicked, too, but made just half of his field goals. Five misses were from beyond 50 yards, and several kicks were blocked or hit the uprights. But the stats don't care about the uprights. Missing half the time doesn't get you drafted.

Tyler was cut by Seattle during training camp in 2004. He was signed by Denver the next off-season and cut before training camp in 2005. He was re-signed by Denver after that season and cut during tryouts for the NFL's European league. Tyler thought his NFL career was over before it had begun, but Denver kept bringing him back. In three years as an NFL aspirant, Tyler has earned about $12,000.

Kickers and punters don't attend many meetings, Tyler says. I ask what they do instead. "Eat, play video games, go on the computer." Tyler notes that the players who perform core football skills—running, throwing, blocking, tackling—will be expected to play at a high level when they are physically and mentally fatigued. Kickers won't face in-game pain and exhaustion. And the finely calibrated and delicate nature of the job means they don't practice nearly as hard as everyone else. "Elam will come out and kick ten balls and be done," Tyler says. "I'll come out and kick a hundred balls and be done. A high-school kid will come out and kick three hundred balls and be done. Everybody's different."

Jeff Williams joins us. We talk about learning to kick. I mention that studies show that people need ten years to develop expertise in a skill like playing chess or the violin. Paul Ernster returns. "How was your lifting?" Jeff asks. "All eighteen minutes of it." Paul says he decided to lift later.

At that, we rise and exit the rear of the room, behind the lockers housing the quarterbacks. (The room is arranged roughly like a game on the field. Offense in one half, defense in the other. At the exact opposite end from the four quarterbacks are the lockers of four defensive linemen.) We hang a left into the players' lounge, which is equipped with six PCs, Xboxes, high-backed leather chairs, a round table suitable for cards. The lights are low. Players nap in here during the twice-a-day-practice grind of training camp, the kickers say.

"Stef, you up for a little video game?" Tyler asks. "Or you can sit in meetings. Whatever you want."

Kicker peer pressure!

We enter screen names into a golf game called Golden Tee 2005. "We've got way too much time on our hands," Paul says. I've never played before, so Tyler conducts a tutorial. After explaining putting technique, he promptly misses one. Paul makes his. On a 615-yard par five, I bomb a virtual drive.

"Look at this," Paul says, "beating us all."

"This is a skill you can learn in ten minutes," I reply. "As opposed to ten years."

Ronnie Bradford enters the room twirling a stopwatch, introduces himself, and invites me to join him. As we leave, the Broncos' special-teams coach shakes his head and glances disapprovingly at the video golfers, as if he can't believe he's in charge of these goof-offs. "In my next life, I want to be a kicker," he says. We walk back through the locker room and up a set of stairs to the team's offices.

Ronnie works in a small room with a black laminate desk, a set of metal bookshelves, photos of his wife and kids, and a couple of extra chairs for visitors. The differences between Ronnie's space and Dilbert's cubicle: a thirty-six-inch flat-screen Sony Trinitron; a laptop loaded with software designed to edit and watch football video; a giant whiteboard adorned with rectangular magnets bearing the names, in uppercase black lettering, of every player in camp, grouped by position. The kickers are joined by one other player, Mike Leach, the long snapper on extra points, field goals, and punts. I don't have a magnet. I'm a little disappointed.

Ronnie is in his third year coaching the players who are on the field during kickoffs, punts, field goals, and extra points. He is thirty-five, with a lean physique, a shaved head, and wire-rimmed glasses. He tells me he played defensive back in the NFL for ten years, retiring in 2002. "Three here, and then one in Arizona, five in Atlanta, and one in Minnesota," he says. "But, um, you know, enough about me. You're here, which is interesting. They called me and were like, 'Hey, we've got a guy coming in. Tomorrow.' Usually I get a little heads-up."

I modify my monologue to emphasize that I'm not some loser reporter but a serious kicker who's been practicing. I tell him I've split the uprights from 35 yards but want to become consistent from 40 and beyond. Ronnie says the team's part-time kicking consultant, Jeff Hays, attends practice every day. Denver is the rare NFL team that employs a kicking expert, he says. I ask what Hays does, and Bradford zips through a directory of kicking fundamentals—the positioning of the shoulders, the direction of the plant foot, the point of the toe, the swing of the non-kicking arm across the body.

"You've learned it," I say, impressed. Even today, when football is an advanced science and the importance of the kicking game has never been greater—in terms of points scored and field position determined via punts and kickoffs—some coaches don't bother with even a cursory study of the mechanics of kicking. Ronnie says he wants to be able to evaluate performance independently, and to establish credibility with his charges.

"Trust me," he says. "I'm dealing with the collective mind. I might be able to fool one, but I'm not going to be able to fool them all."

"When you were playing," I ask, "when you looked at the kickers and punters, what did you think?"

"They live the life. But listen, they have a lot of pressure on them. They take care of themselves as well as anybody. My number one isn't going to be here this week."

"Elam's not coming at all?" I say, surprised.

"Coach doesn't mind if he comes. He bought a hydraulic hip-flexing machine for his house. Stretches constantly. He sees leg guys, a chiropractor guy. Three guys he sees every week. People say if you're a cornerback and you lose your speed you go to safety. If you're a kicker and you lose your consistency, you go home. You can't go to a different position. There's no physical pounding, but there's pressure. You can be a decent lineman, you can be a backup. We don't have any backup kickers."

"Specialist period," during which the kickers work with their snappers and holders, occurs at the beginning of practice, Ronnie tells me. Punting, kickoff, and field-goal drills come later, but not every day. After that, kickers can "get a steam, see their back guy, whatever. I don't do things just to fill time."

My number 9 practice jersey is size 46, and waist-length. It has short sleeves, a mesh chest and back, and a V-neck. The shoulders, arms, and sides are made of stretchy nylon, and there is elastic around the sleeves. The shirt is big enough to fit over shoulder pads but not so big as to look ridiculous without them. Wearing it makes me feel as if I get paid to play football. When my on-field dance in front of the team ends, we get down to business.

"ARMS UP!" The piercing cry comes from the strength-and-conditioning coach, Rich Tuten, a barrel-chested man with chiseled features who strides through the lines of players with the mien of Patton inspecting the Seventh Army. "ROTATE FORWARD!" We windmill our arms forward. "ROTATE BACK!" Back they go. "LEGS SPREAD! OVER TO THE RIGHT!" We bend our right knees and stretch our left groins.

"UP! OVER TO THE LEFT!" Yes, sir. "UP! LEGS STRAIGHT! RIGHT LEG!" Legs spread slightly, everyone bends over the right leg, loosening the hamstrings. "RELAX! LEFT LEG! RELAX! MIDDLE! RELAX! HAVE A SEAT! YOGA!" Soles of the feet together, lean over, stretching the groin and lower back. "HIP STRETCH! LEFT LEG UP!" Left foot over right knee, pull in toward chest. "RELAX! RIGHT LEG UP! RUNNER STRETCH! RIGHT LEG OUT!" Left leg bent and pointed backward, lean over right leg to stretch the hamstring. "LAY BACK!" Stretching the left quadriceps. "UP! LEFT LEG BACK! LAY BACK! LEGS STRAIGHT! ROLL BACK!" We roll backward, some players onto their necks, some barely off the ground, and then pop up. "LET'S GO!"

The airhorn sounds and the players cluster by position for warmups. They push giant pads held by coaches or teammates. They high-step across boxes painted on the field. They pivot around inverted garbage cans. We four kickers turn and jog away from the team, through the end zone, and onto a third field. This one isn't made of Kentucky bluegrass but FieldTurf, a grass impostor. A set of portable goalposts attached to a small John Deere tractor sits in the middle of the far end of the field.

Ronnie Bradford, who is universally known as R.B., joins us, as does the assistant special-teams coach, Thomas McGaughey, who is universally known as T-Mac. T-Mac's NFL career consisted of two training camps and a few weeks on a practice squad. (He also played in NFL Europe and in the indoor Arena Football League.) He coached high school and college, and got into the NFL as a minority intern. Like R.B., T-Mac, who is thirty-three years old, was a defensive back, but he's taller and stockier than his boss.

My first NFL drill is called, for want of a better name, the pole drill. We take turns standing behind a metal stanchion that holds up the goalposts, which, with chipped yellow paint and a coat of rust, appears to be the only worn piece of equipment around. The kicker, a punter in this case, positions one eye behind the pole and reaches out to catch a snap. The idea is to improve hand-eye coordination and focus. T-Mac spirals the ball underhanded, Tyler catches, grips, and extends it with one hand, nose in palm, as if shaking hands, in preparation to drop and kick. Then he tosses it back.

I step behind the pole. I obscure my weaker left eye, catch the ball, extend it with my right hand, and toss it back. I'm a natural. Then I obscure my right eye, catch the ball, extend it with my left hand, and toss it back.

"Stef, are you lefty?" T-Mac asks.

I am not. Oops. I had changed hands when I changed eyes. Only a left-footed kicker would hold the ball out with his left hand. Everyone laughs.

Our part-time kicking coach arrives. "Jeff Hays, rush chairman," he deadpans, extending a hand. In a yellow dress shirt, striped brown tie, and dress slacks, his graying hair neatly coiffed, Jeff looks less like a kicking consultant than a management consultant, which, I learn, is exactly what he is. Jeff works for Booz Allen Hamilton analyzing air force base costs for the government. He played on the Air Force Academy football team in the early 1980s with Broncos general manager Ted Sundquist. They were best men at each other's weddings, and remain pals today. Few NFL teams employ a kicking coach. Jeff's relationship with Sundquist—and Shanahan's relatively progressive thinking about kicking—helps explain why he's here.

R.B. interrupts the pleasantries and gets us back to work. "Playing Golden Tee and watching the cornerbacks scratch their balls is not going to make you an NFL kicker," he says. Jeff has us do "drops." We walk the perimeter of the eighty-yard-long field dropping the ball as if to punt. Right, left, drop. Right, left, drop. Ideally, the ball should hit the ground at its fattest part and bounce straight up. Right, left, drop.

I glance toward the other fields, where a chorus of grunts, shouts, and whistles rises and then subsides. No one is tackling, but the players are moving at full speed. From afar, it looks like chaos, like a crowd gathering around a schoolyard fight. Meanwhile, the kickers are walking—*walking*—around a field dropping a ball. Right, left, drop. Right, left, drop.

After completing a tour of the sidelines, I am, I reluctantly admit, sweaty. It's difficult to maintain pace and technique. More often than not, my ball bounces any way but vertically. Jeff gathers us near the goalposts for the "quick-foot drill," taking the three steps before the punt: left, right, left, kick. We do this without footballs, exaggerating hip and knee movements and avoiding a lunge on the final step. Punting is all swing mechanics, maintaining a stable upper body, he says. "You should look like a prancing pony," Jeff says, a description that surely won't be shared with the rest of the team.

Next we add footballs and take turns punting.

"You're making some nice progress, Stefan. Some spirals," Jeff says. "How old are you?"

"Forty-three."

"I think you're at the tail end of your career. Some guys just don't know when to hang 'em up."

As we prance between two lines of orange cones, T-Mac and R.B. rifle underhanded snaps and Jeff measures the elapsed time from the moment the punter catches the ball until the moment he kicks it. The punt is an exquisitely balanced athletic challenge, akin to a bang-bang play in baseball made possible by first base being ninety feet from home plate. A good snap takes 0.75 seconds. "Catch to kick" shouldn't take more than 1.35 seconds. Anything longer can give a defensive lineman pushing forward or a rusher streaking in from one side enough time to reach the punter and block the kick. Paul gets one off in 1.33 seconds. Tyler blasts one in 1.32 with a superb hang time—how long a punt stays in the air, from kick to catch—of 5.05 seconds. Their kicks fly at least 50 yards. T-Mac doesn't time mine, none of which travel more than 35.

Paul, Tyler, and Jeff Williams are auditioning to punt and kick off, so punts will take precedence over field goals in this camp. When we're done punting, R.B. tells me to placekick a few. Finally, my NFL career begins.

We start at 25 yards. With an audience of three NFL coaches and three prospective NFL kickers, I nervously boot my first ball weakly and to the right. I exhale and make the next one. Then miss a couple more. Then make a couple more. We move back to 30, from where I repeat the cycle. No one is impressed. But they can tell I've had some instruction. A few pointers come about steps and contact points and plant foot position. Then it's time to rejoin the team.

T ake a knee, men," Mike Shanahan says as we gather in the middle of a practice field.

Shanahan is wearing a standard coach outfit: navy Broncos shorts, white Broncos sweat-wicking T-shirt, white cross-trainers. "We've got to get eleven men to play together," he says. "That's why we're working our asses off. That's what we have to do. Eleven people working their asses off. Playing together." The Broncos' conversion rate on third down—that is, gaining enough yardage for a first down—was poor in 2005, he says. "We've got to get better on third down." The team didn't do well enough in the "rèd zone," inside the opponent's 20-yard line, either. "Have to get better in the red zone."

"This is a tough-assed game," Shanahan continues. "You do it here and lose your poise, it's going to carry over to game day. We've got to have the discipline to separate ourselves. Do the little things the right way."

As speechmaking goes, this is less Vince Lombardi than Wayne W. Dyer, and it reinforces the notion that Shanahan is more organization than inspiration. But given his résumé, Shanahan could read *The Cat in the Hat* to the team and everyone would pay attention. Entering his twelfth season in Denver, Shanahan has the third-longest tenure among NFL head coaches. He has won more games—114 in the regular season and eight in the playoffs and Super Bowl—than any coach in that time. As I learned from the second paragraph of Shanahan's biography in the Broncos' media guide, a copy of which is placed in every player's locker, he is one of just four coaches to have spent at least ten years with the same team and have more championships (two) than losing seasons (one). The other three are Paul Brown with Cleveland, Joe Gibbs with Washington, and John Madden with Oakland, who, the media guide notes, are all in the Hall of Fame.

Before practice, I stopped by Shanahan's office to introduce myself. He sat behind a large wooden desk in a recliner swiveled toward a bank of TV monitors on a wall to his left, each with a label: OFF, DEF, QB, LB, OL, DL, TE, RB. Shanahan can tune in to any of the player meetings a floor below. Audio from one played as we shook hands. Shanahan lowered the volume and explained that the Broncos record every meeting. He told me he borrowed the practice from San Francisco, where, as the 49ers' offensive coordinator in the early 1990s, he learned many of the organizational and coaching techniques he employs today. When he arrived in San Francisco, Shanahan said, he watched every meeting under the team's previous coaches to understand how the players had been taught. He told me the 49ers adopted the practice of taping from Silicon Valley.

I thanked Shanahan for letting me inside fortress NFL. He said he liked the idea because I didn't ask for inside access as just a writer. "You kind of come in as a player, where you're actually doing something. If you're just in the press, guys will be saying, 'Keep an eye on that guy.'" The minute-by-minute schedule, the synchronized clocks, the Big Brother television system: Shanahan's reputation for running the Broncos with efficiency and control appears to be true. But he also seems to appreciate the potential benefits of tinkering with the routine, and is secure enough to do so.

After his brief address to the kneeling players, Shanahan observes punt practice. Each kicker gets two or three kicks from a live snap and a modified rush. One-point-three-five seconds comes much faster than it did during practice. Snap, steps, punt. After a short kick, Tyler jerks off his chinstrap. "Practice is a big deal compared to college," he says. "It's like you're always trying out."

The temperature plunges and large drops of rain begin to fall. R.B. points to the top of the camera towers overlooking the field. The videographers recording every second of practice operate a lightning counter to measure storm distance, he says. I put on my helmet to shield me from the rain, watch the rookies run twenty plays, and head inside with the rest of the team.

"How'd it go out there today?" my locker neighbor Chad Mustard asks. Chad is a six-foot-six, chiseled, cue-balled lineman who, with his build and name, looks like he could be a professional wrestler. He leans toward me and pulls up the right leg of his XXXL shorts. "You didn't get kicked like me, I hope," he says jokingly, displaying a purple welt the size and shape of a mussel.

4

There's No Sorries

We reassemble the next morning at 10:30 on the turf field, which I've come to think of as the kickers' field because we seem to be the only players who use it. Carrying the two orange duffel bags, I realize, is a responsibility that falls mostly to me, the rookiest of the rookies. No one imposes the job, though; there aren't any formal rookie chores, like toting veterans' helmets or delivering food, vanished traditions of another football era. "Punt Pro"—short for punt protection, when the punters perform with the rest of the team—isn't until 11:35. "I could drill you guys to frickin' death," Ronnie Bradford says. "But I want to be more realistic. I want everything to be relevant."

So we do more pole catches. We "mold" and drop balls. We wear our helmets because that's how you see the ball in a game. We do prancing ponies. We practice holding for placekicks, catching the snap and positioning the ball for the kicker, a task often handled by the punter, though Jake Plummer does it for the Broncos. (He was the only starting quarterback who held in 2005. Most teams don't want their millionaire signal caller to get bulldozed by a rusher. And most kickers don't want the quarterback to hold, because they worry he will be preoccupied with the last play—in the case of a field-goal attempt, a failed last play—rather than focused on the hold. But Jason Elam wanted Plummer, the coaches tell me, because Plummer is a great holder and because Todd Sauerbrun didn't want to do it and, consequently, did it poorly.) I kick about ten balls held by the punters. One feels solid, the rest tentative, weak, and sad. The sound of my foot against the ball is more of a thump than a thud.

Fatigue is a likely reason. In the twenty-three days before camp, I ran, biked, and lifted weights on thirteen days, kicked on seven days, did both once, and took four days off. I am fitter than ever, which has allowed me to kick as much as I have. But the amount of activity is wearing me down. My workout diary is a chronicle of misery. "Achy. Lower back, hips." "Very sore—outside of right leg, tendon just above knee and lower part of hammy." "Left knee feels wobbly, crunchy. Discomfort when walking." "Concerned about blowing out left ACL on a plant." "Aching everywhere below groin."

I'm a Denver Bronco for only a short time, and I want to kick as much as possible on the manicured grass under the tutelage of the NFL coaches. But the more I kick, the less I'll be able to kick. Everybody's different, Tyler had said, including me. It's probably a good thing that the three kickers in this camp are punters. I could use another month before performing in front of Jason Elam. So after my weak kicks, I quit for the day and snap balls underhanded to my teammates.

Between drills, we talk, the decibel level of the offense and defense rising and falling, simultaneously so close and yet very far away. There's a guilty pleasure in watching the rest of the team work so hard, but it edges toward embarrassment, like we've been summoned by the state to witness an execution.

"I know you guys get tired of standing around," Ronnie says. "But it's a lot of what we do. Even on game day."

As Punt Pro approaches, we pack the orange ball bags and jog toward the other fields. The first distinguishable voice is that of Tim Brewster, who coaches the tight ends.

"Scheffler! You're out of there!" he screams at a strapping rookie named Tony Scheffler. "Get your head out of your ass, Tony!"

As Scheffler trots toward him, Brewster gets more specific. "Eighty-eight!" he says, calling Scheffler by his uniform number. (Saying numbers by their individual digits also is popular football-speak. Scheffler would be "eight eight.") "Were your eyes up so you could see fifty-two?"

Tall, square-shouldered, eyes shielded behind wraparound sunglasses, Brewster—Brew for short—appears to be the Broncos' lone football-coach archetype: windpipe straining, face contorting, riding the green rookie mercilessly. Off the field, Brew tells me he loves the isolation, insularity, and competitive demands of his job, as if toughness and success are determined by who spends the most hours watching film, by who is the most self-abnegating. "Here I can sit in my office and go three or four days without being involved in the outer world per se," he says. "You come in in the dark and you leave in the dark. You're a mole." I imagine him locked in his cell like some gridiron Hannibal Lecter devising new ways to scare the shit out of his Clarice.

The Broncos picked Scheffler in the second round and gave him to Brew to turn into an NFL player, by any means necessary. Brew's claim to football fame is that while coaching tight ends for the San Diego Chargers, he scouted and signed a basketball player named Antonio Gates, and then molded him into an All-Pro.

"You don't have time to develop these guys," he says. "You've got to force-feed them and bring them on quick, because in the National Football League they give up on guys fast. Tony Scheffler's going to have to be a good football player for us this season. Well, hell, I can't wait. I've got to push now. That falls on my head. You don't stand there holding a cup of coffee coaching."

I have no idea whether Tony Scheffler will be a great tight end. But in his wide, frightened eyes I can see that it will be an excruciating journey to get there.

At the end of my first day in the NFL, I showered, dressed, and walked to the team cafeteria for dinner. Tyler said that Rich Tuten was looking for me. I found the strength coach and stretch commandant by the soft drink and espresso machines. "Rich," I said. He walked away. I followed him to a table, where he set down his brown plastic tray. "Rich," I repeated. Nothing.

"Is that how you treat kickers?" I asked lightly.

"You didn't work out today."

"I know. I wanted to talk to you about that."

"You need to work out. You can't write about something without experiencing it. I'm not talking shop now. Get your head on straight and tomorrow you can come in."

I couldn't tell whether Tuten was serious. Regardless, he doesn't look like someone I want to cross. So after practice on Day Two I head immediately to the Broncos Conditioning Center, that is, the weight room. Built a year ago as part of a $4 million facilities expansion, the building is located across the electronically gated players' parking lot from the locker room, cafeteria, and offices. It includes a nine-thousand-square-foot weight room and an indoor practice field twice that size. The paint scheme, naturally, is blue and orange. The floor mats are Broncos colors, too.

"You ready to go?" Tuten says.

Tuten doesn't speak as much as command. He has little use for small talk. He responds curtly to my questions, seemingly uninterested in divulging the secrets of NFL weight training. His facial expression falls somewhere between impassive and intolerant. Or it's possible I'm just out of my league: the wide, muscular torso, the chiseled face, the impassive chest-out power of his being. Tuten is fifty-two and intimidating. Players tell me he is stronger than they are.

Tuten directs me from weight rack to weight rack with directness and without chatter. Today is a legs day. One-legged squats. Hamstring curls. Leg presses. Calf raises. On every repetition of every exercise, Tuten applies manual resistance, pressing down when I lift up, pushing up when I press down. He doesn't ask how much weight I've lifted previously, but decides how much I *should* be lifting based on, presumably, his visual assessment of my age, weight, and physique. On every exercise, he racks up about twenty or thirty pounds more than what I've

been toting back home. And still applies resistance. I assume I'll struggle. Instead, Tuten seems to make me stronger, or at least more determined. During calf raises, facing one hundred pounds of resistance, I
think illogically that Tuten has taken pity on me and is helping to raise
the bar. Then I realize he is making the task harder. Maybe I'm feeling
stronger because I'm in an NFL weight room. Maybe I just haven't
pushed myself hard enough.

"You're getting a real taste today," Tuten says. "Sixty percent of your
job is in here."

When we're done, I ask Tuten about stretching. He walks me to a
machine that operates like some medieval torture rack. I sit on a bench
and extend my legs in a V on two long pads. Tuten turns a crank that
spreads my legs wider and wider. At one hundred degrees, I cry uncle. A
satisfied half smile crosses Tuten's face. He's finished with me. "Good
work," he says, and walks away.

I return to the locker room and do what other players do after a strenu-
ous afternoon: submerge my weary limbs in the ice pool. The six-by-ten
tub is located in the training room, adjacent to the locker room, in a
glass-walled enclosure that also contains a hot tub and a pool that offers
resistance while swimming. Before taking the plunge, I talk to an assistant trainer, Corey Oshikoya, to learn how long I should stay in (about
fifteen minutes) and how deeply I should submerge (to my waist), but
also to make sure someone knows I'm in there, just in case. Corey says
the pool is set at about forty-seven degrees. Immersion, he says, causes
the blood vessels in muscles to constrict. Exiting the cold, blood shoots
into the muscles and speeds repair. Cold followed by heat—a two-foot
trip from cold pool to hot tub—accelerates the healing process.

Use of the ice pool increases directly with the progression of the calendar, Corey says. In the off-season, when players are lifting weights
and running, there's little demand. In the late spring, as bodies begin
acclimating again to football-specific movements—bending over, taking

stances, making cuts on the field—attendance grows. In training camp, when pads and contact are added to practice, it's a liquid mosh pit.

I just want to survive my first visit. I'm wearing my Broncos shorts and a Broncos T-shirt and a long-sleeved Broncos shirt on top of that. I doff my shower shoes and poke in a toe: the Atlantic in March in Maine. I very slowly descend a couple of steps and stand, arms resting on the ledge. I stammer something resembling "Uhuhuhuhuh," and stifle screams.

Through the glass I notice P. J. Alexander and a veteran tight end named Stephen Alexander (no relation, but they've both been friendly to me) lying on training tables receiving treatment—ice, electric stimulation, ultrasound—and laughing at me. Great. I'm David Blaine, encased in ice, in Times Square. My upper body is convulsing. My feet and toes are numb. Slowly, I lean over the side of the pool and read a feature in *Broncos Magazine* about the team's cheerleaders.

After fifteen minutes, I climb out, checking the bottom of the pool for limbs. "Look at him. He's shaking," veteran center Tom Nalen announces. None of the trainers seem concerned, which is a relief, so I take a hot shower. For the next hour, my body occasionally spasms.

It is a truism of professional sports that, as in war, people of radically different backgrounds with radically different personalities are forced to interact. Tyler Fredrickson and Preston Parsons are both tall and white and from comfortable, middle-class backgrounds. But in the spectrum of football personalities, they are more different than alike. Baby-faced Tyler cadges extra sandwiches and Gatorade every night upon leaving. He doesn't drink, attends church on Sundays, and spends much of his free time in Denver watching movies on his laptop—about thirty-five since arriving in early April, according to his Netflix queue. Preston is the unkicker and ur quarterback: solidly proportioned—six foot three and 230 pounds, not skinny-looking like Tom Brady of New England or oversized like Ben Roethlisberger of Pittsburgh—with a sweet, goofy smile and a prom-king swagger. His baseball caps are cocked slightly and his Nike swag drapes comfortably. He enjoys a night out with the boys.

Yet Tyler considers Preston his closest friend on the team, and Preston, though he may not admit it in front of the other quarterbacks, considers Tyler one of his. After Tyler, Preston is the player who makes the biggest effort to welcome me to the team, to show interest in what I'm doing here, and to be willing to hang out. It's clear after just two days that camp isn't packed with hijinks. As far as I can tell, the rookies and free agents staying at the Summerfield Suites aren't pennying teammates into rooms or shooting off fire extinguishers in the hallways. They're channel surfing, playing video games, and sleeping.

So I spend my second night as an NFL player in my hotel room watching the National Spelling Bee with Tyler and Preston. They now know, and seem to respect, that my last act of immersion journalism involved the sport of Scrabble. So I seize my chance to show off. They seem impressed when I nail, like a high and straight 40-yarder, the words *exergue, kamaaina, maieutic, aubade,* and *weltschmerz.* When a surprisingly well-adjusted girl bags *ursprache* and hoists the trophy, we call it a night.

"We'll talk after practice tomorrow," I tell Preston.

"Might as well talk during practice for all you do," he says, demonstrating that it's never too *late* in the day for a kicker joke.

Preston pantomimes the ball-drop drill, exaggerating the motion for effect.

"That's how I hurt my neck!" Tyler says.

"Please don't tell anybody that," Preston says. "That can't leave this room."

The Broncos' locker room is filled with players whose names are unfamiliar to the casual fan. When I first examined the team's roster, I recognized just a few names: Jake Plummer, Jason Elam, Todd Sauerbrun, veteran wide receiver Rod Smith, former Heisman Trophy–winning running back Ron Dayne, All-Pro defensive backs John Lynch and Champ Bailey. In the 1,800-player NFL, though, unfamiliarity is relative. Preston Parsons could have been a longtime backup. The fact that he was staying with the rookies, the free agents, and the writer was a good sign he wasn't.

Rather than talking after practice, Preston stays after the bee and tells me his story. He attended Northern Arizona, didn't graduate, and wasn't drafted. Though he hasn't taken a snap in a regular-season game, Preston has spent two years as a backup quarterback for the Arizona Cardinals. That would be a great start to an NFL career, except for one thing: The years were 2002 and 2003.

Preston was cut by the Cardinals in 2004 and by the Houston Texans in 2005. During the past season, he worked out for nine teams in nine weeks but wasn't signed by any of them. An undrafted quarterback whose last meaningful game was four years ago against Sam Houston State doesn't usually find employment in the NFL. But Preston had a coach who talked him up (Geep Chryst, his quarterbacks coach in Arizona) and an agent whom front-office executives trusted (David Dunn). He got four offers in early 2006, choosing Denver because he believed it gave him the best crack at a job.

The rationale was sound. Preston's good friend and former Arizona teammate Jake Plummer was solidly entrenched as the starter. Plummer had just led the Broncos to a 13-3 regular-season record and the American Football Conference Championship Game, a disappointing 34–17 home loss to Pittsburgh. In the past two seasons, Plummer had passed for a total of 7,455 yards, just 65 fewer than John Elway had in the best back-to-back years of his career. Denver thought enough of Plummer that, unlike most teams, it didn't carry an experienced backup, relying in 2005 on Bradlee Van Pelt, who had completed a grand total of two passes in his two seasons in the league.

That meant the Broncos wouldn't be signing some $2 million veteran as Plummer insurance, which in turn meant that Preston would get to compete with Van Pelt for the number two job. Preston signed in January. Then, in April, at his parents' house in Portland, Oregon, he watched

NFL commissioner Paul Tagliabue announce that Denver had traded the fifteenth pick of the draft and another pick to St. Louis for the eleventh pick, with which it selected Vanderbilt quarterback Jay Cutler.

The Broncos never called Preston to explain why they made the choice or to apologize for signing him when they were considering drafting a top prospect or to reassure him that he still could make the team. "There's no sorries," he says. In an instant, though, Preston's sound decision had backfired. Choosing the Broncos had offered security that he would be allowed to compete. Now he was the fourth quarterback, plunged into deep insecurity. He wouldn't get as many reps under center in practice. The coaches wouldn't feel compelled to encourage his development. He was probably screwed.

Preston says he considered asking the Broncos to let him find another team. But he believed he could beat out Van Pelt. Plus, he was eligible for the eight-man practice squad—which is intended for players with little or no NFL experience—while Van Pelt wasn't. If Denver decided again to carry two quarterbacks, Preston would be thrilled to practice during the week and stand on the sidelines in sweatpants on Sunday. Still, he would prefer fewer ifs. Just today, Dunn told him that Indianapolis and New England were looking for a good "three."

The contacts at least made Preston feel better. Dunn wouldn't risk his reputation by pumping up a lousy player. Plus, to be out of the league as long as Preston had and still have personnel executives spending even a precious few seconds discussing him was reassuring. Preston believed he could play in the NFL—and believed he had been denied his chance in Arizona not because he was untalented but because he was undrafted and inexpensive, because the team had little invested in him. "The political part of it, for a person in my position, is horrendous," he says, twisting his cap. "Someone in my position, someone in Tyler's position, who's scrapping and clawing and trying to get a job, who may be better than someone they're paying a bunch more money."

Preston is twenty-seven. His wife is living with his parents. They want to start a family. He says the $600,000 he made in Arizona is almost gone. There were no crooked financial advisers. Preston says he deposited his in-season paycheck every Monday for seventeen weeks and then spent it: a silver Lincoln Navigator, a houseful of furniture, a Golden Tee golf game. "It's in storage in Portland," he says. "I thought I was going to be there forever." The Broncos gave Preston a $20,000 signing bonus. In the off-season, he's received the league standard of $400 a week.

Preston tells me his family is supportive. His older brother quarterbacked Division I-AA Portland State—they played against each other a couple of times—and appreciates the long odds of an NFL career and the quirks of the business. His wife wants Preston to pursue his dream. His father is the sort of dad who, motivated by nothing but love, believes his son deserves what he wants. His sisters, too. But they don't understand that football isn't a meritocracy. "A quarterback goes down or a quarterback does bad and they're like, 'Why don't they sign you?'" Preston says. "My dad to this day, every day I talk to him, he says, 'You're going to be in the Hall of Fame.' That would be awesome, Dad, but be realistic. It adds so much more pressure. I feel like I'm failing people. Especially my family."

Preston stretches out on the hotel-room couch. He tugs his cap low over his distinctly Cro-Magnon brow.

"I'm not an Ivy League scholar that's going to go be a CEO of a business," he says. "I play football. I love playing football. I can make a lot of money doing it. I don't want to go get a fifty-thousand-dollar-a-year job selling insurance. I see that light at the end of the tunnel. I can get a chance somewhere else, something might happen, and you get your opportunity to play. One opportunity. You're starting on Sunday and you go twenty for twenty-four for three hundred twenty and suddenly you're in. And you're in for a long time."

In the meantime, Preston is just another guy struggling to find work in a cutthroat business. "People think you're a zillionaire because you play in the NFL," he says. "Nope. Four hundred bucks a week. Flipping burgers you make more than that."

My primary goal this week was to ensure that Mike Shanahan was comfortable enough with my presence to invite me back for minicamp in a month and training camp after that. I felt I had to prove something, on and off the field, to the coach and his staff and to the players.

But no one has seemed concerned that there's a reporter around, or that I haven't kicked well. I'm invited into a quarterbacks meeting, where I inspect a four-inch-thick playbook, witness the video review of the day's plays, and listen to conversations in the foreign language of football. ("All it is is the skinny with a tight split," assistant head coach Mike Heimerdinger says.) Team captain Al Wilson sits with me in the locker room after my cold bath and talks, towel draped over his lap, about the Broncos, about the underappreciated nature of playing defense, about his dread of the physical grind of the camp and season ahead. I join a team bowling outing. Shanahan even maps out when we can talk during the coming months.

By the third and final day of camp, I feel like just another kicker. Jeff Hays videotapes us punting, and we crouch on the turf staring at a laptop while he deconstructs the images. For someone who's never learned how to punt, I don't look awful, generating a 3.57-second hang time on a kick that sails about 35 yards. "But you've got that forty-three-year-old flexibility," Jeff observes.

After practice, I ask one of the equipment staffers whether I can stay late to kick. Of course I can: I'm on the team. I grab the orange duffel bag labeled KICKER and stand alone on the turf field, which is scorching. There are eleven balls in the bag. I unfold a red metal tripod to hold for me and kick each ball twice, making a handful from 25, 30, and 35 yards. The last kick is my best kick, and with it I prudently end team camp. I gather the balls and trudge back to the building past a sign outside the orange double doors:

RESTRICTED AREA. AUTHORIZED PERSONNEL ONLY BEYOND THIS POINT. NO MEDIA OR FANS PERMITTED UNLESS ESCORTED BY A DENVER BRONCOS REPRESENTATIVE.

Tyler was right. I'm in.

5

I Just Lost My Punter

The locker I share with Tyler Fredrickson is as I left it a month earlier, helmet on hook, two clean practice jerseys hanging neatly, mesh bag filled with laundered workout clothes. When Jay Cutler, the rookie quarterback, passes by, I casually ask how it's going. He doesn't look at me or break stride. "It's going," he says with a shrug.

P. J. Alexander, the offensive lineman who made me sing, is much nicer. He shakes my hand and smiles. Keith Burns, a linebacker and special-teams captain who's known as Tick, greets me warmly. Al Wilson shakes my hand, soul style. "What? You were taking vacation?" he says. "What have you been doing?"

"Playing with my daughter. Working."

"Working out?" Al says.

"You gonna do sleds?" Tick asks. He wants to know whether I'm going to join them in pushing giant wooden hurdle-shaped contraptions—handmade by strength coach Rich Tuten—from one end of the indoor practice field to the other. He means it as a joke, because even at my new all-time high of 167 pounds, I probably can't budge the approximately 225-pound sleds. The players have to push them down and back a half dozen times per set.

"Oh, yeah," I say, prompting laughter.

I'd like to think I'm showing the players that reporters are people. But mostly I attribute the pleasant greetings to a realization that I'm serious about participating in their mass ritual and understanding it, too. Persistence and dedication matter in sports, and the Broncos can't help but notice that I possess both. At the team camp, I was a three-day novelty. But here I am again. For that alone, I think, I have passed my initiation and been shown the secret handshake. Now I want to earn respect where it is ultimately conferred: on the field.

The Broncos have spent the past month boosting their attendance marks at off-season workouts, which began in April. Under the NFL's collective-bargaining agreement with the players' union, teams can schedule up to four such workouts of four hours apiece per week, and the Broncos do. I have kept a similar schedule at home, following Tuten's advice to lift heavier weights to strengthen my legs and eating constantly to reach Paul Woodside's target of 170 pounds by the start of training camp.

Paul wants to get me not only to look like an athlete but to think like one. At a kicking session in Virginia, I told him I was frustrated at the team camp because I didn't kick well. He replied that frustration is the best lesson. "You want to be able to understand what a field-goal kicker goes through," Paul said as we leaned on the trunk of his battered black Honda Accord at the end of a two-hour practice, during which I liquefied two shirts. "It's the loneliness. It's the boredom. You come in, you're either the hero or the goat. Jason Elam is great because he's the man. But when you look at Tyler Fredrickson, you're nothing but a plebe, forever, until they say otherwise. That's why you can learn more from Tyler than you can from Jason. Tyler's the hunter and Jason's the hunted."

Paul appreciates the hunter, which is why he is training a middle-aged guy who has never kicked in exchange for nothing more than the opportunity to communicate his passion. I will listen, not because my dad has forced me to be here, or because I want a college scholarship, or because I'm *this close* to making the NFL. I will listen because I care, because I'm crazy enough to be kicking footballs on a miserable summer afternoon when other fathers are relaxing in air-conditioning or splashing in pools. And I'm driven enough, or desperate enough, or foolish enough, to think that I can improve. "You're not comfortable in your life," Paul said. "That's the best way to be."

Paul reminds me of a Little League baseball coach who praised me because I tried harder than anyone else. The unspoken subordinate clause—*though he isn't the best player on the team*—never registered. It didn't have to. I knew I wasn't the best player then, and I know it now. To Paul, though, I'm Everykicker. When his chance to play in the NFL arrived, he wasn't ready. He wants to make sure that I am. In the programmed world of professional football, I'm Paul. I'm different. I'm an outsider.

This three-day "minicamp" brings the players one step closer to the monthlong slog of training camp. I arrive a day early. Two dozen players gather on the turf field, which is about ten degrees hotter than the grass, or about ninety degrees. Seeing me, Tuten asks, "What's your name again?" Either I made no impression or he's just messing with me. He leads us in a stretch, then a series of abdominal crunches (one-quarter way up, halfway up, quarter, half, until I can barely lift off the ground). Then we run the fifty-yard width of the field, back and forth and back and forth in gradually increasing combinations, two miles in all, and I keep up with the pack.

"One more week. Then get ready for the long haul," Al Wilson says as we huddle up. "Broncos on three!" he says. "One! Two! Three!" Then we shout in unison. "Broncos!"

Paul Ernster, the second-year punter, looks out the plate-glass windows of the weight room. "Todd's here," he announces.

Todd Sauerbrun is one of the best punters in the NFL, possibly in the history of the NFL. Or so he once asserted himself, saying he was better than Ray Guy, the great Oakland punter. But the numbers back him up. Todd's gross punting average of 47.5 yards for Carolina in 2001 was the highest since 1963. From 2001 through 2003, he had what was at the time the best three-year gross average ever, 45.9 yards. He has made three Pro Bowls. In college, at West Virginia, Todd booted a 90-yard punt. In high school, on Long Island, he made field goals of 57 and 62 yards, still the New York state record. Todd, I am told, is just that much better than other kickers. His ball not only travels farther, it *sounds* different.

At the same time, Todd has a reputation for being a jerk. As one sportswriter put it, his "hang time has always exceeded his attention span." In his second season—the Bears drafted him in the second round in 1995—Todd drove his Range Rover across a lawn at the team practice facility. His teammates in Chicago called him Stifler, for an obnoxious, mean-spirited, and profane character in the teen movie *American Pie*. A court ruled that he failed to pay a former agent more than $50,000 in commissions. While with Carolina, he was arrested for driving drunk. Todd once told reporters he didn't want to fill in for the Panthers' injured placekicker unless the team rescinded some fines against him for being a few pounds overweight.

And while not everyone disagreed with him, Todd made headlines for ridiculing Martin Gramatica's exuberant field-goal celebrations, which Todd said made all kickers look bad. "You don't see me jumping around when I hit a seventy-yard punt like I've never done that before," he said. A week later, Gramatica's brother Bill taunted him outside Carolina's locker room. "That kid is as big an idiot as his brother," Todd said. Replied Martin: "One hundred percent of the people that know him don't like him."

The kicker catfight was the least of Todd's problems. In March 2005, *60 Minutes* reported that he was among three Panthers who filled prescriptions from a South Carolina doctor for performance-enhancing drugs. The program said Todd received a testosterone cream as well as the injectable anabolic steroid Stanozolol and syringes. Stanozolol and testosterone were (and are) banned by the NFL. Todd never tested positive under the NFL's drug-testing program, and neither he nor his teammates were suspended.

As I see Todd standing in the players' parking lot, I know the basic outlines of his career, if not all of the above details. I know that a year earlier, the Broncos traded another punter and a draft choice to Carolina for him. Shanahan told me that the current team is, in coachspeak, one of the best "group of guys" he has directed. But NFL franchises are driven by one thing: winning, and the Broncos have dressed their share of shady characters. While no one considers Todd a reprobate, he hasn't been portrayed as a model teammate. I've heard Todd described as childish, arrogant, irreverent, foolish, irresponsible, and funny. I've heard him referred to as Boom or the Boom—his preferred nickname, intended to describe one of his punts—Sourballs, Sourpatch, and Toddler.

I interrupt my weight lifting to introduce myself. Todd is on his cell phone, texting. His cutoff T-shirt—the only kind, I'll come to learn, that he wears—exposes massive biceps, one tattooed with his uniform number, 10, inside a sun. Todd is just five foot ten but built squarely, and he has close-cropped blond hair. He reminds me of Bruce Willis in *Pulp Fiction,* down to the half smile, half smirk.

I tell Todd who I am and why I'm here and that I'll be around all summer and hope we can talk sometime about the NFL. "I'd have nothing good to say," he says in an unreformed Long Island accent. "I hate it." He plays football only for the money, he says. He hates the culture of the league. He hates the way players are treated. The words come out tough, but matter-of-fact, not threatening. Like a teenager seeking approbation, Todd punctuates sentences with "You know what I mean?" I return to the weight room thinking that the unconcealed disgust is a subconscious act.

Without Tuten's assistance—I suspect he was one and done with me—I work the latissimus dorsi muscles of the upper back, pulling down 130 pounds, more than I've ever lifted at home. I move to the bench press. Al Wilson and Tick Burns enjoy watching me hoist a truly embarrassing 95 pounds.

"Stef, it ain't Humpty Dumpty in here," Tick says. "No one's going to put you back together again."

"Call me when you're forty-three," I reply. I've decided that age will be my fallback defense.

"I'm damn near thirty-four," Tick says.

"That's a long nine years," I say. "You won't want to be doing it when you're forty-three."

"But I've been doing it for thirteen years."

"It's like dog years, though," says assistant strength coach Cedric Smith, an NFL running back for six seasons in the 1990s. "Every year you play in the NFL takes four years off your life."

When I finish my workout, I stop by Todd, who is lifting weights by himself. "Another day at the office," he says. "That's all it is."

WELCOME TO MINI CAMP 2006" reads the projection on the screen in the main conference room. It is 8 a.m. on Thursday, July 6. The Broncos are the only NFL team holding a minicamp. Most clubs had them in May, a few in June. Their thinking: Don't hold a camp too close to regular training camp. Mike Shanahan's thinking: Don't give players too much time away from football. Some players will disappear, some won't work out, some will eat Arby's three times a day.

The players plop down in black leather swivel chairs in the amphitheater-style classroom. Rookies are supposed to be in the first two rows, but I join the kickers and long snapper Mike Leach three rows up along the right aisle. The seating arrangement seems to mimic the formation on the field during stretch: quarterbacks in the front left, lineman in the rear.

"Good to have everybody back," Shanahan says. Then he throws it to Tuten, who supplies what will be the first of many statistics. Tuten says only eighteen Broncos completed fewer than 90 percent of their off-season workouts, and more than three-quarters of the team did every one, almost double the previous best. While the workouts technically are voluntary, the coaches let players know when they fall short, and contracts include attendance bonuses. "It's not easy for a football team to come together and make a commitment in the off-season," Shanahan says. "It's a bitch. It's really a credit to everyone in this room, working your ass off. Especially you older guys."

The Broncos expect to be an elite team. The players and coaches believe they should have beat Pittsburgh in the AFC Championship Game in January. Consequently, Shanahan and the front office tinkered with the roster only slightly. The coach, though, won't laud the players while standing in front of them. So he uses the meeting to set goals the way a corporate vice president motivates his sales force: Tell everyone he is expected to do better. The consequences of failure are unspoken. The defense needs to blitz more effectively and stop teams inside the 20-yard line. The offense has to convert more first downs on third down. When he reaches a stat that demonstrates the team's prowess, Shanahan says it's been that way a long time in Denver and needs to stay that way.

The players slump and rock in the comfy chairs, expectorating tobacco runoff into plastic bottles or paper cups. The veterans have seen a form of this PowerPoint presentation before. The rookies pay attention because they think they have to, but can't help letting thoughts wander. Shanahan doesn't make his dry material dance. But he doesn't need to win converts. He knows he has complete short-term control over everyone in the room. If they don't listen, it's their problem.

Shanahan was raised in Illinois, but his flat midwestern speech seems to have been impregnated somewhere in his peripatetic career by the southern inflections common to football coaches everywhere. He rolls through more stats and talks about how the defense has to improve its zone coverage, in which two or three members of the secondary patrol the deepest parts of the field against long passes. "So if we do get a team like Pittsburgh that throws a little wrinkle, we can switch"—from man-to-man coverage to zone—"and kick the shit out of a team. Because we were a better team than Pittsburgh."

So that's what this is about. A chart called 2005 Composite NFL Rankings goes up. Four numbers are listed: points scored, points allowed, turnover ratio (turnovers caused minus turnovers committed), and a sum of the three rankings. Indianapolis is listed first: 2-2-4-8. Then the Broncos: 7-3-2-12. The Colts are only the second team Shanahan names during his half-hour talk. He doesn't mention that Denver plays Pittsburgh and Indianapolis on successive Sundays in the fall, which the players might notice on the bulletin-board-sized schedule on the wall to their right.

At 9:55 a.m., it dawns on me that I'll be kicking in front of Jason Elam and Todd Sauerbrun in a few minutes. Todd worries me because I don't think he'll appreciate the spirit of my adventure. He didn't scare me when we met, but he didn't offer to be my personal snapper, either. Jason worries me because he's been one of the most reliable kickers in NFL history. And he kicked a record-tying 63-yard field goal in 1998. I'd like to show him that I'm at least competent, contrary to what he might have heard from the coaches and the kickers who have seen me perform.

Jason has been a hovering presence since Pat Bowlen told me I could be a Bronco. If Todd has been portrayed as the petulant adolescent, Jason has been described as the opposite—the sensible father: serious, professional, responsible, friendly. "A true pro," Ronnie Bradford has said more than once. When Jason learned that he didn't have to attend the team camp, he called to let me know. "Believe me," he said, "we'll have plenty of time."

On the first of fourteen pages about him in the media guide, Jason is listed at five foot eleven and 200 pounds. He doesn't look to weigh that much, and he isn't at all physically imposing. His sandy brown hair is flecked with gray around the temples, and there's gray in his goatee, too. Crow's-feet splay from his eyes, which narrow when he flashes his broad smile. When we meet in the locker room, Jason is dressed suburban casual: khaki shorts above the knees, a logo-free T-shirt, slip-on sandals. We shake hands. He says he's glad I'm here, apologizes for not having come sooner, and reiterates how much time we'll have to talk and kick. He couldn't be nicer.

The Broncos' last season ended on January 22. Jason tells me he started preparing for the coming one in April: running three or four miles, lifting weights, reintroducing his muscles to the reflex actions he would need in the subsequent nine months. In May, he did lots of 440- and 880-yard runs. As Paul Woodside had learned the hard way, sprints, which employ fast-twitch muscle fibers, are more useful for kicking than long-distance runs. Once a week, Jason kicked twenty to fifty footballs, no more, to begin reprogramming his technique. He trained mostly at home. At thirty-six years old, after thirteen NFL seasons, Jason is tuned to his body's rhythms and needs. He has no one to impress. Like most successful NFL kickers, he is largely an independent contractor. "I feel pretty good right now," Jason tells me. So good, in fact, that when mini-camp ends he's taking his nine-year-old son fishing in Alaska.

At 10:15, the specialists—kickers, punters, snappers, holders, returners—head onto the field. Todd already is living up to his nick-name, booming punts that seem to pause at their apex before tumbling like bombs dropped from cargo holds. While we stretch, Tyler Fredrick-son watches Todd. "It's a whole different world," he says. Jason loosens up by casually placekicking a few (no snap) from 25 and 30 yards. He seems comfortable, not just with the kicking but with being back on the field. No complaints.

"You want to take a few?" he asks me.

I place a ball under a red metal ball holder, take three fluid steps back—I've finally abandoned my jerky, one-step-at-a-time movement—and two over, make my approach, and kick the ball solidly. But I also push it to the right, to the right of the goalposts, to the right of the pro-tective netting, and onto a black SUV belonging to one of the players, triggering, to my horror, its alarm.

"Kickers should be out of sight and out of mind," Jason deadpans.

The quarterbacks wander onto the field. "Is that Cutler?" Jason asks me. "Number six?" Cutler, Plummer, and Preston Parsons all will prac-tice holding for Jason during Specialist period. Cutler and Preston take turns receiving snaps from Mike Leach. Jason tells his new emergency holders that he likes the ball placed 8⅓ yards behind the line of scrim-mage. He says the ball should be tilted slightly to his right, to counter what he describes as a slight draw when he kicks. He doesn't need to explain that the ball should be tipped slightly forward, to expose more of its lower quarter. That's standard. "And it's a set call," he says, meaning that once Jason gives the holder the high sign—a nod of the head—the holder will shout "Set!" signaling the snapper to start the play.

Twice in a row, Jason's kicks hit trucks in the parking lot, but his balls do it by sailing *over* the netting. Then Jason snaps, winging the ball between his legs to Preston and Cutler. Ronnie Bradford says Jason is the Broncos' second-best snapper. Jason asks Cutler whether he held at Vanderbilt. (He did.) Cutler asks whether Jason likes the ball held with the index finger of the left hand or his right hand. (The left.)

"Stefan, jump in when you want," Jason says, offering me the chance to kick.

I ask Ronnie whether he might prefer that I use someone other than the team's prized rookie to hold the ball for me.

"Yeah, I'd prefer that," Ronnie says sarcastically.

"You kicking or taking notes?" Jason asks good-naturedly.

As I drop my notebook and finally jump in, with Preston to hold, the airhorn sounds. I feel like a dope for being passive. After group stretch, the kickers—six of us now—run to the turf field.

"We're gonna get some pole," Ronnie says. "Wait. That didn't come out right."

We do the pole drill. We talk. We punt to warm up. We do ball drops, crossing the width of the field. We talk some more. We punt some more. Jason talks to Ronnie and T-Mac about the season ahead, excitedly. "If I want Jake, will I get Jake?" he asks. Plummer catches and places the ball quickly and consistently, Jason says. That's important because the kicker begins his approach when the ball leaves the snapper's hands. The faster the holder gets the ball to the ground, the longer the kicker can see the ball during his approach. "Whatever Jason wants, Jason gets," T-Mac says.

A few minutes later, the punters depart for live drills. For each punt, a coaching assistant times and records the duration of the snap to catch, catch to kick, hang time, and distance. I didn't know it, but Ronnie and T-Mac also charted a batch of punts during warm-ups. Ronnie shows me the stats later. Todd averaged 49.3 yards for nine practice kicks and 63.5 yards for two live kicks, with an average hang time of 4.72 seconds. Boom indeed. His live kicks traveled 20.5 yards farther than Tyler's, 19.5 yards farther than Jeff Williams's, and 13.7 yards farther than Paul Ernster's. With a 50.3-yard average, Tyler did output everyone in practice, with no live snap or rush.

Jason and Todd head to the weight room. Ronnie and Tyler stay behind as I kick. After my first batch of ten, Tyler suggests taking slightly longer steps backward and to step to the side on a ninety-degree angle; I'd been inching forward. He says I need to keep my upper body tall and lean forward slightly over the ball on impact.

It works. I start from 20 yards—a chip shot—and work back to 30, bashing the last ball through. "That was *a kick*," Ronnie says.

For ninety minutes after lunch, players watch film of morning practice. The kickers are dismissed. As a rookie, I'm required, however, to attend orientation meetings. Fifteen of us are scattered about the semicircular conference room. Seven are draft picks, eight aren't. Four are white, eleven are black.

"None of you have ever gone through what you are about to experience," Rich Tuten says. "The first ten days of camp all seem to be one long day that never ends."

Tuten talks about food. We should eat all meals and salt everything. Take the bags of trail mix found in the center of each table in the dining room. Drink lots of water and Gatorade. Our urine should be clear. Tuten removes an acetate about food and piss and reads aloud from one about conditioning.

"You should never lose a play, a game, or your job because of conditioning," the overhead says. "This is one aspect of the game you have total control [of]! If the guy in front of you is better, that's one thing. But if he beats you because he outworked you, then shame on you!

"You do have teammates that will try to help you, but at the same time, they are trying to WIN a job and support their families as well. Respect the Vets! Most of them are great guys who have been in the league a long time and have earned that. . . . If you do the little things right in a couple of years you will be in their shoes.

"Listen and learn from your coaches. It's not the end of the world if you make a mistake, just don't make the same mistake twice! If you don't understand something, ask and keep asking until you understand it!!"

Tuten exits and Shanahan introduces Betsy Klein, the Broncos' "executive director of player and organizational development." A small woman with dirty-blond hair that rolls down her back, Betsy is the team psychologist, watchdog, and fixer—counseling players on job issues, helping them enroll in college to finish a degree (for which the NFL will pay), finding them lawyers, quelling personal problems. She talks about a player whose neighbors threatened to go to the media with complaints about noisy dogs and noisy parties. "I squashed that," she says. "Anything I can do to help you get things off your back or help you in your careers, that's what I'm here to do."

Betsy's hardest task might be getting players to understand that they probably won't be playing football for long. She asks the group at what age the average NFL career ends. Jay Cutler says twenty-seven. "Twenty-six," Betsy replies, which works out to an average of three years. The players laugh the black laugh of the doomed. But better for them to get the message as soon as possible.

Then comes the serious stuff. "Domestic Violence: Acts & Consequences" reads her first overhead. Betsy explains that, in Colorado, you don't have to hit someone in order to be arrested. If police receive a domestic-violence complaint, they have to make an arrest, even if both parties say there was no violence. "Oftentimes, that's the male, as you would guess," she says. Another slide appears: "All that needs to be said to a police officer to be arrested and charged." Betsy runs down some offenses: pushing, poking, throwing hot food or a hot drink, pinching. Cursing can be deemed harassment. Pain isn't required. Betsy alludes to the case in which NBA star Kobe Bryant was charged with sexually assaulting a worker at a hotel in Colorado Springs. She doesn't mention Bryant's name or the specifics—which amounted to nonconsensual sex—only that he "did something." (Prosecutors eventually dropped the case.) But the message is clear: Don't "do" anything.

If the police intervene, don't tell them your story, she says. "It will never be written as you say it. If it happens, call me and I will get you an attorney." Prosecutors will pursue charges even when an accuser says nothing happened, she says. "We had a player here who had a girlfriend whose solution whenever they got into it was to call the police." If you are charged and plea-bargain and are sentenced to domestic-violence or anger-management classes, that's bad, because it will be reported by the media.

"Don't do anything wrong" seems a perfectly logical message to send these young, large, gifted men who play a violent game and who, as members of the Denver Broncos, however briefly, pass for celebrities in a football-obsessed city. Making them aware of the consequences of their behavior should be an obligation. Simultaneously telling the players, however, that the police can't be trusted and the law can be a trap—that might encourage a sense of entitlement, not to mention paranoia. To me, it smacks of cynicism.

Betsy concludes with the uplifting. She reads a Hallmarky quotation attributed to Gandhi that has been posted on countless refrigerators: "Words become thoughts, thoughts become actions, actions become habit, habit becomes character, character becomes destiny." Betsy says she told Shanahan that this is the best "character group" she's had in more than twenty years in the NFL. "Just don't prove me wrong," she says.

Up in Ronnie Bradford's office, I examine a list of every player in camp and his weight. Jason weighed in this morning at 190 pounds, Tyler at 200, Ernster at 210, Todd at 213, and Jeff Williams at 238. I scan the two columns for the lightest Broncos. Darrent Williams, a cornerback I can look at eye to eye, weighed in at 174 pounds. Then I see Antwaun Rogers, a cornerback who was on the practice squad near the end of last season: 169.

"What did you weigh in at today?" Ronnie asks.

"One sixty-six."

"You can get 'em!"

Ronnie is working on his depth charts. He says he's got a problem on the punt team with a starter and a backup from last year. "Right now it looks like they might not make the team," he says, shifting magnets around on his whiteboard. "We've got more kickers than tight ends," he announces. "We can take 'em in a street fight!" Ronnie removes two tight ends who tore ACLs this week and slides Chad Mustard, my locker neighbor, from the offensive line cluster to the tight ends, where he has been repositioned.

We examine Tyler's, Paul's, and Jeff's charts for the day. "Now look at my guy," he says. "Todd averaged *sixty-three-point-five* yards per punt." On a laptop computer, Ronnie scrolls through a list of files of this morning's practice video. He clicks on "PUNT PRO," and the video rolls on his television. Ronnie fast-forwards to Todd. We're admiring his punts when T-Mac walks in.

"It just hit the wires," T-Mac says.

"This shit's not happening," R.B. says.

"Here we go again. It's going to be page one. It's going to be everywhere."

I ask what's going on.

"I just lost my punter for the first four games," R.B. says.

"A cool half million out of his pocket," T-Mac says.

Todd. Ronnie says the coaches had heard "whispers" that he would be suspended for four games for violating the league's drug policy. For what, the coaches aren't yet sure. We go online and look for the story. It's not on a site T-Mac mentions. We try ESPN.

"Good. It hasn't hit," T-Mac says.

"It's gonna hit, and it's gonna hit hard," R.B. says.

Ronnie explains that, if suspended, Todd can practice in training camp and play in the preseason. The suspension would start with the regular season. Todd couldn't set foot inside the facility or practice with anyone associated with the team until it ended. T-Mac pulls a media guide from Ronnie's bookshelf and checks the Broncos' first four opponents: at St. Louis, Kansas City at home, at New England, Baltimore at home on Monday night.

R.B. and T-Mac consider whether the team might sign a veteran punter for training camp and the first four games. With the injuries to the two tight ends and the absence of a wide receiver, Ashley Lelie, who has refused to attend camp because of the acquisition of another wide receiver, Javon Walker, the Broncos have three slots available. But a punter with extensive NFL experience might not be eager to enlist for a temporary gig. And the Broncos aren't likely to offer much of a signing bonus, because Paul Ernster could still prove healthy and capable. Or Paul could get hurt, and then the team would have only Tyler. Or Jason—who both coaches say could punt in games and punt well. Ronnie folds his arms and lowers his Broncos cap over his forehead.

"That's the thing about it," T-Mac says. "You're fucked."

Paul hasn't kicked off much so far, T-Mac notes, because he's complained about his knee. But if his knee is healthy, Paul kicks off as well as Todd punts, they agree. But they feel Paul hasn't yet demonstrated the necessary mental toughness and physical consistency. In temporarily replacing Todd, a punter would have to perform at a high level while knowing he's likely to be cut. "All kickers are quirky," T-Mac says. "The ones that have the steel-cage mentality are the ones that play forever. Right now, Paul has not developed that steel cage." He'll be given the chance, T-Mac says, because "he has the ability to knock it out of the fucking park," especially in the Denver altitude. But "he can't shit down his leg."

I ask about other possibilities. "Could Jason kick—" Before the word "off" is out of my mouth, Ronnie interrupts. "No, that ain't happening." I ask why. "Because Jason doesn't like kicking off." I ask whether they would have any input in deciding what to do. Ronnie says he might be consulted, but probably not. One day, Shanahan will just tell him who will be catching snaps.

Ronnie turns back to the computer. We try an NFL news and gossip site, KFFL. "No, the other one," T-Mac says, "Pro Football Talk." Ronnie has the site bookmarked. There's the story: "SAUERBRUN SUSPENDED FOR FOUR GAMES." The Web site reports that two league sources said Todd tested positive for ephedra. It notes Todd's involvement in the steroids investigation when he played for Carolina. It mentions his Pro Bowl selections. And also his selection to the site's "All-Turd Team."

I learn later that Todd had been notified by the league about the failed test a few days earlier—a piece of news that might explain his hello-I-hate-football greeting in the parking lot. I ask Ronnie and T-Mac whether Todd could simply be cut, for affirming the reputation he earned before the Broncos acquired him. "Todd's not going nowhere," T-Mac predicts. "The man brought him in here." He means Shanahan. That helps Todd, as does the fact that he can kick the ball 63.5 yards on his first day of practice.

The calculation ultimately will be whether Todd's behavior hurts the image of the Denver Broncos more than his punting helps the performance of the Denver Broncos. And that will depend on whether someone else punts well enough in training camp and the first four regular-season games to make the team conclude that Todd isn't worth the trouble.

That evening, over free wings and celery sticks at the hotel, I ask Preston Parsons whether the suspension will have a negative effect on the atmosphere in the locker room and on the field. "Not for a punter," he says. "It'll be more like, dumbass for getting caught."

6

Toddworld

At 7:30 the next morning, Tyler Fredrickson spreads the *Denver Post* sports section across the hood of my rental SUV. The lead story carries an inch-and-a-half-high headline: "Sauerbrun suspended." "Well, it's an opportunity," Tyler says. "Now it's even more important to go out and kick well."

We don't have to be on the field until 10:30, but there's a special-teams meeting at 8. Ronnie Bradford delivers a rapid-fire presentation punctuated by frequent interrogatives, "Okay?" at the end of a sentence being his favorite. Special teams are granted little practice time, so they can't waste it, he says. Special-teams players have to perform with "RECKLESS ABANDON AND INTELLIGENCE," he and the Power-Point image he has clicked onto the screen say. Players need to "Set The Tempo," "Make Big Plays," and "Positively Affect The Outcome of The Game" by taking "Pride in Our Performance."

"Put a hat on somebody's ass every time," Ronnie says, meaning that special-teamers should hit someone on the other team—hat is a synonym for helmet—whenever they're on the field. Plays during which an opponent is knocked off of his feet, I learn, are "decleators," and counted by the coaches. And there are observations that, as a fan and a reporter, I've never considered. Ronnie notes that every game starts with a special-teams play, so the unit has a chance to energize teammates and depress opponents. About 20 percent of plays in a football game involve special teams, accounting for 87 percent of the total yardage in a game. The special teams dictate field position, so the kicking game should be used as a defensive and an offensive weapon.

Fueled by the cold coffee that he chugs, Ronnie talks faster and faster as the presentation progresses, motoring through eleven pages of stats and goals. When he's done, Shanahan walks to the center of the floor and repeats that the Broncos need to get better on special teams. Todd is in the room, but neither coach mentions his suspension.

In the cafeteria afterward, I bump into the team's PR chief, Jim Saccomano, who's been with the Broncos since 1978. He expects a pack of more than thirty media members today, including a crew from ESPN, which is a much bigger group than a month ago. That's because this camp is mandatory for players and, under NFL guidelines, open to the media. But practice just isn't that interesting yet, I say. "You know what they're waiting for?" Sacco replies. "For someone to fall down or get hurt or two guys to get into a fight."

I ask about Todd's suspension. "What suspension?" he says. Sacco tells me he hasn't spoken to Shanahan about Todd. Anyway, until the NFL makes an announcement, in Sacco's world nothing has happened. "When they"—the media—"say it's going to happen, well, I'm going to die, but it hasn't happened yet," he says. "Ergo, he isn't suspended."

Given, however, that the team knows that Todd has been informed of his failed test by the league; given that the *Denver Post,* the *Rocky Mountain News,* and *USA Today,* which are dropped on cafeteria tables every morning, have reported the news; given that the flat-screens around the complex, including two in the cafeteria, are turned to ESPN or the NFL Network, which also have mentioned it, not talking about the suspension feels very Oz: Pay no attention to the punter behind the curtain.

Jason Elam rides one of the two LifeCycle stationary bikes in the empty trainer's room, reading a Christian novel. Then he sits for a few minutes in the hot tub to loosen his leg muscles. Then he lies on a training table while one of the summer hires on the staff stretches his legs. After that, a trainer tapes both of his ankles. Most kickers don't tape, but Jason has done so since he kicked well with a taped, sprained ankle in a game in 1995.

From the top shelf of his locker, Jason removes three tins of balms that he rubs into his calves, upper thighs, and groin. One of the ointments contains copper and is designed to minimize tissue damage and stimulate joint healing. Another contains small amounts of silver, the third bronze. Finally, he applies MagnetiCare Cell Activating Skin Cream, another healer, which costs $45 per ounce. He slips on a pair of supertight and rubbery Bio Skin compression shorts, then a second pair of slightly looser shorts, then the standard-issue dark blue Broncos practice shorts. Unlike those of every other player, Jason's shorts don't reach his knees, because he doesn't want them to interfere with his leg swing. He is the John Stockton of the NFL, clinging to short-shorts at a time of exaggerated bagginess just as the retired Utah Jazz point guard did in the NBA.

Next comes the weight room. Jason bikes for five more minutes, as do I, and then stretches himself in the device that Rich Tuten had cranked up demonically on my groins. Jason's legs spread to 125 degrees. I max out at 105 degrees, an improvement from the previous month. Then we hit the field.

Only the specialists need to be out at the start of practice, with the rest of the team due fifteen minutes later. There are no fans at mini-camp, but the reporters watch. On the field next to the main building, Jason tosses a football with one of his closest friends on the team, head groundskeeper Troy Smith. Troy then holds for Jason's warm-up kicks. From 40 to 43 yards, they are impressive in sound, majestic in height, and poetic in their rhythmic, lazy trajectory. The ball zips through the air, turning end over end, breezes past the uprights, settles gently into the protective netting, and drops lazily to the ground. Today, I'm determined to kick, not observe, during Specialist period. So when Jason is done, Troy offers to hold a few for me, and I accept.

We set up at 30 yards, just left of the center of the field. With my right toe, I mark the spot—where I want the ball placed—turn imperceptibly so my body faces the center of the goalposts, and take my steps. Troy holds the ball as he would for Jason. Jab step, right, left, kick. The ball rockets off my foot and climbs, skimming just inside and about a quarter of the way up the thirty-foot-tall right upright, which begins ten feet off the ground, and into the net.

"That was your first kick of the day?" Troy says.

"Yup."

"You're batting a thousand. That was great."

My second kick flies even higher and clangs off of the right post. My third is high and true and down the middle. A few players actually stop to watch.

"That is way better," Paul Ernster says.

Troy returns to work, and I return to Jason, who tutors Preston and Cutler some more in the art of holding for him. Preston, in turn, schools me. The keys to holding, he says, are the lean of the ball and the direction of the laces. A holder typically tries to stand the ball with the laces facing the center of the goalposts. Most holders place the index finger of their left hand (for right-footed kickers) on the nose of the ball and, while the kicker is approaching, spin the ball with their right hand so the laces face forward. Ideally, the holder doesn't have to spin the ball at all, because the snapper thrusts it back identically every time. The holder never releases the ball before the kicker makes contact. To avoid doing that, holders often are taught to drop their finger to the spot after the kick.

"How was that?" Preston asks Jay Cutler after a snap and a hold.

"Walk in the park. He's got the hard job," Cutler says, motioning toward Jason, who's standing to the side, observing.

"That I'm writing down," I say. "Kicker . . . has . . . the . . . hard . . . job." Even Cutler—who with a mixture of teenage indifference and BMOC arrogance has routinely ignored me—laughs.

After we move to the turf field, Jason joins the punters. "In case the appeal doesn't go down?" Todd asks, meaning an appeal of his suspension. Jason nods. He tells Jeff Hays, the kicking consultant, that Shanahan has asked him to practice punting. Jeff offers a few pointers and jokingly puffs up Jason, mentioning how he is the best punter inside the 20-yard line in NFL history. "One for one inside the twenty. Can't ever be beat," Jason says in a mock boastful singsong. The only punt he's taken in a game was downed inside the opponent's 20-yard line, a measured statistic. Jason doesn't mention that the yard line was the 19.

While we're drilling at one end of the field, Todd is at the other. He punts the ball in our direction, nearly hitting Jeff, apparently on purpose. Later, when Jeff is about to snap, Todd tosses a ball at him. (Jeff ignores it.) "More Earl's time for me," Todd says about his suspension, referring to his favorite bar. "He don't give a fuck," T-Mac says. "That's when you know you're in trouble. It doesn't bother him. He lives in a fucking cocoon and it's called Toddworld. The motherfucker's clueless."

But I wonder whether Todd is overcompensating for the news, acting even brasher and drawing even more attention to himself than usual. I also wonder whether the suspension is troubling him more than he's letting on. During live punts, Todd shanks one badly, the ball flying off to the right and traveling just 27 yards. "Shit!" he screams, his face compressing in anger. "Fuck!" He tosses his helmet, which rolls over my left foot.

After Todd, Jason, and Paul repair to the weight room, Ronnie and Tyler stay behind to work with me. I convert just one of six kicks from 20, 25, and 30 yards. Ronnie prescribes a drill. He places three balls at 20 yards in the middle of the field, three balls on the left hash mark at 25 yards, and three balls on the right hash at 30 yards. He holds them for me and I kick one after another. Both men offer pointers and encouragement as I kick, but we don't stop. I process their words and move on to the next ball.

Make, make, make. Miss, make, make. Make, miss, make.

Seven out of nine. I try one more, from 40, but it falls short.

I'm more aggressive, grunting on contact. I'm striking the ball more cleanly. My motion is more instinct than thought. Still, as we assess the kicks, I make a list of problems: I don't flex my foot at the ankle and point my toes enough. I don't snap my lower leg to generate more speed.

My upper body isn't over the ball. My left arm isn't coming across my body. I'm still kicking the football like a soccer ball. If I can correct all of that, though, I could be dangerous.

After practice, Mike Shanahan's no-nonsense assistant, Cindi Lowe, escorts me into his office. Shanahan is seated behind his cluttered desk, today's practice replaying on a monitor. On the bookshelves behind him are binders detailing every minute of every camp he has run. In his how-to-succeed business book, published after Denver's second Super Bowl triumph, Shanahan said his in-season and off-season lives are similarly structured. "No moment is wasted. In my mind it makes for a lot of happy training campers."

Earlier, I watched Shanahan meet the press. He stood on a platform in front of a tarp adorned with logos of the Broncos and the NFL just outside the entrance to the dining room. He was factual but not discursive or revealing. His performance certainly wouldn't make news; he's not Bill Parcells, a coach unable to withhold contempt for the questions and the questioners. As a rule, Shanahan gives the media enough to file their stories but not enough to create distractions for himself or his players, or to draw attention to himself. Reporters are just one more thing on Shanahan's to-do list. He controls the information flow, not the other way around. "A lot of times, [reporters] think they're in control of it," Jim Saccomano had told me. "But when they leave, they'll leave with what Mike tells them."

It's understood that whatever Shanahan tells me is between me and my notebook until this book is published. Granted the protection of time, he seems willing to let the top down a bit. But even in a relatively unguarded setting, Shanahan isn't much more expansive than he is in front of the cameras. More candid, yes. More garrulous, no. It's as if he has been so conditioned by years of cautious sound bite delivery that he can't expound upon a craft he has performed as well as almost any NFL coach ever.

Shanahan grew up in suburban Chicago in the 1960s, the son of an electrician and a housewife. He nearly died when he was speared by a linebacker while playing quarterback at Eastern Illinois, the only college that offered him a football scholarship. A priest was summoned to read last rites. Shanahan lost a kidney, recovered, petitioned unsuccessfully to rejoin the team, and began his coaching career upon graduation. He took a job as a resident assistant in a dormitory at Oklahoma and ingratiated himself with the football staff, eventually ferrying recruits to and from the airport and analyzing game film. Oklahoma won a national championship his first season there. By age twenty-five, he was the offensive coordinator at his alma mater, which won a Division II championship. He took the same job at Minnesota, then Florida, where he rose to assistant head coach. In 1984, at thirty-one, he joined the Broncos as a receivers coach. A year later, he was the offensive coordinator. The next two years, the Broncos reached (and lost) the Super Bowl. At thirty-five, he was hired as head coach of Oakland.

As an assistant coach and coordinator, Shanahan didn't try to get his name in the papers, where it might be noticed by other head coaches and owners. He was withdrawn and cautious, and just wanted to work, says Adam Schefter, who covered the Broncos for both papers in town and ghostwrote Shanahan's book. Shanahan molded himself into an exceptional Xs and Os coach and, by osmosis and design, an astute businessman. When he joined the Broncos, he spent thirty hours a week diagramming plays so he wouldn't forget one at a crucial moment. When he rejoined the team—after the Raiders' mercurial owner, Al Davis, fired him four games into his second season—he told an interviewer that he hadn't taken more than a week off in a fifteen-year coaching career that included a marriage and the birth of two children. After he was hired as the Broncos' head coach, in 1995, Shanahan convened a teamwide staff meeting. "I've got a seventy-two-point program for success," he announced. "Maybe I can hit on a few of them."

In Oakland, Shanahan assigned seats at team meetings. That didn't go over well with the players, and he doesn't do it anymore. But he tried it. Shanahan expects those around him to understand, apply, and enforce his standards of organization, punctuality, and responsibility. He has little tolerance for people who don't work as hard as he works, as restlessly and as constantly. Which doesn't leave much room.

One of my favorite sportswriters, Robert Lipsyte, once described the difference between Vince Lombardi, the legendarily merciless and controlling Green Bay coach of the 1960s, and the generation of coaches he spawned and probably wouldn't recognize. "Lombardi could be a bully but he treated athletes individually and humanely; current bullies tend to treat the athlete as an interchangeable piece in their own intelligent designs," Lipsyte wrote.

Shanahan doesn't seem to be an inhumane bully. If his players, though, are just magnets on a whiteboard, well, he has seen thousands of them come and go. Now fifty-three, Shanahan has honed a style that is part autocrat, part technocrat. His is a reductionist approach to life, but maybe not to modern football. After all, Shanahan has had just one losing season as a head coach in Denver. I'm curious whether he is one of what Lipsyte labeled as the coaching world's "mind-bending manipulators who make athletes believe they alone can make them winners," and whether the players see him that way.

To untrained eyes like mine, I tell Shanahan, the carefully scripted practice sessions, how the players execute the plays, how he responds to them at the end of the day—all make it appear as if the team is ready for the season. It isn't, Shanahan replies, because the players aren't in top physical condition yet, not as quick or instinctual as they will be by September. Practice only seems finely tuned because the players are repeating drills and plays over and over. The NFL-sanctioned "organized team activities" and short camps—seventeen workouts in all—are designed to be a refresher course for players who have been Broncos before, and "a new language, new terminology, a new system" for the newcomers.

"This is basically the fourth time they've been introduced to the first three days of camp," Shanahan says. "So when we go to camp and start with the first practice on July 28, it'll be the fifth time they've gone over it. They can react and don't have to think." The coaches then will be better able to evaluate each player's ability, physically and mentally. No one can complain that he hasn't had enough time to learn the practice routine and playbook.

But Shanahan also tells me he already has a good idea of who's going to make the fifty-three-man roster. Based on performance and salary, he and the coaches and front office assess the team after each camp. The long camp and the preseason games are the final data points. That essentially means that thirty or so players have little or no chance of making the club. They will suffer through training camp with little hope, barring someone else's injury, of playing for the Denver Broncos. They just don't know it.

Shanahan opens a blue three-ring binder: his master playbook, which is at least five inches thick. I scoot up on the edge of my chair and lean over the desk. He flips the binder around and opens to day one of minicamp. "You've got all these passes," he says, riffling a few pages of plays, one per line, denoted by football terminology like FAR DBL WING LT 3 JET X CRASH DIN (T) that explains everything from which players are in the game, to where they stand, to whom they block, to what routes each receiver runs, to where the quarterback should look first to throw. "That's just the passing game. This is just all the pass plays you put in in the first day." He counts them: thirty plays, each with five different formations. Then he scrolls through a few more pages listing running plays.

"This is the first day?" I ask.

"First day," he confirms. I detect the pride of a field commander unfurling a painstakingly drafted map detailing how a battle will be won. And he believes his team will win it. Though the starting lineup hasn't changed much from last year's conference championship game, Shanahan says the Broncos have more depth. And they are ready for training camp. "We'll be good," he says. "You just have to stay healthy."

Shanahan tells me he found out about Todd's failed drug test three days ago, on July 4, and summoned Todd to his office the next day. "You say, 'Dumbshit. What are you doing? You know they're looking at you. Why are you putting ephedra in your body?'" Under the NFL's drug-testing rules—which are posted on a magnetic bulletin board next to a thirty-two-inch Samsung flat-screen just inside the front entrance to the locker room—all players are subject to random testing up to six times between the final game of the season and the start of training camp. Because of his arrest while with Carolina for driving while impaired (he pleaded guilty, was fined $100, and received a year's probation), Todd can be tested year-round up to twenty-four times.

Shanahan says that Todd initially told him he had taken ephedra, available in any vitamin store, to lose weight. "Dietary thing," Shanahan says. "Give me a break." Rather, I learn from Broncos players and officials, Todd took the stimulant to increase stamina and endurance while weight lifting. For Shanahan, the suspension is a bureaucratic and media headache, and potentially a competitive one, too. But it's not a new headache, and not one that especially upsets him. Steroids, marijuana, felony arrests, attitude problems—over the course of his long career, Shanahan has seen it all. "When you're younger, it's life and death: 'Oh my God, how could this happen to me?'" he says. "When you get older, you understand it's part of the profession and you deal with it."

All big-league coaches and general managers dance on a razor's edge, but nowhere more than in the NFL. With its large rosters, its Brobdingnagian bodies, its institutional violence, and its culture of competitive insecurity, the league is naturally susceptible to off-field "character" problems, from simple assault to steroids. More than two hundred NFL players have been arrested in the past six years. In 2006, the Cincinnati Bengals will have more run-ins with police than victories on the field. Apart from an incident in which Jake Plummer may or may not have deliberately bumped a car that may or may not have cut him off, the Broncos have had no off-field problems—until now.

Shanahan isn't sure Todd's action was immoral. "Is it a character issue because he took ephedra?" he asks. He is, however, certain it was stupid. Ephedra had become a bogeyman in the NFL since the death of lineman Korey Stringer, who collapsed of heat stroke at Minnesota's training camp in 2001. But Todd wasn't some three-hundred-pounder who needed to lose weight, and he was already under league scrutiny. After trading for him, Shanahan told Todd the team was taking a risk.

Now Todd had made Shanahan and the Broncos look bad. If the coach keeps him, he appears willing to tolerate recidivists. But if he doesn't, he could weaken his team on the field.

The four-game suspension will cost Todd $328,235 of his $1.395 million salary. He almost certainly will forfeit the chance for a big signing bonus and new, multimillion-dollar contract, which he had wanted. "He's not a bad kid," Shanahan says. "I don't think he's ever had a father figure that's sat him down and said, 'Hey, get your shit together. You can't do this, you can't do that.' I like the guy enough that I think I can get to him, but"—and this is a crucial but—"not at the expense of the team."

I ask Shanahan why he even bothers. Aren't there a dozen guys with big legs he could hire and save himself the headache?

"Not like his. There's three. Not many guys will kick it sixty-five yards from the line of scrimmage, which he does consistently."

In the locker room on the third and final morning of minicamp, P. J. Alexander asks if I want to add my signature to a white souvenir football.

"Hell, yeah!" I reply. "Don't tell anyone."

"Hey, you've got a number," P.J. says.

"Who's it for?"

"A kid having brain surgery. His mom wants him to have it when he wakes up."

Life imitates art imitating life. P.J. hands me the ball and a Sharpie and I sign my name and my number alongside those of the other Broncos.

At the morning meeting, Shanahan cancels the last day of camp in favor of a team bowling tournament (offense versus defense versus coaches). A five-foot-tall trophy stands next to him. "The coaching staff won it last year and obviously expects to win it again," Shanahan says. "The offense really hasn't done anything the last two years. Actually, the offense has sucked."

The Broncos rent an alley near the Summerfield Suites. Players and coaches fill about twenty-five lanes. Staffers organize logistics like handing out shoes to those who don't own their own. I join an all-kicker lane. Paul Ernster enters our names into the electronic scoreboard overhead:

JE

PE

SF

EPHEDRA

Todd chuckles, but TV cameras capture the image. (Some players resent the media's presence. "Why can't we just have time alone to be together, to be a team?" tight end Stephen Alexander asks. "We can't do one team event without someone showing up." Of course, the media didn't just show up; they were invited by the Broncos to record a wholesome team-bonding ritual.) Each player bowls two games. The rollers of the ten best games from each group qualify for the finals: one frame per player or coach, best aggregate score wins. Jason makes the finals with a 212. Todd leaves after one game (111). Paul and I bowl in the low to mid-100s.

During the finals (the offense wins) Paul and I sit on the open flatbed of a pickup truck in the parking lot and talk. Paul tells me he had expected to be cut after the preseason. He didn't believe he could beat out Todd, and didn't think the team would carry him just to kick off. The Broncos had done that his rookie year because he was a draft choice, the punter of the future, cheaper and younger than Todd, and better than Todd at that specific job. Then Paul tore his ACL and became expendable. Suddenly, the job, at least for the first four games of the season, was his to lose. On the first day of minicamp, Ronnie told him, "Don't screw me on this. I need you."

One Saturday the previous August, Paul woke up at the Holiday Inn, the team hotel during training camp, and got out of bed. He took a step, his knee buckled, and he collapsed in pain. The Broncos' head trainer, Steve Antonopoulos, better known as Greek, prescribed ice, anti-inflammatories, and electric stimulation, but no MRI.

When Paul knelt to catch snaps, he had trouble standing up. His knee was sore and tight. But he kept playing. He kicked off three times in the first regular-season game, in Miami. A day before the next game, at home against San Diego, Paul received a shot of Toradol, an anti-inflammatory. During warm-ups, Paul landed on the knee after a kick-off. "The dude shagging balls for me, he was ten yards away and heard the knee pop." After trying to walk it off, he went into the locker room to see Greek, who conducted a routine test for a torn ACL, pressing in opposite directions above and below the knee. Greek asked him if he could play. "I can't kick a ball," Paul replied.

The next day, the Broncos cut him. Paul cleared waivers—meaning no other NFL team claimed his contract, not surprising given the injury—and he was shifted to the practice squad. The team still didn't schedule an MRI, and—stupidly, he admits—Paul ignored his agent's advice to get one anyway. Before a Monday-night game against Kansas City the next week, Paul was jogging on the field. His knee gave out entirely and he was carried off. "All the cameras were right in my grill," he says. The team doctor immediately diagnosed a torn ACL.

I tell Paul he should have had an MRI the day he fell getting out of bed.

"But I'm not Champ Bailey," he says, referring to the Broncos' multi-million-dollar All-Pro cornerback. "Champ Bailey steps on a blade of grass wrong and he's got an MRI."

"But you're a human being."

"I'm not complaining. It is what it is. It was just a really screwy deal."

(Greek tells me that prior to the Kansas City game, Paul showed no clinical symptoms of a torn ACL. He also says that team doctors examined Paul at each step of his injury.)

At the start of the season, Paul was on the fifty-three-man roster and earning the NFL's then-minimum salary of $230,000. If Paul had been placed on the injured-reserve list after the San Diego game, he would have been entitled to about $146,000 for the season. But because he had already been shifted to the practice squad, where his pay was about $4,700 a week, or about $80,000 for the season, that's what he was paid after the ACL finally tore. He was reluctant to complain, or to call the players' union. "I'm a rookie, trying to get my career started. I don't have a name for myself. Nobody knows me. I couldn't do anything."

Paul says he doesn't hold the team responsible. He says the front office was supportive, and he praises Greek, an NFL trainer for thirty years, for pushing him aggressively during rehabilitation. "Your name's on my knee," Paul told him. But he learned a lesson about life in the NFL: Look out for yourself, because the team may not be looking out for you.

Now Paul says he has recovered fully and thinks he is good enough to punt for most NFL teams. The Broncos with Todd aren't one of them, he believes. Paul had been insurance against Todd getting into trouble. Now the policy had come due, which felt strange. Paul had grown close to Todd. They were drinking buddies. While Paul was an award-winning honors student with a 3.6 grade point average in computer information systems at Northern Arizona, he seemed to hide his intellect. Paul, Todd, and I had eaten at Earl's the previous night, and the relationship to me looked like the insecure high-school sophomore trying to hang with the dangerous senior. On the first day of camp, Paul had driven Todd's car out of the players' parking lot to help him avoid the photographers and cameramen stationed there.

Despite their friendship, Paul recognizes that Todd wants him to do badly. "It's nothing personal," he says. "It's just business. He doesn't want me here. I wouldn't either. You've got this young guy who will always compete with you, always push you, so if you screw up they'll just go with him." Todd has told Paul the team will keep him, but he wants to make sure it's only for four games. "He just wants to instill in me that I don't have a shot, which I know is not true," Paul says.

Chris Trulove, the team's pro scouting coordinator, comes over. Paul hops off the flatbed and they walk to the other side of the lot. Chris tells Paul the team will work out a few veteran punters next week and likely sign one to compete in training camp. But he also reassures Paul that he is the first choice to replace Todd, at least temporarily. "That's why I want to stay here," Paul says. "Everyone's been so nice." Last year, after the injury, general manager Ted Sundquist called Paul to his office to encourage him. "At least they're thinking about me and they've got me in the back of their heads, which means something." Kicking well in the next month will mean a lot more.

Mike Shanahan told me that Paul will return for training camp. "He's a little bit of a head case, but he does have ability," the coach said. Of the other kickers in camp, Jeff Williams "doesn't have a chance," and won't be back. Then there's Tyler Fredrickson. "Tyler has done pretty good statistically, but he hasn't done very good when we get together as a team," Shanahan said. Still, he planned to keep Tyler for August.

During live drills the previous day, Tyler shanked a punt that traveled 19 yards. He hung his head but didn't throw his helmet or curse. (He never does.) Immediately afterward, though, he marched off and punted a dozen balls on the turf field. Paul and Todd laughed at him behind his back. I tell Tyler this later, as we watch World Cup soccer highlights in my hotel room. He understands how the scene might have been interpreted. But Tyler says he just didn't want to end the day on a bad kick. "I hate leaving the field in general when the rest of the team is practicing," he says. "I want to be out there. I want to be seen. A coach sees that as, 'He's crying and going to go rip some balls.' I see it as, 'We have a couple extra kicks left, let's go get them.'"

"I see this as an opportunity that God has given me to come out here and do the best I can do. Why would I want to sit around at practice, when we have valuable practice time on the field, and watch and talk about our weekends and get caught up on our vacations? Now we've got the time, we've got the coaches available, the balls are there, we've got nowhere else to be. Let's put the ball in the air."

Tyler would rather work hard than look cool. He says he doesn't respect Paul, whose "little role model has been Todd for the last year—that attitude that, 'I don't give a crap, I'm going to drink and party.'" But in the repressed milieu of the locker room, Tyler's earnestness can seem unhip and his self-analysis whiny. Players are supposed to keep their insecurities private. Tyler is more susceptible to the emotional seesaw of being both a player on the margin and a kicker. He wants to do well so badly—maybe too badly.

"What I want to do is utilize my education, my personality, my ability to lead people, which I think I've got, to manage people," he says. "And also my creativity, to come up with new ideas, new ways around things, to be artistic. In the NFL, none of those things matter for the kicker. They don't care about your education. They don't care about your team management because they don't look to kickers as leaders.

"There's nothing creative about it. It's black and white. Either you drill it or you're out. And there's no personality in it. You can be the nicest guy in the world or the funniest guy. If you don't hit those two punts the way they want to see them, you're done. It's very much a business, but it doesn't correlate to the way the business world works."

Over dinner at a Chinese restaurant, Tyler tells me he's impressed with how I've managed to assimilate into the culture of the team. "Because you've done nothing to deserve it," he says. "You've never gone through the rigors of high-school or college football. And yet you are here." Tyler doesn't mean to sound jealous, but I appreciate his frustration. He's trying, vainly so far, to create a career in a sport in which he isn't entirely comfortable.

"Do you mind if I give thanks?" Tyler asks.

He gives thanks for the food. He asks that I travel safely. He asks that we stay healthy in practice. He doesn't ask that he make the Denver Broncos. That's up to Him, and to Mike Shanahan.

7

There It Is

In the days before training camp, I consider how little time my body has had to internalize the dynamic movements of kicking and how few footballs I have actually kicked—fifteen hundred tops. I had wanted to join an NFL team not as a deluded fantasy camper but as a competent amateur who in a moment of inspiration could pass for a pro. Paul Woodside's unstated goal has been to persuade me that I'm there. He believes. Me, not so much.

In the thick outfield grass of a girls' softball field at Edison High, Paul and I meet for one final practice session. He arranges twelve orange traffic cones in a long inverted V, an airport runway from the cockpit. The shape will force me to zero in on a point in the distance, and remind me that the longer the field goal, the smaller the uprights will appear. Paul crouches about thirty-five yards from the chain-link fence beyond the third-base line. Of my first fourteen kicks, just three clear it. My drive step, the last step before the kick, is too long. My hips are turning more, right leg reaching behind my body, but I'm still pulling left on impact: the soccer problem again. Power and distance, Paul says, come from quickness and leg speed. I adjust, and the ball travels better during the next set, but I still make just three of fourteen.

At this point in my kicking education, psychology may be more important than physiology. My body may not have mastered the technique, but Paul says I know enough to kick well and am smart enough to will myself to kick even better. Stuart Smalley, meet Jason Elam. Anyway,

Paul says, in Denver I need to *forget* everything I've practiced, or at least not think about it. I have to be out of body, number 9, an actual NFL player on an actual NFL team. "Your name's on the back of that shirt," Paul says. "But that's not for you to see. Because you're performing as a functional part of a team. The individual doesn't matter."

This is a repeat conversation for us. Mind over reality—Paul's mind over my reality. After a third, unremarkable set, Paul tells me that from the day I dialed him out of the blue ten months earlier until now, I've done remarkably well. I concede that under his tutelage, I can visualize the technique that will allow me to bang 40-yarders through the uprights every time. But I can't execute it every time, I say, can't bridge the gulf between weekend athlete and professional athlete. I see this as the ultimate obstacle to performance and acceptance in Denver. Paul thinks it's a distinction without a difference.

"How about competitive athlete?" he says. "Who's your competition? Yourself. If you're looking for some scoop, this is actually easier than you're trying to make it."

I had wanted to get beyond Plimpton's "to see how one got along" rationale for mingling with the pros on the field. I had wanted to become an athlete. Paul is saying I've been one all along. Not because I possess reasonable athletic skills; even if I don't ever nail a 50-yarder, taking three steps and striking a football and making it travel relatively high and relatively far and moving fluidly in the process is by definition an athletic behavior. No, I'm an athlete because I can make adjustments on command, Paul says, like I just did, kicking footballs that would have been good from 30 or 35 yards. In his training-camp summer in Buffalo in 1985, Paul says he lacked confidence, didn't know himself well enough to be able to adjust and kick better. In my training-camp summer in Denver in 2006, he wants confidence not to be a problem. He wants me to kick with the understanding that I am Jason Elam's peer, not as a kicker but as a professional.

"You're successful. He's successful. There's no difference," Paul says. "Kicking-wise you have to turn the switch on that turns all the noise off—the perfectionism and the doubt and the fear of failure or looking bad. All of that. Your end-all thing is, 'I want to kick a great ball.' And I understand that. You will, but you're only as good as your next kick. You kick one, it means you've only kicked one. You've already kicked one."

This is a forehead-whacking moment of clarity. I won't kick only "great balls" in Denver, whether I'm alone on the field, in front of my teammates during Specialist period, facing a firing squad of players and fans during a field-goal drill, maybe even in a stadium filled with Broncomaniacs clad in orange and blue. But it won't matter. *I've already kicked one.* I just have to ignore the distractions, forget whether the last ball went through the middle of the uprights or into the snapper's ass, and have fun—for myself, but also for Paul and for everyone who will never get to stand on an NFL field.

As we say good-bye in the parking lot, I thank Paul for paying attention to "a forty-year-old guy who can't kick the ball more than thirty yards." I'm sad that our teacher-student relationship is ending. Paul seems to be, too. He hands me a manila envelope and asks me not to open it until later.

Inside is a DVD of *Rocky* and a handwritten note.

"Thank you for making it possible," it says, "for those who have missed the opportunity or never had one to begin with."

There isn't a professional football player alive who has looked forward to training camp, and the dead ones didn't like it either. In his myth-busting 1970 memoir *Out of Their League,* former St. Louis Cardinals linebacker Dave Meggyesy decried the "dehumanizing conditions" and "enforced infantilization" of pro football generally, but of training camp particularly. A coach, Meggyesy related, once yelled at him to hang up on a call with his wife from the one telephone in the team dormitory and go to bed.

"The whole thing is a pain in the ass," offensive lineman Jerry Kramer wrote on the first day of camp in his diary of Green Bay's 1967 season, *Instant Replay.* Then two-a-day workouts began. "You wonder why you're there, how long you're going to last. . . . You try to block out all the pain, all the gasping breaths, block it all out of your mind and function as an automaton." In his 1982 football recollection *The End of Autumn,* one-time Kansas City Chiefs center Michael Oriard, now a prominent academic voice on sports and society, wrote this of training camp: "Thinking was an unwanted burden; it was easier to stumble from bed to practice field, to meal, to meeting, without much reflection."

The institution of training camp dates almost to the founding of the NFL in 1920. In Denver, it dates to mid-July 1960, when the first prospective members of a charter American Football League franchise convened at the Colorado School of Mines in Golden, at the eastern edge of the Rockies. In the shadow of Lookout Mountain, the burial site of Buffalo Bill Cody, eighty players vied for thirty-three roster spots. They were a ragtag collection. Al Carmichael, a halfback, had worked as an insurance salesman and a stunt man, playing a Roman gladiator in *Spartacus.* A 260-pound defensive tackle named John Hatley was a rodeo steer wrestler. The quarterback, Frank Tripucka, was a former Notre Dame star who had played four seasons in the NFL and seven in Canada.

After arriving in Golden, the players surrendered the keys to their cars, which were sequestered behind locked gates. At night, they slept on dormitory beds arranged three feet apart on the floor of an old basketball court. The players struggled to get into shape. A *Denver Post* columnist wrote that many were "fat enough to butcher." For seven weeks, the new Broncos were whistled out of their bunks at 6:45 a.m., ate breakfast, taped up, and walked three blocks to the fields for three hours of calisthenics and practice. The players dressed in full pads—and used them—almost every day. After breaking at 11:00 for lunch and rest, the team scrimmaged from 3:30 to 5. If there were no evening meetings, bed check was at 10 with lights out at 10:30. "Life in a professional football camp is almost like being in the Army," the *Post* reported.

The modern Broncos camp is more like a short stay in a country-club prison. This year's begins on July 27 and ends on August 18, just three weeks. The players will already be in superb physical condition from the off-season workouts and organized team activities and short camps. They will don complete uniforms only a few times. My teammates won't have to hand over the keys to the Escalades, Bentleys, Navigators, and Ford pickups that fill their gated lot. But they won't be permitted to leave team headquarters during working hours—which can run from 6:30 a.m. to 9:30 p.m.—except in a shuttle bus after lunch to nap in rooms at the Holiday Inn. Driving to work in the morning is a perk for veterans. The rookies and free agents staying at the hotel—more spartan than the Summerfield Suites but closer to team headquarters— always have to ride the bus. As do I. A Broncos staffer checks players' names as they arrive.

Still, twice-a-day workouts in the summer heat are twice-a-day workouts in the summer heat. When I wake with nerves (and still on East Coast time) at 6 a.m. on day one, I check the five-day forecast: high temperatures between ninety-four and ninety-eight degrees. The pressure of camp will be exponentially higher than three weeks ago, let alone forty-six years ago. Broncos scouts have converged on Dove Valley, as the area around the facility is known, from far-flung outposts to help the twenty-two coaches and assorted front-office executives evaluate the players. The physical demands will be enormous. Contact is constant, even during sessions without shoulder pads, and every drill moves at full speed. Fans will assemble on a berm along the farthest sideline. Hordes of media will shoot hours of footage and file hundreds of stories. When I arrive, the visitors parking lot is crowded with television trucks, satellite antennas aloft. And we're not even practicing this day.

"It's a ton more intense," Preston Parsons says when we reconnect in the locker room. The offensive linemen are grimly studying the camp schedule programmed to the minute by Shanahan and inserted in the front of their three-ring playbooks. The good news: no early-morning position meetings before practice, which means only two rounds of meetings per day (after lunch and after dinner) instead of the three some players suffered on other teams. The bad news: everything surrounding the two meetings.

"You ready for this?" a second-year center with a shaved head named

Chris Myers asks. He answers for me. "You're never ready for this. You won't even be hitting and you'll be dying." Chad Mustard, my locker neighbor, needed three Tylenol PM tablets to close his eyes the night before. Tony Scheffler, the rookie tight end, will lose fifteen pounds in the first day and a half from stress, exhaustion, and lack of appetite. Tight end Nate Jackson will empty his bowels seven times the first day. "You know you have to perform at the highest level every single day," Nate tells me. "Your body knows that. Like on game day, I can't eat. This is like game day for a month."

Al Wilson, the linebacker and team captain, spots me. "Hey, man. How you been?" he says. "You ready to do this shit? Ready to have fun?"

"It doesn't sound like fun," I reply.

"It better be fun."

Jason Elam appreciates that as a kicker who doesn't have to compete for a job, he has it far easier than everyone else. "How late can I get here?" he says, paging through the playbook. "When's our first day off?" He laughs, and then turns serious, out of deference to his teammates. "The first week is just brutal."

In the equipment room, teenage and preteen boys in orange Broncos T-shirts push and taunt each other. "Babysitting the ball boys," equipment manager Chris Valenti says, rolling his eyes. "Lots of fun." Inflatable mattresses are scattered around the locker room, a harbinger of the fatigue to come. The coaches get them, too. One is standing in the corner next to the TV in Ronnie Bradford's office. Sheets and blankets are piled on his chairs.

For me, the major changes are in my locker. Imposing gray shoulder pads on the top shelf. Two pairs of white football pants hanging on hooks, one with an orange stripe, one with a blue stripe. My name centered on the nameplate overhead. I have the locker to myself now.

Two days earlier, Tyler Fredrickson's name flashed on my cell phone, and I knew what had happened. To replace Todd during his four-game suspension, the Broncos had a choice: Let regular-season punting virgins Paul and Tyler compete for the job along with a veteran. Or give just one of the novices a chance. General manager Ted Sundquist told Tyler that Paul was a draft pick and that the team had signed thirty-one-year-old Micah Knorr, who had started for the Broncos in 2002, 2003, and most of 2004. Sundquist promised to help any way he could.

Tyler hung up, lay on the floor of his apartment in Oakland, and told God how he felt. He said he was frustrated and confused about what God was doing with his life. Why had He carried him this far for this long—hanging on in football for three years—only to leave him disappointed again? Why did He keep closing one door only to open another? "There's no justice here," Tyler told me. "The good thing with God is that there is justice with Him. And all things work according to His plans and according to His glory. I can rest on that." But he still believed the Broncos were making a mistake.

When a player is released, coaches and teammates don't dwell on it for long. A cut guy is like a communicable disease. "That's the business," Chad Mustard says. "I've been cut enough times to know." (Five times in three years by two NFL teams, to be exact. Chad also played for the Rhein Fire of the NFL's European league and the Omaha Beef—yes, the Omaha Beef—of the National Indoor Football League, whatever that is.) Ronnie Bradford dispassionately shifted the magnet bearing Tyler's name from the whiteboard to a stack of rejects on a shelf below, his "fallen soldiers pile."

I move on, too. I spread my belongings across the width of the locker. I extract my workout clothes from my mesh bag: XXXXL shorts and an XXXL shirt. I've been punked. When I walk into the equipment room holding the shorts aloft like a mainsail, the equipment guys are laughing. "We wanted to see if you gained weight," Valenti says. Well, I have just hit a record 172 pounds. But I am still X-less for shorts and tees.

The first team meeting of training camp is like the first team meeting of minicamp, only more crowded. Sixty Broncos staff members sit behind Mike Shanahan: eight coaches for the offense, eight for the defense, two for the special teams, and three for strength and conditioning; front-office personnel; trainers; equipment managers; media-relations staffers. They look like a high-school band without instruments.

Shanahan reminds us that camp is shorter than it used to be. But also that it's not easy. Out come his favorite phrases: "It's a bitch . . . do the little things the right way . . . a chance to do something special." For the nth time, he reminds us to be punctual, mentioning the year he forced Jake Plummer to sleep at the Holiday Inn because he was fifteen seconds late to a meeting, a story the antiestablishment quarterback must just love hearing.

Shanahan introduces the coaches individually. He praises Ronnie Bradford as "not only a great defensive back but smart enough to know that to stay in this league you've got to play on special teams." Context is everything. In his book, Shanahan recalled a sideline moment from the Broncos' second Super Bowl win, over Atlanta, for whom Ronnie was playing. "They're dead," Shanahan told quarterback John Elway. "We've got a good play, especially if we're going against Bradford."

For two hours and five minutes, we are lectured on minutia from how much Gatorade we can take from the practice facility at night (more than one twelve-ounce bottle, less than a case) to the daily autograph routine (four players and one coach for ten minutes after practice) to the need to shower before entering the hot and cold tubs to deter the spread of the potentially lethal bacteria MRSA, which has appeared in some NFL locker rooms. Ted Sundquist enumerates a new leaguewide fine system "to protect your teammates from distraction, the distraction being your conduct." Operations manager Chip Conway asks us to use the Port-O-Lets by the fields to relieve ourselves during practice. "Don't go behind the trees." Media chief Jim Saccomano encourages us to give interviews but to let him know if we don't want to do a particular one. The media, he says, want their "pound of flesh" and will be gone.

Betsy Klein, the team psychologist, discusses a survey of 15,700 current and former NFL players about their playing days. If the dawn of training camp and a season of ceaseless violence and pain don't make the players question their career choice, the survey results might. Frustration and/or irritability was cited by 68 percent of the respondents, Klein says. Fatigue: 50 percent. Sleep difficulties: 30 percent. Anger: 38 percent. Poor concentration/distractibility: 25 percent. Anxiety: 24 percent. Headaches: 20 percent. Unwanted thoughts/lack of confidence: 11 percent. Depression: 10 percent. "Every one of these things can be resolved," she tells us. "If they haven't, my question is, why not? That's what I'm here for."

Don't buy over-the-counter medication, head trainer Steve "Greek" Antonopoulos warns, don't take weight-control medications, check with the NFL drug hotline before taking vitamins. Performance-drug testing in the locker room starts tomorrow (photo ID required). "If you test positive, we can help you—or you're stupid," Greek says. "Every swinging dick in this room is counted on. Think about your teammates." At this, I swivel slowly and look at Todd Sauerbrun, seated two leather chairs away. He is glaring at the podium.

After minicamp, the NFL officially announced Todd's four-game suspension, and now the wayward punter has to perform his mea culpa. At a team meeting after dinner, Shanahan dons gold-rim half eyeglasses and reads twenty-nine more team rules. (1. Must attend every meal. 5. Double parking a $500 fine. 10. No vulgarity in front of fans. 14. Don't chase too many women. 19. No distractions because of religion, politics, business, or personality. 25. No hotel room-service. 26. No hotel-room guests. 27. Minimal end-zone celebrating. "If you do a lot of that shit in the end zone," he says, "you better be good.") Then he removes his glasses, leans on the podium, gazes sternly from his narrow, intense, piercing eyes, and summons Todd. The room is silent as Todd, in a bright red sleeveless tee, walks past me and down the aisle.

"I just really want to apologize to all of you guys," he says. "I did a stupid thing that I regret now. You guys are the best group of guys I've ever been around since I've been in the league." Todd admits taking ephedra—and not to lose weight but to work out harder. "It was for a good purpose, but it was stupid. It backfired on me. All I can say is it'll never happen again. I'll be more than ready when I come back and we'll go to war together. When I come back I'll be more than ready for all you guys."

Todd steps away and Shanahan speaks.

"The thing I appreciate about Todd is he said, 'I fucked up.'"

And that's it for the Todd "situation." Shanahan will never mention it in front of the team again.

There are three methods of passage from the locker room to the field: out the frosted-glass-doors main entrance, left, and through two sets of orange double doors; a zigzag through the trainer's room and a quick left through the orange doors; out the rear of the locker room and through doors near the media workroom. The last is used predominantly to dodge the reporters and cameras clustered near the main entrance, behind a yellow rope and a sign at the field's edge, new for training camp, reading: RESTRICTED AREA. BRONCOS PERSONNEL ONLY BEYOND THIS POINT.

As we emerge in ones and twos and threes, photographers snap the first moments of 2006 training camp like paparazzi. Fans also are shooting, from under a shade tent reserved for a group of disabled visitors who apparently don't miss a practice. I play it cool, ignoring the lenses and sauntering confidently into the restricted area.

"When do we break camp?" Jason Elam deadpans.

"Shit, you don't even have to kick for the next ten days," T-Mac says. "You're just here for the camera work."

"Stefan, drink plenty of water out there today," long snapper Mike Leach cracks as he jogs by. "It's going to be hot."

We stretch, we trot to the kickers' field, we get some pole. I ask Jason to explain the lingo on the daily practice schedule. Jason keeps a copy of the schedule folded in quarters and tucked inside his helmet. At the top is the date, the practice number—1 to 28, the last one on the day before our second preseason game—and the duration of the practice. AM or PM is boldfaced and underlined, as is the manner of dress: shorts, which in terms of protection means just helmets; shells, which are light shoulder pads worn by linemen and some other constant-contact players; or shoulder pads, usually with shorts, a few times in full uniform with pants.

An eight-columned chart establishes the type of activity, its duration, and its specifics. Practice always begins with a five-minute warm-up and ten minutes of Tuten-led stretching. After that, this day, comes thirty-five minutes of Individual, in which players work with their position coaches. Next, while the wide receivers and defensive backs go One-on-One, the rest of the team does Nine-on-Seven: nine offensive players (no wide receivers) against seven defenders (no backs). That lasts twelve minutes and is followed by twenty-five minutes of Seven-on-Seven, which includes no linemen at all. "That's fun to watch," Jason says.

Next is twenty minutes of Team, with full complements on both sides of the ball. Ten of those minutes are devoted to a formation known as Tiger and ten to a formation called Base. I ask Jason to explain them. "Uh, I don't know what that is," he says. (Tiger, I learn later, features two tight ends, two wide receivers, and one running back. Base is one tight end, two wide receivers, and two running backs.) Then comes ten more minutes of Individual and ten minutes of Team with an empty backfield. Then Punt Pro. Total time: one hour and fifty-two minutes.

With Tyler and Jeff Williams gone, and the punting competition narrowed and focused, the stakes have changed. Paul Ernster and Micah Knorr have been told they are fighting for a four-game job. But whoever wins that beauty contest wants to demonstrate that he is worthy of replacing Todd permanently. No matter how confident Todd might try to appear, his roster spot isn't guaranteed. With its voidable contracts, the NFL conditions players to be territorial about their jobs. Todd needs Paul and Micah to fail, Micah needs Todd and Paul to fail, and Paul needs Micah and Todd to fail. Go for it, boys.

Micah, who is left-footed, takes snaps from Jason and practices punting to the right side of the field. Todd nonchalantly asks, "Where you going with that?"

"Right," Micah says.

"Straight and long is all I know," Todd says.

Unlike Paul, who has let Todd inside his head, Micah is unmoved. Ronnie told me the team chose to sign him sight unseen over four punters they auditioned because he was a familiar quantity who "had played up under the lights." If Paul stumbles, the Broncos will be safe with Micah.

The night before, Micah and I talked for two hours in his room at the Holiday Inn. Sitting cross-legged on the bed, in a T-shirt depicting vintage Coca-Cola bottles, Micah described a winding road from a blue-collar section of Orange County, California, to the NFL. Micah said he is estranged from his parents, and from his siblings. As a kid, Micah took kicking lessons from "Bootin'" Ben Agajanian, one of pro football's first kicking specialists. (In a career that lasted from 1945 to 1964, Agajanian, who kicked with the stub of his right foot after his toes were sheared off in a freight-elevator accident, suited up for ten teams in the NFL, the AFL, and the All-America Football Conference. He is one of only two men to play in all three major pro leagues.) Micah managed to land a scholarship to Utah State, but the NFL wasn't a realistic prospect. A couple of years after graduating, Micah was managing a Champs sporting goods store when a coworker persuaded him to give pro football a shot.

The Cowboys saw him at a tryout camp for kickers in 2000 and signed him. When the regular punter was injured, Micah suddenly was starting in the NFL. He was cut by Dallas during the 2002 season and picked up by Denver. Micah had been ill with what was probably bronchitis when the Broncos released him. He didn't play in 2005. But it wasn't so bad, he said. The New York Jets had given him a $75,000 signing bonus before releasing him during camp.

"I added it up," Micah told me. "What I made my first four or five years, it would have taken me twenty years at Champs to make."

I connect with Micah instantly. He is friendly, modest, forthcoming, and passionate about kicking. In stocking feet in the hotel room, he demonstrated details about the craft that came up in conversation. Ronnie had described him as reliable, dedicated, and consistent. So why, I wonder, didn't the Broncos save themselves the headache and keep Micah or someone like him? In five NFL seasons, Micah posted a gross average of 41.4 yards per punt and a net average (deducting return yards) of 33.5 yards. Todd's career numbers were 44.0 and 36.0. The difference: 2½ yards.

On a football field, though, that's a lot. Field position is one of the game's most underrated components. The game is a tug of war, with the two sides pushing instead of pulling. The farther back a punter pins the opposing offense, the farther the offense has to travel to score. An NFL team averages about eighty punts per season. In raw numbers, then, Todd's punts position opponents a collective 200 yards deeper than Micah's punts. And that distance correlates to scoring. By one calculation, every five yards of field position equals about 0.4 points in scoring. Todd's extra yards, multiplied by those eighty kicks per season, are "worth" about 16 points for his team.

Mike Shanahan understands Todd's ability to "flip the field," to instantly transform the Broncos' lousy field position into their opponent's lousy field position. That's why Shanahan traded for Todd, and that's why Todd is still in camp. Shanahan further acknowledges the importance of the kicking game with his willingness to carry three kickers— one to kick off, one to punt, one to placekick—as he did in 2005 before Paul's injury (and still could this coming season). Most teams don't want to spend the money.

"If I were a coach, I'd go out and get the best punter and then I'd go get the best field-goal kicker and then I'd go get the best kickoff guy and I'd carry three," Jason Elam tells me. "So it's an extra roster spot. Who cares? If you had a linebacker who could impact a game and make a difference of five or ten yards on every kickoff, that guy would be making ten million a year. What does it matter that it takes a roster spot? It's a whole perception—'Ooooh, those roster spots are so important. I don't want to sign a guy and pay him two hundred fifty grand to come out here and kick off four or five times a game.' If that's the way you look at it, yeah, it's probably not a good investment. But if you look at it the way you *should* look at it"—Jason laughs—"in my opinion, it makes a huge difference."

After the last set of Team drills, the 1,103 fans who showed up on a weekday morning to watch what amounts to touch football—without the scoring—are ushered out of the complex and back to their cars. They aren't allowed to stay for special-teams practice. What they miss is the sound of footballs shooting at seventy-five miles per hour from a Jugs Football Machine, which consists of two six-inch-thick discs tilted skyward and spinning in opposite directions like deranged pottery wheels. On a coach's command, an equipment staffer drops footballs into a slot like mortars into a launcher. The balls slingshot out with a metallic clang, float on the air, and land in the arms of wide receiver Javon Walker forty yards away.

Jugs never misses a kick, unless it's instructed to by changing the settings for speed, angle, or direction. Todd steps in to replace the machine. Keith "Tick" Burns announces the formation, shouting out the rushing team's alignment so his charges can react. Tick screams, "Six man center stack! Six man center stack!" meaning the receiving team has six rushers clustered around the middle of the line of scrimmage, with four other players guarding the punt team's two "gunners," who will race downfield to the returner. "Spacing and leverage, guys!" Ronnie Bradford yells at the line. "Spacing and leverage!" Mike Leach snaps the ball, Todd crushes it, and Javon retreats to catch it.

"You *better* back your ass up," Todd says.

His second kick doesn't travel as far. "Dumped it," Jason says, meaning that Todd dropped the ball with the nose pointing down. "Yeah, I did," Todd says, moving his right hand in a diving motion.

Micah is next, and he shanks his first official kick of training camp to the left.

"Come on, Micah," Ronnie says. "Gotta show something."

On the next two, he does, blasting balls with hang times of 4.75 and 5.08 seconds.

"Nice one," says Paul Ernster, waiting his turn. "Attagirl."

Jason turns to me and says, "It's more fun listening to the head games."

Though the number of diners has increased by only a few dozen, the offerings and amount of food has tripled from minicamp. For this lunch, there are four kinds of salads, two vegetables, two soups, three pastas, two entrées, two starches, two desserts, and bread, not to mention a staffed sandwich counter, ice-cream freezer, espresso machine, drink fountains, and drink refrigerators (two). Some players, as instructed, pile mounds of sloppy joes and hash browns and salads and banana pudding on their plates. Some pick at their food. Some force themselves to eat.

One player, at least, is exultant. Offensive left tackle Matt Lepsis, who had stared and laughed during my locker-room arrival, says that Shanahan summoned him with very good news. While others will toil twice a day during training camp, he will practice only in the mornings. That's a reward Shanahan bestows on a few veterans. Lepsis, in his tenth season, all with Denver, is joining a cadre of elites who stand on the sideline, a pinch of chewing tobacco behind their lower lips, watching their teammates suffer in the afternoons. "One of the three happiest moments in my life," Lepsis says. "It has restored my love for the game."

If he weren't a kicker, Jason Elam would long ago have been on a diet of one-a-days. But he knows not to complain, even if it does get hot in shoulder pads in the afternoon. The trick to being a kicker and to being accepted is not making yourself a target, Jason says. So when camp starts, don't pretend to suffer what everyone else actually is suffering. "I've never been treated like an outsider. Never," he says. But, he points out, "I've never said stupid things. If you say stupid things and do stupid things you're going to be treated like a stupid person." Just this morning, Paul Ernster sat at a table with Stephen Alexander and said what might be viewed as a stupid thing: "You looking forward to this as much as I am?" he said sarcastically. Paul probably was just trying to fit in, but, as Jason could have counseled, he should be the last guy on the team to whine. Not only will the kickers not be bashing each other's heads in, but Todd had just gifted Paul a chance to make it—permanently—in the NFL.

"Let me show you my office," Jason says after lunch. "I have a secret place."

We walk outside, through the weight room, down a short set of metal stairs, and into a warehouse space filled with groundskeeping equipment. Pat Bowlen's dark blue Porsche Cayenne Turbo is to the right. (Bowlen parks here because he likes walking to his office through the places the players frequent.) Turf manager Troy Smith's office is to the left. When the Broncos rebuilt the weight and groundskeeping facility, Troy set aside desk space for Jason, including an Internet connection for his silver Apple PowerBook G4.

I haven't seen Jason work under pressure—or, frankly, work at all—but he navigates the locker room, hallways, and back corridors of the building with Clintonian ease. Jason doesn't gripe, is liked by everyone, and seems to want to like everyone. And he appears sincere. We spend an hour and a half schmoozing in Troy's office, and each manifestation of Jason's personality and revelation of his life outside of football makes me feel like a lesser human being.

Jason tells me he has a real-estate broker's license and owns two RE/MAX franchises in suburban Denver. He is a licensed commercial pilot and a flight instructor for single-engine planes, with 1,500 hours of flight time. To gain experience, he delivered emergency medical specimens (urine, mainly) for a pharmaceutical company. For fun, he flies a bright red 1957 de Havilland Beaver. Jason hunts and fishes with ardor. He has caught salmon in Alaska and marlin in Costa Rica, bagged a mountain lion in Colorado and a giraffe in South Africa. Even his love life is storybook: Jason tells me he wooed a Broncos cheerleader with a single rose and a sappy note. Five months later, he and Tamy Cline were engaged. Today, they have four kids, whose names all start with the letter J. They home-school the two oldest.

From Troy's office, Jason is working on a master's degree in divinity through the Denver Seminary. He still needs two years of Hebrew and two years of ancient Greek. Jason calls himself "a very committed Christian," but he's not an in-your-face one. "I don't have a problem talking about it," he says, "but I don't want to be a goofball either." He has joined Christian relief missions to distant corners of the world. He helped build an addition to an orphanage in Uganda. He visited a Kenyan village with a ministry that gets the Bible translated into languages in which it doesn't exist.

When he retires, Jason wants to study religion at Oxford and take his family on a yearlong world tour. He watched the 2004 Super Bowl from a U.S. Army multinational force base in Kosovo, where he shot a .50-caliber machine gun and a Mark 19 automatic grenade launcher. Oh, and he and a buddy are producing a fishing and hunting show that he wants to call *The Off-Season*. They've shown segments to television executives, and are compiling more footage.

As adventures go, the past off-season includes Jason's most harrowing. He took his family on a Holy Land tour and stayed on to deliver food and supplies to refugee camps in the Gaza Strip. Jason and his colleagues were stranded for three days amid bombings and shootings; a missile landed a block and a half from where they were staying. A few weeks later, he was flying a single-engine Piper Pacer over the Kenai Peninsula in Alaska when the engine conked out. Elam safely landed the plane on a narrow, muddy stretch of coastline—next to a grizzly bear. After a few minutes, the bear ran off and the engine restarted.

As a successful NFL player, Jason has earned millions—his current contract paid a $2.675 million signing bonus and has a 2006 base salary of $1.3 million—but without the attendant threat of debilitating post-career injuries. Plus, for two or three hours in the middle of the workday, while his colleagues are recovering from various physical traumas, Jason can take a master's course or check on his real-estate business or schmooze with a fellow kicker. But he recognizes that he has performed one of the most unsettling jobs in sports long enough to be the most tenured member of his team. He has remained relatively injury-free because he has paid attention to his body.

"There's a lot of guys who can kick the ball a long way," Jason says. "And there's a lot of guys that may be pretty decent in practice. But when you get into a game situation, it's different. Can you still kick the ball the same when the adrenaline's really flowing? Even in a preseason game, your nerves are there. In the NFL, you always feel like you've got to prove yourself. Every day."

"Even you?" I ask.

"Oh, yeah. On Monday, I want to do well." The following Monday is the first field-goal session on the camp schedule. "I want my coach to be proud of me: 'Okay, he hasn't lost anything.' I worry more now about them thinking that. I still feel good. I'm not doing the kickoffs and I don't have any desire to do the kickoffs, because it takes a lot out of you. That's really helped me. But at the same time, I better make my field goals. Because they are always trying to upgrade their team. Because you are a replaceable part. It's just that unknown. What are they thinking and how long am I going to be here?"

I'm trying to understand what Jason has experienced, but also how it might apply to me. I ask what he considers the hardest part about playing in the NFL.

"Just being under the microscope," he says.

"Which microscope?" I say. "The microscope from the coaches? The microscope from the fans?"

"Um, yes." He laughs. "The whole thing. It's not easy when you are giving your best shot and you're in front of millions of people and you have an off day. As a professional athlete, you can't have off days or you get replaced. Just hearing the criticism—I mean nobody likes that, especially when they're giving it everything they've got. Sometimes you roll with it. Sometimes it gets to you. You've just got to develop a thick skin. You're never going to make everybody happy. It could always be a higher ball. It could always be a longer ball. Instead of being ninety-eight percent it could be ninety-nine percent. But that's just part of it, being part of the NFL.

"The biggest thing is you've got to be okay with the outcome either way. Trust your swing is number two. Let it rip and more often than not you're going to make it. If you miss it, oh, well. It won't be a whole lot of fun for a few days. But, what is it, a billion Chinese won't care?"

During two-a-days, the afternoon practice begins with a fifteen-minute special-teams meeting and fifteen minutes of Specialist. The regular practice follows, with a ten-minute Punt Pro session halfway through. Stepping outside, on my right foot I wear a new size-7 Reebok cleat over a thin, NFL-issue, 85 percent cotton sanitary sock; on my left foot one of my size-7 Adidas with a thick, NFL-issue, 90 percent Duraspun Acrylic "coach quarter sock." The Reebok shoe feels tight—but I feel morally obligated to wear the free gear that the company has sent me.

Before training camp, I decided that a shoe contract would help me feel like a real NFL player. I first called Nike, which shoes about 70 percent of the league's players. But the company's public-relations guy didn't get back to me for days. Reebok quickly connected me with its "NFL Footwear Specialist," Doug West, the sales rep for fifteen teams, including the Broncos. (Nike and Reebok are licensed NFL footwear suppliers. Kickers, however, can wear whatever brand they want.)

West also happens to be Chris Valenti's predecessor as the Broncos' equipment manager. He instantly agreed to play along. "Look at it this way," he said. "You're one of the guys on the team. We want to take care of you like that." Since my Copa Mundials don't fit like sausage casings, I told him I might need a size 6½ for my right foot. West had never been asked for anything that small, but he promised to find something similar to the Adidas model. He also e-mailed me Reebok's standard five-page endorsement contract, filled out in my name. Under the agreement, I will wear Reebok products "exclusively during all athletic workouts, practices, tournaments, games, events, exhibitions, media interviews and during all public activities where it is appropriate to wear Products." I will keep "all Reebok trademarks visible, and with no other trademarks affixed thereto." In exchange, Reebok will compensate me with $3,000 worth of merchandise a year, the standard for unknown NFL rookies.

For reasons of journalistic propriety, I didn't sign the contract. Still, when I arrived in camp, five boxes from Reebok were stacked in my locker, each labeled in marker with my uniform number: two pair of black NFL Casparo II cleats, size 6½ and 7, plus running shoes, cross-trainers, and shower shoes in my civilian size 8. My teammates were amazed—both that Reebok sent me product and that I rejected the contractual swag.

Shanahan and some of the position coaches wander out and make small talk and observe casually. There are no whistles or shouted orders, but the players attend to their jobs regardless. The kick returners, accompanied by some ball boys, trot to the far end of the near practice field. Mike Leach, Chris Myers, and Tony Scheffler hunch over and intermittently snap. Jake Plummer, Preston Parsons, and Jay Cutler catch and hold. Todd, Paul, and Micah swing their legs and arc balls downfield. Jason does too, but only after playing catch with Troy Smith.

During minicamp, Jason had told me to jump in, and I didn't, and the airhorn blew. No more. I've decided to take an ax to the wall separating writer and player. With the exception of Todd, my teammates have fully accepted my presence. I'm even fooling the fans. As I walked from one field to another earlier in the day, a boy of about six waved. "Hi, number nine!" he called. An adult fan asked my name and where I went to college. "So you've been around," he said. "A while," I replied with a smile, before confessing.

So when Preston offers to hold, I don't hesitate. Paul Ernster bends over the ball at the 16-yard line to snap. Preston kneels just beyond the 24-yard line to hold. I dab a spot for him with my right toe for the 34-yard field goal. I make three of five kicks, the last one, to my eyes, an airborne wonder, a confirmation of my progress since the first camp. Micah Knorr and kicking consultant Jeff Hays stand sentry, offering casual observations: I'm leaning back too far at impact, I'm approaching the plant on a curve instead of a straight line. But they are observing seriously, and I am as attentive as if *my* job were on the line this month.

Todd, naturally, is less impressed. During a second set with Preston and Paul, I leave a ball short and to the right. I hear Todd's Long Island nasal behind me.

"*There* it is!"

"I'm surprised it took you so long to give him shit," Paul says.

Todd smirks and sniffs. "There it is" is one of the catchphrases he tosses like a firecracker when someone screws up. "Bottle it!" is another. In an all-male environment, where shit giving is mandatory, this is funny, of course. It's funnier still when Todd mis-hits a ball and Jason barks "Bottle it, Todd!" giggling while Todd curses the world a few yards away.

I still haven't heard Jason swear and don't expect I will. Yet Jason not only tolerates Todd as a coworker—as placekicker and punter they are the NFL equivalent of cubicle mates—he seems to like him. Jason is the kid in high school who gets along equally well with the jocks, the brains, the geeks, and the slackers, and influences their behavior. His unadvertised commitment to doing well unto others allows him to appreciate why Todd might hate life in the NFL—the rules, the scrutiny, the monotony—and also to look past his acid commentary. " I don't think he means it to be mean," Jason tells me. "I think he's just joking around and as bored as everybody else around here."

As an athlete who wants his team to do well, Jason knows that Todd is a valuable football player. And he understands that NFL players feel pressure to perform and face decisions about how far to push for an advantage. Todd pushed too far. Jason believes the suspension wounded Todd emotionally, as well as financially. "It hurt him more than it hurt anybody else," Jason says. "It crushed him in a lot of ways." Jason, I think, saves his moral judgments, if he judges at all, for offenses greater than Todd's.

"I try to stay out of Todd's business," he says. "But at the same time, without him thinking I'm in his business, just tell him, 'You need to be smart about this thing.' Because he's so talented. He's the most talented punter I've ever seen. Oh man, by far. He hits balls I've never seen hit. He misses balls better than most guys can hit 'em perfect. He could play for twenty-five years if he doesn't upset—well, I'm sure they're pretty upset with him right now. And it put doubt upstairs in their minds: 'Can we trust him?' I'd like to be there to help him any way I can. At the same time, a lot of people don't want any outside help."

In other words, Jason doesn't feel sorry for Todd. And he certainly isn't unwilling to pick at him. When we reassemble, Jeff Hays has the punters practice ball drops. Jason knows how Todd feels about instruction, especially Jeff's sober, analytical instruction, so he dives right in. "Mold it, Todd," Jason says, at once tweaking Jeff and Todd's forced participation in the drill.

I vow to ignore Todd as much as my fragile ego will permit. Micah, it becomes clear, intends to be my guru. After the afternoon Punt Pro, we stay on the defense field, the one farther from the locker room. Micah tells me I need to kick more than I have been. I remind him that I'm forty-three. "You have to pretend you're a twenty-three-year-old free agent trying to make the team," he says.

Micah is channeling Paul Woodside. If I need a reminder to get into character, to block out reality, to willingly suspend disbelief, Micah will supply it. I've known the guy for only a day, but better than anyone here he understands my goal: not to make the Broncos but to feel what it's like to try to play in the NFL, and to challenge myself. I have one more month as a kicker. I should kick.

Micah says to kick with the wind, as a psychological aid more than a practical one; a steady wind doesn't help or hinder much inside 40 yards, he says. Everyone watches, even Todd. We start at 34 yards. Jason snaps to Paul, and I kick comfortably. The ball thumps off my foot with authority and sails through with distance to spare. Micah, though, reminds me to start my approach with the snap, to step in a straight line to the plant, and to explode through the ball. Micah places a ball under the red metal holder and smashes one through. "You're just kind of lofting it up there," he says, swinging his leg lazily. I shouldn't be happy just to clear the crossbar. Micah suggests imagining that I'm kicking through an endless line of goalposts every five yards from the spot of the ball.

I kick one more from 34, two from 35, two from 36, and so on back to 39 yards. Jeff has me don my helmet. Ronnie times me from snap to kick: 1.12 seconds, too fast, a sign that I'm anxious. "Just wait till you have a line of guys coming at you, in a packed stadium with the clock running," Jason says. "The adrenaline rush is huge." Todd is talking on the side with his personal trainer, whom he brought from Chicago. Shanahan agreed to give the guy an on-field credential. (Other players are incredulous. "They let that dude out here after he's responsible for him taking ephedra?" Jake Plummer speculates.) I notice the trainer say something to Todd, then Todd look at me and blow out air.

My penultimate kick is textbook: end over end, high, and authoritative. All that's missing are the referees lifting their arms overhead. Ronnie high-fives me. T-Mac says the kick was good from at least five more yards. I'm proud, of what I immediately consider a 44-yarder, and of shutting out Todd while I kicked it.

The rest of the team hasn't done as well. During our usual end-of-practice midfield gathering, Shanahan pronounces the afternoon a failure. The young players did especially poorly. And that's no way to make the team.

"Guys get the opportunity," Shanahan says, "they shit in their hat."

8

Someone Else's Game

The little stuff hurts the most," P. J. Alexander tells me in the locker room before the second day of camp. "Stepping on your toe—that might be the most pain. Someone's got on like a seven-stud shoe. Oh my God. It is unbearable."

"Or like this pinkie," Chad Mustard says, holding up one in the shape of a gnarly tree branch. "Dislocated."

"The fingers," P.J. commiserates, as if the thought alone were painful.

"These guys' thumbs are the worst," Chad says, motioning to the offensive linemen.

"They're always getting caught in a jersey, jamming, twisting back," P.J. says. "Benny!" P.J. calls over to starting guard Ben Hamilton. Ben holds up his hands and spreads his fingers. Cracks in a shattered windshield. Not a single digit remotely straight.

It's like the scene in *Jaws* where Robert Shaw and Richard Dreyfuss, waiting for the great white to show, compare scars. ("Moray eel. Bit right through my wetsuit.") The linemen recount a few more broken bones and surgeries, then finish wrapping their wrists and taping their fingers so they can go outside and break more bones and have more surgeries. We're not kicking at all on this day, which is just as well. My right groin, lower back, and left knee are especially sore. The second toe on my right foot is inflamed, its nail broken. Eighteen relatively comfortable minutes in the ice pool didn't cure a thing. I don't dare mention my ailments to my teammates, and spend the afternoon watching the parade of nicks and bruises and worse that are common in the first few days of training camp, when players' bodies reacclimatize to life as human bumper cars and the training room begins to fill like a theater after intermission.

Halfway through practice, starting offensive guard Cooper Carlisle emerges from a scrum grimacing with pain in his right shoulder. "It's killing me," he says. "It's still real numb."

Steve Antonopoulos scampers over. Greek is mostly bald, with a walrusy build and a matching gray walrusy mustache. A fanny pack bulging with medical supplies bounces on his belly.

"Give me a minute. Give me a minute," Cooper says to him.

Greek has Cooper squeeze his thumb and tells him to try to rotate his lowered arm in the shoulder socket. *Click.* "That normal?" Cooper asks. He has trouble lifting his arm to shoulder height. He takes a long pull from a water bottle, much of which rolls down the number 65 on his chest. It's ninety-four degrees, a staff member announces, receiving the information via walkie-talkie from Troy Smith's office, where an online subscription service provides a micro-forecast for the area around the Broncos' facility.

"I couldn't play in a game," Cooper says. "This one's real."

"The pain's probably going to stay a while," Greek says.

"What's a while?" Cooper replies. "A day a while or ten minutes a while?"

"Ten minutes," Greek says.

Greek has Cooper raise his arms to a ninety-degree angle at the elbows and push out. He examines both hands.

"He'll be back in a minute," Greek says to a coach standing nearby.

Starting linebacker Ian Gold walks by. "Dirtiest guy on the team," he announces. "What goes around comes around." I don't know whether Gold is joking, though it doesn't sound like it. (Opposing teams generally don't like Denver's offensive line because of its frequent use of the "cut block," in which a player blocks an opponent below the knees. The block is legal as long as the lineman's helmet remains in front of the opponent.) If true, Cooper's personality is the opposite of his game. He's

Baby Huey, a cuddly guy with a mischievous smile and a Mississippi twang.

"Fatsis, what are you doing?" Cooper says when he sees me scribbling in my notebook. He then talks to me, perhaps violating the starting offensive line's decade-old prohibition against speaking with the media. On the whiteboard in the unit's meeting room, fines are listed for breaking the rule: "Quotes $100." "Sports Show Guest $1,000." During last season's AFC Championship Game, the NFL threatened a $10,000 per-player fine for boycotting the media, and the linemen agreed to talk. No one asked them for an interview.

Cooper tells me he fell on his shoulder, then someone else fell on him. The linemen are wearing shells, not shoulder pads. Hitting in practice is supposed to be incidental—players are instructed to "thud up," to release after making initial contact, which works better in theory, especially on the line. Cooper tries to lift his right arm straight up.

"That hurts right there," he says.

"Then don't do it," Greek replies.

"Why don't you tell Cooper what I said?" Tom Nalen, the center, says to me. "I said if he's hurt it's going to fuck up our Blitz time." Every afternoon between practices, four of the starting linemen—Nalen, Cooper, Hamilton, and Matt Lepsis—cluster like overgrown ten-year-olds around a football video game.

After ten minutes, Cooper announces that he's returning to practice. "I'll be all right."

Jake Plummer walks over. "You get hurt?"

"Yeah."

"You going back in?

Cooper nods.

"Because you're tougher than that. You looked at these guys"—Lepsis and Nalen—"and were inspired." Plummer is being sarcastic, but he's also showing concern for his lineman. It's part of the quarterback's job description.

Cooper trots back to the sideline after a few plays.

"Okay?" I ask.

"Nah, it hurt."

An x-ray later reveals a bruised rotator cuff; nothing that will cause Cooper to miss practice, or Blitz. There are other casualties. Wide receiver David Terrell tries to self-treat a cut on the back of his ankle, poking a hole in layers of tape to relieve pressure. Surrounded by Terrell's cleat, his bloody sock, the carcass of his ankle tape, and his catching gloves, Greek rebandages the wound. "Sweet," Terrell says, popping back up. Mike Bell, a rookie running back, crosses the yellow rope behind which everyone but the drilling players and coaches must stand, kneels over, and vomits a stream of water. Dehydration. A trainer pours water on his back. "I'm all right, I'm all right," Bell says, and returns to the field.

If you're not a veteran starter or a big-bonus rookie, and you're getting treatment in the hot tub or the ice pool or on a training table instead of practicing, you're not likely to be among the final fifty-three. Players often don't report little injuries, in part because they don't want to have to arrive at 6:45 a.m. for treatment, but also because they don't want to be perceived as injured. Obviously, it's illogical. But players believe they can overcome pain more easily than they can a coach's perception. So they avoid treatment and suck it up, playing at less than full ability and possibly risking further injury. "Everybody's hurt. Nobody feels good," wide receiver Charlie Adams says. "If it's something you can walk off, shake off, you do that."

Midway through practice, a young offensive lineman with a red beard and a gentle face named Erik Pears leaves for the trainer's room holding his left pinkie. When I see him later, I ask what happened. "I punched the pass rusher. It just felt weird. Then when I looked down it was facing the wrong way." A team doctor "cranked on it so darn hard" but the finger wouldn't pop back into its socket. An x-ray revealed that ligaments had slid off the finger to one side. Erik is to have surgery the next day. The doctor said he'd miss five days of practice, which doesn't sound like much recovery time to me but sounds like an eternity to Erik. He played in

Cologne, Germany, in NFL Europe in the spring, which means he is no sure thing to make the Broncos. "I'm just at the bottom of the barrel trying to work my way up," he says. "Five days is a big deal."

P. J. Alexander slumps his three hundred pounds into a chair in the empty offensive-line meeting room. I ask him what hurts.

"Honestly, everything. From my waist down, everything hurts. Ankles, feet, quads, calves, shins—everything hurts. My arms are just beat up from getting swatted and banged with helmets. Having to go down into your stance all the time and drive-block people"—pushing defensive linemen away with the hands—"and brace up and use all your leg muscles all the time. Your hands are unbelievably sore. Trying to grab jerseys, smash the helmets, you jam 'em on people, people jam your hands, they come down and chop your hands, your hands get banged up."

"This is after one day," I say.

"One day. That's what's amazing to me. How bad I feel right now. And it's just one day."

With the Broncos, the trade-off for not hitting as much as other teams—shoulder pads are required for just fourteen of the twenty-eight practices—is that the tempo is faster. That speed produces unintended, high-impact collisions, their intensity magnified for linemen wearing shells. Go full speed for ten seconds. Recover for twenty seconds. Repeat.

"It's maximum effort every single time," P.J. says. "It has to be all out or you don't have a job. You can't just sit out because your legs hurt."

A year ago, P.J. had expected to compete for a starting spot on the line, and the money that went with it. As a group, the Broncos' current starters—the four Blitz players plus right tackle George Foster—are among the best paid in football. Three of them are among the top eleven under the team's salary cap. Matt Lepsis, who as a left tackle protecting the quarterback's "blind side"—his back side when throwing—plays one of the most highly valued positions in the NFL, received a five-year,

$30 million contract extension. Tom Nalen, a possible Hall of Famer, just extended his contract three seasons for $9 million.

After a Friday practice in May 2005, P.J., Cooper, Tom, and some friends of Tom's drove into the Rocky Mountains to ride all-terrain vehicles. P.J. didn't own one, and he didn't have much experience behind the wheel. Descending a mountain trail, Cooper was in the lead, P.J. in the middle, and Tom in the rear. They were traveling no faster than ten miles per hour, with ample space between them. P.J. cleared a small hill, then squeezed the brake too hard or hit a log. He's not sure. The right rear of the ATV flipped toward him. P.J. leaped out, landed on his left leg, and rolled down the hill. Cooper heard a scream and turned around. Tom crested the hill and saw the overturned vehicle. He thought P.J. was trapped underneath, that he had broken his neck or was dead.

When P.J. stood up, his left knee collapsed. He stayed in the mountains all weekend and arrived at the Broncos' facility at 6 a.m. on Monday. Greek iced the knee and, P.J. says, told him he didn't think the ACL was torn. P.J.'s agent advised an MRI, which showed the ligament was indeed torn. (Greek says he is sure the team suspected a torn ACL right away.) P.J. expected Shanahan to scold him and cut him. Short of arrests, nothing upsets front offices more than boys-will-be-boys injuries off the field. Instead, Shanahan said he was disappointed for P.J. but that the team would keep him on its "non–football injury" list.

During minicamp, I had asked P.J. whether the team added a clause to his contract banning him from riding ATVs. "No, but they took *out* a lot of things," he replied. "A lot of zeros." In 2004, he made $305,000, the league minimum for his experience level, and was due to make $380,000 and become a restricted free agent after the next season. If he had won a starting job, the team likely would have rewarded him with a long-term contract. The Broncos picked up medical costs not covered by insurance and gave P.J. $75,000 to live on during rehabilitation, which they didn't have to do. But now P.J. was further than ever from the security of a seven-digit payday.

During practices this spring, P.J. tried to stay off his rebuilt left knee as much as possible, which aggravated preexisting tendonitis in his right knee. Vioxx helped. (It is the anti-inflammatory of choice for many players even after being pulled from the market because of studies linking it to heart attacks and strokes.) But P.J. sees himself limping on practice film, and he worries. Not so much about his long-term health, because he knows that NFL players—especially heavy, often clinically obese players in hit-every-play positions like offensive line—make a bargain: the thrill of the game and the potential compensation in exchange for a lifetime of pain. "You don't get any hundred-year-old NFL players," P.J. says. No, what worries him is failing to capitalize on what he understands is, in the best of circumstances, a long shot to make lots of money in a short time.

NFL fans don't know, or care, much about revolving-door players like P.J., who was born to a sixteen-year-old mother and a seventeen-year-old father and grew up in public housing in Springfield, Massachusetts. His parents beat the odds. They married after high school, and remain together. His father joined the marines, survived testicular cancer, and became a letter carrier, a job he kept after moving the family to Tallahassee, Florida, to escape the projects. (A picture of a cousin shot and killed in Springfield while dealing drugs is tattooed on P.J.'s right biceps.) His mother has worked steadily through the years as a secretary. P.J. won a scholarship to Syracuse. He wasn't drafted into the NFL, but was signed by the New Orleans Saints as a free agent. He received a $6,000 bonus and made the practice squad. The next year, 2003, he made the Saints' roster. Then he was released during the season. Then he was re-signed. NFL teams can poach each other's practice-squad players, and Denver poached P.J. He dressed for every game in 2004, and played on special teams.

P.J. knows that he is struggling and knows that the coaches know it, too, and are upstairs *right this second* watching tape and talking about him. This morning, for instance, P.J. made a mistake. He was playing right tackle, the farthest lineman to the outside. His assignment on a running play was to engage the defensive end. If the end came straight at him, P.J. had to tie him up so the running back could scamper to the outside. If the end tried to run wide around him, P.J. had to push him even farther outside so the back could cut to the inside. After the snap, though, P.J. crossed his left foot over his right and lost his balance. The end shoved P.J. out of the way and ran straight into the backfield. "And that's all completely my fault. Because I didn't block the guy. My footwork was wrong. I crossed over instead of going at him, so I wasn't able to get back on him and get a club on him."

Part of P.J.'s problem is that the Broncos have switched him from guard to tackle. On the offensive line, the center is closest to his opponent. He has to snap the ball to the quarterback with one hand and raise both arms before the rusher can make a move. Adjacent to the center, the two guards have slightly more space, but still need to get their hands up quickly. Typically, the heaviest and hence slowest defensive linemen face the guards, allowing a few extra milliseconds to act. Tackles are responsible for holding off the quickest defensive linemen, the ends, who take a stance farther from the line than the interior linemen. Offensive tackles have to neutralize the extra space with fast footwork. At guard, P.J.'s ability to quickly punch and grab his close-in opponent compensates for whatever mobility he has lost because of the knee injury. Playing tackle marginalizes that strength and magnifies his weakness. It doesn't help that Denver's zone-blocking system favors linemen who can pivot and move agilely enough to, on certain plays, block speedy linebackers.

At practice, I had watched a one-on-one drill in which a defensive lineman tries to get around an offensive lineman on the shriek of a coach's whistle. A Broncos scout named Ed Lambert crouched to show me the basics of body positioning and explained the moves and countermoves, which sound like dances from the 1950s, or other less wholesome activities: the swim, the rip, the club, the bull rush, the jerk pull. The offensive lineman, Lambert said, has to keep his arms within the framework of his body, staying square and balanced with his opponent directly in front of him. The defensive lineman, meanwhile, has to whack and shove to get his opponent off balance because "when you get that three hundred pounds going in one direction, it's hard to stop." If the defensive lineman spies his counterpart leaning too far forward, for instance, he'll do what Lambert did to me: tug on my jersey, sending me stumbling forward. That would be the jerk pull. If he feels him listing to one side, he'll do what happened to P.J., push him in the same direction.

Sixteen offensive linemen are in training camp. Eight or nine are likely to make the team, and five spots are spoken for. That leaves three or four openings. P.J. talks about fighting through the pain to regain his timing and quickness, and he frets over whether he'll have a job in October, when his girlfriend, who lives with him in a rented apartment, is due to give birth. But, like a man on his deathbed taking stock of his life, P.J. also says that just having made the NFL is an achievement he never imagined.

"This is living a dream for me. Whooo!" he says. "I know how easy it is for me not to be here. I respect it. Every day I come in here I'm happy to see stuff in my locker. I really am." P.J. returns to the locker room, grabs an inflatable mattress, and lies down on his stomach, staring blankly at a television twenty feet away.

That night, before returning to the hotel, I drop by Ted Sundquist's office. The general manager is watching tape of practice with player-personnel director Jim Goodman. Goodman is possessed of a fabulous southern accent and uncontained enthusiasm for a well-executed move, which when combined are a thing of beauty. ("*Look* at *Braaan*-din Mah-*reeeee!*" he exults as fullback Brandon Miree makes a nifty spin move.) The two men scrutinize the one-on-one showdowns and then break down the performances of the linemen during Team. Sundquist props his stocking feet on his desk and highlights players or moves with a red-dot laser pointer. After admiring Matt Lepsis and Ben Hamilton coordinate a blocking sequence with the intuitive grace of ballroom dancers, Sundquist focuses on a slow-footed play by P.J.

"P.J.'s just missing something," he says. "It's not back. He's just not the same." When P.J. does better on the next play, Ted offers praise, as if he's rooting for him to succeed.

Tim Brewster wastes no time making Tony Scheffler's camp life miserable. He yells at him for running the wrong pass route. "Out, Scheffler, out! Get him out of there. What the fuck was he running? Y Right Shallow Cross, Tony." He yells at him for not blocking well enough. "We should have more movement on that two-hundred-forty-pounder there!" He yells at him to be more aggressive. "This is where you got to compete and get better! You hear me?"

Everyone hears Brew. Everyone can't help but hear Brew. Tony's teammates sympathize. They think Brew's old-school badgering is a show for Shanahan that doesn't impress the coach and doesn't work on players. "We're all self-starters. We're all very ambitious people," tight end Nate Jackson says. "We're all here because we had the motivation internally to not need someone screaming at us to get here. Me personally, I would prefer you pulled me aside after a play and said, 'Hey, Nate,' instead of, 'Fucking Jesus, why'd you fucking, what the fuck?' I don't need that. That doesn't motivate me."

At the same time, Nate and other players understand what Brew is trying to accomplish. Tony is six foot five, 255 pounds, fast and strong with big hands that pluck the ball out of the air. But he doesn't know how to block well—he didn't have to do it much in college—and has scant understanding of intricate pro defensive coverages. In his lack of NFL readiness, Tony is no different from other rookies. But his potential, his team's expectations, and his coach's techniques are different. If Brew can make him a complete player, Tony will be a beast in the league for years.

The shouting is purposeful, not gratuitous, Brew says. The NFL mandates precision and consistency, because opponents are skilled enough to capitalize on the slightest technical imperfections. Brew knows Tony has the ability to perform like a wide receiver, running into "seams" in the defense twenty yards downfield, whereas other NFL teams might not send a tight end out more then twelve yards. What will make Tony special, Brew says, is turning him into a road-grading blocker who can stifle a three-hundred-pound defensive lineman and open a hole for a running back. To create an aggressive player, Brew believes he has to be physically and emotionally aggressive himself.

"How you coach them is how they're going to play," he tells me in his office one afternoon. None of it is personal, he insists. "Tony Scheffler knew coming in here that my reputation—what's the term?—precedes me. So he knew what he was getting. And I don't think I've disappointed him."

Brew is a forty-five-year-old former tight end who captained a University of Illinois team that played in the Rose Bowl. After sixteen years as a collegiate assistant, most of them at powerhouse Texas, Brew has been an NFL assistant for five years. He is tall and broad, favoring sleeveless Broncos windbreakers that accentuate his size. And he is relentlessly upbeat. Every morning I ask him how it's going and every morning he replies, "Outstanding!" Brew enunciates clearly, often looking at the ceiling or staring over a shoulder while delivering what can feel like a lecture. He projects the no-bullshit assertiveness of an NFL head coach, which is what he wants to become.

One evening, Brew invites me to a tight-ends meeting. Two "Brew-isms" are written on the whiteboard: "DEMAND PERFECTION FROM YOURSELF" and "ATTITUDE & EFFORT ARE NON-NEGOTIABLE." ("He loves that one," Stephen Alexander tells me.) The meeting amounts to an hour-long ransacking of Tony's performance that afternoon on tape in front of the four other tight ends, S.A., Nate, Chad Mustard, and Mike Leach.

When Tony drops his head during a block: "It's like you're in the dark there and you're trying to find something. Eyes up and bite 'em. You know what I'm telling you, Tony. You got the courage. Get it done."

Critiquing Tony's stance at the line of scrimmage: "Sit your ass on the barstool. When you come up to hit, get off the barstool. Then sit your ass back down."

When Tony pushes with his hands instead of plowing his face into a defensive lineman: "It fucking drives me crazy when you go in there and reach with your hands. I mean, shit. Go in there with your facemask and hit him in the earhole. *Shiiiiit*. If you're going to block him, block him."

After another poor pass-protection sequence: "Is that you, Chad? No, that's fucking Tony. Come on, Tony. Tony, come off the ball. Knock his ass off. Would you say you were in an attack mode here?"

When Tony has trouble getting past a defensive end to run a pass pattern: "Pitch a fit on the son of a bitch. Take your outside hand and slap his ass and go by him. You have to do better than this."

Brew praises Mike for a block. He praises Chad for a block. (S.A. is one of the veterans who don't have to practice in the afternoon; Nate is nursing an injured ankle.) When Tony's body turns upfield before the ball arrives, Brew rewinds the tape and replays the instant of the poor maneuver about ten times. Rewind, play, rewind, play, rewind, play. Finally, Brew rips someone else (Chad) for "horseshit technique" on a foot pivot before a block. And he even praises Tony. Once.

"You feel better about that, Tony? I feel better about that."

"Uh-huh," Tony says.

"You look more like a football player."

Tony is sweet and wide-eyed, bashful and gullible. He grew up in a small working-class town near Ann Arbor, Michigan. Coaches from Harvard visited Tony in high school, but he wanted to stay close to home. He also wanted to play both football and baseball, which ruled out in-state giants Michigan and Michigan State. He sailed through Western Michigan with a 3.55 grade point average, majoring in marketing. He excelled at the NFL "combine" for prospects. And then, before the draft, he visited the Broncos and met Brew.

"He roughed me up in the car a little bit," Tony says, recalling their first meeting. "Grabbing me by the back of the neck. 'You ready, boy?' That sort of thing. He was feeling me out. I knew what was going to happen. Just from that one interview. I knew he was going to ride me the whole way until he got me to where he thought was acceptable." When they arrived at Broncos headquarters, Brew queued up a highlight reel of Tony in college and savaged every play.

Tony knows that Brew is trying to make him a better player. He's heard Brew tell him to ignore the tone of his voice and listen to his words. But it's withering. "As a man, to be put down to this level on a daily basis, it eats at you," he says. Tony is a pleaser. He wants to live up to the expectations of the coaches and the media and the fans and his friends and family. He wants to reward Mike Shanahan for picking him in the second round. But the NFL is so demanding, Tony says. In college, he could run a pass route nine yards instead of ten and compensate because he was a better athlete. But there's no error margin in the NFL, so he's "getting totally motherfucked for being six inches to the right of where I was supposed to be."

And if Brew weren't enough, there's Tony's personal life. He just learned that his girlfriend is pregnant and wants to get married—now. Thanks to a signing bonus of close to $1 million, he has bought a 5,600-square-foot house. His parents—his father is a meat cutter and his mother worked at a Target after getting laid off from an auto-parts plant—have moved here from Michigan. Tony is devoted to repaying them for sacrificing so much so that he and his brother could have all the sports equipment they wanted and attend all the practices and games and camps they wanted. But they don't understand what he's suffering, and neither does his girlfriend. He feels responsible for all of them, and a failure at his first job.

S.A. talks to Tony every day and assures him that it—and he—will get better. He tells him that he felt lost when he was a rookie, too. S.A. also reminds him that while Brew's approach might be demoralizing, he is a fair coach and a decent man who cares about Tony and wants him to succeed, which is high praise for an NFL assistant. Tony knows that, but he also wants a pat on the back, he wants to exhale, he wants to have fun.

"Being the only one out there on the field that's being berated, that's hard," Tony says. "And they're all looking at you: Is this kid a total fuckup? Two thousand people there, they hear everything. And you just have to listen to it and every play hope you don't screw up."

When the NFL is compared to the military, which is often, the most commonly cited similarities are an inviolable chain of command, inflexible rules, structured rituals, and physical exhaustion. More than anything I've witnessed so far, though, the psychology of the NFL seems its most militaristic trait. College football isn't without its tyrannies, its red-faced coaches and demanding schedules. But players describe it comparatively as a Caribbean vacation. "It was the time of my life," P. J. Alexander said a minute after describing a coach at Syracuse who snapped him around by his facemask and spit in his face. Even with the physical, emotional, and time demands that football imposes, college is still college, fun and free.

The stress in the NFL derives partly from a fear of unemployment. My teammates recognize the long odds of even getting to the league, let alone playing for a decade and making millions. There are about 20,000 intercollegiate football players and about 1,800 NFL jobs, only a sixth or so of which turn over each season. The Broncos are affected far more, though, by something more temporal, the fear of making a mistake. Players resent the tactics coaches use to see if they can hack it: the reminders that they are under pressure, that someone else wants their job, that their every step is being observed, that they need to be perfect, as if that were possible.

As we gather on the field at the end of a morning practice, Shanahan tells the players that for the next two hours, while they are lunching and napping and listening to iPods and playing Blitz, the coaches will be one floor above them reviewing everything—*everything*—that has just transpired. The intent is to thin the herd of the weak and the unready so the team can go to battle with only the most physically and mentally capable soldiers. Among the players, the consequences of this strategy include cynicism, paranoia, and disillusionment.

"Someone's getting yelled at every single play," Nate Jackson tells me. "Half the guys out there fuck up, basically, every single play. You've got be able to separate the yelling and posturing and bravado and be able to see it for what it is. The ultimate plan is creating a synchronized machine that makes no mistakes. That's the ideal. But we're human. That's what makes football so great. If we were perfect it would be boring. Who wants to watch two robots fight? Not me."

And yet, even the most intelligent and self-aware players like Nate, a twenty-seven-year-old from northern California who is in his fourth NFL season, find their self-esteem bestowed like a prize from the coaches for performance. "When you can't perform, you feel worthless," Nate says while standing on the sideline, unable to practice. "You don't feel wanted. You don't feel respected. It sucks."

When I ask if that applies even though injuries, like his current one, can be random and relatively minor, Nate takes it a step further. "Even though what we're doing is an unnatural thing for the human body. Completely unnatural. The things we're asking our bodies to do, God didn't make us to do these things. To feel worthless because my body is breaking down under these conditions is totally irrational. But you're in an environment where all you see is physically gifted athletes running around, and you're one of them. When you get hobbled and you see them performing and feeling okay, you feel like shit. It's a mind game. Football's a mind game. How many people are in the NFL? About eighteen hundred? In the world there's probably a hundred thousand guys, if not more, physically talented enough to play football in the NFL. But mentally they don't have it. You see it all the time. Guys come in here who are physically great but mentally break."

Whether Shanahan recognizes those paradoxes, the players have no idea. They praise him for taking care of their basic needs—the plush environment, the relatively humane approach to practice—and for his football intellect and preparation. And while they also credit the coach for leveling with his players, they say he doesn't do it until absolutely necessary, leaving them to twist and squirm in the dark. The problem with that, Jake Plummer says, is that the coaches have their own agendas. He recalls Shanahan eviscerating a player for running the wrong pass pattern, then watching an assistant coach privately apologize to the player for having assigned him the wrong route—and then not tell Shanahan that he, the assistant, was responsible. "Are you kidding me? Go tell Mike," he says. "It's my job, my family, my fucking livelihood that's getting fucked up here." Jake describes assistant head coach Mike Heimerdinger turning off the overhead camera during quarterbacks meetings to discuss "reads" on particular plays—where the quarterback should throw based on the defensive alignment—in order to shield the players, and coaches, from criticism. Jake says he asked Heimerdinger to stop it. "What can you not say that can't be said no matter what?" he tells me. "And then you're giving us info and [the camera is] off? What are we supposed to think about that?"

Consider Preston Parsons. After a few days, camp isn't going well. To compete for a roster spot, Preston needs repetitions during Seven-on-Seven, Nine-on-Seven, and Team. Of the couple hundred plays in those drills so far, Preston has quarterbacked fewer than ten. He had no reps in the first morning practice, three that afternoon, two the next morning, a couple that afternoon. Preston is reluctant to approach any of his coaches—Shanahan, Heimerdinger, or quarterbacks coach Pat McPherson—for a status report. He won't because he believes it smells of insecurity and annoys the coaches. So Preston keeps a mental tally of reps and pats on the helmet and, like an FBI agent listening to a wiretap, tries to interpret the coaches' remarks. His day can turn on a single "That's the way to throw it, Pres" from Shanahan.

Holding his helmet in his right hand, his arms crossed against the number 5 on his chest, a single bead of sweat rolling down his left cheek, Preston watches impassively as Jake Plummer, then Bradlee Van Pelt, then Jay Cutler quarterback plays. To stay engaged, he asks Pat McPherson for the next play, and Pat whispers it like Allen Ludden giving a clue on *Password*: "Strong Right 16 Power," "I-Right Bump 18 Box," "3 Jet Scissors X Shallow." When a pass from Bradlee falls incomplete, I ask Preston whether the receiver should have been there. "Should have been a better throw," he says.

To outsiders, there's no story in the quarterbacks. Jake is the veteran starter. Bradlee is the young, incumbent backup. Jay is the touted rookie. And Preston—for anyone who's even noticed him—is the camp arm. Everyone assumes the Broncos will keep the first three. Preston hopes something will happen to change that.

That something could involve Bradlee. Drafted by the Broncos in the seventh and last round in 2004, Bradlee spent his rookie season on the practice squad and his second as Plummer's only backup. As an athlete, Bradlee is a brute: a solid six foot two and 220 pounds, with a swaying, cocksure gait. In college, coaches wanted to convert him to running back or defensive back to utilize his strength and speed. But Bradlee was determined to be a great college quarterback and is determined now to be a starting NFL quarterback, no matter how much he still has to learn about the mechanics of passing and the complexity of the position and the demands of life in the NFL—and no matter how much the pressure of simultaneously learning, performing, and competing at the most scrutinized position on the field gnaws like termites on his brain.

If P.J.'s story is about what can happen to an NFL body, then Bradlee's is about what can happen to an NFL mind. On one play while I'm watching, Bradlee is indecisive about a pass and gets sacked. (In training camp, that means being touched by a defender. Hitting the quarterback is verboten.) "Fuck! Fuck!" Bradlee shouts, whacking his helmet on the grass. Plummer waves him over for a pep talk—and raises his hand to stop me from joining them. "He's such a head case," Preston says. "I hate to say that about a friend. But he's got some head issues."

Elite athletes are as unique as snowflakes, but they can be separated into two piles: those who absorb—or ignore—on-field errors and move on and those who dwell on them. Bradlee belongs to a subset of the second group: players who dwell on their errors so deeply that it affects their performance. Even in high school, Bradlee was a dweller. But his physical talent was such that his introspection could be dismissed as a potentially healthy quirk. In the pros, it is considered a liability, especially now, when Bradlee hasn't been playing well in practice.

"They think I think too much," Bradlee says in a breathless sideline monologue between reps one morning. "But it's a thinking position. You've got to be able to comprehend everything at once. That's the point. You're worried about one thing, you're looking at another, then when you come back you have to look at the route. It's just a flicker." He snaps his fingers. "I'm talking like a half second and all of a sudden you're like, 'Oh, fuck.' And then you sit there and go, 'Why did I do that?'"

He nods at the coaches. "They're up there watching with all their video cameras. You're getting evaluated and scrutinized every minute. This ain't easy. They don't want to make it easy. I'm not complaining. Hey, that's the world I live in. The invisible world no one sees that I go to bed with. Why do you think I can't sleep at night? Because my head won't let me. It won't relax."

Bradlee pauses. He points out that not only does he have Shanahan, Heimerdinger, and McPherson as his coaches, but two younger assistants often attend quarterback meetings. Ten eyes. Five mouths. I ask him whether the focus on the quarterback is greater in Denver than in other cities because of the legacy of John Elway.

"It's because of the legacy," Bradlee says. "But it's the position. We're the Intel chip. It can't run without us. They've got to train us to a higher degree. But you can't go through these days—" Bradlee stops. He seems to suppress an urge to justify self-doubt and instead forces himself to be positive. He's thinking about the sack a few minutes earlier. "When you mess up once—I'll forget about it, I'll bounce back. It's not about perfection, it's about persistence. That's kind of like my motto. I'll fight through it. But it's hard, fighting."

"Hey, Ding," Bradlee says, trying to get Heimerdinger's attention. Dinger, as he's known to everyone, either doesn't hear Bradlee or ignores him. "Yeah, he doesn't want to talk to me," Bradlee says.

"Because of that one play?" I ask.

"That one particular play." Bradlee made two mental errors. He screwed up the snap count and then misread the defensive coverage and reacted too slowly. In the West Coast offense that Denver employs, the quarterback typically looks first to a designated primary receiver. If he's covered, the quarterback pivots his feet quickly and looks for the secondary target. If he's also covered, the quarterback pivots again and tosses the ball to the tertiary target, usually a running back peeling off to one side. Dinger finally walks over. Bradlee barrages him with a step-by-step dissection of the play. Complete with pantomimes of passing motions, Dinger explains where Bradlee went wrong.

"Where you went, that's no problem—it's one-on-one," Dinger says. "But you've got to go there faster. You looked over here to see if he was protected, then you went over there. You were here, then you were waiting, and it was a little late."

In other words, it's a thinking position, but Bradlee thought too much.

———

Bradlee's father, Brad Van Pelt, played fourteen seasons in the NFL and was an All-Pro five times. He was one of my childhood favorites, partly because he wore the unlinebacker number 10. Brad didn't push any of his four sons to play football, and as they grew older, he was a distant presence. After his parents divorced, Bradlee lived with his mother in Santa Barbara, California. Brad lived in Michigan.

Bradlee says he wasn't close to his father growing up and wasn't consumed by football. But he did want to succeed, like his father, and chose Michigan State, where Brad had been an All-American safety, a second-round NFL draft choice, and a first-round draft pick as a baseball pitcher. When the Michigan State coaches told Bradlee they were switching him to defense, he refused, and transferred to Colorado State. The coaches there wanted to make him a running back. This time, though, Bradlee was allowed to decide, and he decided to plug away at quarterback. Four weeks later he was starting, and he never relinquished the job, leading the team to three bowl games and winning conference most-valuable player honors twice.

Bradlee stood out as much for his personality as for his accomplishments. He didn't hang out with other football players, he skateboarded to practices and to class, he wore his blond hair long, he taunted opponents, he partied, and he spoke colorfully and honestly about everything from his defiant will to play quarterback to the death of his twenty-three-year-old brother of a drug overdose, which was ruled accidental, in 2001. After the one and only arrest of his life—for yelling at a guy outside a campus bar—Bradlee took responsibility for his actions, in his own words, not through a canned statement written by a lawyer. "The cops were just doing their job," he said. "I don't hold any animosity toward them."

In an emotionally closeted and ritually conformist sport, Bradlee was openly introspective and goofily different. But because he was so energetic about learning the game—and because he completed passes and ran for touchdowns and won—the coaches at Colorado State let him be himself. "Sure, Bradlee has been a handful at times, but he has also been a great football player," the team's quarterbacks coach, Dan Hammerschmidt, said on the eve of Bradlee's final game. "He has taught us all a good lesson, and that's to live life."

In the NFL, though, Bradlee discovered that coaches aren't interested in life lessons. Bradlee's NFL stock wasn't high. He was a freelancing playmaker, not a central-casting quarterback who could effortlessly sling seventy-yard spirals. He loafed through the Wonderlic intelligence test given to NFL aspirants, scoring 23 (out of 50), which didn't help his prospects. When he stared down the psychologist evaluating players at the NFL's predraft meat market and answered a question about marijuana use confrontationally, that probably didn't help, either. As we sit across from each other after lunch at one of the metal picnic tables near the field, Bradlee reenacts the interview.

"Yeah, I smoked pot."

"When was the last time?"

"I don't know."

"So you condone drugs?"

"No, I don't condone drugs."

"I was just on my own listening to myself," Bradlee says. "It took me a little while to go, 'Aha, I see, this isn't my game. I have to play someone else's game.'"

As a rookie, Bradlee skateboarded through the locker room. He slept on a futon in an apartment in central Denver that he shared with an unemployed college buddy. It was a forty-five-minute rush-hour drive to Broncos headquarters and a five-minute walk to downtown bars. Bradlee made both commutes just about every day. Shanahan lectured him about drinking and scolded him for being late a couple of times. But the coaches seemed to have a bigger problem with his living downtown rather than in a suburban apartment complex close to work. It reinforced Bradlee's reputation as someone who had to be different, especially when he screwed up. *See? We told you. He's living downtown!*

In his second season, Bradlee roomed with two other college buddies in a loft near the University of Denver. Making six figures—about

$218,000 his first season and $260,000 his second—Bradlee bought a metallic blue Porsche 993, traveled to Hawaii and the Cayman Islands, took his friends out for steaks and red wines. He was living how a guy in his early twenties with a little money might. Who could blame him?

The public image of NFL players is one of excess: young, brash, violent, reckless, out of control. But for every Chris Henry, the Cincinnati wide receiver just arrested for the fourth time in six months, there are a hundred guys like Domonique Foxworth, the Broncos' second-year defensive back who lives a few minutes from the practice complex in a neat two-bedroom town house equipped with a single TV, a Scrabble set, and framed diplomas on an office wall. "After Long Day at Office, Football Player Returns to Subdivision, Watches *SportsCenter,* Goes to Bed" isn't much of a headline, but for most players, it's a daily reality, and not just because of the rigors of training camp. The rules and demands of playing in the NFL force players into a sort of premature middle age. Single or married, they rent or buy in sleepy new developments a short commute from "the facility," which invariably is located well beyond the urban center of the team's name. To me, a city dweller since college, the style of life seems unnatural for a twenty-something guy with a brain. It did to Bradlee, too. "I wanted to hold on to my life," he says. "I didn't want to give it up. I was doing everything in my power to hold on."

During training camp in 2005, Jake Plummer invited Bradlee to stay with him. Plummer understood. He was a sometimes-long-haired iconoclast with a rowdy but mostly harmless past himself. Plummer also was an improvisational quarterback. Coming out of college, though, Jake was a better player, a higher draft choice who started almost immediately. When he was Bradlee's age, twenty-six, he could afford to act up once in a while, reputation be damned. Bradlee couldn't. So this year Bradlee capitulated. He moved alone into a house near the facility. He tells himself he has to conform and perform, or else. But he doesn't seem happy about it. He misses the carefree and irreverent dude who was caught on camera giving the finger to some Colorado University fans during a game between his alma mater and its rival, the guy who got a kick out of fans seeing him 'boarding downtown. "That's who I want to be. But I can't," Bradlee says.

The Broncos trusted Bradlee enough to let him back up Plummer exclusively in 2005. Plummer had a fabulous and virtually injury-free season. Like most backups, Bradlee barely stepped on the field. But he assumed the Broncos were grooming him to succeed Plummer. Both were adept scramblers who were more comfortable throwing on the run than passing upright from the "pocket." Bradlee believed he was learning from Plummer, and progressing. Then the team drafted Cutler, a pocket passer. Bradlee has to prove that he is worthy of remaining the number two, even though he knows intellectually the team wouldn't have chosen Cutler if it believed he, Bradlee, was the heir apparent. And that's making him nervous. "They're not expecting him to walk out here and be everything," he says. "Then here I am. I can't do anything right. There's always something wrong that I'm doing."

Bradlee sometimes feels overwhelmed by the information: having to know all the personnel groupings, all the formations, all the players' assignments and how they change depending on the defensive alignment. If a defense shows blitz, for example, the offensive line's protection scheme changes, the receivers' routes change, the quarterback's primary target changes. "It's one thing to have all that. It's another to go and physically perform it," he says. "And all the audibles. You have a run and they bring a certain defense. You might have a possibility of three different audibles you can check to," that is, change the play at the line of scrimmage. "Maybe there's one you should. And you should have known that." The reason to check to a certain play can be as subtle as whether a linebacker is standing to the inside or outside of the tight end. "It's overwhelming. Right now I feel I don't have enough time to study everything I need. I gotta find time." Last night, after the quarterbacks' meeting ended at 9:30, Bradlee watched the day's practice again, writing down each mistake, each mental error, each self-deflating moment.

Practice in the NFL, Bradlee says, is a misnomer. The players aren't practicing, the way a clarinetist practices scales or a tennis player practices serves. Practice in the NFL is what players do on their own time, in front of an open playbook, on the field in the winter and spring, in the film room, in their heads lying in bed. What occurs on the field in the summer is execution. Coaches explain a formation or an audible and expect players to know it. But they don't *teach* it, Bradlee says. Just today, the defense blitzed two players, and Bradlee had to choose where to throw before he was sacked. He chose wrong. "Even though I hadn't done it, even though I hadn't seen it, you execute, no excuses," he says. "No one's saying, 'Hey, you know what? It's the first time. I know you'll get it next time.'"

For someone like Bradlee, who can't let the summer wind carry away his mistakes, the pressure is demonic. Especially now, when each new error feels exponentially more significant than the last. Maybe, Bradlee thinks, he should go have a beer after practice, to unwind. Not three, one. One beer. Or maybe he should just have a bowl of ice cream and study the playbook some more. Maybe he should just go to sleep. He can't decide.

At practice that afternoon, Bradlee throws a couple of terrible balls and makes a couple of obvious mental errors. Pat McPherson pulls him aside afterward and asks what's wrong. The coaches can tell that Bradlee is sinking, that he knows his hold on the number two job is more tenuous with every laser thrown by Cutler and every errant ball thrown by him. Pat talks to him gently. When Bradlee mentions his lack of sleep, Pat asks whether he has considered taking Ambien.

I join the quarterbacks for their evening meeting. Dinger reviews each play, red laser darting around the screen. Bradlee, Jake, and Preston take notes like students in a graduate seminar. After a few minutes of technical analysis about one play, Dinger says, "That make sense to you guys?" It doesn't to Bradlee, so he asks questions. Then, as the other quarterbacks flee, Bradlee asks Dinger to review the same play with him. The defense shows a blitz by the safety. The quarterback should call an audible at the line of scrimmage. But what? "Blue Ninety,"

Dinger had said during the meeting. That instructs the offensive line to slide to the left to handle the blitz and the tight end to slip out toward the right sideline for a short pass.

"This is going to be real simple," Dinger says. "If the strong safety is over here, just check the motherfucker to Ninety. You see any strong safety, Blue Ninety. Throw the fucking dagger. Ninety. Ninety. Ninety. And that ain't even nuclear physics."

Dinger leaves. Bradlee continues questioning Pat, who looks bewildered but tries to be patient. After Pat leaves, Bradlee spends ten minutes diagramming the play for me, racing through every aspect of the formation and every question it raises. And this is just one audible, one that probably won't ever materialize in a game. "But if I get it and fuck it up?" Bradlee says. "Fucked."

Bradlee decides a beer is a good idea. We climb into his Porsche and drive to JD's Bait Shop, a nearby strip-mall sports bar. Bradlee gets a draft. I get a nonalcoholic beer. (I don't drink.) Bradlee orders another draft. Then he tries a nonalcoholic beer. We talk about Shanahan, how Bradlee is fascinated by his rapid rise as a coach. Bradlee respects him, but says he's not a "players' coach." Bradlee wants more help on the field, not on a whiteboard in the classroom. One comfort, Bradlee says, is that, whatever happens, he will have obtained from Shanahan "the equivalent of a Navy SEAL's training." He will have learned a complex football system.

Not that he understands the need for the ever-increasing intricacy or the vicious cycle it creates, at least for Bradlee: more study, more film, more meetings, more exhaustion, worse play, more study, more film, more meetings, and so on. It's stressed Bradlee out, and pissed him off. On the field, Bradlee wears a sweatband on each wrist. Before every play, he twists one and then the other, calling an audible he has no trouble remembering: "Fuck." (Twist.) "You." (Twist.)

Fuck whom? I ask.

"All those cameras and those guys watching me. Fuck it all," he says. "It is really strange how they've gotten me to think this way."

9

A Few Seconds of Panic

During the team camp and minicamp, I felt like I was trespassing. On the field, I didn't want to steal time from the kickers fighting for a chance. Off the field, I didn't want to attract any more attention than my presence already did. In twenty-five years of reporting, I'd never felt so tentative. An NFL locker room, not surprisingly, is an intimidating place.

Time, though, is a good relaxant. Nervousness about my ability and my physique—showering next to my huge, sculpted teammates instantly destroyed the pride I'd taken in my dozen pounds of new muscle—is fading. My presence is no longer noteworthy. Journalistically, this is terrific. The players don't care anymore that I'm carrying a notebook, and when they remind themselves that I am—as Cooper Carlisle did when he hurt his shoulder—they keep talking anyway. And they seem to respect that, no matter my skills, I have the guts to be here at all. "You're doing this stuff," Amon Gordon, a sensitive, soft-spoken 312-pound defensive tackle, tells me one day. "You're doing it."

("It" doesn't compare to Amon's own story. He was born in Queens, lived for a time with his grandparents in Virginia, and spent most of his childhood with his poor, single mother in Seattle. As a high-school senior, Amon moved to San Diego with the family of a football teammate in part to escape what he calls a "really hairy" environment at home. He received a scholarship to Stanford and was picked in the fifth round of the draft by Cleveland. Amon, who is twenty-four, tells me he recently went to court and won full custody of his seven-year-old daughter, Jasmyn.)

I'm falling somewhere between team mascot and ribbable rookie kicker. On the day we don full uniforms for the first time, someone remarks that I'm wearing no leg pads. "You never know when you'll get a helmet to the thigh!" Stephen Alexander says. In my notebook, I spot a message: "Kickers suck dick!" I'm sure I know the author. "Hey, Plummer," I say. "Did you leave me a little love note?" "What?" he replies. "I don't know what you're fucking talking about." Plummer flashes the notebook at Preston Parsons, who laughs.

Still, I want to be accepted not just as a teammate but as a player. The nonspecialist Broncos rarely watch me kick. If they wander out early and witness only one of my inevitable pop-ups or line drives, that kick defines me. That's a performance issue. Then there's a confidence issue. I fear failure and its attendant embarrassment, which argues deeply against attempting what I'm attempting. It's one thing to try, in early middle age, to become an expert Scrabble player. It's another altogether to try to become a professional athlete.

All of which makes me an ideal candidate for a sports psychologist. Matt Stover had introduced me to the Ravens' "performance enhancement specialist," David McDuff, who invited me to call to discuss my issues. Before the start of camp, I did. We began with a prosaic but potentially calamitous one: a concern that my reconstructed knees will fail midkick. The surgery on my left ACL—a rather important body part connecting the femur and the tibia through the knee, enabling stability and lateral movement—is ten years old, and a series of complications long ago convinced me the doctor did a lousy job. Every creak and tweak, I told McDuff, is a sign that the ACL graft, a slice of my patellar tendon, will snap. His answer: Apprehension is a derivative of fear. Without medical evidence, I'm unnecessarily directing attention to that area.

"No one's told you to pay attention to your plant knee as part of a good kicking process, have they?" he asked. No, they haven't. "So you don't want to have any attention there. You should just let yourself transfer that certainty in a much more rigorous test than sitting at your desk."

Transfer is textbook sports psychology. McDuff explained that successful athletes override physical and emotional anxieties by "shifting" and "narrowing" their attention. For instance, when I mentioned that my knee pain mysteriously vanishes when I kick, McDuff said I'm subconsciously directing attention away from my knee to my environment— a bumpy high-school field in Virginia, the perfect turf in Dove Valley, the gaze of my teammates. If there were a medically diagnosed problem, I wouldn't be "distractible." I'm willing to accept that some endorphin rush lets me kick pain-free even though I walk on Rice Krispies knees, but I'm skeptical.

So I visited my current orthopedic surgeon, Thomas Wickiewicz at the Hospital for Special Surgery in New York. Wickiewicz, who himself tore both ACLs playing college football, handled the knees and other joints of the New York Giants from 1984 to 1992 and has two Super Bowl rings to prove it. In the exam room, he grabbed my right shin and thigh just below and above the knee, pressing the former down and lifting the latter up: a solid clumping sound and limited movement. "This is about as normal an ACL as you can have," Wickiewicz said. "And I'm not just saying that because I did the surgery." He repeated the process with my left knee. No solid thunking, rather a looseness indicating that there's nothing connecting the shin and thigh.

I asked about the ACL. "Ain't there," Wickiewicz said. The graft and the screws are still inside my leg; they're just not doing what they're supposed to do. The stand-in ligament is like a floppy rubber band when it should be taut. The knee isn't buckling, so I don't need more surgery. But an "arthritic malalignment" is causing a "varus deformity" in my left leg. Translation: My leg is getting progressively bowlegged, and kicking is stressing the knee, so it hurts. The good news, Wickiewicz said, is that kicking is a unidirectional movement. My legs, my knees, and my plant foot move toward the goalposts. My hips rotate above them. So my left leg shouldn't snap like a wishbone when I jam it into the ground before a kick.

I asked whether my journalistic folly is worsening the left knee. "Maybe a little bit," Wickiewicz said. "But guess what? For three and a half weeks you're going to suck it up and do it. Just don't let their medical staff put their hands on your knee. You don't want to get kicked out of camp." We laughed, and the irrational, instant-gratification, short-term-thinking-athlete part of my brain was thrilled. Medical clearance! I get to play! The rational, rest-of-life part of my brain, though, began worrying about my left knee and bowing leg.

A little after dawn one morning at camp, I call McDuff. I mention that my ACL is slack, my left knee is weakened, and the varus could require surgery someday to straighten the leg. My language is too strong, McDuff says, and it will be distracting. "It's a little lax and a little varus. But it's not relevant to your venture. It's relevant to your future."

If NFL players thought about the future they couldn't possibly play in the present. My knee has held up this far, so I have to trust that it will survive camp, too. To help generate that trust, McDuff wants me to find a positive phrase I can repeat before kicking. When we worked out together, Matt Stover told me his: "I see it. I feel it. I trust it." (Stover utters the phrase after banishing the unwelcome thought of missing that inevitably intrudes on his brain. "Get off of me!" Stover says out loud.) McDuff asks what I want in a kick. A good plant and a solid hit, I reply. "Good plant, solid hit. I like that language," McDuff says. "G-P-S-H. You can use a little shortened version of it. But you really start to create very strong images of success. Good plant, solid hit. Good plant, solid hit. If those are the words you like, you start becoming obsessive with them. It's the sound of it, the view of it, the sense of it."

Now that I have a mantra, I have to work on my confidence. Paul Woodside said that only one kick matters: the next one. McDuff reinforces that idea. When I mention that I'm still making only about three kicks out of ten, he tells me to stop keeping score. Failure shouldn't be my last experiential memory. Walk in a circle after a miss. Turn away from the goalposts. Take some clearing breaths, in through the nose and out through the mouth. Redirect attention to the body. Decide on a place to go and develop a routine to get there. Dismiss the miss, McDuff says. Let go and go to.

Finally, I confess that my biggest insecurity is that, next to Elam, I look like the amateur that I am.

"You're not an amateur," McDuff says. "You're a kicker. How many soccer balls have you kicked in your life?"

"Thousands," I say.

"Right. You're a kicker. If you start chanting, 'I'm an amateur, I'm an amateur,' it's devastating. That language has to be filtered over with something strong."

Success, McDuff tells me, depends on activating several areas in the brain, all different but all part of the action an athlete seeks to repeat. "It's not a perfect action," he says. "You don't have to have a perfect hit. You just have to have a good hit."

"And," I tell him and myself, "I'm capable of having a good hit."

The fifth day of training camp is the first to include "FG/FG Rush" on the schedule: field-goal practice, with a live rush from the defense. In the training room, I rub Flexall, a mentholated aloe vera gel, on my quadriceps, hamstrings, and groin (a little too close to the private parts), and I slather my neck and face with sunscreen. A training staff summer hire stretches my legs. To make the environment I might encounter feel familiar, I close my eyes and visualize the full assemblage of Broncos watching me kick, the thousand fans gathered on the berm, my technique. I imagine good plants and solid hits.

Still, I don't think Shanahan will let me kick with the team. It's too early in camp. Jason hasn't even kicked yet. Ronnie Bradford won't give me a straight answer on whether I will. We have forty minutes before FG. We stretch, punt, loosen up. I ask Jason the plan.

"We're going to kick field goals," he replies. "The idea is to kick the ball between the tall yellow things."

Jason will kick ten balls, two apiece with the ball on the 10-, 15-, 20-, 25-, and 30-yard lines, or field goals of 28, 33, 38, 43, and 48 yards. With twenty minutes to go, I pace back and forth on the turf field. When a rabbit runs across, Ronnie, T-Mac, Todd, and the gang joke that Jason the big-game hunter should keep a bow and arrow in our duffel bag to take advantage of such opportunities. I need to pee. Inside a Port-O-Let, I hear fans talking about me.

"He hit four in a row the other day," one says.

"But they were ten yards out and didn't get ten feet off the ground," another replies.

Everybody's a critic. I jog back and kick a dozen balls from 25, 30, and 35 yards. *Good plant, solid hit.* When I connect from 35, Ronnie says, "That's going to be your distance." This isn't casual stand-around-and-schmooze kicker talk. Ronnie is dead serious. Under the lights. Bullets flying. If Shanahan summons me, Ronnie is saying, I'll be kicking from 35 yards.

"One kick?" I ask.

"One kick."

I have to pee again. Two more fans are standing near the sideline of the kickers' field.

"Jason was kicking from here," one says.

"Number nine's pretty good, too," the other says before I trot by. "Way to go, nine!" he says.

I scoop up the orange duffels and we migrate to the empty grass field. Paul Ernster snaps and Micah Knorr holds. From 40 yards, I strike with foot sideways, skip through directly toward the goalposts, and land with my toe pointing straight ahead. Perfect execution. "Way to go, dog!" a fan screams. But I'm growing visibly nervous. I ask Paul to hold my Broncos cap and my notebook. "Relax, dude," he says. "Just do what you do. You make a hundred out of a hundred if you do what you do. No sense making it harder on yourself."

I nod. I'm hungry. Inside my helmet, I feel perspiration form beneath my forehead and burst through the skin. We walk to the sideline. General manager Ted Sundquist mimics John Facenda's voice-of-God baritone on the classic NFL highlight reels: "The hot breath of the defensive end. The beads of sweat pouring down his cheek . . ."

The airhorn sounds: FG. I jog onto the field with Jason for our first moment in the spotlight. Shanahan shoos me off. While Jason kicks, I stand a couple of yards in front of the team, shaking out my right leg, pacing, breathing the way David McDuff recommended to relax and focus: in through the nose for four counts, hold for seven counts, out through the mouth for eight counts. It's supposed to release tension. But it's not working. The players are watching. The coaches are watching. The fans are watching. This scene doesn't feel familiar at all. A few days earlier, Jason had described the kicker's job as "hours and hours of boredom surrounded by a few seconds of panic." My few seconds feel like a lifetime.

Each of Jason's kicks is a tracer bullet that soars through the goalposts and smacks into or passes through the hydraulic video tower scaffolding beyond the end zone. I try another breathing technique, one used when the body's physiology kicks into overdrive: hyperventilating through the nose to tighten the muscles, then taking some clearing breaths to release the tension. I want to look like I'm preparing to kick. Instead I look like I'm having a nervous breakdown. Paul writes in my notebook: "Pacing rapidly, rigid, frantically breathing, looks like a man awaiting execution. Elam is drilling field goals effortlessly. More pressure on SF."

Then the horn sounds to signal the end of field goal, and I suddenly realize I'm not going to kick. I'm deflated that Shanahan has left me out—this is why I've come to Denver—but also relieved. My mind had been invaded by an army of tiny, hectoring kickers. Smooth steps back! Stay down! Be aggressive! Good plant! Bend over! Chippin' and skippin'! Head down! Leg to butt! Hips open wide! Foot perpendicular to ball! Solid hit! Follow through toward the goalposts! I couldn't have made a 35-yarder if you had spotted me the first 25. Having experienced the prekick stress, I think, will help me when I actually do have to kick. Phew.

Shanahan motions the team to the middle of the field before the next drill. "In this business," he says, "there's a lot of pressure, and a lot of pressure put on kickers. We're going to put some pressure on our kicker, Stefan. He's going to kick. If he makes it, meetings will end at nine instead of nine thirty."

A war whoop rises from the team. As I record Shanahan's words, defensive back Nick Ferguson snatches my notebook. "Quit writing!" he shouts. The special teams line up on the 12-yard line—a 30-yard field goal—and the fans realize what's happening. Applause builds. "Come on, nine!" "Let's go, nine!" "Come on, Fatsis!" Jason approaches. "Stefan, you know there's a twenty-five-second clock," he says with a grin. I'm too frightened to ask whether he's joking.

In the movies of our lives, the most meaningful moments occur in slow motion. We want to preserve them and relive them, find a way to recover the most evanescent details: the first upturn in a smile, the bounce of a bob of hair, the instant when two pairs of eyes meet, the flutter in a skirt. We want to savor the experience. We want to enjoy. Intellectually, I recognize that this should be one of those moments. I am comfortable with my teammates now, and comfortable in front of crowds. I have spoken to audiences in the hundreds, appeared dozens of times on national television, talked to millions of people on the radio, had my work critiqued in the pages of influential newspapers and magazines. I am comfortable with spotlights. I couldn't have conceived, arranged, and carried out this extended performance with an NFL team if I wasn't.

In sports, there is nothing quite so appealing as the split second before execution. There's the anticipation of what will happen, for sure, but also the exquisite beauty of the pause: the moment of nothingness before the explosion of everythingness. But instead of soaking in the attention, in appreciating the most unlikely moment of nothingness in my life, I am *totally freaking out*. I can't find a way to slow things down. I can't smile. I can't high-five the other players and skip into place. I can't acknowledge the fans with a rock-'n'-roll finger point, the way Todd does. I can't pat my long snapper, Mike Leach, on the ass and my holder, Micah, on the helmet. I can't call the field-goal team together for an impromptu huddle and a self-effacing joke. I can't see anything around me—but I can't shut out the fact that I'm surrounded, either. Nothing looks clear. It's as if I'm standing a few inches from an impressionist painting, the players, the Broncos staff, the fans on the berm all dissolv-

tant strength coach Cedric Smith, comforts me best of all. "Close, Mr. Stefan," he says, either too young to realize just how badly I have performed or too well raised to say anything different.

I sit on my helmet and wipe sweat from my brow while pretending to watch [...] me not to. Ronnie Br[...]rders with room to spa[...]easy." Then, as curtai[...]quist says that, in my

W[...]layers standing behin[...]k up on Preston Parso[...]even talk to me!" he sa[...]f hour off. "That was p[...]fensive lineman, want[...]for jumping offside i[...]tape you up and throw[...]."

Rick —
Here's an early Xmas gift — I love this book!
Xo xo — Jim

W[...]s my embarrassment and disappointment. I say that I'm dumbfounded by how I could have missed so badly.

"You play long enough in the NFL, you'll miss some kicks," Jason says.

"But I'm not playing long enough in the NFL," I say.

"That's what I'm saying. You've played long enough to miss some kicks."

To the media, actual practice in training camp is incidental. Very little occurs that is newsworthy, and most reporters know that drawing major conclusions from the on-field minutia is foolhardy. They don't understand enough about the purpose of each drill, or the intent of the coaches. The media are present to make sure all the players are present, to transcribe Shanahan's daily thoughts, and to gather material for ritual camp profiles and features: who's up or down on the depth chart, who's poised for a big season, who's recovering from an injury, who's a new face on the team, who's got into trouble. Most training-camp stories are the product of quotation, not observation. So when something different does happen, reporters converge like ants to a breadcrumb. I'm today's breadcrumb.

A posse of about thirty reporters and cameramen awaits me as I stroll off the field alone. I handle them with greater ease than I did the kicks. They ask who I am and why I'm here. They ask how it's been going, and I in turn ask whether they saw me bagging 40-yarders. They want to know if I have any kicking experience. They want to know who's taken me under his wing. They want to know what the stakes were for my kick. They want to know how it felt. They want to know whether it changed how I appreciate and perceive the NFL. I answer honestly, in sound bites.

From his nearby daily news-conference perch, Shanahan is kind. He tells the throng that I didn't choke. "What was great about that, since he's been around, he knows what a kicker has to go through," my coach says. "When you miss a kick in a game, you're by yourself, nobody talks to you for a week until the next game. It was a lot of fun."

Not for me it wasn't. But I'm grateful that Shanahan is at least charitable. At the back of the crowd, still in shoulder pads, I pretend to be just another reporter. "So will you give that kicker a second chance?" I ask. Shanahan sees that it's me, flashes one of the tight, white smiles that often cross his permanently windburned face, and says that he will.

Amid a pulsing dance beat, I do a perp walk through the locker room. The reviews are not good. Tick Burns: "I was thoroughly disgusted." Tom Nalen: "Thanks for fucking us." Chad Mustard: "Shit the bed! Call housecleaning! We need new sheets!" Jake Plummer: "Don't fucking come near me. Get out of here." But when the abuse subsides, the players (the more sympathetic ones, anyway) seize on my failure as a happy confirmation of their reality, a big, fat I-told-you-so. My going down in an intergalactic fireball illuminates their struggles to play professional football.

Athletes complain that the reporters who smugly judge their performance and behavior can't possibly understand what they experience. Before joining the Broncos, I was sympathetic to the Atticus Finch principle, that you can't judge someone unless you walk around in his shoes. I'd watched and reported on enough sports, and talked to enough jocks, to conclude that fans and reporters often absurdly consider athletes as automatons who should never fail. *How could that jerk have missed?* (That night, when a local TV sports reporter cracks in his report that my book should be titled *Worst Kicker Ever,* I say to the screen: "Asshole.") But, trite as it may sound, now I have learned the lesson because I have lived it. And my teammates love that. A half dozen tell me that I got a taste of their lives, that I should multiply the pressure I felt by twenty-five or fifty or a hundred, that I was lucky to have had just a half hour of meetings riding on my performance instead of my future employment.

I skip the ice pool out of fear one of the offensive linemen will drown me and instead walk directly to the showers. Just outside, next to the urinals, fullback Kyle Johnson is wearing a white towel and his Broncos ID, waiting to take a drug test.

"How was that for pressure?" he asks.

"More than anything I've felt in my life."

"That's what it's like every play of every game. It'll keep you up at night—if you let it."

By the end of lunch, my folly seems forgotten. Either I don't matter much to my teammates, or, I prefer to think, they understand that there but for the grace of God go they. The coaches may expect perfection. The players understand it's an impossible standard. "You're all right," Jake Plummer reassures me. "We'll get you another chance."

My spirits lift even more when Preston Parsons and Chad Mustard want to play Scrabble. At their behest, I've stashed a deluxe board, a bag of plastic "Protiles," and a copy of *The Official Scrabble Players Dictionary* in my locker. I'm thrilled for the chance to assert my dominance at something. We set up in the quarterbacks' meeting room. As we draw tiles, Plummer studies his playbook. "I don't know how you guys can play that right now. All I see when I see those letters is, 'Where is Y lined up? T is Tiger,'" he says, referring to some playbook shorthand.

Jake thumbs through the dictionary and says that Scrabble makes him realize how dumb football players are. I disagree. I note the parallel between learning the hundreds of plays and formations in Jake's playbook and the thousands of unusual words in the Scrabble lexicon. In both games, competitors face ever-changing alignments, the complex geometry of a playing surface, the pressure of a clock ticking down to zero, and incomplete information—in Scrabble, not knowing the opponent's tiles or the contents of the bag; in football, not knowing what the other team will do once the ball is snapped. Both great football players and great Scrabble players say that when they're in the proverbial zone, the game decelerates and they instantly see the answer. I, for one, think that's easier to accomplish without the continual threat of being steamrolled by a charging goliath, which is not a major concern in Scrabble.

Chad is a good living-room player, as we say in the game, and Preston is an eager learner. Jake is naturally smart and curious. He looks up a couple of words that I've laid down: DIRK, to stab with a small knife; CURIA, a court of justice. (Another day, I play TURK, who in football is the person who summons players to the coach's office to be cut. Preston checks the definition. "One who eagerly advocates change," he announces. "That's fantastic! I've seen the turk a couple of times.") We don't finish our game before practice, but the board will be there when the quarterbacks and their coaches meet later, and Jake will use the game to lighten the mood. "Come on, this isn't a curia," he says during a debate over a play. "I'm gonna dirk your ass," he tells quarterbacks coach Pat McPherson.

Regaining confidence through Scrabble is step one of my recovery program. Step two is regaining pleasure, and a feeling of competence, in kicking. At that afternoon's practice, Jeff Hays is eager to help. I suspect that after hearing about my performance in the morning, the part-time kicking coach feels guilty about not having worked much with me. His lesson for the day: Focus on a tiny spot on the ball where I will make contact, and sustain that focus straight to the ground after the ball disappears. We work on locking my foot and following through to my left shoulder. From 20 yards, I try to hit the right upright, and when I do it pings like a tuning fork. Practice ends, and the field clears. Jeff, Micah, and I keep working. It's liberating. No one is watching, no one is yelling, no one is laughing. There's no sneering Todd or amused Jason. Just me and two guys who love kicking and love teaching kicking, immaculate grass, a cooling breeze, a fading sun.

For step three, I want to show the players I am actually capable. Since most of them rarely or never see me kick in practice, they don't think I can make a field goal of any distance, let alone a 40-yarder. Nalen, Lepsis, some other offensive lineman, Plummer, too—none of them believe me. So the next morning, when I insist I can indeed kick, they challenge me. Jason holds. I crush one that is easily good from 40, but it fades wide right. Still, I prove my point, to them and to myself. I can do it.

The fourth and final step is recognizing that every player is too busy worrying about his own issues to care about mine. P. J. Alexander is limping badly, and the Broncos have signed a former Indianapolis Colts lineman who has come out of retirement, Adam Meadows, worsening P.J.'s chances of making the club. One day, I walk into the training room and see P.J. on a table with a purple gash on his left shin and a large bruise on his right. A trainer bandaging the cut calls it gruesome. P.J. says it's the least of his problems. He slides a pad under his legs to elevate them. The trainer attaches two conducting pads to his left knee and applies a pressurized wrap filled with cold water. He asks P.J. how much electrical stimulation he wants. "As much as possible, man," P.J. replies.

Preston Parsons is miserable. In the first six practices, he has received a total of just four reps during offense-versus-defense drills, compared to 129 for Jake, 83 for Bradlee, and 74 for Cutler, we learn from the printed log posted in the quarterbacks' room. Without reps, Preston can't show that he is capable of beating out Bradlee for the number two job.

"Every coach in the world says, 'Go stand there and get mental reps and watch what's going on and study the playbook,'" Preston says after we adjourn the Scrabble game. "But there's absolutely no substitute for doing it. Look what you did today. Sitting here, you can say that in theory we should do this, that, and the other. When you're under center, it looks totally different. You've got the play clock running down, you've got motherfuckers breathing down your neck, yelling at you, you're trying to run the best play. There's no substitute for that."

Bradlee is still struggling mentally and performing erratically. "I've got three people in my ear," he says. "It's always chaotic out there. How am I supposed to perform? I can't handle it. You're trying to get mentally focused while these guys are up in your shit." But Bradlee's troubles aren't helping Preston's confidence. Preston calls his agent, David Dunn, from the locker room to ask him to scope out other teams.

The punters, meanwhile, are generating their own drama. Paul Ernster yells at an equipment staff intern who can't find his cap. Ronnie tells him that second-year kickers enjoy no such authority. A position player earns some respect after four or five years in the league, Ronnie says, a kicker maybe after eight years, if he has some money kicks on his résumé. Todd Sauerbrun shows up on the field wearing the wrong color jersey and no shoulder pads or helmet, and then doesn't do a ball-drop drill as instructed. Ronnie chews him out in front of the other kickers, saying if he doesn't want to be here, he should talk to "the man," meaning Shanahan.

"They can both be out on the street together," Ronnie tells me. "I'll cut both those motherfuckers and keep number four," Micah.

"You don't want a fucking punter to distract the team from what's going on, all the good shit that's going on," T-Mac adds. "A fucking punter."

In other words, Todd should shut up and do his undemanding job. But he can't, either because he's angry and depressed about the suspension, because it's his nature, or, most likely, because of some combination of the two. Ronnie and T-Mac think he's a lost cause. But they'd like to reach Paul. T-Mac tells the young punter bluntly: Todd doesn't want you here. Todd wants you to kick the worst balls you have ever kicked. "Todd wants us to want him back," Ronnie tells me. "He knows that if

Paul's successful his chances of coming back with us are slim and none."

In the afternoon, Todd and Paul average 54 yards each on live punts, Micah just 44 yards. But Micah is consistent, and better at angling the ball to one side of the field or the other. Practicing kickoffs, Paul squibs one and Todd says, "There it is. Bottle it." Todd kicks a wobbly line drive and Jason says, "There it was, Todd. Bottle it." Paul's foot pops out of his cleat during a kick. Micah kicks one seven yards deep in the end zone.

"Micah's gonna sneak in the back door," T-Mac says. "While they're over there talking crazy with one another, Micah's gonna say, 'I stole another year from the NFL.'"

I just want to steal another kick from the Denver Broncos. Two days after my debut, FG is on the schedule again. Jake Plummer asks if I'm prepared for redemption—and says the stakes are always higher the second time. But my fellow kickers aren't concerned with whether I'll have an encore. It's just another day at camp for them. Jason regales us with tales of buzzing a herd of antelopes in Colorado in his 1957 de Havilland. T-Mac notes that Jason would rather be killing antelopes than buzzing them. Todd makes the sound of propeller blades and suggests that Jason could do both at the same time.

I laser the ball from 35 yards on the turf field. T-Mac calls it my best hit yet as a Bronco and announces, "He's full of piss and vinegar!" I hand him my tape recorder. He hits the red button and talks. "Stefan, do not shit down your leg today. Focus. Don't be scared. Execute. Swing. If you shit down your leg today, your reps will be limited from here on out."

I line up for another from 35.

"You better get the fucking ball up. Get it up! There it is!" T-Mac shouts, not sarcastically. "Whoa ho ho! He's on the driving range!" he says in a falsetto.

"Back him up," Ronnie says. "He'll hit a forty-yarder."

"Next on the tee box, from New York City, Stefan Fatsis! Whaaaaaaaa . . ."

I make the 40-yarder. I'm completely comfortable. Nervous, yes, but in a good way. After my flop, Jason told me that if you're not nervous, you don't care. He said he's nervous kicking an extra point in a preseason game. We repair to the weight room to count down the time to FG. I pee, eat a chocolate brownie Myoplex protein bar, and read the *Denver Post*. With ten minutes to go, I make two kicks from 30 on grass and patrol the sideline calmly, stretching my legs and breathing methodically. Paul writes in my notebook: "Looks much better today. More relaxed." Instead of standing alone to await my fate, I stick close by Micah while he ingathers snaps from Mike Leach. Snapper, holder, and kicker are a unit, after all.

"Field goal and field-goal rush!" Shanahan shouts. "Let's go!"

Jason again converts all ten kicks from the same distances and locations as the other day. The last ball skims the right upright and bounces through. I watch with stupefied awe, but no intimidation or worry. I'm not shaking or hyperventilating, and I'm not afraid.

"Offense!" Shanahan barks. "Fifty-yard line!" The horn sounds. Redemption will have to wait. "At least you were ready," Paul says.

10

Here's Your Rope

Wearing an NFL uniform on an NFL field in front of an NFL crowd is every fan's fantasy. *Here I am slicing through the Dallas secondary! Now I'm doing a sack dance over Tom Brady's crumpled body!* But the image of the guy on the field isn't an actual self. It's an athletically gifted fantasyland other—one I haven't conjured since I was Fran Tarkenton scrambling for backyard touchdowns for the early-1970s New York Giants.

So when Paul Woodside pulled me aside at a kicking camp in the spring and said that at 4:30 that morning he'd had a vision that I would play in a preseason game, I laughed it off as one more motivational one-liner. That camp was my worst; ninth-graders outkicked me. Even though the NFL and the Broncos had agreed to let me play, I didn't believe they would let me play in a game. Plimpton didn't get to, and that was long before the NFL was a multibillion-dollar business that operated as if it controlled the codes to the nuclear arsenal. Journalistically, the idea was appealing. Practically, it was frightening. I knew enough about professional athletes to understand that every task they perform is exponentially more difficult than fans believe it to be—and that they are much bigger up close.

Now, though, I've been to Denver, trotted onto the field, worn shoulder pads, rehabbed in the ice pool. Dressing at my locker, shampooing in the communal showers, rubbing Flexall on my thighs, I've stopped worrying about my comparatively unmuscled self. The players are just people, their bodies no longer intimidating. More important, I've tasted the pressure and failed, but emerged intact. The two bad kicks feel like necessary dress rehearsals for success. So while I fear Shanahan won't live up to his postkick podium promise to give me a second chance—the kicks were that bad—I now want not only that but the real thing. I want to fulfill Paul's dream of me nailing an extra point or a short field goal in the preseason.

There's no middle ground this summer. The Broncos don't stage intrasquad scrimmages, Broncos versus Broncos, under the lights in front of fans. (In *Paper Lion,* Plimpton quarterbacked a set of downs in one such game.) Too many millions of dollars already are at risk during full-speed, minimal-contact practices to increase the possibility of injury in a gamelike environment. Shanahan did try to schedule a few days of joint practices, including some controlled scrimmaging, before preseason games against Detroit and Tennessee. To my disappointment, the other teams turned him down.

But I have a plan. I will ask the Broncos and the NFL for the harmless favor of letting me "dress out" for the first game in Detroit—wear a uniform, kick during warm-ups, and stand on the sideline. That will give me additional time to practice and persuade the powers that I should be allowed to kick in one of the three remaining games.

I pop the question to Pat Bowlen in the weight room. He's in there daily, grinding away for forty-five minutes on the stair climber, bathed in sweat and looking deceptively near collapse. Bowlen is a former Ironman triathlete who, at sixty-two years old, can't withstand the pounding of running anymore but whose resting heart rate still hovers around forty beats per minute. Bowlen tells me to ask Shanahan, but to go to Ted Sundquist first.

Since arriving in Dove Valley, I've shuttled among the offices of the Broncos' top three football executives. When Bowlen isn't in Hawaii—his two daughters from a first marriage live there; he also has five children from his current marriage—we have long, rambling conversations in his capacious two-room office. We talk about everything from his family background in ranching and oil in western Canada to his acquisition and management of the Broncos to the emotive Aldo Luongo paintings that hang on the walls along with assorted Super Bowl and team memorabilia (pictures with presidents, signed jerseys, miniature statues of players). Black cowboy boots propped on a mahogany desk, speech liberally punctuated with expletives, Bowlen is one of the most casual sports owners I've met, one reason the Broncos players are respectful but not obsequious in his company. That he doesn't constantly meddle in football matters—though he is constantly informed, talking to Shanahan daily, and does weigh in on major personnel decisions—further enhances his reputation.

"You could pay a guy fifty million to play every year, but if you don't get the little things that make you feel appreciated, fuck it," Jake Plummer tells me one day. "I can walk up to Mr. Bowlen and be like, 'Hey, Mr. Bowlen, those are sweet boots, where did you get 'em?' 'Aw, these are some fuckin' ostrich skin. You got to get yourself a pair of these, you little fucker.' You're like, 'All right, I will.' The little bit you get from that makes you feel like, goddamn, they appreciate you here, they know what I'm doing, they know what everybody's doing, if you're a first-stringer or a third-string snapper. They take care of their people."

That includes Shanahan, whose title might as well be Coach for Life. When I ask Bowlen to describe their relationship, he stares past me. "I don't want this to come out in the wrong way," he finally says, "but it's almost like a marriage. You know, you grow with that person and you develop a certain level of confidence and trust over a period of years. And so you know the right questions to ask, you know the right, the wrong buttons to push. It's not like you put all your faith and trust in this person and then they're not doing the job or cheating on you. That's not happening."

For all of his job security, though, it's hard to get Shanahan to talk about himself, his career arc, his motivations, his style. Our meetings, which require two people to schedule, are more question-and-answer sessions than stream-of-consciousness conversations. His linear, directed life is circumscribed by the business of football, his philosophies are simple and logical, and his answers reflect that. Shanahan isn't distant. He's been friendly, informal, and straightforward in all of our interactions. But after three months he's still a cipher to me, though I imagine that holds for people who have known him for three decades.

Sundquist and I have the most casual relationship. I show up at his office door unannounced, usually between practices or during evening meetings. If he's free, we talk. If not, I come back later. As a source in the journalistic sense, Sundquist is more valuable than Bowlen, whose dish about his fellow owners is interesting in my day-job life but less so in my kicker life. Sundquist also is a more valuable source than Shanahan, whose orderliness precludes unplanned bull sessions. Sundquist instantly understood what I'd hoped to accomplish, on and off the field, and wants to help. At forty-four, Sundquist is a year older than I am. As a former college running back who tore an ACL, he appreciates the folly of my venture. He likes that I'm interested in how the personnel side of the team functions, and he likes explaining it.

Sundquist isn't a typical front-office grind. He didn't join the Broncos, his only NFL employer, until he was thirty. After graduating from the Air Force Academy in 1984, he stayed on as a second lieutenant and football-team graduate assistant. Then he was assigned to the 6912th Electronic Security Group, a military intelligence unit at Templehof Central Airport in Berlin, and was at the Brandenburg Gate in June 1987 when Ronald Reagan challenged Mikhail Gorbachev to "tear down this wall." Sundquist was released from his commitment to join the Air Force football coaching staff. When it was time to return, the Berlin wall had fallen and the Soviet Union—his specialty—had crumbled. Already behind his peer group, Sundquist accepted a buyout from the military.

Through a coaching colleague, Sundquist was hired as a gofer for the Broncos' general manager. His military training had taught him to accept his role without complaint. Within a year, he was a scout. Impressed by his organizational skills, Shanahan in 1996 appointed him director of college scouting. After he was a finalist to become the general manager of two other teams, Bowlen promoted him to that position in 2002.

When he nearly was hired as president of the Seattle Seahawks, Bowlen extended his contract until 2010.

Now Sundquist says he doesn't want to leave. Few NFL general managers know their team will spend whatever it takes to win, season after season. This year's per-team salary cap is $101,866,000, and the Broncos will come as close to that number as possible. Fully funding the team was a condition Shanahan set when he became head coach in 1995; a few years earlier, he had spurned an offer from Bowlen for reasons of internal politics and authority.

Bowlen says he wouldn't do it any other way. "I'm not going to be judged on how much money this organization made," he tells me one day. "I mean, fuck, that doesn't even enter the equation. Zero. It's, 'How many games did he win? How many Super Bowls did he win?' There's not a lot of things that I really want other than winning Super Bowls. I mean, what do I want, a bigger house? No. More space in Hawaii? Own my own jet? I mean, none of that makes a hell of a lot of sense to me at this stage in my life." For Sundquist, knowing that football decisions aren't predicated on their bottom-line impact eliminates a major job hassle. "You can't just freewheel—at least show me where it's going," he says of Bowlen's approach. "But it's not heavy-handed by any means."

As a former military man, Sundquist respects what he calls the "culture of leadership" that Shanahan has imposed. In it, failure is not an option, and fear—fear of disappointing, and ticking off, Shanahan—comes with the territory. Slavish attention to detail and consummate professionalism are as basic to the Broncos as orange and blue. Practicing at full speed. Fretting about punctuality. One evening in his office, assistant head coach Mike Heimerdinger—who roomed with Shanahan in college—looks at the digital clock on the wall and cuts short a conversation. "Don't *ever* want to be late for one of Mike's meetings," Dinger says while moving for the door. I mention to Sundquist that I heard one of the equipment guys exhort a ball boy before practice to "bring your A-game today!" Sundquist replies with a story about the same staffer congratulating another ball boy, a coach's son, for racing to hold the yardage chains during a drill.

"That's us. That's our organization," Sundquist says. "And that more than anything is the profound effect that Mike has had. It hasn't been that he has come in here and added XYZ play, although he is thought of as one of the masters of game planning and he should be respected for that. It's not in the systematic stuff with regards to how to travel efficiently, how to put together a good draft, how to manage your cap. He didn't come up with this." Sundquist flaps a salary-cap accounting ledger created by him and his deputy, Mike Bluem, whose title is director of football administration. "But we know his standards. What he's done is accumulate people with high standards themselves who take great pride in their work, and, voilà, you put together very efficient systems."

Within the Broncos, it is understood that Shanahan has the final word on almost every decision, from who starts at left guard to where fans stand during training camp. But while Shanahan had named Sundquist college scouting director, he wasn't behind his promotion to general manager. "Pat made me GM. Mike didn't," Sundquist says. "I replaced Mike's guy."

There is a natural tension between a general manager, whose job is to evaluate, procure, and sign players, and a coach, who often thinks he can perform all three tasks as well if not better. Sundquist was elevated in part as a check on Shanahan's omnipotence. When he led the Broncos to back-to-back Super Bowl victories in the 1997 and 1998 seasons, Shanahan was dubbed the Mastermind. But when he signed more than a few busts and bad apples in the subsequent, lean years—the Broncos had a record of 34-31 in the four seasons after Elway and before Plummer—his ability to coach and identify talent at the same time were called into question. As mediocre as the team's on-field performance was, more worrisome was that Shanahan's signings had placed the franchise on course for financial trouble.

NFL teams maintain two sets of books. One is the salary cap, an accounting system for the complex contracts that players sign. The other is cash allocations, or the actual money spent on players. Like other teams in the 1990s—most notably two of the decade's other successful franchises, the San Francisco 49ers, where Shanahan was the offensive coordinator for one Super Bowl champion, and the Dallas Cowboys—the Broncos often lured players with huge up-front cash bonuses prorated for salary-cap accounting over as many as seven years.

The Broncos didn't have a cash budget at the time. (Sundquist now gets one every off-season from the business side of the building.) If Shanahan wanted a player, the front office found a way to make his contract fit under the cap. The team pushed its maneuvering to the league's limits and beyond. The NFL twice fined the Broncos nearly $1 million and docked them a draft choice for violating financial rules in the late 1990s. In one case, the league said the Broncos manipulated the cap by getting players to defer compensation with interest and by timing a player's release to reduce the team's cap obligation. The first punishment was announced in December 2001. Sundquist was named GM a month later.

He and Mike Bluem analyzed contracts across the NFL and quickly identified a root of the team's woes: Players who signed seven-year contracts completed on average less than two years of their deals. For the Broncos, that meant that as much as 22 percent of the cap would be consumed by players no longer on the team—"dead money" in NFL parlance. "That's the way Mike knew how to do it," Sundquist says one night in his office. "Trying to convince him otherwise that that was not necessarily the right way to go was not a real easy thing to do at first."

Creating and managing an NFL team is an exercise in balance, among ownership, management, coaching, and scouting. Ownership wants to win—but also to make money. In 2001, the Broncos moved into a new stadium, Invesco Field, and instantly jumped into the top quarter of the league in revenue. But Bowlen also spent some of his own money on the stadium, bought out his siblings' ownership stake, expanded the practice facilities, and fought lawsuits from a former club owner demanding a piece of the franchise. (Bowlen eventually prevailed.) The big cash outlays on players translated to financial pressure, which no owner appreciates, especially one who has made the game his primary business, as Bowlen has, and especially in the cash-rich NFL.

Scouts target physical abilities like size, speed, quickness, strength, and body structure, and mental capabilities like reaction time on the field and intelligence off of it. Which of the 12,000 football-playing college seniors deserve our attention? Can they become great? At the Broncos, five staffers observe, live or on tape, the top 250 college prospects two times each. Coaches, meanwhile, focus on execution: Does a player line up properly? Does he run a pass route to the proper depth? Is he paying attention in meetings? Will he make me look better—and preserve my job? Then there is management—Sundquist's office—which has to concern itself with issues material to ownership, coaching, and scouting: the present and the future of the franchise, on the field and on the payroll.

The conflicts can be especially knotty when the head coach is accustomed to blanket authority over player acquisition and roster composition, increasingly common in the era of the celebrity coach. Sundquist quotes Bill Parcells, who upon leaving the New England Patriots told reporters, "They want you to cook the dinner, at least they ought to let you shop for some of the groceries." "Okay, fine," Sundquist retorts. "Here's your rope. Hang yourself."

Sundquist and Bluem rescued the Broncos from their salary-cap burden by waiting for old bad contracts to expire and avoiding new bad ones. The Broncos drafted players who could play immediately, because younger players are cheaper than older ones, and acquired young free agents who might blossom rather than veterans in their peak earning years. The approach kept the team from making a big splash in the free-agent market, but in 2003, 2004, and 2005 the Broncos posted records of 10-6, 10-6, and 13-3, making the playoffs each season. Now, Sundquist and Bluem tell me proudly, the team's dead money amounts to less than 10 percent of the salary cap, below the league average. The Broncos can spread the remaining $90 million or so among the fifty-three players who make the team, plus the eight-man practice squad and anyone placed on the injured reserve list, who also count against the cap.

To help Shanahan understand the team's financial status, Sundquist gives him the daily balance sheet detailing cap and cash allocations, which change based on when players are signed or released, on when various contract provisions kick in, and on unusual circumstances. For instance, the Broncos will receive a credit against the cap of four-seventeenths of Todd's salary—$328,235—when his suspension officially begins on September 1. "Whether Mike reads it or not, I don't know," Sundquist says of the ledger. "But it gives him information he doesn't always want to talk about."

Through his organizational skills, loyalty, and track record in player decisions, Sundquist has gained meaningful influence. One player agent who deals with the Broncos regularly tells me that Sundquist isn't a "full GM" with ultimate authority over free-agent signings and trades and draft picks. But, the agent says, he has earned more power and deference than any general manager under Shanahan. If the team does poorly, though? Sundquist knows that while Bowlen promoted him, he ultimately serves at Shanahan's pleasure.

On this particular day, the Broncos are $1.7 million below their cash target of $100 million and just under the cap, based, per league rules, on the fifty-one players with the biggest cap numbers in camp. (Accounting for fifty-one players during camp winds up giving teams flexibility, because some lower-paid rookies and minimum-salary players inevitably displace some higher-paid veterans, for competitive and financial reasons.) Even just a week into camp, Sundquist and Bluem are compiling mock fifty-three-man rosters with contractual details input into a spreadsheet. The projected cut players, currently worth a total of $32 million, are listed below them, with a practice squad grouped in red ink. Sundquist, Bluem, and player-personnel director Jim Goodman assemble the mock teams using their own evaluations, plus what they glean from informal chats with Shanahan and other coaches at practice, in the cafeteria, or late at night. They'll begin sending the financial projections to Shanahan when the preseason starts. Shanahan then will supply more-definitive roster plans, which will be entered into more spreadsheets. Sundquist predicts that his current roster won't differ by more than six or seven players from Shanahan's final one.

The most celebrated new contract belongs to Jay Cutler of Santa Claus, Indiana, and Vanderbilt. When Cutler signed, the media reported the deal at $48 million over six years. As with most NFL contracts, the gargantuan figure is a chimera. Less than a third of it, $15.1 million, is guaranteed. The rest consists of incentives, some of which Cutler will likely earn, most of which he probably won't. It's also highly unlikely that Cutler will play under the contract for six years. Virtually all big NFL deals are eventually restructured to reduce the player's salary-cap cost. The big number is leaked largely at the insistence of agents, because big numbers attract attention and can influence impressionable young men who might become clients.

Sundquist flips around his black binder and shows me the details of Cutler's deal. The incentives read like *Jeopardy!* categories. *Super Bowl for $500,000.* Cutler will earn that much every time the Broncos win the championship with him as the season-long quarterback. The team would be delighted to pay it every year, but it's not going to happen. *Starter for $3 million.* The Broncos expect to pay this onetime bonus in a year or two, when they project Cutler will become the starting quarterback. *Division championship and playoff wins for $200,000. Pro Bowl for $100,000. Statistical prowess for $325,000.* Finishing the season in the top five in the NFL in passer rating, completion percentage, interception percentage, total yards passing, touchdown passes, and yards per pass, is worth that much—per category.

If Cutler doesn't pan out as a star or even a starter, the Broncos will have a backup quarterback for about $2 million a year—less this year, when he will get the NFL rookie minimum salary of $275,000 plus $1.275 million of his $7.9 million signing bonus. "It's a significant investment but it's not a backbreaking investment," Sundquist says. It's certainly not one that pressures the team to play him now. Cutler will cost less this season than a veteran backup would have. "Why would you spend that on a guy that may be with you only a year or two?" Sundquist says. "At least right now I know I'm spending it on a guy who is continuing to be groomed and eventually will become your starter down the road."

And if it doesn't work out? If Cutler's a bust?

"We're a team that's not afraid to cut our losses. So we never feel handcuffed by a particular investment. You wouldn't want to cut him today. But two or three years down the road, if it was conceivable that it didn't make a whole lot of sense, there are ways to break even."

Now, though, the Broncos are doing the opposite of cutting losses. Shanahan promotes Cutler to number two and drops Bradlee to number three.

Bradlee breaks the news of the demotion to me at dinner before Shanahan announces it at the team meeting. He was getting treatment on his back a half hour earlier when Shanahan summoned him from the trainer's room. Shanahan told Bradlee that, while he was having a good camp, he wanted to give Cutler more reps. "It's their duty in their eyes to do what's best for the team," Bradlee says. "Whether I believe it is or not is not the point." He doesn't feel sorry for himself, but he does wonder if this is a defining moment in his career. "You'd be a liar to say you don't think about things like that."

Bradlee left Shanahan's office resigned and disappointed. Shanahan's quick-and-dirty message didn't satisfy Bradlee's desire for *more*. He didn't need to hug it out with the coach, but he would have liked to talk it out. Instead, Bradlee has to shrug it off and plug away and keep his head up—pick a sports cliché. "It's part of the business," he says. "Either you hang or you can't." But I know that's not enough for Bradlee. I can't imagine the demotion won't render him an emotional basket case.

Either Shanahan can't see that or he can but, with Cutler's emergence, doesn't find it relevant. Bradlee is an excellent athlete, Shanahan tells me, but Jay is a better NFL quarterback already. "He's six three and a half, he's two hundred thirty pounds, he can make all the throws, he's got mobility, he can escape the rush," Shanahan says, and goes on. Cutler started four years in college, the last two in a passing offense. He played in one of the most competitive conferences in the nation. He hasn't faltered under the weight of the playbook.

After twenty-five practices in the spring and summer, with their attendant hours of direct observation, video, and statistics, Shanahan believes he can trust Cutler to run the team now if Jake gets hurt, in a year if he doesn't. Jake, who will turn thirty-two during the season, relies on his mobility, which will worsen with age. Shanahan insists that Cutler's promotion isn't a coaching head game to pressure Jake, but simply designed to prepare Cutler to play.

Sundquist is equally emphatic about the rookie's progress. "He's got as strong an arm as I've ever seen," he says. "John Elway had a very, very strong arm, but this kid's got a really strong arm as well. And mentally, I don't judge that part of the game, but the feedback that I've gotten from the coaching staff, and especially Mike, is that none of this has been too big for him so far. So far. Now let's see if you can go out and execute on the field, read and react and adjust accordingly to some stuff you haven't seen."

I ask Sundquist whether the team trusts Cutler enough to keep just two quarterbacks on the roster.

"Potentially. But I think that remains to be seen."

"But it's an option? If you're that confident in Jay, in theory you could—"

"You could go with two and carry Preston Parsons on the practice squad. So from Bradlee's perspective it's probably, uh-oh. But as of right now every model that I've put together has consistently had a three-man quarterback rotation."

"With Bradlee being the third?"

"Yeah."

"And Preston?"

"Preston's a talented kid. But Bradlee's been here before. He's our guy. I think Preston in any other year certainly has shown the talent to be a number three."

"But it's still conceivable when you get down to that final move—"

"Could go with two."

I just want one roster spot for one preseason game, and one play.

Pat Bowlen probably could make it happen with a phone call to Paul Tagliabue. But in the weight room he tells me he won't do that. The

owners are searching for a successor to the commissioner, who is retiring, and Bowlen says he doesn't want to do anything that might upset
his colleagues, some of whom already resent Bowlen because he's close
to Tagliabue. A special favor might be an excuse to oppose the candidate
for whom Bowlen has been lobbying, a career NFL executive named
Roger Goodell.

I bump into Sundquist in the lunch line. I stress how important it
will be for me to dress for an actual game, and to kick in one, to truly
understand what it feels like to play in the NFL. He appreciates that,
but he's unwilling to bring it up with headquarters. While he knows the
league has sanctioned my presence, he has never mentioned me to officials. He's worried that the control freaks who enforce roster rules might
punish the team if they realize I'm occupying a locker. Why? Sundquist
says the NFL could argue that my kicking in practice means that Jason
Elam has to kick less in practice, which is advantageous to Jason Elam
and the Broncos. By that rationale, I am actually helping the team prepare for the season. It's a stretch, especially given the kickers' light
workload. Jason kicks when Jason wants to kick, period; you could add
ten more of us and there would still be plenty of kicks to go around. But,
given the NFL's fine-print rules enforcement, Sundquist doesn't want to
take any chances and have the team fined or me kicked out of camp.
"That's how they think," he says.

So while the official team position on me is don't ask, don't tell,
there's just a week until our first preseason game. I tell Sundquist I'll
call the NFL. I state my case to PR guy Brian McCarthy. He says he'll
bring it up with the executive in charge of roster bean counting. A
few days before we fly to Detroit, word comes back: I can dress but not
kick.

And that's enough for now. My teammates are happy for me. The
equipment guys are, too. I stop by and tell them to get a game jersey
ready. "That's what we're planning for," Chris Valenti says. "I hope you
don't mind that we spelled your name F-A-T-S-U-S."

11

Groundhog Day

Every day of training camp should be, for me, new and exciting. But after a week I begin exhibiting the same symptoms as my teammates: exhaustion, boredom, claustrophobia. Am I that easily influenced and subconsciously desperate to fit in? Am I experiencing a reverse Stockholm syndrome in which I identify with my fellow captives rather than with my captors? Or is training camp actually as exhausting, tedious, and claustrophobic as advertised, even for journalist kickers?

The routine is unchanging and paralytic: Holiday Inn to shuttle bus to facility to cafeteria to locker room to field to locker room to cafeteria to meetings to field to weight room to locker room to cafeteria to meetings to shuttle bus to Holiday Inn. "Groundhog Day," Tick Burns says, referring to the movie in which a Pittsburgh TV weatherman covering the insipid annual small-town ritual is forced to relive the day until he discovers virtue and meaning in life. Like Bill Murray's character, the Broncos wake up to the alarm clock playing "I Got You, Babe," praying that today isn't yesterday. But it is. The drills are the same. The practice film is the same. The lectures are the same. The weather is the same. Even the free chow—copious, varied, and not terrible—begins to irritate. "If I have to eat any more food on a stick, I'm going to stab myself with the skewer," a player says over dinner.

The monotony is broken the way young men break it, with games, humor, time wasting, and irreverence. Two pieces of paper are taped inside the locker of Ashley Lelie, the AWOL wide receiver. The "Lelie-O-Meter" lists how many days of camp he's missed and a running tally of fines: $140,000 so far. The video games, computer terminals, and inflatable mattresses are fully occupied. Some guys recline in their four-feet-deep lockers reading playbooks; some nap there. Others watch movies on their laptops. Others download music. A group of defensive backs and linebackers—Champ Bailey, Ian Gold, Domonique Foxworth, and others—plays hand after hand of Texas hold 'em on linked Sony handhelds for hundreds of dollars. Preston Parsons and Chad Mustard play Scrabble nightly, with or without me.

Before practice, Jason Elam, Paul Ernster, and Mike Leach compete to see who can hit the crossbar with a ball thrown from forty yards away. After twenty misses, they hit four in a row. One afternoon in the cold tub, Tom Nalen works on a Sudoku puzzle. Paul Ernster, submerged to his waist, faces him. Cooper Carlisle and Matt Lepsis stand in the water behind Paul. Over Paul's shoulder, Nalen makes eye contact with his fellow linemen. Like a middle linebacker, I read the play as it's developing and lift myself out of the pool. Nalen pushes Ernster backward into Lepsis, who pulls him fully underwater. Mike Leach jumps in—*jumps in!* Then he gets out and does a cannonball, triggering a cascade of water and laughter.

For the kickers, our on-field dead time is filled with mindless high-school banter. Between playing catch and getting some pole, we talk. Someone mentions that second-year cornerback Darrent Williams and veteran linebacker Al Wilson each drive $200,000 Bentleys. "I could have bought two of those with my fine money," Todd says. Todd might be deeply embarrassed about his suspension, but at least he can joke about it. "Two hundred thousand?" says Jason, who drives a Ford pickup equipped with a winch. "Put a mailbox on it."

The conversation turns to 1980s and '90s television, a favorite Todd subject. He has encyclopedic knowledge of the teen sitcom *Saved by the Bell*. Todd offers a few trivia questions—"What was the name of the principal's brother?" "What did Screech's mom do for a living?"—that only he is able to answer. Jason mentions that he was on *Wheel of For-*

tune, when the show paired an NFL player with a fan, and he missed RECORD-BREAKING FIELD GOAL. Then Todd asks everyone to name his favorite show. We debate whether to go with current or all-time. After we settle on current, Todd goes first, ignores the criteria, and, along with *Entourage,* names *Saved by the Bell* on grounds that he watches reruns every day. I also pick *Entourage* (*The Sopranos* is on hiatus). The others go with *CSI: Miami* (Ronnie), *CSI: Las Vegas* (Micah), *House* (Paul), *Forensic Files* (T-Mac), and *24* (Jason).

Punt Pro is at the end of practice on this morning, so we troop into the weight room to wait. Todd, Jason, and Micah set their helmets on the round table in the rear of the room alongside a couple of boxes of Myoplex bars. Paul removes his shoulder pads and sits cross-legged on the floor. Micah stands watching a flat-screen. And I plop down on a machine with the pin inserted at twice the weight I can lift.

"Fifteen minutes, girls," Todd says.

"Fifteen minutes to what?" Paul asks. We've got much more time than that until the punters have to perform.

"Rain," Todd says.

Jason decides to check Todd's forecast, so we head to Troy Smith's office. The isolated weather map of the area is open on Troy's computer. Todd was close. "Six minutes away," Jason says. A storm, in green and yellow, inches across the screen. "That's where I live," Jason says, moving the cursor to the southwest. He moves it some more. "That's where I killed my mountain lion," he says. He moves it some more. "That's where I killed my elk."

Jason's deep Christian faith and his affinity for hunting confound some of his teammates. "I like Jason and I don't want to dislike him because of what he's killed," Jake Plummer says. Jason, though, has no qualms about his hobby. "God says go subdue the land, that the animals are under our authority. He says go kill and eat," Jason tells me. "I'm not going to just kill something to kill it."

I ask Jason about his safari in South Africa. He says that the head and shoulders of a giraffe that he bagged are being stuffed and mounted. Then he flips opens his PowerBook and clicks to a photo album. There's

Jason leaning on the dead giraffe, a .300 Winchester Magnum rifle in his hands. There's Jason posing behind a fifty-five-inch-tall kudu, a chevron of white hair between its cold, dead eyes. There's a gunned-down zebra trailing a stream of blood. There's a close-up of ticks in the ear of an eland. There's Jason in front of a sable. "I'm doing a life-size mount of him in a big wildlife scene," he says.

A guide drove Jason and a friend on private land, sometimes chumming for game with carcasses, animal feces, and a tape broadcasting mating calls. A price list set the cost per kill. Jason acts out the scene in the back of the Jeep: sighting an animal, quickly asking the price, and then firing away. A picture pops up of a gemsbok, a regal animal with a black-and-white head and long, straight antlers resembling screws. "That cost eleven hundred dollars," Jason says. He killed eighteen animals, his friend killed twelve. Almost all of the meat, and the internal organs, were given to locals, who skinned the carcasses. After a year-long quarantine, the skins were sent to Jason. The tab for the month-long adventure was $22,000.

Glancing at the clock, Jason says, "Oops. We better go out."

I share neither Jason's conservative politics nor his evangelical Christian religion. ("You've got this goo man they want you to think we came from," he tells a reporter regarding evolution. "It doesn't make sense to me.") Rather amazingly, Jason manages to make those personal details seem no more noteworthy than the fact that he grew up in suburban Atlanta. From killing kudus to saving souls, everything is related matter-of-factly. One day I see Jason reading a book called *Christian Apologetics* and he says he plans to take a nine-month course at Oxford University to study the subject, which holds that the life and miracles of Christ are historically demonstrable. During the season, he'll inform me that all summer he'd been writing, with his church pastor, a Christian thriller about football and terrorism. And that it was bought by the publisher of the best-selling, apocalyptic *Left Behind* series. And that the publisher had contracted a sequel. The literary merits of *Monday Night Jihad* aside, I'm amazed again by Jason's oh-by-the-way accomplishments.

Here's his greatest football one: On October 25, 1998, the Broncos played the Jacksonville Jaguars in Denver's old Mile High Stadium. With about fifty seconds left in the first half, a Denver drive stalled on Jacksonville's 40-yard line. If the Jaguars had called a time-out, Denver would have had to punt; it couldn't risk missing a 58-yard field goal and giving Jacksonville the ball in excellent field position with enough time to advance far enough to score. So Shanahan sent Jason in but told him not to kick. Denver had no time-outs. The play clock expired with four seconds remaining. The field goal now would be 63 yards. "Just stay out there and kick it," Shanahan told Jason. Three years earlier, he had authorized a 66-yarder, which fell short. Jason had once converted from 72 yards in practice.

"I'm lining up from sixty-three," Jason recalls. "The crowd—I had no idea they even knew—the crowd just started going nuts. I mean, really loud, when they saw we were trying one from that far." Jason's holder, punter Tom Rouen, looked up at him and said with a grin, "You know this is for the record, don't you?" Jason was unnerved. "That was pretty cool," he says now.

The long snapper, David Diaz-Infante, was playing for the first time since undergoing arthroscopic surgery. His snap was high. Rouen pulled it down, tilting the ball forward a bit more than usual to give it a lower trajectory. "I hit it about as good as I can possibly hit a ball," Jason says. "I knew it had a shot. It really was one of those slow-motion things. I went nuts. I chased it down the field. I was like on the twenty-yard line by the time it went through."

Jason retrieved the ball and was mobbed by his teammates on the field and in the locker room. He had to escape to the trainer's room to calm down. After the 37–24 win, Shanahan handed a game ball to running back Terrell Davis, who had surpassed 1,000 yards rushing in the Broncos' first seven games, victories all. John Elway whispered to Shanahan, "Hey, Mike, you forgot Jason." The actual 63-yard ball is in the

Hall of Fame, along with Jason's size-10 kangaroo-skin Nike Tiempo cleat. Jason received a congratulatory fax from the man who had held the record alone for eighteen years, Tom Dempsey, who kicked straight on with a stub-nosed shoe designed for his deformed right foot.

This is what Jason told reporters after the game: "The truth is, three quarters of the guys in the league can make this kick. They just don't get the opportunity to do it." This is what Jason said after watching a Broncos camp leg named Ola Kimrin kick a 65-yard field goal in a pre-season game in 2002: "It was great to see him to do that. He's the nicest guy in the world." Jason's mark stood because the NFL record book doesn't recognize preseason games. But he knows it won't last forever. "That record and all the records will be broken," Jason tells me. "It was just a really fun moment for me." He almost broke the record himself, narrowly missing the left upright from 65 yards in a *Monday Night Football* game at home on September 10, 2001.

At the top of their report on the University of Hawaii placekicker and punter, two Broncos scouts described Jason as "a class person" and "a strong student who is also very active in community affairs." As with most such reports, Jason's moved quickly to his football attributes. "Shows good athletic ability . . . Has good body balance and leg explosion . . . Fine foot quickness . . . Makes the big kick. Does not let the pressure get to him . . . Rarely makes mistakes. Shows natural instincts to adjust quickly to change . . . Has the ability to decide the outcome of the game . . . Expect him to go early in the draft . . . He will kick for someone in the National Football League."

Jason was the seventieth player, and first kicker, chosen in 1993. The Broncos already had two placekickers on the roster, David Treadwell and Brad Daluiso, who handled kickoffs. Not only didn't they talk to Jason much, they trashed his locker and pennied him into his dorm room. "It was two against one," Daluiso tells me. But Daluiso sensed that Jason knew he was the best placekicker of the three, and good enough at kicking off to unseat him as well.

In thirteen seasons, Jason has missed just four games—one with a pulled groin muscle and three after he fractured parts of two vertebrae in his lower back when he tried to tackle a kick returner. He's proud of that. He's also ambitious. Jason would like to reach 2,000 points for his career, something accomplished by only two kickers in NFL history, Gary Anderson and Morten Andersen. (The kicker/quarterback George Blanda amassed 2,002 points, but 54 of them came on rushing touchdowns.) Jason could get there with four more productive seasons. "I just think it would be kind of cool to have two thousand points in my career," he says.

Cool? Along with the 63-yarder, two Super Bowl rings, a record 371 consecutive extra points, the distinction of being the only NFL player ever to score more than 100 points in each of his first thirteen seasons (two more and he'll break the total record of fourteen), an 80 percent field-goal success rate, and (maybe) a career spent with one team, 2,000 points should, I think, get him into the Pro Football Hall of Fame. In this disposable job, accuracy and longevity matter.

The nature of the position should matter, too. Kicking, I'm not the first to observe or experience, is the most isolated and isolating task on a football field. In a game of maddeningly intricate and indecipherable choreography, kicking is the only job that could be understood by someone—a gaucho on the Pampas, an Albanian goatherd—watching the sport for the first time. The act of kicking is so simple that Garo Yepremian kicked five field goals in the first football game he ever saw. But it is so complex that kickers study video slowed to the tenth of a second. Everyone knows when a kicker misses. Almost no one can tell you precisely why.

For the first eight decades of football, kickers weren't considered outsiders, because they played other positions first; kicking was a sideline. Even the greatest of the straight-on kickers, Lou Groza of the Cleveland Browns—who played from 1946 to 1967, retired holding ten NFL kicking and scoring records, and was nicknamed "the Toe"—didn't want to be known as a kicker. "I was a left tackle," he bristled when the Browns once introduced him as a kicker.

When the NFL expanded rosters in the early 1960s, teams began adding kicking specialists. Then came the soccer-style revolution. When he joined the NFL in 1966, after two seasons in the AFL, Hungarian-born Pete Gogolak began a jobs-taking influx of foreigners that would turn kickers into punch lines—and change the game. In the 1970s, NFL teams scored more than two offensive touchdowns for every field goal made. Today, the ratio is less than one and a half to one. Field-goal accuracy has climbed from 53.8 percent in 1965 to 64.2 percent in 1975 to 72.2 percent in 1985 to 77.4 percent in 1995 to a record 81.0 percent in 2005. Kickers account for nearly half of the points scored in the NFL these days, compared to just over a third in the 1970s.

Since this great leap forward began, the NFL has changed the rules to make field goals more challenging, for kickers and coaches. In 1974, the goalposts were relocated from the goal line to the rear of the end zone. In 1994, the opposing team was given the ball after a missed field goal at the spot of the kick rather than the line of scrimmage. In 1999, kickers were forced to use stiff, fresh-from-the-box "K balls" in games. (The move was designed to end the practice of kickers cracking, beating, and generally softening the leather of game balls—using knees, weights, hot towels, dryers, and saunas. The foot compresses a softer ball more deeply, helping it fly farther. With a factory-fresh ball, "you're hitting a brick wall," Jason says.) More recently, the NFL has discussed narrowing the uprights and, to force kicks from more difficult angles, widening the on-field hash marks. In short, kickers have improved so much that the NFL would like to *discourage* their participation in games.

So the fact that just one full-time kicker is enshrined in Canton, Ohio—Jan Stenerud; success rate: 67 percent—is absurd. Halls of Fame are supposed to honor players whose achievements exceed those of their contemporaries and rise to some subjective level of all-time greatness. Shunning kickers was easy when making a 40-yard field goal was a coin flip and a 50-yarder was as rare as a UFO sighting. No kicker was particularly accomplished. Now, though, to stand out means to be perilously close to perfect. That's why modern kickers deserve busts. "It has to happen," Dick Vermeil tells me. Before a long head-coaching career, Vermeil was the NFL's first special-teams coach, with the Los Angeles

Rams in 1969. "The contribution is becoming more glaring and more consistently important every Sunday," he says.

When Jason said that three-quarters of NFL kickers could have made his 63-yarder, he was being only half truthful. Physically, they can kick that far, absolutely. But what separates Jason and the other greats of this era is what has prevented me from being even good enough to kick well in front of the team: sangfroid, complete self-confidence and unflappability, kick after kick, year after year. Slip up once, and a kicker's career can be forever tarnished, like that of Scott Norwood of Buffalo, who (five years after beating out Paul Woodside) missed a 47-yarder to win Super Bowl XXV in 1991, or Mike Vanderjagt, who is the NFL's most accurate field-goal kicker ever but was let go by Indianapolis after missing a game-tying 46-yarder in the playoffs in January 2006.

One missed kick could recast Jason's image, too, or that of others who deserve to be in the Hall of Fame. But it shouldn't. No matter how his career ends, Adam Vinatieri's game-winning kicks in the final seconds of an unprecedented two Super Bowls and a legendary last-second kick in the snow to tie a playoff game, all for New England, should ensure entry. Matt Stover of the Ravens also deserves to be there. He owns the third-highest career field-goal percentage and, in the 2006 season, will pass Stenerud and others to move into the top five in career points. Gary Anderson, who retired in 2004 as the career leader with 2,434 points, and Morten Andersen, who will take over the top spot in 2006 while kicking at age forty-six (and who will kick again in 2007 at forty-seven), deserve busts, too.

If there's one knock on Jason, it's where he has kicked. Denver is indeed mile high—actually, at 5,183 feet above sea level, just short of a mile. The density of the air at Invesco Field is about 20 percent less than what it is at Giants Stadium in New Jersey, which is just 60 feet above sea level. University of Nebraska–Lincoln physics professor Timothy Gay, who has literally made a science of football, writes that punts and kickoffs should travel four or five yards farther in Denver than at lower elevations. Field goals, however, are a different matter. The vast majority of field goals don't test an NFL kicker's leg strength or range. Placekickers don't need an altitude steroid for anything inside of 50 yards. Micah Knorr maintains that the thin air doesn't help at all inside of 40 yards. Professor Gay agrees. "I don't think altitude is a super big effect" on field goals, he tells me.

Jason's overall statistics show no meaningful disparity between home and road performance. Through 2005, he had made 81.2 percent of regular-season field goals in Denver and 77.6 percent elsewhere. From distances of 50 or more yards, though, there does seem to be some effect. Jason is 21 out of 32, or 65.6 percent, from 50-plus yards at home—with the rate climbing above 70 percent without his four attempts from 60 yards or more. On the road, he has made 14 out of 26, or 53.4 percent, from 50-plus. Mike Shanahan clearly thinks Jason is more likely to make a long field goal in Denver: He's let him try ten more of them at home than on the road. Still, to better determine whether the air has made a difference—and not, say, field conditions, the crowd, or psychology—you would have to examine each kick to see how far short of the crossbar the misses fell and how far beyond it the makes flew. Eyewitnesses said the 63-yarder was good from at least two or three additional yards.

Other variables should diminish the thin-air rap. Denver is colder than many other NFL cities, so kicking there later in the season can be tough. Only one in every 7.4 of Jason's kicks has been from 50 or longer. And atmospheric density doesn't impact a kicker's composure or his accuracy. Even an occasional altitudinal gift doesn't alter the basic facts of Jason's brilliant career.

On the field, Mike Shanahan ignores the crack of thunder and urges the players to push through the drudgery of the first week of camp. "The great teams [*crash*], this is where [*rumble*] they pick it up [*roar*]." When he's done, everyone scatters but the special-teams players.

Micah kicks first.

"Rain coming in right behind you," Todd says.

Then it's Paul's turn.

"Overcome the wind, Paul," Todd says. "Overcome the wind."

The wind accelerates, gusting mightily, carrying footballs aloft as if they've been inflated with hydrogen and fitted with propellers. And I am *pissed off*. In these conditions, I'm convinced I can make the elusive 50-yarder. Gale at my back? If the ball clears the crossbar, no one would have to know. But my leg is dead. Right groin, left quadriceps, left hip: They all ache. I feel as if I have no muscle mass, no strength. I take three one-steps to test my leg, but each ball skitters limply to the right.

"Shut it down," Ronnie orders.

It's not a kicking day for Jason, and he's too cautious to be tempted by a little tornadic field-goal fun. Micah and Todd aren't. From 60 yards, Micah hits the netting behind the goalposts in front of the parking lot. Not to be outdone, Todd takes it farther back, kicking from what would be the opponent's 40-yard line. His first four balls have the distance but blow one way or the other. Then he splits the uprights, raising and pumping his arms like a fan at an AC/DC concert: a 70-yard field goal.

What's physically required to be a kicker in the NFL? "Strength, speed, balance, coordination, and timing beyond the capacity of most people," Jeff Hays tells me. Consistency is important, too, he says. Since placekicking and punting are repetitive actions, kickers need to be able to replicate their form time after time. Even mistakes need to be consistent so that they can be eliminated. Explosiveness sets apart the best. Good kickers don't need to be sprinters, but, like sprinters, they must be blessed with a preponderance of fast-twitch muscle fibers.

When it comes to consistency and explosiveness, Todd outranks his Broncos colleagues, and most of the NFL. Jeff has charted Todd's punts on a bell curve and compared them to other kickers. Todd's chart shows a heavy concentration of punts of between 45 and 50 yards. Other punters have a greater range, especially on the crappy end. As for twitchiness, in high school, Todd ran the 40-yard dash in a pro-level 4.5 seconds. Otherwise, he's anomalous. Punters traditionally are tall, lanky, and flexible. When I think of punters, I think of photos of Ray Guy in full extension, his right knee kissing his chest and his toes above his helmet pointing skyward. That's not Todd. He's compact, thick in the thigh and broad in the foot, which Jeff calls a "forgiving striking surface."

"Todd dispels a lot of myths," Jeff says. "Static flexibility is not that important. It's your active flexibility and how fast your leg can go through the point of impact. What happens after the ball leaves your foot has no effect on the height and distance of the ball." So a kicker's follow-through, when the leg is decelerating, can be a poor indicator of what happened at contact. Jeff shoots video of kickers at thirty frames per second, and he freezes one or two clicks before and after impact to observe the foot. While Todd might appear to be kicking the ball as hard as he can every time, Jeff says he isn't. "But his eighty-five or ninety percent is generating so much more power and leg speed than other people's eighty-five or ninety percent," he says. "I think that's a genetic gift. I think he's just kind of born to kick. I don't even think he likes it that much. I think he'd rather be a lacrosse player."

But no one's signing lacrosse players to multimillion-dollar contracts, a fact Todd recognized while at Ward Melville High School in East Setauket, New York. In lacrosse, he played for a Hall of Fame coach and was an All-American. In football, he played wide receiver, returned kicks, ran the ball a little, and placekicked and punted. Not only did he kick a state-record 62-yard field goal, he hit the top of an upright on a 68-yard attempt. Syracuse offered him a scholarship to play both sports. As much as he loved lacrosse, Todd decided that football could be a career. Lacrosse would be a fun prelude to a corporate day job, and Todd didn't want a corporate day job. It is indeed hard to imagine Todd in a nine-to-five with a thirty-minute lunch break, cold-calling stocks, suffering an overbearing boss, stressing to meet a sales quota. He hasn't even been able to cope with the alfresco corporate culture of the NFL.

Todd has mostly ignored me in camp. I can understand why. His career is hanging by a thread because of an indiscretion he admits was dumb, and some reporter is hanging around him all day taking notes.

After a team meeting one evening, Todd and I are the only two players in the vast locker room. I approach and say that while I appreciate why he's angry, I'll be writing about him regardless and want to make sure he's represented fairly.

Todd tells me he's just been too bitter to talk. He can't stand the mental strain, the game of musical chairs that front offices stage with players' lives, the salary-cap cuts, the absence of guaranteed contracts, the constant threat of being released. He loathes the perceived lack of respect, the bureaucratic inflexibility. On this day, Todd notes, none of us were scheduled to kick in the afternoon. But we had to stand outside while everyone else practiced and then we had to wait for the postprandial team meeting, at which Shanahan spoke for a total of three minutes before adjourning for position meetings, which the kickers don't have. "Good thing we stayed around three hours for that," Todd says.

Todd was always brash and irreverent. But until reaching the NFL, he tells me, he didn't hate football. In Chicago, he was hazed mercilessly by veterans who resented that the Bears had drafted a punter in the second round. Teammates shaved his head, constantly made him carry equipment, lobbed snide remarks when he walked by, made him lose confidence in himself for the first time in his life. (He had a terrible rookie season.) In Carolina, he says the team abandoned him after he was linked to the steroids doctor and drank and drove. Now in Denver, since the suspension, he has had a gut feeling the team wants to cut him loose. Todd admits he has made mistakes, but he doesn't view them as horrific, not in a league dotted with felons.

At this point, Todd says, he's playing only for his daughter, Brooke, a third-grader who lives in Chicago with his ex-wife. Todd clearly adores her. His locker is decorated with eight pictures of her—and a player-payroll schedule on which he's written, "JUST PAY ME!!$" "If I didn't know I was that much better" than other punters, Todd says, "I'd quit." He feels this way despite believing, after playing for five organizations in twelve years, that the Broncos treat players far better than other clubs. Shanahan has chewed him out, and is possibly orchestrating his departure. Yet Todd praises him, not, I think, because he wants to kiss ass to save his job but because, if he has to play football for a living, he wants to play it here.

Still, Todd can't help himself. On the second weekend of camp, 2,630 fans show up to watch a morning practice. It is the largest crowd since the Broncos shifted training camp to Dove Valley in 2003, so big that the berm fills and the overflow is stationed between the two practice fields. While Jason plays catch with some kids, a few feet away Todd drops F-bombs when he mis-hits a punt.

"Class act," T-Mac says. "Three more weeks."

"Of what?" I ask.

"Of this. Then he's gone for a month. I'm going to push as hard as I can to make it permanent."

On the one hand, I dislike Todd for his sneering contempt. It's also hard to feel sympathy for a recidivist screwup. On the other hand, I like Todd because he's a caustically funny smart-ass who doesn't suffer fools or filter his opinions. After one of Todd's cutting remarks while Paul is punting, Jeff Hays says, "Attaway to pump air in his tires, Todd," to which Todd replies, "I'm here to *slash* his tires." He's a character, and he relishes it. Last year, the equipment staff made cutoff T-shirts emblazoned on the front with MUST BE NICE—Todd's favorite sarcastic retort—and BOOM'S TOP TEN on the back, above a David Letterman-style list of his other catch phrases. (10. THAT'S HOW I ROLL. 9. JUST PAY ME. 5. BALL! 4. THERE IT IS. 1. WHO'S BETTER THAN ME?) I'm convinced that if this were last summer, if he hadn't been suspended, Todd wouldn't scorn my presence. I think, as fellow New Yorkers, we might even be friends. In the locker room, Todd promises to talk once his black cloud lifts.

While Todd is sulking, Paul is realizing that the starting job is his to lose, while Todd is suspended and after. But Paul has to demonstrate that he can be trusted with the ball five yards deep in the end zone in the fourth quarter of a tie game in the playoffs. Ronnie and T-Mac have already lectured him. Now Jeff Hays has a come-to-Jesus talk with Paul. They stay on the empty field at day's end, and I join them, just the three of us and a brilliant sky bathed in softening late-afternoon light. After practicing kickoffs, we sit in the grass. Jeff, still in his management-consultant clothes, tells Paul he's not taking advantage of the available coaching or the ample practice time. "If Shanahan sees you doing ball drops, that shows commitment," Jeff says. Paul has to forget about Todd's peer pressure, he says, and demonstrate that he's "not just some goof who's standing in his shoes."

"I'm going to prove them wrong," Paul says.

"No, you're going to prove them right," Jeff corrects, "because they drafted you."

In the locker room, Paul confides that he's been an emotional wreck. Ronnie and T-Mac told him that he has changed. They told him he is becoming like Todd. "I couldn't sleep," Paul says. "I was broken. I've been thinking about it constantly." He went to Ronnie later and apologized. I've noticed that Paul keeps team psychologist Betsy Klein's cell phone number on a yellow Post-it in his locker, and he tells me he's talked with her—about the coaches' perception that he isn't mentally tough enough for the job, and about Todd. "No one knows how hard it is to compete with Todd," Paul says. Todd, he says, can be such a prick on the field and such a pal off of it that it's hard to know where the line is, or if there is one, hard to know what's sincere and what's "just business."

Paul also is suffering like other players: He gets lots of pressure but little feedback or encouragement. "Every night you're on pins and needles," he says. "You're snapping at people. It's so stressful. You feel like you have a deadline you can't make." That's compounded by the fact that he's a virtual rookie the team needs to see if it can trust. The coaches don't criticize Micah when he shanks one, but they do criticize Paul, because they're testing him. Paul is recognizing that he has to channel the pressure from the coaches—and from Todd—to prove his competence. "Me following Todd Sauerbrun is intimidating enough," he says. "If he hits a seventy-yard punt and I follow up with a seventy-yard punt—do you think I could do that if I wasn't mentally tough?"

When we finish talking, I point out another challenge to Paul's mental state—a piece of paper taped inside his locker. It reads:

Shanahan Saw You Move Your Car At Lunch!
That's a No No!
Your car is now locked!
Your keys are in the cold tub!
Go Fish!

Earlier in the day, Paul received a call that his dog had run away. He got permission to leave the facility, but as he was pulling out of the lot he got another call that his dog had returned. Paul tossed his keys on the front seat of his car—which many players do—and went inside. But some teammates saw him. I've been sworn to secrecy by the pranksters.

Paul is mad. A couple of players are recuperating in the ice pool, but they've been tipped off and won't grab the object submerged in its depths. Paul drags it up and out with a skimmer. No keys, but a soggy note instructing him to inspect the freezer. In the cafeteria, he finds another note among the ice-cream sandwiches and frozen Snickers bars telling him to look under one of the toilets. Paul goes to the stalls, but emerges keyless.

I confess that in the event he came up empty, I had been authorized to point him to the first stall. Paul returns with a giant ball of white athletic tape inscribed with sophomoric barbs that reveal themselves as Paul unspools it into a garbage can. He finally extracts his keys. But he decides not to retaliate (which is good, because he's wrong about the identity of the tormenter—Nate Jackson, who has been stealthily watching Paul storm from room to room). "The funny thing is, it took them an hour to do that and me five minutes to figure it out," he says.

Strength coach Rich Tuten has witnessed the operation from conception to execution. "Training camp boredom," he says.

In Mike Shanahan's finely calibrated world, every second of every day has a purpose. During training camp, he arrives at 5 a.m., exercises, watches film, and leads an 8 a.m. meeting of the coaching staff. Shanahan knows that the succession of two-a-days is brutal. It's intended to be. But after thirty years as a coach, he has a sixth sense for when to pull back, when to toss a bone. "When you're younger, you're so into wanting to have a good practice that you forget you're getting ready for the games," he tells me in his office.

One of those bones is a bit of levity at the end of almost every day. The team meeting begins with players drumming on the desktops until Shanahan calls a rookie to the front, where he has to answer questions, tell a joke, or "suffer the consequences." Where fight-song singing was once instigated by players in the locker room or cafeteria, today even the standard rookie hazing ritual has been co-opted by management. It's a departure from the usual church-service reverence of the team meeting, but it's also controlled, like everything else, by Shanahan.

"Who *are* you?" the players scream one night after Shanahan orders a rookie to the podium.

"Greg Eslinger."

"No! Who *are* you?" The pack wants the red-cheeked, peach-fuzzed Eslinger to say his nickname, and he knows it, and eventually capitulates.

"Wee-Man," he says into the microphone. The room explodes. Eslinger is a six-foot-three, 290-pound center who won the 2005 Outland Trophy as the nation's best interior lineman. But he also looks a bit like a four-foot-seven actor on the MTV show *Jackass*.

Every joke told in these sessions is crude, sexist, or homophobic. The players usually find them on the Internet. Tony Scheffler modifies one about a Russian who, granted a wish by a genie, asks to be able to urinate vodka. In Scheffler's version, he is the Russian. His ball-busting coach Tim Brewster is the Russian's wife. The first day, Tony pees into two glasses and gives one to Brew. The next day, same thing. The third day, he pees into just one glass. When Brew asks why, Tony says, "Today you're drinking from the bottle."

The team roars. Scheffler has handled the ritual well. Woe to the player who doesn't. When running back Mike Bell chooses to suffer the consequences rather than tell a joke (the players will shave his head, unevenly), Shanahan says, "I sure hope you're better prepared for Detroit." When a soft-spoken lineman named Antwon Burton says, "I don't really know any jokes," Shanahan replies, "Well, you come tomorrow and be ready" to tell one, and the room falls silent as the rookie lumbers off the stage in shame. To Shanahan, "the little things" that must be done right in the pursuit of football excellence apparently include telling a joke.

In anticipation of my moment in the spotlight, I compose some original material, test it on Preston Parsons, who laughs sincerely, and carry it around in my notebook for days. Finally, Shanahan tells me in the hallway that my time has come. The drumming begins and Shanahan summons me.

"Who are you?" ninety large men shout.

"Stefan Fatsis," I announce strongly. "University of Pennsylvania."

My alma mater provokes titters.

"What year?"

"Class of . . . class of . . . 1985!"

Peals of laughter, guffaws, wails of joy.

"What position do you play?"

"Kicker!"

Hysteria.

"All right, all right," I say. "Since I'm talking to a bunch of football players, I've got a couple of light-bulb jokes."

"Ohhhhhhhhh!!!!!!"

"How many NFL coaches does it take to screw in a light bulb?" I begin. "Nineteen. You've got your sixty-watt bulb coach. You've got your sixty-watt bulb assistant. You've got your seventy-five-watt coach and your seventy-five-watt assistant. Your hundred-watt coach and hundred-watt assistant."

I thought they might appreciate a swipe at the bloated nature of the coaching staff. But they're getting impatient. I sweat, and plow ahead.

"You've got your special coordinator in charge of removing the bulb. You've got your lightbulb-box-removal special assistant."

Boos and groans.

"You've got your counterclockwise turning instructor. You've got your ladder coach. You got your light-switch-flipping coach."

More boos and catcalls and laughter—not with me, *at* me.

"This went over much better with Preston," I say. "You've got your coach in charge of yelling at Scheffler. You've got six coaches who carry stopwatches and clipboards but really don't do anything."

That line they like.

"And, finally, you've got your head lightbulb coach, who at the end of the day tells everyone that if they screw the little things the right way . . ."

Score! Making fun of the boss! Points for bravery!

". . . if they screw their asses off, they've got a chance to screw something special this lightbulb-changing season."

Chris Rock could have written my material and they still would have dissed me. Writer. Rookie. Kicker. "Okay," I say. "How many quarterbacks does it take to change a lightbulb? One. But he needs six three-hundred-pound guys to stand in front of him, nineteen coaches to tell him what to do . . ." A momentary swell of appreciation! ". . . and six referees to make sure nobody touches his pretty blond head."

On the way back to my seat, I am roundly mocked, which I take as acceptance. Shanahan makes no comment and moves on to team business. Mike Leach tells me later that he appreciated the original material. "I'm not sure the other guys did," he says.

"Right," I say, "no penises or sex."

"Or pussy or vomit or other bodily functions."

Beyond creating a few yucks at the rookies' expense, Shanahan's main carrot is time off. In recent days, his end-of-practice lectures have grown more scolding. He's angry about dropped balls, missed blocking assignments, and lack of concentration. The team has run every play four times since the spring and still is making mistakes. It's hard to know how much is honest evaluation and how much is purposeful motivation. But Shanahan knows that pain and exhaustion are setting in, and that the monotony is breaking some spirits. So, after nine straight days of practice, and meetings every night until 9:30—no thanks to me—he grants thirty-one hours off (at least for players who don't require treatment). "They need this," he tells me.

You'd think he was releasing inmates after a year on a chain gang. After practice the next morning, the locker-room mood is jubilant. The rap music is louder. The chatter is happier. Players bring their kids in for a visit. A ball boy is dragged into the shower. "Turn on the cold! Turn on the cold!" wide receiver Charlie Adams shouts. A few minutes later the kid wanders the locker room, drenched and elated. When I walk past Charlie's locker, I knock a washcloth off his shaved head. "You could get a shower, too!" he says. "You *are* a rookie, after all!" Fullback Kyle Johnson agrees, and when I spot their conspiratorial smiles, I exit quickly.

Later, I ask Charlie if he wants to go out on this night of liberty. "Yeah, but *you* can't *go out* go out," he says, poking at my wedding ring. I join Charlie and some other players, first for dinner at Earl's, then at an overcrowded, overloud club in downtown Denver, where they guzzle free drinks—one player knows the bartender—make dopey conversation with college-age and slightly older women, sing along to Prince and Nelly Furtado, and are hammered before midnight. (Most are smart enough to take cabs home.)

It's a small release, one that Shanahan considers necessary to create a winning football team—and one that the players consider necessary to escape football. The psychology of training camp is such that a single evening out seems like a diamond necklace. In the off-season, after six months under the high-resolution microscope of the coaches and media, the freedom translates into a nonstop whirl of travel and partying.

"We go all out. Pretty hard," Kyle Johnson tells me. "And you never had the capacity to go as hard as you go now. You're not breaking any league rules, because they're checking your piss. But you do it so hard. It's almost like you're out to get revenge. You're drinking. You're not sleeping. You don't give a damn.

"Fans think you live this glorified lifestyle where the women flock and you just have to pick who's next. The women may flock, but you never noticed all the bottles of booze that we bought. You never noticed how we called all these girls to meet us before we left the house. Because you want some release, you want something to feel good about, something you feel like you're in charge or in control of.

"The world on the outside thinks it's so wonderful and it's so glorified. 'What a job they have!' And it does have its days. But you are seeing us at our highest point on Sunday at two o'clock. That's the best it gets. And then you see us on Sunday at ten and maybe we won the game, we're maybe having some drinks and you think we're sitting there with our chests out, boasting, trying to glorify ourselves. No, we're trying to shake it off and get ready for week number twelve or week thirteen.

"When we get out of here, I see pleasure. What can I do when I get out of here to feel pleasure? Is it a relief? No, it's not a relief at all. It's week to week. If I had to think about Kansas City on Thanksgiving, I wouldn't make it."

12

The Bottom of the Trickle

As I drill deeper into the minds of my teammates, I discover an understandable, if possibly oversimplified, split. The locker room isn't divided along financial or social or racial lines but intellectual ones. There are the players who love playing football, for whom the ceaseless pain and pressure are occupational facts, the way sweat is part of a line cook's job or soot part of a chimney sweep's. They don't think too much about what they have to do to play football, they just do it.

Then there are the players who grapple with their motivations. Some compose internal lists of pros and cons, weigh each, and decide that the goods outnumber the bads, or at least the goods make the bads tolerable. Some accept that the bads outweigh the goods and play anyway. Some play in constant turmoil. They are the thinkers and, for whatever reasons, my closest friends on the Broncos. If we sound like complainers, they say, you try doing what we do. Do you really think this is a glamorous life? The overbearing bosses, the zero job security, the risk that every play could result in a life-altering or life-threatening injury?

"This job isn't all it's cracked up to be," Kyle Johnson tells me one afternoon. National Football League player, he says, is a job for a technically proficient worker—the very best at what he does—with a very specific and limited skill set. "Then you get here and the day-to-day rigmarole, the stress levels, are through the roof. It's not necessarily the satisfying Valhalla that you expect it to be. And it can be a heartbreak.

Is this a dream? No. It's a good job that pays extremely well. Or, really, it's a bad job that pays extremely well is what it is. Last year, we started in July and went into January. I played in twenty-one games and we played twenty-two games. That's a lot of football. Two college seasons. And it's not like they're any easier on you in week twenty than they are in week one."

Kyle has been the Broncos' starting fullback for two seasons but, despite scoring six touchdowns in 2005, he has no guarantee of a third. In fact, he's been demoted to second on the depth chart because the coaches were displeased with how he performed toward the end of the past season. ("I was worn out. I viewed myself on film. Who is that guy?") Jobs in the NFL are far more tenuous than in baseball or basketball, where guaranteed contracts force teams to have more patience with and loyalty to players.

Football coaches, naturally, think NFL contracts are terrific. "The great thing about football," Mike Shanahan tells me when I ask how he motivates players, is that only signing bonuses are guaranteed. In Major League Baseball and the National Basketball Association, coaches "have absolutely no leverage," he says. In the NFL, "guys understand that you do have some leverage, and if they want it a certain way they better perform." Plus, the sheer volume of roster spots in football increases the disposability factor. When a player disappears from a twelve- or twenty-five-man roster, it's obvious. In football, Kyle Johnson is part of an anonymous herd of veterans of whom only the most dedicated fans are aware.

Kyle can accept being cut. "They've got to do what they've got to do because they want to win and they want the best players," he says. And he knows he's an easy target because the Broncos didn't draft him and have never paid him more than the minimum salary—$500,000 this coming season, his fifth in the league (but fourth for salary purposes). Kyle isn't sure what he wants to do after football, but he's secure with the idea of a life after football. He has a smooth, deep voice, and his words come quickly and crisply and cleanly, and he also loves to write. He can see himself working as a sportscaster or in the entertainment industry. For Kyle, the questions are more complicated than whether he'll make the team: Is playing professional football rational? If not, then why is he doing it?

Kyle grew up in suburban Woodbridge, New Jersey, the son of a contractor and an inner-city public high-school teacher. Football wasn't a way out of the ghetto. "You know how people always say they're the first person in their family to go to college?" he says. "I wouldn't be the fourth person in my family to get their master's." Recruited by Columbia and Penn, Kyle accepted a football scholarship to Syracuse, where he was a Big East conference football scholar-athlete of the year. Making the NFL was a goal. But now that he's achieved it, he wonders: Was it his goal or his father's? Has he been playing football for twenty years—he first padded up at age eight—just to give him and his father something to talk about? Has it taken the NFL to make him finally resent football and what it does to young men, and make him confront his relationship with his father?

"My dad was on my ass when I was thirteen years old about dressing up, going out in the game, being out there regardless," he says. "It didn't matter whether or not I was hurt. Nobody gives a shit. If you can play you can play. And if you can't you best not be able to move. You best be fucked up." Kyle remembers fracturing his pelvis as a junior in high school. "I was fifteen years old. My dad's like, 'Are you all right? Why aren't you putting your pads on? Other guys put their pads on because they just want to be out there. Even if they're not playing they just want to feel the pads on.'" During the first week of his first training camp with the Broncos, Kyle broke a thumb. After surgery, he played with a cast halfway up his arm.

Kyle was drafted by Carolina in the fifth round in 2002. He was the last cut of training camp. He drove ten hours home to New Jersey. Twenty-seven hours later—he remembers exactly—the Giants signed him to their practice squad. Two months later, they released him. Three weeks later, Detroit signed him to its practice squad. A month later, Denver signed him off of Detroit's practice squad. In 2003, Denver brought Kyle to camp. Then, in the space of four months, the Broncos released him, re-signed him, released him, re-signed him, released him, and re-signed him, all to the practice squad. "You see how the psychosis is evolving," he says. "They need a man at a certain position for a certain week. The problem is, every time you get cut, you don't know if they'll ever call you back again."

Because their salaries are virtually public—leaked by agents or general managers or the players' union—and because so much coverage of pro sports focuses on money, players don't blanch at the subject. Kyle tells me he made $225,000 as a rookie, including a $120,000 bonus; $37,000 in his second season; $305,000 in his third season, the minimum salary for a player of his experience; and $380,000 in the fourth season, also the minimum. "The money is what it is," he says. "We always say it is what it is." Kyle has used some of his to take stress-relieving trips to places like New York, Las Vegas, and St. Thomas with teammates Nate Jackson, Charlie Adams, P. J. Alexander, and other friends. Kyle says he lives like a twenty-seven-year-old who maybe works on Wall Street or as a corporate lawyer. But he says he's not playing for the money, that the money isn't his inspiration, the way it is for some NFL players.

"What is?" I ask.

"I don't know. There's the rub. There's the rub. Used to love it. Used to love it. I don't hate it now. But it's not the same."

P.J. said the same thing. Bradlee did, too. Yes, they understand that the NFL is a professional sport, that the coaches' jobs depend on winning, so they will do whatever they consider necessary to win. In college, coaches at least had to show some concern for the maturation and general welfare of their players, only a small percentage of whom would play football for a living. In the pros, excepting prized rookies, concern for anything more than a player's current value to the team won't be found in the playbook on which Kyle will be tested before every game. In college, Kyle says, he felt as if the coaches were working to get the best player out of him. In the NFL, he feels as if they're sucking him dry.

The feeling manifests itself in what Kyle calls "the exacerbating process of always getting judged and evaluated," especially the demeaning tone of voice that coaches often use when addressing players. "Unless you were a dunderbrained Neanderthal you would know they've got to be assessing who's better because they've got to make a team up. Duh. But no, they're going tell you every five minutes. We've got to make cuts, we've got to make decisions, who's up, who's down, we've got to make a move, blah, blah. They threaten you every day. It's going to take a lot of the pleasure out of it."

Some players let it wash over them like a thundershower: loud, yes, but just water. Kyle says that being signed and released thirteen times in two seasons has made him feel vulnerable. How couldn't it? "Finally, you barely make the team and then you make it. And you feel like, 'Am I good enough to be here? Do they want me here?' Those are two questions that ring through my head in my subconscious every day."

But the same way Kyle accepts that he might get cut, he also accepts that Shanahan is just the guy in charge, the guy with the power to decide, and by NFL standards a likable guy at that, one who will invite a group of players to the exclusive Castle Pines country club for twenty-four hours of golf and steaks and beer and scotch—and drink right with them. "Shanahan's loyalty is three or four times bigger than Belichick's," Kyle says of the infamously, among players, cold and single-minded Patriots coach Bill Belichick. "Belichick plays guys on Sunday and cuts them on Tuesday. Literally in pads on the field. Shanahan doesn't do stuff like that. He might not dress you for three weeks and then release you. But usually during the season he keeps his crew. If he was a terrible tyrant of a man you wouldn't like him. He's just a guy with a lot of power."

And he uses that power to keep his coaches on edge, who in turn put their players on edge.

"It's almost like he's read the book on how to lead. He understands the philosophy of leadership," Kyle says. "If the ends justify the means, then he's good at his job."

"But do they?" I ask.

"Let Plato, Socrates, and Aristotle argue about that. Because in the world, yeah, they do. Let's be street for a second and talk money. Wins mean cash and he gets wins. Super Bowls mean even more cash, prestige, all that kind of stuff. He's basically a Super Bowl championship away from being a guaranteed Hall of Fame coach. And I'm sure he wants it. But there's a trickle down, though. And the problem is that you're at the bottom of the trickle."

I tell Kyle that for all of that, he's one of the lucky ones. He, Nate, Charlie—they'll be successful at other things. I say he's almost too smart to be hugely successful at football, because that would mean he's either unwilling or unable to examine and question the way his profession operates.

"I totally know what you mean," Kyle says. "You take the Wonderlic test to get in the NFL and that's what they use for soldiers so that they'll follow orders in a crisis situation. Could we have scored too highly on our Wonderlic, to the point where it's like, this is irrational? I contemplate that every day. Is this rationally what we are destined to do?"

Sitting in his compression shorts after practice one day, Kyle tells me I'm spending too much time with the quarterbacks, wide receivers, and tight ends—his and my best friends on the team. "You need to go to the other end of the locker room," he says. Kyle doesn't mean I need to learn the intricacies of Denver's 4-3 defensive alignment or the nuances of the Cover Two zone. He means that I will find a far less intellectually and emotionally complicated approach to football among the huge men whose job is to flatten the quarterbacks, wide receivers, and tight ends.

In purely operational terms, this makes sense. As a general rule, players love hitting, not getting hit. For the "skills" players on offense, the ideal is to throw or carry the ball into the end zone untouched. For defenders, the ideal is to lay someone out. They are paid to seek out contact, to hit, hit, and hit some more. If they didn't like the core brutality of football, there's absolutely no way they could play.

"It's grimy down here," fourth-year defensive tackle Demetrin Veal tells me. "But you're certainly welcome."

I spend time watching the linemen huff and grunt through one-on-one drills against their offensive counterparts, deploying balletic spins and cuts as well as pure force to push and shove and juke their way into the backfield. Playing defensive line, one of the unit's coaches, Andre Patterson, tells me, requires speed, strength, agility, finesse, technique, precision, and brains. There are specific ways to position the feet, specific times to lift the arms, specific moments and spots to strike the offensive lineman. The Broncos employ five basic defensive alignments, but they all include permutations based on how the offense assembles. Each defensive lineman needs to work in intuitive harmony with the lineman next to him. "You can't be a dummy and play it," Patterson says of the d-line.

And you can't be ambivalent about it, either, I learn. Unlike Kyle and my other introspective friends on the offense, the defensive linemen I get to know don't seem troubled or conflicted about how they make a living. "I love what I do, man," six-foot-four, 325-pound tackle Gerard Warren says, crossing himself and looking up at the ceiling. "It's my life. This is what God blessed me with. I asked for this. I prayed for this early."

Warren is no Bible-thumping Athlete in Action. On the contrary, he is perhaps the loudest, scruffiest, and most unkempt, profane, and physically menacing guy in camp. More than once he seems a step away from depositing me upside down in a garbage can or knocking me on my ass, for fun. A self-described country boy from a rural town in northern Florida, Warren couldn't wait to get to college when he was winning state championships in high school, where he obtained the nickname "Big Money" because of his pro potential. And he couldn't wait to get to the NFL when he was in college; he left a year early after being talked out of trying to go pro two years early. Warren has a rap sheet—marijuana possession, a brawl, carrying an unlicensed firearm—from his days at the University of Florida and the Cleveland Browns, who drafted him third overall in 2001—and a reputation for loving the night life. But he's no dummy. One day I hear him discussing, in detail, the Israeli-Palestinian conflict.

Warren tells me he loves the demands of defensive line. "It's an art form, man. It's all about angles and body lean, kind of like a martial art." He loves the challenge. "It's like having a six-shooter. Okay, the ball is snapped, I shot him dead." He has been portrayed as an under-performing problem child whose game doesn't match his bragging mouth, but he loves that, too. "In no way could it ever break my confidence of me being who I am on the football field. I define that role. The papers never made me. I made the papers."

Pressure? "There ain't no pressure," he says calmly. "There ain't *no* pressure, Stef."

Pain? "The first time a football player ever felt pain, he had a choice to make right then." Warren made his choice in the seventh grade, when his mother saw him wince after bumping a forearm he had bruised at practice. "And my mother was like, 'You come home wincing in pain and I'm going to make you quit football.' From that point on, it was like, you take the pain, but you love it that much."

The prospect of an injury-racked life after football? "The guys talk about after. What about before?"

Before for Demetrin Veal was the gang-infested Compton neighborhood of Los Angeles. His mother worked two jobs. He didn't meet his father until he was sixteen. Demetrin had a paper route at ten, ran errands for a roofing company at eleven, sold newspaper subscriptions, bussed tables, picked up his two younger sisters at school every day. "It kept me out of a whole lot of trouble," he says.

The NFL wasn't a life goal—he didn't watch a game until he was thirteen years old—but it wound up being a life raft. Demetrin didn't play until his senior year of high school. He spent two years at a junior college, and then received a scholarship to the University of Tennessee, where he became more studious and spiritual. That's reflected now on his body, which is covered with tattoos—across his back, on his neck, along his arms. Seven flaming lamps and "Holy Holy Holy Lord God Almighty Who Was and Is TO COME," from Revelation 4:8. A crucifix and "Romans 3:25," in which Jesus is sacrificed to atone for the sins of others. The name of a dead friend. A Native American water symbol. "Villin," a nickname given to him by his mother. "Pleasure" on his right arm, "Pain" on his left. "It was in my head and my heart so I put it on my skin," he tells me at his locker one afternoon.

Demetrin keeps his hair in dreadlocks, one for each thing he is thankful for. He travels to places he never imagined visiting. (In the off-season, he will backpack alone through Europe.) To escape the grind of football, he writes poetry and music, or closes his eyes and imagines he is surfing. At home in the morning, he writes pieces of a novel set in Los Angeles he has titled *Dying Young*. He began writing about himself one day, then wrote about a friend, then transformed them into characters. One is abused by his family, another comes from a generation of gang members, another is drugged out. "Half of it is real," Demetrin says. An eight-year-old friend killed in a drive-by shooting. A sixth-grade friend shot in the head for his jacket. "It makes you grow up quick," he says.

That the position he wound up playing requires unrestrained aggression—Demetrin is six foot two and close to 290 pounds, and chiseled like Michelangelo's *David*—seems bizarrely antithetical to his centered personality. Or maybe the position is the release he needed from his life. "You've seen what we do," he tells me. "Every play you're smacking somebody. It's not for the weak. You have to have a few screws loose to do this."

"So what are the rewards?" I ask.

"Besides the money?" Demetrin hits me with a knowing, cunning smile. He played in fifteen of the Broncos' sixteen regular-season games in 2005, and expects to make the team again this year, when he would earn $500,000. "The money's huge." The stress, not so much. The scrutiny is nothing like what a quarterback faces, he says. "My stress level is performance. You go into this knowing everyone can do the job. You have to be something special to keep you here." Compared to how he grew up, that kind of pressure is inconsequential. Football becomes a gift, not a burden.

If Kyle Johnson is the equivalent of a patient in football psychotherapy, then Ian Gold is the Broncos' resident pragmatist. After repeated afternoon retreats to empty conference rooms and silenced practice fields to talk with my teammates, I'm convinced that his worldview comes closest to embodying what players injected with truth serum, promised complete anonymity, or maybe just having a terrible day would say about the game.

Ian is the Broncos' starting weak-side linebacker, lining up on the side of the field with fewer blockers on the offensive line. (In football lingo, the weak-side linebacker is known as "Will," the strong-side linebacker is "Sam," and the middle linebacker is "Mike.") Ian plays with scholarly intensity and evident passion. He led the Broncos with 106 tackles in 2005. Off the field, he seems utterly bored, constantly retreating into video poker, which he plays with childlike impatience, needing to see every flop.

His detachment is a journalistic turn-on. When I tell Ian I want to talk not about the team or the season but the game itself, he responds like Todd Sauerbrun did when we first met, saying he won't have much good to report. But there's no woe-is-me bitterness. Ian hasn't failed a drug test. He just views football from a critical distance. He's convinced of management's disdain for players. He's resigned to the inevitability of injury. He's inured to a joylessness that, based on my camp interactions, anyway, does seem to infect the sport. Ian has answers to every question about the game but one: Why do you play?

"I don't know," Ian says. "There's not a day that goes by I don't ask myself that question. What am I doing here? Why am I playing football? What am I getting out of it? I ask myself that only about football. It's providing, of course, a solid foundation financially, that it is doing. Then I ask myself, does the good outweigh the bad or the bad outweigh the good, as far as the temptations. I'm a Christian. I want to live my life righteously. It's tough when you're in an environment where you've got gambling, you've got women, you've got all kinds of stuff you can get into.

"Everybody plays this game for a different reason. You've got some cats, and I'll be blunt, who want to play for women. Some cats are going to play for status, the fame. Some cats want to play for the money. I don't love football. I'll be the first to tell anybody. I don't love football. I love to compete. I don't care if I was playing jacks, playing a game of cards or a ten-yard race. I just love to compete. It's the only reason I'm out here. I can compete at the highest level of competition known in the world."

Ian's mother was the first person in a family of eleven children to graduate from high school. A single mother of four boys who was working multiple jobs, she announced one day, Ian says, that she was going to school. She attended a community college and transferred to the University of Michigan. She graduated and teaches high school in Ann Arbor. "I'm out here sweating on a hot day," Ian says. "My mom had four boys, going to college and working. What am I complaining about?"

Ian followed his mother to Michigan, where he majored in political science and intended to go to law school. (He says he still intends to.) But Ian improved so much at football that he started for the Big Ten power and was drafted in the second round by the Broncos. After three seasons, he had made the Pro Bowl for his special-teams play. At that point, as a reward, the team could have renegotiated Ian's contract. Ian viewed its refusal to do so as an act of disloyalty. When he tore his right ACL in the sixth game of the following season, he wasn't pleased exactly, but he believes the injury was a response to the front office. "I got my salary and they didn't get anything out of me," he says.

Ian rehabbed to full recovery in five months, for which he praises Greek. But the Broncos, assuming he wouldn't leave as a free agent, offered him a contract for half of what he wanted. During the 2004 draft, Mike Shanahan called Ian to ask whether he was returning. Ian said if the team paid him what he was asking, yes. Fifteen minutes later, the Broncos drafted a potential replacement at his position. Ian signed with Tampa Bay. His knee held up, he played well, and at the end of the season he was a free agent again.

"Who comes knocking at the door?" Ian says. "I wasn't surprised. I knew they would come back because I was healthy and I knew Shanahan likes me as a person. No hard feelings, no bitterness." In Tampa Bay, he says, the facilities were "worse than my high school," with half the weight room outdoors under a tarp, where a trainer would ask him what exercises he wanted to do to rehab his knee, not vice versa. He was happy to return to Denver. Ian doesn't use an agent; he has dumped three during his career, two of whom, he says, acted unethically. Instead, he negotiated his current contract himself, running the paperwork by a college tutor of his who's now a law professor at Indiana University. Ian told Shanahan the team knew what he wanted. This time, he got it, signing a six-year deal with $7.75 million guaranteed over the first two seasons.

Ian isolated the business of the sport from the performance environment. "I could have said, 'Fuck you, no way I'm coming back.' I could have gone to Kansas City and played Denver two times a year. For me, it was almost as if I went for a ride around the block and I saw what was out there. I knew where I wanted to be. Because Mike's a good coach. They've got a good thing going here, a good organization." But good to Ian isn't great. While he has forgiven the Broncos, he hasn't forgotten. The way he believes he was treated has shaped his broader view of the game.

"The hard part for me is dealing with the lack of loyalty, dealing with people who have such a lack of integrity that it's just sickening," Ian says. "You have coaches that will smile in your face and they'll shit on you the next second. You got head coaches, owners, 'Oh, yeah, we love you,' and the next minute you're gone. But *you* go out there and you play your ass off. You play hurt, you play with tight hamstrings, with sore shoulders. You lay it on the line for these people, for the organization, and all it is is a moneymaking machine. When it comes time for them to take care of you, you think they'll do the same thing for you? No. They're looking for your replacement the day you step foot in this door. That's the truth. That's the reality of this whole deal."

The NFL, I think, rolls that reality into its Lombardiesque code. The breathtaking sound of a locomotive hit on a speeding ballcarrier, the drama of a blood-vessel-popping coach chewing a player a new one, the permanent state of impermanence imposed by the absence of guaranteed contracts: All are equal parts of the culture of toughness the NFL has helped manufacture around the game. "As they preserve that image, they're going to make a shitload," Ian says. "If they have to go through running back after running back, linebacker after linebacker, guy breaks his neck, breaks his arm, whatever, get another guy in there. Keep 'em coming."

Ian's hard shell of embittered indifference helps him cope with the stresses and indignities of professional football. But that still doesn't answer some fundamental questions. If he has so little respect for how the NFL operates—and this is a guy who says he works for one of the best organizations in the league—how does he tolerate it? How does he maintain self-respect?

"Play every game with an effort to win. If I lose, is my heart broken? No. Because I know I've put everything I had into that game. When we lost to Pittsburgh [in the AFC Championship Game]? We made it that far. Why should I be upset? Things happened the way they did for a reason. Now if I put shit on the field and didn't play hard, I have a problem.

"I keep things in such a clear perspective that it's ridiculous. This is business. When I'm here on this field, it is absolutely business. When I'm in the meeting rooms, it is business. Don't hug me, don't touch me, don't call me your buddy, don't tell me you love me, because I know you'll motherfuck me as soon as I leave the room.

"That's how I deal with it personally. I keep everybody at a clear distance, more than arm's length away. Since I've been in the league, I've befriended maybe two guys. Coaches? No. You've got a dinner over at your house. For what? What are you having the linebackers over to your house for? This is bullshit to me. Everybody thinks I'm an asshole because I am this way. I go home to the people I really love and care about—in Michigan, my family. Those are the people I really give a fuck about. Everybody else out here, I hate to say it, when we're on this field, we'll play together and we'll play our ass off together. But when we leave this facility, peace out."

When I arrive from the Holiday Inn one morning at 7:30, I discover that I've been kicked out of my locker. My equipment is gone, my nameplate is missing. Around the corner, Paul Ernster is griping that he has to share space with me. A few minutes later, the equipment guys arrive like the Seven Santini Brothers and relocate me again, to a locker belonging to a tight end recovering from a torn ACL. I'm now sandwiched between a running back and a wide receiver, across from Kyle Johnson and some other ball carriers, catercorner from my fellow kickers.

The interloper in my old space is newly signed offensive lineman Adam Meadows. I was moved so he could locker with the other plus-sized blockers. Dressed in plaid shorts and oval, wire-rimmed glasses, a thatch of blond hair decorating the chin of his completely bald head, Meadows is six foot five, polite, and friendly. He tells me he played seven seasons for Indianapolis and, after two years out of the league, is trying to make a comeback. Once he gets his bearings, he says, he'll be glad to talk; he's intrigued that the Broncos have let a writer into camp. As for the offensive line's media omertà, he just shrugs. He's too old and too mature to worry about that sort of stuff, even in a new locker room.

By NFL standards, Adam, I learn, has had a remarkable career. He started ninety-six games and played in more than a hundred before suffering a major injury. When the injury left him unable to lift his left arm above his shoulder, unable to punch at opposing defensive linemen, on a steady diet of painkillers, and in need of regular cortisone shots—all of this *after* corrective surgery—he had the good sense to cut his losses and retire to his beautiful wife and two beautiful daughters. Not only that but—and I'm astounded when Ted Sundquist relays this bit of information—Adam returned a $2.5 million signing bonus from his new, post-op team because he didn't feel right taking the money when he realized he couldn't perform. He started a real-estate development business. So why then, after this series of rational and conscientious decisions, would he return to the NFL?

A few days after his arrival, Adam and I sit in the empty offensive-line meeting room. He holds a prescription bottle of anti-inflammatories he procured after disappearing into the training room with Greek. His return to football hasn't been easy. His legs feel heavy, almost as if they're swollen. His surgically repaired left shoulder aches, and he still can't lift his left arm over his head. (But he dismisses that as an unnecessary movement for an offensive lineman.) His right shoulder is sore, too. His lower back is extremely tight, from bending over at the line and from ramming into defensive linemen and linebackers. His reaction time is slow and his foot speed diminished. On top of his physical woes, he has to learn the Broncos' zone-blocking system and the quarterback's play calls and the line shifts announced by the center based on the defensive formation. Adam hopes he'll feel more comfortable soon, but he can't be sure.

Before I ask why he came back, I ask what happened to make him leave. During the 2003 season, while lifting weights, Adam noticed that his left shoulder was getting weaker. He thought the muscles were just fatigued. When he took a hit in the neck during practice, a doctor performing a strength test noticed the diminishment and said he was concerned Adam might have a cyst compressing an important nerve in his shoulder. Adam decided to wait to check it out: The Colts were in the playoff hunt and the shoulder weakness wasn't preventing him from doing what offensive linemen do: push and punch in a narrow plane in front of their bodies. But on the first play of the second half against Atlanta on December 14, 2003, someone fell on Adam's knee. The team doctor ordered an MRI on the knee and, while they were at it, on the shoulder, too. The knee was fine. The shoulder wasn't. Adam had a nickel-sized cyst in the spinoglenoid notch of his shoulder big enough to permanently disable two muscles.

On Christmas Eve, Adam underwent surgery. It was supposed to last forty-five minutes. It took two and a half hours. When the anesthesia wore off and the doctors explained the extent of the damage, Adam broke into tears. He told his wife, Courtney, to not let him forget that moment. "I don't ever want to do this again," he said.

Three weeks later, he signed a five-year, $15 million deal with Carolina. He just wanted to play and, after seven months of rehab, thought he would be fine. Instead, Adam got to training camp and couldn't function. He couldn't throw punches. He had difficulty sleeping. He couldn't wash his face with his left hand. The cyst was gone and with it the threat of permanent nerve damage. The new diagnosis was simpler: eighteen years of football with a bad shoulder. A week into camp, Adam couldn't go on. Carolina's general manager, Marty Hurney, told him he could practice minimally or not at all and just play in games. But Adam didn't want to collect a check to sit in the training room. He returned the $1.5 million the Panthers had already paid him, forfeited the remaining $1 million, and retired.

"When you play football long enough, you see guys take advantage of that situation," he says. "I didn't want to be that guy. I didn't want the guys in the lockers next to me to go out there and bust their tails five, six days a week and then on day seven, when they're calling out your name and the fans are yelling and the smoke's going and the jets are flying over, run out there. I think you make your money Monday through Saturday. Sunday's fun. Sunday's what it's all about." He pauses. "Toughest decision I ever made. Right decision. I felt like a thousand-pound gorilla jumped off my back—the burden of the team paying you and you can't perform to their and your own expectations."

The family moved to Macon, Georgia, Courtney's hometown. Adam also is from Georgia and graduated from the University of Georgia. He had been active in real estate, and now started building homes in the Florida Panhandle. In the fall of 2004, he was too busy to have any regrets. By the next season, he was angry at himself: Other players had returned from worse injuries. Why couldn't he? In the spring of 2006, he decided he wanted to try to play again. Courtney told him he was crazy, but also that she would support him.

To test his shoulder, Adam lifted weights with Jeff Saturday, a fellow Colts lineman who lived a few doors down on Amelia Island in Florida, where Adam had a weekend home. Adam pressed through the pain. In a couple of months, he went from 258 pounds to 289 pounds. He didn't tell his agent he was contemplating unretiring until July. Four teams—Atlanta, New Orleans, Green Bay, and Denver—expressed interest. Denver's offer was for three years, a $400,000 signing bonus plus salaries of $850,000, $1 million, and $1.5 million, which could increase based on playing time. Adam liked that he would be rewarded for performance, because he wasn't coming back for the money—he had earned almost all of a $20 million contract in Indianapolis—he was coming back to play more football.

Adam knows his decision looks idiotic. He's not some angry, asocial, macho man who feels inadequate for having quit football. Yes, the sport is what he knows best, but he proved he could work hard and succeed at something else. Adam also knows that he's fortunate. He left the NFL rich, in relatively good health, with an intact family—his girls are six and four, with a third one on the way. Why, I ask him, risk that?

"I missed it so much, man," he says, drawing out his vowels in a gentle southern way. "I love the game. I love the locker room. I love the guys. I love Sundays. I love competing. Yeah, two-a-days suck, training camp sucks. But it solidifies a team. It draws you closer. And that stuff's hard to find. The competition is impossible to replace. You can't do that in real estate."

The inner workings of the offensive line are far more choreographed than fans understand. Linemen depend on one another, and the rest of the offense depends on the line. The job is the most primitive in the game: explosive, at close proximity, and central to the overall success of each play. When I'm not kicking, I like watching the o-line.

"If our job doesn't work, nothing's going to work," Adam explains. "You're not going to complete a pass, you're not going to gain any yards rushing. While it's often a thankless position, I think you'll find that the guys on the offensive line are the closest group on the team. The obscurity bonds them. They know the onus is on them. If they don't work together, it's all going to fall apart. There's no better competition than lining up across from a guy and whippin' his ass, or him whippin' your ass. You're doing it play after play after play. Maybe you do it sixty-five, seventy times a day on a Sunday. It's hard work, it's painful, but it's very rewarding. It's extremely rewarding."

Adam knows that he and his fellow players are heading for knee replacements and hip replacements, a lifetime of mangled hands, bad backs, limps, and worse. That's just part of playing in the NFL. One afternoon in the locker room, thirty-five-year-old Tom Nalen mocks my physical ability, and I good-naturedly remark that I doubt he'll be on any field at age forty-three. "Why?" he says, half jokingly but disarmingly. "Because I won't be able to walk?"

The players are aware of a recent spate of heartbreaking, and infuriating, reports about NFL retirees suing in vain for disability benefits from a league and a players' union portrayed as indifferent to the ravages of the game: to the unseen toll of often undiagnosed concussions, to the tales of former players in their forties, fifties, and sixties suffering from depression or Alzheimer's disease. Adam says he has struggled with depression, as have many of his teammates, and with the way day-to-day pain interferes with his being a good husband and father.

But he and Courtney haven't discussed the life-altering damage he already could have suffered that won't reveal itself for two or three decades. To think about it would prevent Adam—and every other player—from doing what he has decided he should be doing. Practically, Adam avoids making contact with his helmet, avoids any unnecessary contact at all. In the cauldron of battle, though, avoidance isn't possible, and out of one's control. "You almost just hope it's not you," he says.

"You're talking about guys compromising their health short term, and then long term, to play a game. And once that season's over, they can get kicked to the curb and not get another dime. That's bullshit. I think long-term health care for everybody—those who play now, those who played before—that's a major concern. Imagine our list of preexisting conditions. Try to go find a policy." He adds, "If you're fortunate to play longer than a few years, you realize the ramifications on your everyday life."

Ultimately, Adam says, players play for the intangibles, the things that drew him back: camaraderie, team, competition, Sunday. Those things blot out the frustrations: the culture of secrecy and distrust created by poor communication between coaches and players, the relentless focus on making money, from players to owners. Adam is thirty-two, a "borderline dinosaur" in the NFL, he says. Attempting a comeback at thirty-four wouldn't be possible. Adam wants to recover what made him a starter in every one of his NFL seasons and help a team. If he fails, at least he tried. Even for someone as self-aware as he is, short-term reward trumps long-term risk.

13

If It's In, It's In

Until now, I haven't troubled the trainers with my minor maladies. Instead, I've relied on gobs of Flexall—there's a gallon squirt jug on a training-room counter, next to a gallon jug of sunscreen—applied with a rubber glove to my thighs, hamstrings, and groin, along with visits to the ice pool and hot tub and regular days off. Each of these simple measures has prompted verbal pokes from my teammates, who can't believe so little activity requires so much attention. As I often repeat, I'm forty-three, I have two surgically reconstructed knees, and I've never done this before. They know all that, but feel morally obligated to give me shit nonetheless.

"Look at this," Jake Plummer announces loudly and with incredulity one morning when he joins me at the Flexall bar.

"I'm one step away from tearing every muscle in my legs, Jake," I say.

"I'm just messing with you, man," he replies. "You can't make the club in the tub."

This is one of my favorite locker-room expressions. It means a player can't make the team taking cures instead of practicing. I'm no different. As my orthopedist warned: Don't let the team doctors get too close. If they spot the scars on my knees and perform one simple motion test, I'm convinced they will tell Shanahan to cut me for liability reasons. (The Broncos didn't have me sign a waiver.) So I lie down for the massage therapists who set up in the hallway beneath a giant photo of retired running back Terrell Davis. My soft tissue gets manipulated by a specialist in something known as Active Release Technique, which is de-signed to repair overused muscles. I stretch a lot and pop Advil.

But I don't take up a trainer's-room table, for reasons of pride and practicality. I scan the room one afternoon. Bradlee Van Pelt lies on his stomach, a garbage bag of ice held against his upper back and throwing shoulder by a five-pound, sand-filled leather weight. Tender groins be-longing to John Lynch and Cooper Carlisle receive treatment. With a peach-colored Ace bandage encasing a small mountain of ice on a knee, Tick Burns looks to have elephantiasis. Mike Leach's face contorts in pain during an A.R.T. session. Charlie Adams naps with ice on a knee. When he wakes up and limps away, I kiddingly ask whether he needs some help. "Yeah, I need a body double," Charlie replies.

Finally, though, I capitulate. The days on which I have no leg strength—compared with the tiny bit I possess when healthy—are in-creasing in inverse proportion to the number of days remaining in camp. I fear that if I don't get better I'll have to shut it down permanently: no redemption, no preseason game, no story. So on the morning of our Sun-day off, not needing to sleep off a hangover like many of my teammates, I ride the shuttle bus alone to the facility, make a peanut-butter-and-jelly sandwich, and visit the trainer's room. An assistant trainer named Scott Trulock waits like Hawkeye Pierce for the inevitable incoming.

I tell Scott my symptoms: the long-standing pain in my right groin plus newer pain in my left quadriceps and left hip. Scott diagnoses a strain in my hip flexor, the muscle group that moves the hip forward when walking or running. Because it often occurs during an overly forceful contraction, a strained hip flexor is a common kicking injury. Scott speculates that my body compensated for the hurt right groin by shifting weight and pressure to the left side, and now I've injured the muscles I use when planting my left foot to kick. He suggests a daily regimen of ten minutes in the hot tub, followed by a ride on the sta-tionary bike, stretching, and weight lifting on a machine designed to strengthen the hip flexors, all of which I do immediately.

The next day, with FG in the afternoon, I add to the routine some-thing suggested by tight end Stephen Alexander: wrapping my left hip and thigh to cinch the muscles in place. A trainer does the wrapping, and my leg feels taut, secure, and strong, and I feel confident. "Oh my God," defensive back Nick Ferguson says when I hike up my blue shorts. I just laugh. I'm way beyond caring. "At this point," I tell S.A., "I'd wrap my entire body if I could run out and kick."

Not only am I wrapped, I'm wired. NFL Films, the league operation that since the 1960s has turned football games into hundred-yard epics, has arrived to interview Shanahan, shoot B-roll of the Broncos, and prepare a piece about my exploits as a latter-day Plimpton. I'm hoping that Shanahan, mindful of the cameras, will let me kick on this overcast and humid afternoon. During warm-ups, Jason Elam notices the tape beneath my jersey. "Are you miked up?" he asks, incredulous. Word quickly spreads. "Donnie Brasco!" players shout, using the term for a wired player, after the eponymous movie about an FBI agent who infiltrated the mob. When I run through a gauntlet of tight ends, Nate Jackson shoves me in the chest, hard, aiming for the hidden mike.

Backup center Chris Myers offers to snap. Preston Parsons offers to hold. He asks after my hurting legs, and I tell him I'm wrapped now. "That's what happens when you're forty-eight years old," he says. I swipe the ground on a kick. "Would you please quit kicking fucking dirt in my face," Preston says. The next kick is better. "No dirt in my face," he says. "I appreciate that."

Whether playing to the cameras and mikes or not, everyone is helpful this day: Chris, Preston, Jason, Paul Ernster, Micah Knorr, T-Mac. Almost everyone. "You're getting progressively worse," Jay Cutler states flatly after a bad kick. The experts ignore him and tinker. Jason notes that I'm still swinging soccer-style, and not generating enough power with my hips. Micah says I'm too "narrow," and suggests that I expand my sideways steps two to three inches to increase the angle between me and the ball. And, Jason reports after timing me with a stopwatch, I'm too slow: 1.7 seconds from snap to kick instead of the optimal 1.25 to 1.3 seconds.

But the wrapping works. By temporarily masking my injuries, it allows me to kick through weakness and pain, consequences be damned. That's what players do, with ice, balms, painkillers, injections, or Ace bandages and medical tape. I lunch with my Scrabble companion Chad Mustard, his shoulders encased in ice twice as high as pads. "I don't have a job yet, so I have to keep playing even if I'm hurt," he says. In the training room, defensive end Kenard Lang dips his hands in a bowl of paraffin, which he says alleviates the arthritic pain in his crumpled fingers. The day before, Lang reports, Demetrin Veal stepped on three of his fingers, straightening them. "So he did you a favor without doing you a favor?" a trainer asks. "He didn't do me any favors," Lang replies.

The kicking drill for the day is known as FG Down by Two. A portable game clock in the end zone is set at two minutes. Hypothetically trailing by two points with no time-outs, the offense begins on its own 30-yard line. Its goal: to get the ball into field-goal range with enough time to kick. The team, Jason explains, needs sixteen seconds from the spot of the ball by the referee—time for Jason and the kicking team to run onto the field, for the players to set their positions, and for the ball to be snapped. Jason preps me for what could follow. For instance, if the team attempts a field goal on third down, and the snap is botched, and the ball rolls to, say, me, I should throw it away so we can try to kick again on fourth down.

"The biggest thing is don't rush it," Jason says. "Everybody's screaming and yelling, there's a lot of chaos going on. But we've got ten seconds, nine, eight." He counts down calmly. "You've got plenty of time."

"Six, five, four," I say, taking my three steps back.

"It doesn't have to be snapped until zero," Jason says.

T-Mac holds, and my first attempt is good from 30 yards.

"You are hitting that so much cleaner," he says.

"That sounded good, too," I add.

"Like a kick," T-Mac says.

I boot the next one wide left. Then wider left. Then off my toe. Then at the cars in the parking lot. Then I kick the ground, a clump of grass protruding like Bart Simpson's hair from my cleat.

"Still hurting a little bit?" T-Mac asks.

"A little bit. I feel like I'm not getting my leg through."

"That's because you're not. Keep your head down all the way through contact and swing through. Don't worry about looking."

On the next kick, I emit a grunt worthy of Monica Seles. The contact sounds like a boxer's punch—*bip*—and the ball sails powerfully through the uprights. Simple.

"See that? You hit through the ball," T-Mac says. "Head was down, hit through the ball, went straight. The crowd will tell you where it went."

Paul takes over the holding duties and T-Mac snaps. We move back for a 35-yarder.

"Straight as an arrow," Paul says.

T-Mac makes an errant snap. "Fire! Fire! Fire!" I yell, the kicker's signal to his blockers that the kick, and all bets, are off.

"Run for your life," Jason advises.

I exhale once and make one, off of my big toe, from 35. When T-Mac snaps one high, I stutter-step with uncertainty but still manage to kick it far enough, though just wide right. "It's going straight and it's going forty yards," I tell Paul. "And that was off my toe. I'll take it."

"Are you kicking today?" he asks.

"Maybe."

As T-Mac heads to the sideline to attend to other business, he suggests that I keep kicking until FG Down by Two starts, to stay in sync. Paul holds without a snap from 38 yards. I smack it through the uprights to the foot of the netting.

"Forty-five," I say, meaning the kick would have been good from 45 yards. "Best one I've hit all day." Paul holds up a palm, which I hit backhanded. "Thanks, dude."

I don my helmet and trot confidently to join the team. Tick Burns says I look like one of the kids in the movie *Little Giants*. No, he amends, I look like the diminutive, chain-smoking, soccer-playing Australian kicker in *The Replacements*. The airhorn sounds. "Field goal!" Ronnie Bradford shouts. "First-team field goal!" The offense moves downfield, Jason makes a single kick, and the airhorn sounds again.

"That's it?" I say.

"That's it," T-Mac says apologetically.

After my failed kicks the previous week, Nick Ferguson was one of the first players to console me. His already enormous eyes opened like garage doors and he nodded slowly a half dozen times. "Now you know what it feels like," he said. "Welcome to our world." This time, Nick asks, with complete seriousness: "Were you ready?"

I assure him that I was and head inside for a ten-minute cold tub. A few feet away, Jason floats in the endless swimming pool. "You're getting better," he says. And it's true. My steps are fluid. I'm striking the ball with greater consistency. This day, after a brief round of poor hits, I made contact with the side of my foot, kept my head down, and skipped through. Most of the kicks felt like the result of a trained reflex, not like random swings. Taking several days off helped. The wrapping did, too. "Pace yourself," Jason advises with a smile. My tubmates, Matt Lepsis and Kyle Johnson, shake their heads in tandem. *Kickers.* I don't care. For the first time, I feel like I've kicked well enough to call myself a football player.

Mindless endurance, I've concluded, is the secret to success in training camp. Everyone has issues. I miss my wife and daughter. I'm not sleeping well at the Holiday Inn, rising with daylight and anxiety, slightly woozy from my nightly five milligrams of Ambien. I'm burning the notebook at both ends, kicking and standing in the sun and lifting weights by day, chatting with coaches and management by night. I'm at the office fourteen or fifteen hours a day, less than Shanahan's typical eighteen or nineteen, to be sure, but more than my teammates, and more than my body would prefer. I may be only a kicker, but I'm also the only player on the field born in the 1960s—and the early 1960s at that. I shower every morning in the hotel *before* practice, to ease the stiffness in my neck, back, and legs that has accumulated overnight.

One morning I ignore the 6:45 wake-up call and the subsequent 7:00 backup alarm and doze. At 7:30, a time I'm usually at the facility with granola, fruit salad, juice, a bagel, and the local papers, I'm in the shower. Wrapped in a towel, I peel back the window curtain and see the shuttle bus idling in the parking lot. When I hustle downstairs at 7:45, it's gone. A replacement doesn't arrive until 7:55. I race into the building at 8:00. I'm supposed to be on the field in thirty minutes.

I scarf down breakfast and rush to the locker room and then realize: FG is on this morning's docket. Oh, shit! Not today! I need to dress, bike, get stretched by a trainer, rub on Flexall, and get wrapped, all in fifteen minutes. And we're in shoulder pads, and I still can't quickly hook the elastic straps that secure the pads against my back and chest. Ronnie Bradford strolls through the training room while I'm being wrapped.

"Oh, no. Oh, no," he says with disdain, and turns to a trainer. "What time do rookies get taped?" he asks, though he knows the answer.

"Seven fifteen."

"Seven fifteen," Ronnie repeats.

The digital clock reads 8:27.

"Two and a half minutes," Ronnie says.

My hip flexor locked in place, I grab the pads and drop them by the bike. As if decorating a headless scarecrow with a flannel shirt, I've slid my jersey atop the pads in advance, a time- and contortion-saving move.

"Two and a half minutes," Ronnie repeats.

"One and a half," corrects assistant equipment manager Jason Schell. He's conducting a sweep of the locker room, walkie-talkie at the ready to relay the names of stragglers to a colleague on the practice field, who relays them to Shanahan.

I pedal for a minute, hop off, and insert myself into my pads on the fly. I run through the double doors and onto the field. As I hit the grass but—significantly—just before I cross the white sideline onto the play-ing field, the airhorn wails. I'm late. And busted. Al Wilson is the first to notice. Then word spreads. In an unbroken stride, I jog to the daily stretch, feigning innocence while reaching under my jersey in a vain attempt to connect a recalcitrant shoulder pad strap.

"Fatsis, were you late?" Rich Tuten asks.

"First motherfucker to be late for practice so far!" someone shouts with evident glee.

I take my place next to Jason Elam in the rear of the pack. "Let me give you one piece of advice," he says. "Do not do *anything* to stand out. Especially as a kicker." As we line up for the stretch, Micah Knorr sidles away as if I'm contagious. "You're going to get called up," he predicts.

A second later, Al Wilson speaks.

"Only one motherfucker was late for practice this morning!" he announces, eliciting a you're-going-to-the-principal's-office chorus of *ooooohs*. "Only one motherfucker has been late for practice all camp! Coming up to break it down for us, my man, Stefan Fatsis!"

I toss my cap next to my helmet, and the eyes of all—players, coaches, fans—turn to watch as I trot to the front of the group. I begin a rhythmic clap. Then I drop into a squat with my arms bent forward as in a Maori war dance. My teammates follow my lead, simultaneously crouching and grunting, and I'm loving the power and the attention. I jump up, perform a few faux disco-dance moves, and escape whence I came to high laughter, slapping palms along the way. When I return to my spot among the kickers, Ronnie says jokingly, "Expect a fine in your locker."

FG/FG Rush doesn't start for seventy-four minutes, so we attend to our rituals: outdoor drill work, indoor bull session, periodic time checks, slow march to the offense field. The temperature is in the upper seventies, and yet, after just a few warm-up kicks, sweat pours from beneath my helmet onto my forehead, nose, cheeks, and neck. My first ten kicks are uniformly terrible. So I visualize Shanahan calling me out to kick, and imagine myself as focused and powerful as someone hoisting a Volkswagen off of an accident victim. With Paul holding, I drain three in a row from 33 yards. One kick, I tell myself, gather strength for just one kick. No panic.

Veteran players know when to bear down and accelerate, which drills matter and which don't. In kicking, the important moments are few and therefore obvious: On the field, in front of your teammates, you'd better perform. I'm no exception, especially after my earlier misses. The pressure is greater now. Miss again and I'll lose whatever little interest and small stake my teammates have in my journey, and whatever credibility I have with them, too. As much as anything, I crave their respect. Human nature makes it so.

Mentally, I'm at ease. I've been here before, waiting vainly—in both senses—for Shanahan to summon me from the bench. I've had more practice quelling the internal storm when it matters most. An e-mail from my sports psychologist, David McDuff, helped. "Quiet the mind by sending your attention down into your body," he wrote a couple of days earlier. "See yourself making a solid hit, feel the rhythm of your steps and then good contact and follow through, smile at a good kick." How pleasing!

Another reason for my relative calm is a group of visitors at practice. About a dozen members of the 759th Military Police Battalion based in Fort Carson, Colorado, stand between the two practice fields, guests of Jake Plummer. Through his charitable foundation, Jake has brought personnel from various branches of the military to camp and traveled to bases around Colorado to show support in memory of his close friend and former college and pro teammate Pat Tillman, who quit the Arizona Cardinals after September 11, 2001, to join the Army Rangers and was killed by friendly fire in Afghanistan in 2004. One of the MPs watching practice, Doug Billiot, tells me he's returning to Iraq in two weeks for a second, yearlong tour of duty. I, meanwhile, might in a few minutes be allowed to attempt a field goal during an NFL practice. All things considered, I should be able to handle that.

I don't pace, shake, or hyperventilate. I just fasten my chinstrap and wait for Jason to make his ten field goals. Unbeknownst to me, as Jason finishes, Al Wilson asks Shanahan to let me try again. The coach consents. "The guys want Stefan to get another chance," Shanahan tells us at midfield. The stakes are the same as before: If I make a kick, meetings will end a half hour early. The players cheer, slap my helmet, hit me on the back and ass, implore me to make it this time. Al and Jake high-five me as I take center stage.

Don't think don't think don't think, I tell myself. *Blow out blow out blow out.* My steps back are precise. I exhale three times and waggle my arms. It's a 28-yard field goal, I remind myself, a chip shot for me on any field. My heart is racing, but it should be; I'm under pressure. I'm not frightened, though, or self-conscious. Watching the video later in Ronnie's office, I realize that I am oblivious of my surroundings, locked in, in a good way. I have no idea that the cheering players aren't off on the sideline but crowded in five yards away. To most of the Broncos, whose livelihoods really are on the line here, my presence remains a happy goof. But I've wanted to believe that they understand that I care the same way that they care. "I do want to be able to walk off the field and have my teammates know that I came through in the clutch for them," I told my NFL Films interviewers a few days earlier. Seeing them shout encouragement, I realize they wanted me to come through for them, and for me, too.

I look down at Micah, who's holding, and give the nod to commence the play—no freakish "Go!" this time. Mike Leach's snap is textbook. Micah's hold is laces out. Nothing goes wrong—until that is, my right foot sweeps down too low and the front of my Copa scrapes the ground and my lower leg decelerates and my foot strikes the ball near its bottom point.

The instant my failure becomes distinct—when my cleat hits the ground or, perhaps, the nanosecond later when the ball departs my foot—is one of my life's most clearly identifiable moments of agony. A weak line drive barely clears the offensive line and skitters under the crossbar. The same collective groan I'd heard before rises from the field, accompanied by players leaping and twisting and, ultimately, laughing. Groundhog Day indeed. This time, I don't collapse to the turf. I just shake my head in resignation and chuckle in stunned disbelief. During camp, I'd been told a story about a kicker who was signed in the morning and cut in the afternoon, a fate that seems far more merciful than what I'm experiencing.

But Shanahan doesn't allow the failure to take root. He blows his whistle and lines us up once more from the same distance: no penalty this time, just a second chance on a second chance. The coach, I see on the tape, stands just beyond my left shoulder. The players gather even closer the second time, some just a couple of yards away. Though I'm supposed to forget about my last kick—zero for zero, Paul Woodside would say—I'm demoralized. Some of Todd's leftover ephedra would be helpful right now. I have no choice but to proceed. I take my steps. I nod to Micah. When the ball is snapped, the offensive and defensive lines, fearing another line drive, drop to the ground. The snap and the hold are perfect. I make the jab step with my left foot and go.

It takes less than two seconds for a kicked ball to travel twenty-eight yards. As this one leaves my foot and climbs—the first second—I realize two things. That it isn't much of a kick. But also that it should be enough of one to spend the second second carrying above the crossbar and between the uprights. I see arms rise above heads in anticipation. And it's good.

Players and coaches jump and hop and slap each other's hands in exaltation. Fans on the berm applaud and cheer. A wave of confirmation envelops the field, a happy mix of "Yeah!" and "Woo!" and "All right!" Jake Plummer is the first to reach me. He rattles my helmet with both hands and shouts congratulations. I'm too dazed to concentrate on what he's saying, but knowing Jake it's probably something like, "Fuck yeah!" John Lynch, Al Wilson, and Tick Burns—more veterans—arrive next. I'm pounded on the head and whacked on the shoulder pads and then, suddenly, hoisted into the air. Guys are high- and low-fiving, wagging index fingers in the air. "Rudy! Rudy! Rudy!" some players shout, reenacting the climax of the tear-jerking movie about a shrimpy Notre Dame practice player in the 1970s who plays in a single game because his teammates demand it.

I've come through under pressure. I've performed when it mattered. I've done it.

And I'm as disappointed as when I missed.

During the kicks, I learn, some Broncos were saying they can't understand why I keep choking, because I look good in practice, sometimes like a real kicker. It's why I find the cheers undeserved and the trip on my teammate's shoulders patronizing. "No!" I say as the players lift me overhead. I'm not worthy. On tape, it looks as if I'm struggling to get down. When I'm returned to earth, I say to no one in particular, "That was awful."

And it was! The kick's physical properties were atrocious: I struck the ball the opposite of thunderously. I didn't rotate my hips to generate force. I didn't extend through to the target. The sound was unthreatening. The ball's trajectory was low and its flight lethargic. The football cleared the crossbar by no more than ten feet. On good kicks, I'm at least ten feet higher from that distance.

Six months ago, I would have been thrilled to have made a 28-yard field goal before the entire Denver Broncos organization, the phalanx of media that covers the team, and 1,160 fans loyal enough to skip work or spend a vacation day to attend practice. My standards are higher now. "DEMAND PERFECTION FROM YOURSELF," Tim Brewster had written on the whiteboard in the tight ends' meeting room. Like many players, I have scoffed at the idea of perfection. But the truth is that, when performing, I expect it. I expect a perfection proportional to my abilities. I don't believe anymore that, barring the reappearance of Category Three winds, I will improve enough to kick a 50-yarder. But I do expect to make a 28-yarder. Every time. Under any circumstances. So while I've finally come through for my teammates, the victory is Pyrrhic.

My kicking colleagues see that I'm hurting. Jason raps me on the helmet. "At least it went through," T-Mac says. "You made one," Micah offers. "Now you get better at making them." Todd, bless his cold heart, offers that the kick probably would have been blocked had the linemen raised their hands rather than dropped to their knees.

The rest of the team, though, is unconcerned with the kick's aesthetic shortcomings. "Way to go, Fatsis." "Finally made one." "Nice kick." "The monkey's off your back." In the deterministic world of field-goal kicking, style doesn't matter. "If it's in, it's in," Kyle Johnson says. Plus, I have granted every member of the Denver Broncos thirty minutes of downtime. That's something. And I have avoided the sure humiliation of being taped to the goalposts or submerged in the ice pool or deposited in a laundry hamper. (When he sees me later, Shanahan gives me a high-five and a handshake. "Man, I'm just glad I wasn't you if you missed the second one," he says.)

On the sideline, the members of the 759th Military Police Battalion, who will be shipping off to war soon, offer me hearty congratulations, and a dose of reality.

"Think of how many guys would love to be doing what you're doing," Lieutenant Colonel Chad McRee, the battalion commander, tells me in honest awe.

But it was an ugly kick, I say apologetically.

"Who cares? You're in the NFL. You kicked a field goal in the NFL."

14

My Dogs Adore Me

etween practices, I sit in the quarterbacks' room with
Jake Plummer, Preston Parsons, and Nate Jackson.
Preston and I play Scrabble. Nate reads *How the Other Half Lives,* the
pioneering study of the urban underclass by Jacob Riis. We'd talked
about the book, and Jane Jacobs and Robert Moses, while Nate soaked
an injured left ankle in the ice pool. Knee bobbing, Jake studies for our
first preseason game, in two days in Detroit.

A special playbook for the game contains thirty-nine running plays
and sixty-eight passing plays. It also includes rosters, depth charts, dia-
grams of Detroit's offensive and defensive fronts, and analyses of the
Lions' personnel. The plays are part of the basic offense Shanahan and
his staff have been "installing" since the spring. During the regular season, many of the basics will go unused, replaced weekly by dozens of
new schemes designed for a particular opponent. It's as if the cast of a
production of *Macbeth* is told a few days before opening night that it
will be performing *The Tempest* instead. Then the next week it's handed
King Lear.

That's maddening for players, who think the playbook already is too
fat and complex "without the hundred and five new plays we have to put
in every week," as Jake says, barely exaggerating. One might think the
coaches are getting paid per play, or are just overeager to demonstrate
their mastery of ever more intricate NFL offenses and defenses, and

their ability to outsmart the opposition. "What coaches do way too often in the NFL is think it's about them, not about us," Nate says.

During practice, Preston quarterbacks the third-string offense in "cards," diagrammed plays that Detroit might employ, drawn on large cards and held up in the huddle by a coach with his back to the defense. Jason and I watch a video compilation of every field goal and every extra point the previous season in Ford Field in Detroit. He does this before road games to develop a mental image of the stadium and to glean tendencies about the wind, grass, and ball flight.

During practice, Shanahan told Micah that Paul will handle every punt and every kickoff in the preseason. The team, he said, needs to see whether Paul can perform under pressure, how he does when territory and situation matter. But if Paul screws up, the job is Micah's. Most players would complain privately that they're getting shafted. After all, Micah has more experience than Paul and has kicked well in camp, and he couldn't work any harder. But Micah doesn't even disagree with the decision. "I think it's a great coaching move," he tells me. "I'm only bummed because I won't be on film—and I haven't been on film for a year." His one request, which he makes in Ronnie's office, is to be given a couple of punts in the last preseason game if Paul has already won the job.

Though he's been told he won't play at all in the preseason, Todd will travel with the team. Shanahan likes the idea of Paul having to deal with Todd's head games during a real game. He also likes the idea of Todd having to follow road-trip rules when he has little reason to care. "If he screws up on this trip, if he doesn't do everything that he's supposed to do, he won't be around anyhow," Shanahan says in Ronnie's office. After the coach leaves, T-Mac chirps gleefully: "Ding, ding, ding, ding! Not a whole lot of wiggle room, brother."

In the quarterbacks' room, talk turns to Shanahan. "He is a fucking scientist," Jake says. Bradlee Van Pelt, who's just walked in, adds, "A mad scientist." Bradlee describes watching film once with Shanahan, the coach's pointer zooming around the screen, his mouth drag-racing with analysis, his brain processing the tiniest digression from perfect. "What's the word when nothing exists except within your own imagination?" Bradlee asks. When nothing outside this room, he says, is real, not the practice fields, not the goalposts, not the painted lines, not the blocking sleds, not the greater world beyond?

"Sort of what they'd like you to think," I say, pointing upstairs.

Jake looks up from his playbook.

"Yeah."

In March 2003, on the day of Jake Plummer's first news conference as a Bronco, Mark Kiszla, a contrarian, often mean-spirited *Denver Post* sports columnist—"every paper's got one," Shanahan says—wrote that for $40 million, the team deserved a quarterback who was "fully loaded, with Super Bowl guarantees and legitimate Hall of Fame aspirations." Except in the imaginations of sportswriters, though, this love child of Joe Namath and Peyton Manning doesn't exist. Anyway, the Broncos structured Jake's contract to protect them in the event of a flop. (The team could opt out after two years, having paid $8.2 million.) But never mind. "Neither his arm nor his reputation is golden," Kiszla wrote. Plummer is "full of swagger in the huddle, but short of savvy in the pocket." His nickname shouldn't be the Snake, he quipped, it should be the Scarecrow. "If he only had a brain, Plummer would be dangerous."

Welcome to Denver, Jake!

The Broncos had missed the playoffs three of the four seasons since winning their second straight Super Bowl under John Elway, who still hovers over Denver like the giant statue of Jesus in Rio de Janeiro. Plummer was hardly the second coming the city's fans, and writers, had been demanding. In six seasons with the Arizona Cardinals, he had thrown 114 interceptions against 90 touchdowns. His passer rating was an abysmal 69.0. His record as a starter was 31-53.

But what Kiszla didn't offer readers—because to do so would have undermined his argument—was context. Plummer played for one of the NFL's worst organizations. Yes, he sometimes scrambled crazily and chucked the ball into triple coverage and hoped for the best. But he had to do something: His supporting cast was lousy. Plus, taking risks was

Plummer's style. When it worked—in college, he led Arizona State to the brink of a national championship; in his second year as a pro, he engineered a string of fourth-quarter comebacks that delivered the Cardinals franchise its first playoff appearance in sixteen years and then its first playoff win in fifty-one years—Plummer looked like Joe Montana. When it didn't work, he looked like Joe Pisarcik. The question Kiszla should have asked was: What did a relentless empiricist like Mike Shanahan see in a risk-taking freelancer like Jake Plummer?

Before deciding to sign him, Shanahan examined every one of the 2,831 passes Plummer had thrown for Arizona. He examined how Plummer played when the Cardinals were trailing (often) or leading (not often). He examined what Plummer did when no passing options were available, and what resulted. The conclusions: Plummer's arm was strong enough to make the necessary throws. He played better on the run than standing in the pocket, which suited the Broncos' mobile offensive line. His athletic ability allowed him to create something out of nothing. Many of his interceptions occurred when he was trying to mount a comeback, at which he succeeded more than any of his peers. And his laid-back, go-for-it, whatever personality might help him cope with the inevitable Elway comparisons. The bottom line: Plummer didn't care about statistics. He cared about winning.

But numbers become part of a quarterback's permanent record, and columnists don't watch film or do nuance. So a coach and front office have to figure out which stats are relevant and which are red herrings. The Broncos decided that Plummer's numbers reflected Arizona's lack of talent, not his own. Jake told Geep Chryst, his position coach with the Cardinals, that Chicago had offered him more money than Denver. "You don't need more money," Chryst replied. "You need better players."

In Denver's run-first offense, Plummer was an ideal fit. I ask quarterbacks coach Pat McPherson—whose father, Bill, coached on the staffs of all five of San Francisco's Super Bowl championship teams in the 1980s and '90s—to explain why. He says the running game's best weapon is the cutback, in which the ballcarrier heads toward his blockers but cuts by design in another direction. The effect is to neutralize the defensive end, who has to hesitate a split second to figure out which direction the runner is going. With a drill-team offensive line, Broncos runners are a perennial threat. So Plummer's ability to fake a handoff and roll out toward either sideline further destabilizes the defensive end and, in a domino effect, the rest of the defense. The run sets up the pass, and often the pass is a short one.

Such conservatism was new for Jake. But he respected the team's offensive coordinator, onetime Elway backup Gary Kubiak, and bought into the system. Jake just wanted to win. In 2003, he never passed for more than a pedestrian 277 yards in a game. But he threw just seven interceptions, half as many as his previous low, and his quarterback rating was a career-high 91.2, fifth-best in the NFL. The Broncos went 10-6 and finally returned to the playoffs. Though they lost in the wild-card round to the Indianapolis Colts, 41–10, the franchise had found its quarterback. "The fantasy stuff is so far away from where we're thinking," McPherson says. "If Jake Plummer has a monster game numbers-wise, we probably lost, because we ended up throwing a lot."

In 2004, Jake had a lot of monster games. He threw for more yards, 4,089, than John Elway ever did in a season, and he had as many touchdown passes, twenty-seven, as Elway at his best. For the Broncos, that wasn't good. McPherson says Jake was put and found himself in too many situations in which he thought he had to win games on his own, "kind of going back to what he did in Arizona." Passing 521 times, as Jake did, sixth-most in the NFL, is not Broncos football. Throwing a league-worst twenty interceptions, as Jake also did, was the by-product. He was booed at home. The Broncos managed to finish 10-6, but they were whomped again by the Colts in the first round of the playoffs, 49–24.

To the media, the story line was Good Jake/Bad Jake. In some respects, it was true. He did make mistakes. He did take risks. But it was the coaches' job, too, to minimize them. Before the 2005 season, they drilled Jake in reading coverages better to discourage him from throwing into areas clogged with defenders. They restricted the game plan even more than the year he arrived. And the Broncos rarely trailed, so Jake didn't feel burdened with winning single-handedly. The success spawned a new media creation: No-Mistake Jake. He threw for 3,366 passing yards, eighteen touchdowns, and just seven interceptions. As measured by a newish statistic that offers a holistic assessment of performance—analyzing each play according to game situation and comparing it against the league average—Jake was the fifth-best quarterback in the NFL. The Broncos went 13-3 and beat New England at home in the playoffs.

And then they lost to Pittsburgh in that AFC Championship Game.

Forget the season. Plummer, Mark Kiszla wrote, had failed to "escape the shadow of John Elway." With a chance to "capture the city's heart, Plummer dropped the ball." He left the field as "the loneliest man in Colorado."

A less sexy interpretation was that, as several Broncos tell me, everyone played poorly that day, for no apparent reason. Sportswriters try to impose clear and simple narratives on events. But the reality of what players do on the field, and how they are perceived off of it, often defies simple storytelling. Players dutifully grant interviews but, I learn, often don't check to see how their words are used. They consider the life-and-death devotion and red-faced opinions of writers (and fans) bizarre and troubling. Jake thinks it's pitiable that Denver is still hung up on Elway.

Jeff Legwold, a longtime Broncos beat reporter for the *Rocky Mountain News,* tells me one day that Plummer is the "anti-Elway." Elway went to Stanford, was built like Adonis, had a cannon arm, was a conformist, flashed a big smile, courted the public and was courted by corporate sponsors, protected his image. Plummer went to Arizona State, is scruffy and skinny (his ass sticks out, his calves have no definition), talks like a surfer, plays with finesse not power, wears jumpsuits and second-hand flannel shirts, keeps his distance from the public, doesn't sculpt his image.

"Every breath you take is supposed to be about being a football player," Nate Jackson says. "Jake's not like that."

Jake has quietly donated hundreds of thousands of dollars through a charitable foundation in his name for Alzheimer's care (his grandfather had the disease), at-risk youths, and animal welfare. He shows up unannounced at the local humane society to walk stray dogs, and has adopted two, Ray Ray and Kosi. Pat Tillman's death, Jake says, inspired him to do more with life outside of football, during and after his career. If, along the way, he betrays some of the purported responsibilities of the modern athlete, so be it. Jake has given the finger to a fan during a home game, chewed out a gossip columnist for writing about his girl-friend, a Broncos cheerleader, and said during the media storm over his recent fender-bender, "Image tarnished, whatever. Role model, blah, blah. I'm here to play football and play the games and whatever happens, that's what I've got to deal with."

Jake doesn't deny looking forward to being done with the game, but while in uniform he pledges to be passionate and determined and ag-gressive, a team leader, whether insisting on privacy while giving Brad-lee Van Pelt a pep talk or lifting me on his shoulders when I make a field goal. During a practice, Jake gathers the offense on the 30-yard line. "Young guys, you've got to concentrate," he says. "We're doing some good shit. Coaches are going to motherfuck this and motherfuck that. But we're going to be a *bad* motherfucking offense. We were bad last year. We're going to be even better this year." He almost sounds like a coach. "We've got to seek perfection. Let's come out tomorrow and put it to the defense. We've got to pick it up."

In the locker room, Jake and I play an old board game called Shut the Box. He's one of the few players I see reading books. One day it's *The Giver,* a Newberry Award–winning young-adult novel about a utopian society. Another day it's *Before the Legend,* a biography of Bob Marley, whom Jake calls one of his heroes. Jake treats me like a kid brother (who just happens to be twelve years older). I think his early acceptance of me signaled other players to accept me, too.

Jake tells me he has no regrets about coming to Denver, despite the criticism he has faced about his playing style, his statistics, and, now, his "failure" to win the big game. "It was a good decision. A big-time place to come. And they were hungry. I brought in an attitude that was not like the one they had here." Rod Smith, the twelfth-year wide re-ceiver, once told him, "You must have Alzheimer's. You make the shittiest play I've ever seen and then you go out and make the most amazing play I've ever seen, like you didn't just make a shitty play." Jake replied, "How the hell can I survive if I can't go back out after failing?"

At thirty-one, Jake isn't old for a quarterback. His seven-year contract, through 2009, is reasonable for a starter at his position: salary-cap numbers of $7.357 million this season, $8.6 million in 2007, $9.6 million in 2008, and $10.1 million in 2009. Yet after completing their best season since Elway, and Jake's best season as a professional, the Broncos scaled the draft ladder to pick a quarterback. Jake was in his unwinterized two-thousand-square-foot cabin in Coeur d'Alene, Idaho (he grew up in Boise), unreachable. "I'm sure they knew not to try to call me, because I would have said, 'Do whatever the hell you want to do,'" he says.

But it bugged him, the way the business of football naturally bugs players, no matter how much money they've made or how successful they've been. Jake understood that teams do as they please, and that winning teams like the Broncos don't often get to select high in the draft. But Jake had the franchise "a game from the bowl," and believed he could take the final step.

"And then all of a sudden they draft him, when I think we could have drafted other positions to make us better. But they drafted him. When you do that, bam, the whole world changed here. I tried not to change though, because that would show my weakness. Is it a slap in my face? Was it? Ahhh, maybe a little bit. But if that's a move they felt they had to do, then they've got to do it.

"In certain cities, that could probably work, but not this one. They've been waiting for the next gunslinger, the next Elway. I'm going to wish [Cutler] luck at some point because he's going to deal with the same shit I've been dealing with. I got booed my first preseason game here. I threw a pick and got booed off the field. Right then I was like, this is going to be fun. But I knew we'd win games, so I wasn't worried."

Since coming to Denver, Jake has the third-best winning percentage among NFL starting quarterbacks, behind future Hall of Famers Peyton Manning of Indianapolis and Tom Brady of New England. But Jake wasn't bred by Denver the way Elway was. And he didn't have time on his side the way Elway did when he took the Broncos to three Super Bowls in his first fourteen seasons but lost every time and was branded a loser, like Jake after the Pittsburgh game.

"Cracked under pressure I guess, according to the guys with the pens in their hands." Jake laughs. "There will be a loser and a winner in every football game you play. And it sucks that we happened to be the loser, but we were. We brought this city back something it hadn't seen in a long time. Two home playoff games. An AFC Championship Game. And they were not satisfied."

As a player, Jake certainly wasn't satisfied, either. "But it's a sin. It's like sacrilegious to say we had a good year, we had a great season, and our team was amazing, because we didn't win the Super Bowl. In these parts, if you don't do that it's blasphemy against the almighty Super Bowl god—when we're all chasing the childhood dream, really. I'm chasing the childhood dream. It was a dream of mine to win a Super Bowl. But, damn, it's hard as shit. There's thirty-one teams that are failures, that have to go back to the drawing board, that have to go reevaluate all the shit they did wrong.

"But that was the first time I'd been in that situation. I did what I'd been doing all year. I prepared my ass off and went in and plays just didn't happen for us. Shit that had been happening wasn't and we lost. If that prompted the whole, 'Let's go get another guy,' then . . . I don't know, man."

Jake never asked for an explanation and never got one. I, however, did ask Ted Sundquist and Mike Shanahan why they drafted Cutler, knowing how it would play in town. They said there were two main reasons: finding a replacement for Jake, whose mobility and durability would eventually decline, and finding themselves in the position to obtain an elite quarterback who could play until 2020. Sundquist's rationale was the latter. Shanahan's was the former.

Jake had spent much of the off-season in Idaho, away from Denver and the "voluntary" workouts that teams nonetheless monitor obsessively and reward monetarily. Jake attended 85 percent of the sessions, but it was the lowest attendance mark on the team. Shanahan inter-

preted that as a loss of interest. "A big part of it was the off-season program," he says of the decision to draft Cutler. "Jake is a guy that I could
tell going into this year was not as enthused about the off-season program, working out, wanting to be away. He gave up two hundred grand
because he didn't hit his percentage. Well, when my quarterback is
missing . . ." Shanahan pauses. "John Elway, he's in here sixteen years,
he's making those guys work because he wants one thing, and that's to
win the Super Bowl. He wasn't playing for the money. He wanted to win
the Super Bowl and knew his only chance was to get the team going in
the off-season.

"When I knew [Jake] wasn't too excited about the off-season, that
made me think that, hey, a guy gets to a certain age and it's just not
what it used to be. So in the back of my mind it was going to be through
either free agency or it was going to be through the draft. I was going to
get somebody that I knew really wanted to play the game, that I could
hang my hat on, that loved the game. What you want to do is cover yourself. You're never sure if somebody says, 'I've had enough.'" I ask Shanahan whether he addressed it with Jake. "You bet your ass. That's
between me and him. Obviously, [I was] not very happy."

Jake admits that he thinks more now about life after football. It's
only natural. "When you get into your tenth year, some guys realize,
'Oh, God, I'm going to have to give this up soon,' and they can't live without it and they start going harder and harder. I love football. I love playing it. It's fun. Take it away, I've got a lot of shit on my plate that I can
go do and want to go do and have been waiting to go do but can't because
of the time commitment." Jake has two brothers with two kids each, a
mother he adores and talks to every day, a father in treatment for alco-
holism. There are other sports and activities: handball, skiing, back-
packing, mountain biking. He'd like to work with children. He wants to
raise a family. He imagines joining the Peace Corps. "I'm not a big ego
guy," Jake says. "My mom, my dad, my two brothers, anybody who's
family and friends to me, they know what I'm about. My girlfriend, my
dogs. My dogs adore me.

"You won't even hear my name after I'm done. You will not see me at an NFL old-timers' game. You will not hear me [on television saying], 'Well, that was one of those plays, if he just turns out it's a completion, I don't know what he's thinking.' I'm not going to be that fucking jackass. I refuse to. I'll go coach high-school football, where it's pure. Not to say I haven't loved this and enjoyed it. I have. It's provided me with a life that I never dreamt of living. I have more money in the bank than I could ever spend, and that's if I started having a really nasty drug habit, bought all kinds of shit, and started throwing money out on the street. I couldn't get rid of all of it by the time I die."

For now, though, in camp, Jake is playing well, and says he is fully committed to trying to win a Super Bowl. And Shanahan seems pleased. Rather than harp on the off-season workouts, Jake says, Shanahan told him, "You need to be in Coeur d'Alene more often. You're throwing the ball like crazy." While Shanahan has praised Cutler, and promoted him to number two, publicly the coach has knocked down talk of a quick ascension to the starter's job. That hasn't stopped the speculation: Would the overthrow take place sometime this season? Next year? The year after?

Jake says he's not worried about it. Whether fans like it or not, whether his accomplishments are ever enough for the city of Denver, he's the quarterback until further notice. "They have to put up with crusty-assed old me for however long I can take it," he says before the Detroit game. "Which means they have to put up with thirteen-win seasons. I think they can put up with it."

To players like Jake, the preseason is meaningless. He isn't clawing for one of the fifty-three roster spots. He doesn't need to appear on tape so other teams' personnel directors can see him perform under the lights. He doesn't even need to refresh his game instincts against players wearing differently colored jerseys. After nine years, 133 regular-season and playoff games, 4,230 passes, somewhere in the neighborhood of 9,000 total plays—plus thousands of hours of book, film, and field repetition—Jake's brain and body quickly assimilate each year's new basics. The only thing he hasn't experienced this summer is the one thing he doesn't need or want to experience now. "I just don't want to get hit," he says. "Every time you step on the field there's a chance you can get hurt. You just don't want it to be in the preseason."

In the 1950s, teams played six games in the preseason and twelve in the regular season. The starters often played every down of every pre-season contest. As football's popularity grew, and as the NFL warred with the new AFL, the league in 1961 expanded its regular-season sched-ule to fourteen, but kept the preseason the same length. The current format—four preseason and sixteen regular-season games—was adopted in 1978, and it's not changing. Fans are forced to buy tickets to their team's two home exhibitions—the NFL hates the word "exhibition"—as part of season-ticket packages. Teams reap the usual concessions and parking dollars. And because player salaries are paid during the regular season only, preseason wages are cheap: for rookies, the training-camp standard $775 a week; for veterans, $1,300, a $200 bump over the nor-mal camp stipend.

Someone in the media always suggests playing two exhibitions and eighteen games that count, which would raise everyone's income. The television networks would pony up more money for more real games, and the additional revenue would get passed on to the players via a bigger salary cap. But two and eighteen would increase injury rates, because the best players would play more downs in more meaningful games. Players rationalize getting hurt in contests that matter. But teams would rather not increase the likelihood of injury to their stars. While the most logical solution would be to ditch two preseason games altogether, that would mean turning down free money. The NFL didn't get rich doing that.

So veterans like Plummer play to not get hurt, and the backups play to protect their spots, and the guys on the roster bubble—a group smaller than the players might realize—play to impress the coaches and the audience of other teams that might be interested if and when they are cut. Before leaving for Detroit, Shanahan tells me he tries to win preseason games simply to keep the knee-jerk Denver media and fan base from overreacting.

The Broncos won't employ a game plan tailored specifically to the Lions. The formations will be the basics the team has been implementing. "We just throw plays together," Shanahan says. The regulars will play about a quarter of the game. (They will take twenty plays in the second game and forty in the third, which will include an actual plan, and get the final game off.) To Shanahan, the preseason exposes the starters anew to game conditions, and lets him see whether everyone else understands the offensive and defensive schemes, how they react in real-world situations, and how they perform on special teams, composed almost entirely of second- and third-stringers.

At a practice before leaving for Detroit, Jason Elam tells me he's scheduled to kick only one quarter of the game. He says that I'm listed on the special-teams depth chart after that.

"Yeah, right," I say.

"No! Really!" he says. "Come on. I'll show you."

We walk inside and there it is on the locker-room bulletin board:

K

1ST Q: ELAM

2ND Q: FATSIS

Ronnie Bradford has no doubt put my name there as a joke; he knows the NFL isn't letting me play. But I see it as a gesture, a message. The season is starting, and I'm part of the team.

15

Nice Form, Though

O n the morning of our departure, a Broncos duffel bag
sits on the floor in front of my locker, labeled with a 9.
Into it I place my helmet, shoulder pads, cleats, and workout clothes. It
will be loaded with the rest of the player bags into two trucks carrying
the twelve thousand pounds of equipment and gear that the Broncos
haul on the road: hampers filled with game jerseys, game pants, and
coaches' clothes; steamer trunks packed with medical supplies; video
equipment for the hotel and the stadium.

The NFL's drill-team regimentation is never more apparent than before a game. Like kindergarten teachers, the coaches can't trust that
their charges will be where they are supposed to be, on or off the field,
so we rehearse. Shanahan has the offense stand to the right of the 50-
yard line, the defense to the left. Kickers, punters, and snappers will
take the field first in Detroit, seventy-five minutes before kickoff, he
says. So Ronnie runs us to the right side of the field, where we'll take
our first practice kicks, and then he runs us to the left. Jason will take
seven or eight warm-ups, 28 yards to 53 yards, from each end of the
stadium, he says. The punters will punt. R.B. mimes a kickoff. "When
the linebackers and d-backs come out," he says, "we go off."

Then Shanahan calls out groups in the order and formations in
which they will appear. Players trot on and off like performers auditioning for the chorus of a Broadway musical, so the casting director can get
a look. "Okay, we've got third-quarter Zebra," Shanahan says, and vari-

ous offensive players jog to the middle of the field. "Third-quarter Tiger on offense. Third-quarter goal line." Chad Mustard trots out at the wrong time. "That thirty-four test score's not helping you now!" Shanahan says. Freakishly, he recalls Chad's score on the Wonderlic exam.

"First-quarter kickoff," Shanahan announces, and Paul Ernster trots out.

"Way to go, Paul," Todd shouts.

Shanahan subs individual players on various teams. "Nick's out. Karl's out. John, out." He even summons the team that will be responsible for a kickoff return in the first half in the rare event of a safety. Shanahan can't control the execution of the plays on the field, so he programs his players within an inch of their patience and sanity. "We want this to be fun. Part of fun is winning," Shanahan says as we fidget. "But we have to be organized."

Between the walk-through and departure, players watch TV, play video games, and download music. Some take the tests that position coaches administer before games. Running backs coach Bobby Turner walks through the locker room distributing a multipage exam. Each question has room for two answers, one for the tailback's responsibility on a particular play and one for the fullback's. "That test is hard as hell to fill out and I wouldn't do it by myself the first time," Kyle Johnson advises rookie tailback Mike Bell. Bell nods, then writes and erases but solicits no help. Next to "H2 PROTECTION vs. NAVAJO," he writes "Edge." He pauses at "2-3 JET PROTECTION" before writing "M.S. Secondary Blitz." Next to "PASS 14 MAN (HOT) PROTECTION vs. WOB on LOS," Bell writes "Will and FS" and "Safety C.D."

Kyle tells me he learns his and the tailback's assignment on each play. In his playbook, he draws his path on the field for a block or a pass route. "I call it the pretest," he says. "The test is tomorrow night." It's not news that NFL playbooks are thicker than Bibles, or that players who can't process the information in them stand little chance of surviving. Rote memorization is important—Kyle notes that offensive linemen operate under different sets of rules for running and passing plays; that tight ends must know every formation in the offense; that a single running play can vary based on six different defensive alignments—but instinct is equally important. The name of a play has to be a trigger: for a mental diagram of the play, for the path a player must take, for any necessary adjustments based on how the defense lines up or how the play evolves after the ball is snapped.

I've gone through camp mostly oblivious of the meaning buried in football's complex language, which derives from at least the 1950s. Cleveland's Paul Brown instituted a numbering system to denote positions and spaces in the line of scrimmage. George Halas, who coached the Chicago Bears for five decades, used numbers and colors to call plays. Word strings were introduced by Sid Gillman of the Los Angeles Rams. The Broncos use a system combining words and numbers that was created by San Francisco 49ers head coach Bill Walsh and was spread through the league in the 1980s and '90s by disciples including Shanahan. Terminology varies widely from team to team, but there are enough similarities that learning a new system is like learning another Romance language rather than tackling Arabic. Play long enough and the linguistic complexity is largely forgotten. "There's only so many ways you can run a route," says Stephen Alexander, who is with his fourth team in nine seasons. "Everybody runs the same plays."

That doesn't make the plays any less complicated to outsiders like me. Kickers are required to learn scant few plays that don't involve kicking—the rare fake or doomsday scenario. Jason doesn't even know much of the basic shorthand. So while I have recorded the names of the Broncos' six offensive personnel "packages"—Tiger, Base, Zebra, Eagle, E, and Cinco—I'd fail a spot quiz on how many running backs, wide receivers, and tight ends are in each. I ask Kyle Johnson to deconstruct one of the sixty-eight plays in the playbook for the Detroit game. He flips a few pages and settles on a pass play called "Near Right 3 Jet Y Spot Disk (Disk O)."

"Near Right" means the tight end lines up on the right side of the field and the fullback lines up in the backfield on the left side, "taking him away from the strength," Kyle says, meaning the more heavily populated side of the offensive line. "3 Jet" establishes the duties of the line.

It tells the left tackle to block the left defensive end and the rest of the line to slide to the right. The sliding linemen will be responsible for any defenders blitzing from the right side of the field. The tailback will be responsible for blitzers from the left. "Y" is a symbol for a tight end. "Y Spot" tells the tight end to run a "spot" route: six yards straight downfield, then rounding to the right toward the sideline eight yards from the line of scrimmage.

"Disk" is a contraction of "Drag Skinny." "Drag" is Kyle's assignment: a "flat" route, three to five yards to his left. "Skinny" refers to the pass pattern for the wide receiver also on the left. In a "skinny" route, the wide receiver takes seven strides—ten yards—and then cuts slightly to the right and keeps running. The route is called a "skinny" because the angle between the receiver and the end zone is less than the typical forty-five degrees for a similar "post" pattern, so his path is narrow, or skinny. The parenthetical "Disk O" modifies the route. Two steps after making his cut, the receiver aborts the diagonal path and heads straight downfield. The placement of the Disk combination at the end of the play's name makes it a "tag" route—"an addendum," Kyle says—because it happens on the "weak" side of the field, opposite where most of the personnel are clustered. The name of the play doesn't specify the assignment for the wide receiver on the strong side. He needs to know from the rest of the information that he is to run a "go" route, straight downfield in an effort to outrace the covering defender.

While all that's happening, Kyle says, the quarterback is determining how the defense is responding to the offensive formation so he can decide which of his receivers is the best target. Y Spot is the first choice, hence its placement first in the play name. Kyle says the quarterback, for instance, might see what the Broncos call a Cover Eight zone, in which the two safeties and two cornerbacks divide the deep field into quarters, each with responsibility for a slice. In that case, the first "look" would be to the overloaded right side, with the tight end and wide receiver. If they're covered, Kyle explains, the quarterback might turn to the play's safety valve, the fullback in the left flat. If the defense lines up in a run-stopping Cover Three zone, with the two cornerbacks and one safety dividing the field into thirds, the quarterback might look to the wide receiver running the skinny route on the left side—a pass pattern that often succeeds in finding space between the defenders, each of whom has substantial territory to cover.

"And the funny thing is," Kyle says after completing the lecture, "people think we're pretty dumb."

Traveling to Detroit feels like a vacation. The mood is discernibly lighter. We're like a fourth-grade class taking a field trip to the circus. In this case, the kids will have to ride the elephants and walk the tightrope and tame the Lions, but no one minds. The game means three days without two-a-days and weight lifting. Even for players who expect to get cut when training camp technically ends in a week, the break in the grind is comforting.

We roll in a convoy of five buses, bypassing the main terminal and driving directly to a United Airlines jet on the tarmac. Ten airport employees at two tables inspect our luggage. As I watch the players climb the stairs and disappear into the charter, I imagine them stooped and struggling in old age and wonder how they'll look back on their football careers. Inside, we get two seats apiece. My row-mate is reading Bill Clinton's autobiography, *My Life*. When I ask him about the book, Patrice Majondo-Mwamba observes that "it is a very complex world, but a small one."

If any football player is qualified to make such a statement, it's Patrice. He is the unlikeliest Bronco—and that includes me—a six-foot-four, 300-pound defensive tackle from the Republic of Congo via Waterloo, Belgium; Atlanta; Salinas, California; Lubbock, Texas; Rhein, Germany; and Amsterdam. He speaks French, Swahili, Flemish, and English. Patrice casually mentions that his father has multiple wives.

As we settle into the flight, Patrice relates how he came to the United States in 2000 to learn English and attend college. His journey began at Georgia Tech. One day, he saw big students coming in and out of the gym and asked the head football coach, George O'Leary, if he could play, too. O'Leary advised him to go to a junior college, so Patrice went to California and then was recruited by Texas Tech, where, over two seasons, he made thirty-three tackles and had one sack. An NFL scout wouldn't read far enough down the stat sheet to see Patrice's name. But the league was recruiting foreign players for a program to seed the sport abroad. Patrice played in Rhein in the NFL's European league in the spring of 2005, was assigned to the Broncos' camp and practice squad, went to Amsterdam to play this past spring, and is back in Denver.

I watched him in practice one day. Patrice is obviously slower than the other linemen, his footwork and reactions less precise. "Come on, Mwamba, show me you're learning," defensive line coach Andre Patterson shouted. As if on cue, Patrice muscled past an offensive lineman. "It only took two years!" Patterson said playfully. In the next drill, a two-on-two, Patrice spun around his foe. "You're on a roll, Mwamba!" Patterson said. "Let's see if you can give me three in a row!" One defensive lineman had to make contact with his opponent while the other cut around him. Patrice rolled off of a block by Tom Nalen, but got no penetration. He pushed hard again, but still couldn't do it. Finally, he succeeded, sheepishly accepting praise.

In a football sense, Patrice is me: underskilled, unprepared, attempting to learn a sport while performing alongside the very best. "For most of them, it's second nature," he says. "I have to repeat over and over and over." We also have the same NFL dream. "One play," Patrice says. "One play. That's the goal. That's the goal. I want to play one play."

Shanahan, the coaching staff, and team officials sit in first class and business class. But when we land, the players file past them. It's a small gesture that Shanahan believes shows the players that they come first, and, psychologically, it does feel empowering, looking down at the authority figures while exiting into waiting buses to be escorted by police to the hotel. There, two elevators are curtained off for us, and an entire wing of the hotel. An off-duty state trooper is stationed on the players' floor. The Broncos' logo decorates our room key cards.

The VIP approach isn't surprising. NFL franchises are highly lucrative businesses that pay their key employees—the players—nearly $2 million apiece a year on average. They attract those workers based partly on their reputation for how they treat them. The Broncos' annual revenue is about $200 million, and the franchise was about to be valued by *Forbes* at $975 million, fourteen times what Pat Bowlen and his family paid in the mid-1980s. According to the magazine, the team is the sixth-most valuable in the NFL. It can afford to fly charter and book a fancy hotel.

But that's not the point. Amid the strict rules and physical deprivation of the NFL, the psychology of small things rules. Shanahan says perks like traveling well—or holding a Hat Day, when the players wear a cap of their choosing instead of helmets, or a bowling outing during camp, or cutting thirty minutes off of meetings for a field goal made by a writer—matter to players as a reward and a show of respect. When you bunk at the Holiday Inn and suffer fourteen-hour days and put your body on the line constantly (private deprivations), a night in a Ritz-Carlton (public luxury) seems special. So the players deplane first, sleep in individual rooms on the road (except for the rookies during preseason), and are permitted one pay-per-view movie a day (two during the regular season, though Shanahan tells us that Tom Nalen's contract calls for three).

The usual routine doesn't break entirely. There are meetings at night and more meetings the next morning, with plenty of video of the Lions from the previous season—Lions against Bengals, Lions against Packers, Lions against Bears. There is video of Tampa Bay's defense, because Detroit's new defensive coordinator just arrived from the Buccaneers. There's a repeat of the who's-in, who's-out on special teams that we performed on the field, this time standing up and sitting down in a conference room. The offense meets at 11 a.m. "to go over the same shit we've gone over ten times already," Jake Plummer says. Indeed, assistant head coach Mike Heimerdinger conducts a play-by-play review of the script of the game's first fifteen plays (allowing for variations depending on situations). Shanahan knows the players tire of the repetition, so he reminds them why it's done. "In order to have a chance to play well, you have to go over those scenarios time and time again." Regardless, Shanahan says, "you're practicing against better guys than you're going to see on game day."

The players also receive more of the same unintentionally contradictory messages about playing football. They are told, as usual, that their futures depend on their performance. "Everybody's going to see this fucking tape," T-Mac reminds the special teams. They also are told to "have fun."

And then I see it, perched atop the locker I share with Paul Ernster, the first one on the left inside the no-doubt-intentionally small visitors' locker room at Ford Field. The letters of my last name are stitched individually and perfectly onto the back of an authentic NFL jersey and predressed on my authentic NFL shoulder pads ready to be worn on an authentic NFL playing field and read by thousands of authentic NFL fans. My helmet rests on the top shelf of the wooden stall; my Copas are arranged neatly on the bottom one, next to a game program. My game pants hang on a hook opposite my laundry bag containing my socks, compression shorts, shorts, and T-shirt.

Kickoff isn't for three hours, but I took the first bus from the hotel to the Lions' red-brick downtown home, which from the outside looks more like a factory than a domed football stadium. We got another state police escort, one car and one motorcycle, and the journey was much quieter, with most players listening to iPods or texting. Jason read another Christian novel. Training camp is agonizing, but at least the environment is secure, the drills meticulously controlled to guard as much as possible against the unexpected. An actual game is its own form of relief from the grind—a reward for enduring the grind, really—but it carries fears far more profound. It's what players love and what they dread.

The suits at No Fun League headquarters in New York may have barred my participation, but I've decided to treat the experience as if my number could be called at any time. (That is, any time the Broncos score a touchdown or a drive stalls inside the Lions' 20-yard line.) Pregame will be my game. Blockers will protect me. Mike Leach will snap for me. Micah Knorr will hold for me. Visualizing the circumstances in which you perform is a tenet of sports psychology. I will step on the Ford Field field, visualize, and perform. As I try to convince myself this is a reasonable compromise, reality intrudes.

"So are they going to let you kick?" Tom Nalen asks outside the locker room, where he is pedaling a stationary bike. "The big, bad NFL?"

"Nope," I reply.

"What would happen?"

Nothing, I tell Nalen. I'd either make it or miss it, like every other kicker. I'd take the same breaths, the same three steps back and two same steps over as every other kicker. I'd look down, nod at my holder, and break with the snap, like every other kicker. It would take the same 1.25 seconds from snap to kick as it does for the others, and the ball would rise up and split the uprights, or sail right or left, or be batted down by a leaping lineman or a rusher flying toward me from the edge. I would be elated or disappointed and would unbuckle my chinstrap, and the kickoff team (if I made it) or the defense (if I missed) would take over. Play would resume. No time would have elapsed from the clock. Nalen and my teammates understand that. They'd like to see me kick for comedic value but also, I think, because it would represent a rare subversion of the rules and bureaucracy that govern their professional lives.

While Jason massages various creams into his legs, I walk down a semicircular ramp to the field. The thump of music from the PA system grows with each step. There are no fans in the stadium yet. Players test their footing on the FieldTurf, dropping into a stance and breaking as if with the snap of the ball. P. J. Alexander crouches in the end zone and grimaces every time he springs up. His knee is "on fire," he tells me, but he might have to play. He hasn't taken any painkillers—yet. Erik Pears lines up to P.J.'s right. "You and me, partner. To the end, buddy," P.J. says. "Hopefully that won't come too soon," Erik replies.

Seeing the Broncos and Lions mingle in the empty stadium reminds

Anatomy of a kick. My guru, Paul Woodside, holds while I blast one through the uprights at Edison High School in northern Virginia. Note the leg extension. And the celebration.

© PAUL WOODSIDE

The facility: The team offices, locker room, and dining room are in the building on the left. The players' parking lot is next to the weight room and indoor practice field on the right. The "offense" field is the one nearest the main building and the "defense" field is behind it. We kickers congregate on the fake-grass FieldTurf field with "Broncos" painted in the end zones. Fans camp out beneath the trees along the sideline farthest from the locker room. © TREVOR BROWN JR./RICH CLARKSON AND ASSOCIATES LLC

Jason Elam does it all. He kicks record-tying field goals, he snaps, he holds, he punts, he hunts, he flies planes, he studies theology, he writes novels about Islamic terrorists attacking a football stadium, he makes me a better kicker.
© JAMIE SCHWABEROW/RICH CLARKSON AND ASSOCIATES LLC

Boom! As Todd Sauerbrun's nickname attests, his punts are a thing of wonder—and he'll be the first to tell you so. But Todd's suspension after testing positive for the stimulant ephedra leaves him depressed, angry, and embittered toward the NFL.
© RYAN MCKEE/RICH CLARKSON AND ASSOCIATES LLC

Paul Ernster in full extension on the turf field as Todd Sauerbrun watches. The second-year punter must cope with recovering from a torn ACL and his conflicted feelings toward his friend Todd, whose suspension opens the door for Paul to take the veteran's job.
© RYAN MCKEE/RICH CLARKSON AND ASSOCIATES LLC

I've never met an athlete trapped as deep inside his head as quarterback Bradlee Van Pelt. His struggles to cope with the rigid NFL workplace, the voluminous playbook, and his own shortcomings are poignant to watch.
© RYAN MCKEE/RICH CLARKSON AND ASSOCIATES LLC

Veteran quarterback Jake Plummer on the first day of training camp. His freewheeling play, antiestablishment personality, and outward indifference to public opinion make him a polarizing figure among fans waiting for "the next Elway." But those features are why I come to admire Jake. © RYAN MCKEE/RICH CLARKSON AND ASSOCIATES LLC

My first few seconds of panic. I collapse in a heap after missing my first field-goal attempt in front of the team. Nick Ferguson tries to help me up. Domonique Foxworth (22) rushes over shouting "Offside!"—a pretend penalty to give me a second opportunity.
© KYLE SONNEMAN/DENVERBRONCOS.COM

The second kick is worse than the first—the worst, in fact, of my short career. I'm devastated and humiliated, and suddenly appreciative of the massive, constant pressure that professional athletes face. I tell a teammate afterward that it's more pressure than I've ever felt before in my life.
© JACK DEMPSEY

I face the media mob after the missed kicks. Later that day, one local sportscaster cracks on the air that this book should be titled *Worst Kicker Ever.* © JACK DEMPSEY

Head coach Mike Shanahan's postpractice lectures are succinct. Shanahan isn't a rah-rah motivational speaker, which the players appreciate. They also praise his organizational abilities and his football mind. But he remains a cipher to many players who chafe at the culture of paranoia his top-down management can create.

Wide receivers coach Steve Watson (wearing cap in huddle) addresses his charges. While I never stop taking notes, I do get comfortable enough to forget about the obvious size disparity between me and my teammates. These guys aren't even among the big ones.

I hit the ice pool and hot tub, do targeted weightlifting, and, at a player's suggestion, tightly wrap my left hip and thigh to combat what a trainer diagnoses as a strained hip flexor. The players mock my fragility, but the Ace bandage becomes my personal fountain of youth.

© NFL FILMS

Quarterback Preston Parsons awaits the snap while I prepare to kick. This is during Specialist period, the fifteen minutes at the start of practice when the kickers, holders, snappers, and kick returners work on their individual crafts.

© NFL FILMS

Micah Knorr and I wait to shag punts. The former Broncos starter is signed to give Paul Ernster competition after Todd Sauerbrun's suspension, and he immediately takes me under his wing. Micah urges me to kick more, supports me when I fail, and stays after practice to work with me on technique.

© NFL FILMS

During Specialist period, Jason Elam points out that I'm swinging my leg across my body. I have difficulty shaking a lifetime of playing soccer, in which the kicking motion is like that of a windshield wiper. In placekicking, it should be like a pendulum: straight through after impact toward the goalposts. © NFL FILMS

Hanging out with the NFL's cool kids: the quarterbacks. From left, Jake Plummer, Jay Cutler, me, coach Pat McPherson, Bradlee Van Pelt, and Preston Parsons. © JOHN LEYBA

Redemption! Micah Knorr holds and Mike Shanahan watches as I get a second chance to prove myself in front of the team and the fans. On my first kick, I keep the nerves at bay until my foot grazes the ground and I send a line drive *beneath* the crossbar. When Shanahan gives me a second chance on my second chance (above), I make good.

© DON SCHWARTZ/DENVERBRONCOS.COM

I kick a field goal in the NFL. Quarterback Jake Plummer is the first Bronco to congratulate me when I make it from 28 yards, and he shakes me by the helmet with pride and joy. In a moment, the Broncos will lift me onto their shoulders.

© DON SCHWARTZ/DENVERBRONCOS.COM

Jason Elam looks on as I line up for my first attempt during warm-ups before our first preseason game at Ford Field in Detroit. Though everyone in the Broncos organization is willing to let me kick in an actual game, the NFL won't allow it. So I treat the pregame as my game. The glimmering uniforms, the cavernous stadium, the throbbing music— it's fantastically empowering. © NFL FILMS

Standing on the field as a player and not a reporter, I'm initially nervous. But I come to embrace the feeling of superiority: I'm playing while everyone else is watching. © NFL FILMS

Jason Elam—with assistant special-teams coach Thomas McGaughey—puts a whammy on me as I attempt a 30-yard field goal in Detroit. My form does improve during camp: better right leg drawback, a more upright body at impact, a follow-through more directly at the goalposts.
© NFL FILMS

Special-teams coach Ronnie Bradford and me on the field before the Detroit game. Ronnie and Thomas McGaughey treat me no differently from the other kickers—and they want me to succeed like the other kickers, too. Unlike some special-teams coaches, they also understand the nuances of kicking a football. © NFL FILMS

Broncos general manager Ted Sundquist, team owner Pat Bowlen, and their rookie kicker on the field in Detroit. Accessible, candid, and thoughtful, Sundquist and Bowlen instantly understand my desire to be both a writer and a player. © NFL FILMS

Hanging out on the sideline with Preston Parsons during our home game against the Tennessee Titans. With limited "reps" during camp, and as much playing time as me in the preseason, Preston grows increasingly despondent as the summer progresses. "I need something good to happen in my life," he says.

Chatting with Jake Plummer and Preston Parsons on the sideline during the Tennessee game. The starters play a limited amount in the preseason, and the games, naturally, lack the off-the-field intensity of the regular season. So once Jake's work is done he becomes a cheerleader and general goofball. During one game, he ambushes me with smelling salts. During another, he jaws back and forth with taunting fans. © JOHN LEYBA

Ultimately, I'm just another rookie. Carrying the orange K and P duffel bags loaded with footballs, tees, holders, and other kicking paraphernalia often falls to me. I'm happy to do it—to do anything, really, to be on the field. © NFL FILMS

me of the Looney Tunes cartoons in which a sheepdog and a wolf ask after each other's families and punch a time clock before spending the day sparring mercilessly over a flock of sheep. Fans would like to think that every player believes the guy across the line of scrimmage is his mortal enemy, the way we imagine it was in the mud-and-guts days of snarling legends like Dick Butkus and Ray Nitschke and Chuck Bednarik and Alex Karras. The NFL is no less violent than it was before the advent of a players' union and billion-dollar TV contracts and $15 million signing bonuses and bilateral postgame prayer sessions on the 50-yard line. If anything, the escalating size, speed, and strength of players—via natural and unnatural means—has made it more dangerous. But the game is surely sleeker, cleaner, more organized, more professional. Nothing is personal (usually); everything is just business.

The kickers, of course, have absolutely no reason to dislike one another. Apart from membership in the NFL's most alien subculture, opposing kickers are never on the field at the same time. The only game-related grudges I've heard involve home teams pretreating and then hoarding some of the "K balls" that kickers are required to use in games, giving the visitors rock-hard new ones. Gathered at midfield, we're like the geek table in the high-school cafeteria. No one else understands us. We're comfortable together. Jason, Paul, Micah, and I make small talk with Lions kicker Jason Hanson and punter Nick Harris. If I get in a game, Harris advises, "Kick it hard. Don't play it safe."

I tuck and smooth my game jersey, which flows nearly to my knees, and retie my pants and adjust the "Broncos Navy Blue" external socks—leggings that cover my knee-high whites—and tighten my Copas. Five minutes until kickers and punters and snappers are due on the field for actual warm-ups. "Wedding ring!" Mike Leach says. I didn't know I was supposed to take it off. "Don't want to get a fine out there!"

Compared to our cozy practice field, the 65,000-seat dome, as tall as a ten-story building, seems vast and borderless, the athletic equivalent of the New Mexico landscape Georgia O'Keeffe called "the faraway." As a reporter, I have always felt invisible standing on a pro sports team's playing surface. As one of the featured athletes, I feel conspicuous. I'm not here to watch but to be watched. I grab a few balls and the white PVC-pipe ball holder from the K bag on our sideline and set up from 25 yards. A ball boy in a royal blue vest emblazoned with the NFL shield shags for me. For the moment, he has no idea that I'm an interloper, and I savor the deception. I stare at the neon goalposts. They look indistinct, amorphous. I steady myself with practice swings, because everything's good when you're kicking air.

My first kick on an NFL field riffles the netting. Then I miss six of seven from 30 and 35 yards, spraying balls wide right. I'm suddenly aware of the clutches of fans taking their seats and wondering why that kicker can't make a 30-yarder. Then I turn around and see Jason behind me, beginning his warm-up routine with comfortable strokes from 39 yards. He loosens me up with a Todd Sauerbrun rock-star point. I don't need to worry about anyone seeing the fucking tape (even though an NFL Films cameraman is, in fact, recording me, so millions of people could wind up seeing the fucking tape). I set up another from 35, relax, and make it. I bang another one through from 35, with enough leg to be good from 40 or more. I high-five Jason and bop to the bass line thumping through the stadium and my body. I look around in giddy wonder. The players are right: This is fun.

Jason takes a tour of the field, the follow-up to the video of a season's worth of kicks here. He tries to imagine what the stadium will look and feel like once it is filled with fans. The natural light pouring through windows at the upper reaches of the four-year-old, half-billion-dollar building is another variable. Jason envisions the lighting after the sun goes down. Then he stands in different spots on the field identifying landmarks beyond the goalposts.

When Jason kicks, I kick, and the Lions' two kickers kick, too. Paul and Micah and the Detroit punters punt. Other groups of Broncos and Lions slowly begin populating the field. Within a half hour, it's a Busby Berkeley production in pads. Quarterbacks throw to receivers. Linebackers throw to one another. Linemen crash into one another. Defenders backpedal furiously and then stop suddenly. It seems faster than in camp, which is mostly an illusion. The exquisite surroundings, the skin-tight uniforms, the bright lights, the massing crowd, the overloud music: The artificial stimulation makes it hard not to be pumped up. As the chaos and the tension mount, my confidence grows. I'm less and less self-conscious. I chat up fans between kicks. I stroke another one that just clears from 35 yards.

"Nice form, though," a ball boy says.

16

The Gladiators March into Battle

Fuck the bullshit! Fuck the crowd! Fuck everybody!" Al Wilson screams when we gather in the far end zone before retreating to the locker room one last time. "Play football! Win on three!"

We count together: "One, two, three. WIN!"

The locker room is bursting with eighty-six players, eighty-one of them in uniform (including number 9, who isn't listed on the rosters distributed in the press box), and another forty or so coaches, trainers, and staff members. Excepting the sound of tape ripping and pads adjusting and cleats clacking to and from the urinals and stalls, though, it is silent. There are no exhortations or rah-rah speeches. Mike Shanahan stands passively in blue slacks, a Broncos golf shirt, and crosstrainers. Suddenly, he shouts, "Bring it up!" The players gather and drop to a knee. "We're coming here for one reason—to win the game," Shanahan says. He is so blasé that he could be ordering a sandwich. "Let's win it." Then he leads the team in the Lord's Prayer, which jars me. Only later do I discover it's a ritual that's been practiced for decades. Football is both church and state.

Four giant linemen—SAVE, PEARS, ENGELBERGER, GORDON, their jerseys read—are my blockers down the ramp. We stop en masse at the tunnel's end. Jake Plummer is at the head of the pack, squatting and stretching and slapping each player's hand as he passes by. Preston looks at me and taps his helmet. I need to put mine on. I toss an energy bar in a garbage can, drop my notebook and pen in my cap, and follow Preston. I high-five Domonique Foxworth. Chris Myers whacks me on the shoulder pads. I hop with childlike wonder amid the roiling bouillabaisse of boos and whistles and applause and cheers. Preston had said nothing compares to the adrenaline rush of running onto a professional football field. He wasn't kidding.

Every tension felt by every player since the start of camp rises like steam toward the stadium roof. On the sideline, Tom Nalen tries to slip a packet of smelling salts under my nose. The atmosphere is loose, almost casual. Yes, it's the preseason, so the pressure is a fraction of what it will be when the real games start in three weeks. More important, it's the first on-field release of the summer, the first time football can be a game again. Paul Ernster kicks off to the goal line and I rap him supportively on the shoulder pads afterward. My buddy Nate Jackson makes the tackle, the first official takedown of the Denver Broncos' 2006 season, and I congratulate him, too.

"It felt good. It felt real good," Nate exults on the sideline. "No more coaches yelling at you. Now you can just play."

Watching an NFL game from ground level is like watching a school of fish dart past in shallow waters. Movements that seemed visible and comprehensible in the controlled environment of camp are blurs now. And the absence of all-out hitting and tackling to the ground in practice— just once all summer—makes unrestrained blocking and tackling that much more dramatic. "Violent game, isn't it?" Mike Leach deadpans when running back Mike Bell gets pile-driven to the ground a few feet from where we're standing.

Leach is my sideline companion. Practicing with the tight ends, as he does, rather than hanging with the kickers all day, as a few long snappers do, gives the Broncos an emergency backup. It also helps him prepare for the contact he experiences on punts and kickoffs, when he has to rise from his bent-over position and stabilize himself so he isn't flattened by rushers trying to reach the kicker. But there's no confusing

Leach's job. His nickname is Snap and his golden retriever is named Snapper.

In college at William & Mary, Leach set school records for receptions by a tight end and for punting average. He made the Tennessee Titans as an undrafted tight end and backup punter. When he snapped a ball for fun one day, the special-teams coach said he had a better chance of making the league as a tight end who could snap than as a tight end who could punt.

Leach's snaps on placekicks invariably make three and a half revolutions; the extra half revolution allows the holder to bring the ball straight to the turf with the laces pointed directly at the goalposts, the way Jason and most kickers want them. On punts, Leach whizzes the ball at the punter's kicking hip. There are indeed stats for snappers: stopwatched times for snap to catch. Leach averages about 0.75 seconds on punts and about 0.45 seconds on field goals and extra points. One day in camp, he snapped a couple of punts to Paul Ernster in 0.64 seconds. "Way to go, Snapper! You are great! You make it easy for them!" he jokingly wrote on a printout of the kicks that I carried to a team meeting, where we sit next to each other every day. Another day, he wrote, "Maybe the best in the business! Can you say 'Pro Bowl'?"

Snapping looks simple—chuck it between your legs—but it's incredibly difficult, as I learn when I try it. Leach grabs the ball by the laces as if throwing it overhand. His nonthrowing, left, hand rests lightly on the ball as a guide. He whips the ball on a low diagonal to the target, then simultaneously lifts and pulls back his upper back to block. He practices by firing balls into tipped-over garbage cans. *Thwap, thwap, thwap.* During camp, the Broncos' coaches had a few players snap, to try to develop backups. Most guys just couldn't do it. Chad Mustard's snaps waddled weakly and awkwardly in the air, traveling nowhere near the requisite fifteen yards for a punt. After a few days, the experiment was abandoned.

NFL snappers have to be consistent first, and quick enough to block the usually bigger and faster guys who line up across from them. Leach often is one of the first Broncos downfield on punts, and he makes a handful of tackles every season. When he recovered a muffed punt against New England in the playoffs, his cell phone filled with congratulatory messages. In team meetings, when Leach appears on game film making a tackle, the quarterbacks snap their fingers. "My tackles are touchdowns," he told me one day. "If Jason kicks a game winner, I take a little pride in that."

That's plenty. At six foot two and a roundish 240 pounds, Leach realizes he's not designed to be a regular NFL tight end. But he's nearly indispensable as a long snapper. After a series of one-year contracts, the Broncos this past off-season offered him a four-year deal. The salaries all are at the veteran minimum—$585,000 this season, into the $700,000s and beyond after—but with a $300,000 signing bonus, his first as a veteran. "We said make it four hundred, a hundred a year. They said no. We said okay, we'll sign anyway. We didn't really play hardball."

Like kickers and punters, snappers can have long, prosperous, and relatively safe NFL careers. Coaches like Shanahan understand what Leach provides when the Broncos are down by two on the road with the clock ticking down and Jason lining up for a game-winning 42-yard field goal: security. Intellectually, Leach doesn't feel challenged by football— if he hadn't made the NFL, he planned to go to law school and maybe into federal law enforcement—but the financial security for his wife, Julie, and new son, Ryan, is terrific. He doubts he'll play deep into his thirties. When football is done, he'd like to be a stay-at-home dad while his wife pursues a career in college athletic administration. She's followed him for football. He'll take a turn as a trailing spouse.

Eight minutes into the Detroit game, when Plummer and the Broncos face a third down and 7 from our 32-yard line, Leach announces, "Let me snap a few."

"To who?" I say.

"You. All you have to do is catch it."

"Cool!"

Whenever the Broncos have a third down, Leach dons his helmet, grabs three balls and a snapping partner, sometimes the punter, sometimes an equipment guy or a ball boy. Until now, I've been roaming the sideline, patting guys on the shoulders as they come off the field, chatting with Nate and Micah and Preston. When Leach drafts me, I suddenly feel useful—not just part of the team but part of the game: Designated Sideline Snapper Warmer Upper! I'm nervous even for that, worrying that I'll fumble the ball onto the field. I stand fifteen yards behind Leach, bobble the first snap, and catch the second and third.

"Keep me off the field!" Leach shouts to Plummer. It's not that Leach doesn't want to play. It's that his entry into the game usually means the Broncos have failed: The offense has failed to make a first down and the team has to punt or try a field goal. In 2005, Denver punted seventy-three times and attempted thirty-two field goals and forty-four extra points. So 70 percent of Leach's snaps followed some type of failure.

Since it's almost impossible to decipher what's happening from the sideline, we watch the play on the gigantic video screens towering over the end zones. Jake completes a short pass to Stephen Alexander on the right side for eight yards and a first down.

"I owe S.A. five bucks," Leach says.

"Why?" Nate Jackson asks.

"Preseason first down, five bucks. Regular season, ten." It's Leach's thank-you for keeping him off the field.

The world of the game is divided into two realms: on the field and on the sideline. On the field, the players apply everything they've learned with passion and intensity. The consequences are too great not to. They exit to another dimension. On the sideline, when they need to, the players concentrate with deep conviction, as when they huddle around their coaches examining black-and-white still photos relayed to the field from video shot by two Broncos cameramen, one perched in a luxury box and the other high above an end zone. (Each play is numbered and inserted into a spiral binder, one binder per series.) Again, the consequences are too great if they don't. Off duty, though, the players are happy, loose, animated, irreverent. Kyle Johnson sees me taking notes. "The gladiators march into battle . . . ," he intones in the standard NFL Films voice of God. Kyle is being ironic: The NFL isn't the biblical confrontation the league wants fans to imagine. It's a game. The players take it profoundly seriously when they are engaged in it—it's their livelihood, after all— but also not that seriously at all.

Whenever the Broncos cross midfield, Jason puts on his helmet to prepare mentally and physically to kick. He spends the entire game pacing to keep active, jiggling his right leg intermittently as if a piece of paper were stuck to the bottom of his shoe. He doesn't take practice kicks into the stationary net on the sideline as other kickers do. In the second quarter, Jason makes field goals of 36 and 35 yards. They're kicks I conceivably could attempt in an actual game, but watching the Lions go after the snapped ball like a pack of cheetahs chasing a wildebeest makes me for the first time seriously consider the inherent, if remote, danger in what kickers do. I consider the fear, and then dismiss it. I'd gladly have trotted out there in Jason's stead.

Paul Ernster punts and kicks off credibly, improving his chances of replacing Todd for the first four games of the season, and possibly longer. He has one amusing screwup, though. In the third quarter, after Jay Cutler's first NFL touchdown pass, the ball falls off the tee just as Paul is about to kick it. Shanahan chides him. "You've got to see that and stop," he says. "You've got to be like Tiger Woods and stop." Paul tells me he saw the ball listing but couldn't halt his momentum. "I was like, 'Oh, fuck, *this* isn't good.'"

Jake Plummer's day is done after throwing four passes, completing three, and handing off the ball five times. He spends the rest of the game alternately encouraging Cutler and Bradlee Van Pelt, who split the last three quarters, and goofing around on the sideline. He and S.A. succeed in ambushing me with smelling salts, filling my nose, eyes, ears, mouth, and lungs with a clarity-inducing shudder of ammonia. Another moment, Jake gives me a hard time for wearing my cleats. "I'll kick farther than you with my left foot," he says when I challenge him to a contest. "You're dealing with an *ath*-lete here." Between the third and fourth quarters, Jake sits alone on the metal bench bopping and singing to Kim Wilde's 1981 hit "Kids in America," which reverberates through the dome. Nate Jackson looks over and laughs. "What a retard," he says.

Bradlee's evolving breakdown continues. Over two possessions, he is sacked four times in a row and then throws an interception. Preston watches with folded arms, knowing he won't play no matter how poorly Bradlee does. The first sack occurs on a three-step drop—three quick steps back from the center and an immediate throw, usually just a few yards downfield. "You should never get sacked on a three-step drop," Preston says. On the second sack, Bradlee is indecisive about where to throw. "He's got to let it go," Preston says. Despite Bradlee's performance, here and in camp, Preston has been increasingly discouraged about his own chances of making the roster.

"I need something good to happen in my life," he says.

"Maybe it just did," I say after Bradlee's interception.

Preston shakes his head. He knows from experience that Bradlee won't be benched, not in the preseason. "Coaches want a guy to do well," he says. Their time, effort, judgment, ability, and reputations are wrapped up in Bradlee's performance. The game ends with a delay-of-game penalty by Bradlee and an incomplete pass into the end zone that would have brought the Broncos to within a point. (Shanahan would have attempted a two-point conversion to win or lose the game outright; no one wants to play overtime in the preseason.) We lose, 20–13.

On the bus to the airport, a media intern hands out cans of Bud Light. Most players, though, swig Gatorade or water and eat the boxed dinners—sandwich, apple, mini Snickers bars—that we grabbed from a cart outside the locker room. We board the 767-300 well after midnight. Flight attendants carry trays of beer down the aisles, and now more players partake. Preston had a few beers on the bus and has a few more on the plane. "I've never heard of any other team in the NFL that would allow that," he says. "It's awesome."

The mood is boisterous but by no means out of control. The five-foot-eight cornerback Darrent Williams—whom I sought out on the sideline because he made me appear normal sized—says it won't be as relaxed during the regular season. Players gamble on video poker, watch movies, talk trash. No one buckles up, stows his tray table, or puts his seat in the upright and locked position. Preston, Chad, and I play Scrabble on my laptop. When Chad finds DETAINEE on a triple-word-score line, we bump fists. Ian Gold hands out slices of a delicious homemade cake his mother gave him at the game to Preston, Paul Ernster, and me— white guys alls. From a couple of rows back, Domonique Foxworth asks, "Aren't the coloreds allowed to have any?"

We pull into the facility at 2 a.m. Denver time, 4 a.m. in Detroit. An elderly woman bedecked in orange clothing nicknamed Bronco Betty waits by the entrance to the players' parking lot, as she does after every road game, regardless of time or weather. We get back to the Holiday Inn at 2:20. Since we lost, we have to run and lift between noon and 4 p.m.

Because they need to say something, the morning papers make Jay Cutler the story of the game. "Nothing against Jake Plummer," Mike Klis begins his account in the *Denver Post,* saying that Jake played well in his one-drive night. "But explain again why the kid isn't supposed to play much this year? If Jay Cutler represents the future, then the Broncos have no choice but to deal with a quarterback dilemma in the present."

Cutler told reporters that one preseason game doesn't mean much, that the Broncos used a basic offense, that the Lions used simple defenses, that plenty of quarterbacks could have moved the ball the way he did. No matter. Completing 16 of 22 passes for 192 yards is "sure to get Broncoland yakking," Klis writes. His reporting is normally fair and balanced and he has a gentle touch with words. But here he asks "whether Broncos fans [will] begin applying pressure to open up the competition for the No. 1 quarterback." His counterpart at the *Rocky Mountain News* plays it straighter, writing that Cutler might someday be good. But a cartoon in that paper depicts a scruffy Plummer spotting

Cutler in his Honda Element's side-view mirror, which reads, "OB-JECTS IN MIRROR MAY BE CLOSER THAN THEY APPEAR."

Not that anyone disputes Cutler's fine debut. "The good news is that number six was—*pfft*—off the charts," Pat Bowlen says, pushing a hand skyward like Kramer on *Seinfeld,* when I see him in the afternoon. Shanahan is impressed, too. The rookie's performance validates the decision to promote him to number two. But no one foresees a quarterback battle. The media have no insight into Plummer's state of mind or Shanahan's interpretation of it or even the frame-by-frame analysis of Cutler's progress. Passively deploying nothing-againsts and whethers and sure-tos only confirms the stereotype of Denver impatiently waiting for its quarterback Godot. I like Mike Klis, and he might prove correct, but his story is the sort of verbal lighter fluid that makes Shanahan dislike the local media.

In reality, the quarterback most affected by the game is Bradlee, who, unsurprisingly, doesn't handle the aftermath well. "I was trying to find something that wasn't there," he tells the editor of the Broncos' Web site. "Maybe I was seeing things that weren't there. I don't know. I don't think I've ever felt that way coming off a football field." He tells another reporter, "It was almost like it wasn't meant to be complete. . . . Half slow motion, half I don't know what."

After the game, Bradlee went to sleep at 3:15 and woke at 7. He took a drive in the country in his Porsche and had breakfast with his brother. When I find him in the weight room, he's watching a local-television replay of the game on a small screen attached to a stationary bike. He's already studied on the team film the "reads" made by all of the quarterbacks, where they looked and threw the ball. The review made him less depressed. "It wasn't as bad as I thought," he tells me. "It was small stuff." He "busted one read" because he didn't roll out when he should have. On two others, the primary receivers weren't where they were supposed to be. On the sack on the three-step drop that Preston criticized in real time, Bradlee says he failed to "check wide," or dump the ball off to the tailback. He led a seventeen-play drive to end the game, which was good, but failed to score, which wasn't. And he took the delay-of-game penalty because he was slow calling an audible, switching the play at the line of scrimmage, to counter a perceived blitz. "For some reason I didn't look at the play clock. My fault."

A *Post* columnist suggests that the Broncos make Bradlee a defensive back. Despite his summer of woe, Bradlee remains determined, stubbornly perhaps, to prove that a strong, mobile, nontraditional quarterback who, in only his third season, is still learning the basics of the position can eventually start in the NFL. He considers his evolution a matter of time, more reps and more games. Lots of great quarterbacks, he says, are given time to work through their problems. "You have guys that have never played a lick who assume because I got bumped to number three I'm a failure," he says of the newspaper piece. "It does get to me. So you're out there judging me on two throws. Fucking idiot."

The Detroit game demonstrated that Bradlee isn't yet comfortable doing what a starter needs to do: decode the defensive formation while preparing to receive the ball from the center and then adjust strategy accordingly. But it also indicated that the Broncos aren't interested in helping him do that. On the game-ending drive, Bradlee handed off twelve times in seventeen plays. His education as a quarterback was less important than seeing whether a backup running back could carry the ball downfield. Shanahan's conservative play calling let the clock run down on the game and, metaphorically, on Bradlee.

17

How Far Was That?

The end of training camp means the end of two-a-day practices and the start of a schedule more closely resembling the regular season's: meetings in the morning, practice in the afternoon, weight lifting and more meetings after practice, dismissal before dinner, two days off a week. We're finally and fully inured to the monotony—Todd's swapping *Saved by the Bell* trivia with an offensive lineman? What's so strange about that?—just as it's about to end. The transition from summer to fall is palpable. The players complain a little less. The stress of doing well in games mitigates the stress of doing well in practice. Even the temperature falls and a just-so morning breeze cools the field, as if Mike Shanahan controls the weather, too.

In the no-man's-land between the offense and defense fields, we make small talk, in this moment about high-definition television. Jason asks if it's worth it, and I'm stunned that he doesn't have at least one high-def set. "Imagine if *Saved by the Bell* was in HD," Todd says, smiling. The conversation turns to kickers hitting or getting hit. Todd recounts last season's playoff game versus New England, when he launched himself at a Patriots kickoff returner, forcing a fumble that was recovered by Denver. Jason didn't see the play and, when Todd came to the sideline, asked him what happened. "I dropped him, bro'," Todd recalls saying, now in a deadpan that cracks everyone up.

Then Todd relates an opposite experience. In the 2001 preseason, when he was with Carolina, he was blindsided on a punt return in front of the Baltimore bench. The Ravens exploded in celebration. "Deion was doing his little dance," Todd says, and he mimics defensive back Deion Sanders's signature juking motion, two hops on one foot, two on the other.

"Your helmet was still on?" Micah asks.

"Hell no!" Todd says. "I think one of the cheerleaders handed it to me." Todd mimics the hit. "Todd! Look out!" he shouts, remembering a teammate's admonition. Then, *boom!* Todd leaps backward with arms flailing, falls down, rolls over backward, and then jumps up, tugging on his jersey and looking around nonchalantly.

Jason goes next. He describes the lone 15-yard penalty of his career. In 1995, his third season, Jason tried to break up a fight after an extra point. A gigantic Cardinals lineman swatted Jason away like a kid brother. Jason instinctively swung at the guy. At which point an Arizona cornerback named Lorenzo Lynch grabbed Jason by the facemask and flung him aside. Jason's helmet spun around on his head. "I looked like *The Exorcist,*" he says.

Jason can throw a football fifty yards. In high school, he ran a fast 100-yard dash. But never in his career has he had to throw or run the ball. Jason looks at me as if I have never seen a game of American football, let alone met his head coach, when I ask the last time Shanahan ordered a fake field goal. "The Nixon administration," he says. When someone says we should postpone fake-field-goal practice on this morning because the NFL Network is filming at camp, Jason chuckles.

Other teams practice field-goal gimmickry and gimcrackery with regularity. Not the Broncos. Fakes are on the practice docket just twice, for five minutes apiece. I stand with Shanahan watching Jason take a direct snap from Mike Leach and throw the ball to a receiver peeling off the line of scrimmage. On another fake, called Rainbow Right, Plummer receives the snap and tosses the ball blindly backward over his head. Jason catches it on the run and hightails it toward the right corner of the end zone.

"Might have to put that one in!" Shanahan shouts. Then he says to me quietly, with more than a bit of sarcasm. "That'll scare 'em."

"That'll scare Jason," I reply.

Shanahan doesn't invite me to take a flip, so I head to the offense field to kick. I'm fully Flexalled, wrapped, stretched, and loosened. Ready to go. R.B., T-Mac, Paul, and Jason offer a batch of advice: Don't swat the ball, swing through it. Get your shoulders over the ball at impact. Follow through straight, not to the left. I hit one with a bass-drum resonance from 28 yards. "Listen to the coach," T-Mac says. "Imagine that."

To simulate the noise and pressure of actual kicks, the group stands close by and heckles me while I line up and go. Thud, thud, thud: three good ones in a row.

"Now, stop," T-Mac advises.

"Don't want to go for five in a row?" R.B. asks.

Nope. I just want to prepare for another summons from Shanahan, to be ready as if the practice fields were ringed by seventy-five thousand Broncomaniacs. But, once again, the call doesn't come. I glumly unsnap my chinstrap and trot to the center of the field for Shanahan's ritual postpractice analysis.

"I think we're feeling sorry for ourselves," he says, and for once his lecture applies to me. "We do that, we're going to get our asses kicked."

I don't want to get my ass kicked! I just want to kick again!

"You either get better or you get worse. We got worse."

No! I've got better, Coach! Let me prove it! Forget about these other guys! I was ready, Coach! I just needed a chance!

There have been no fights in camp, on or off the field. Then I look up while getting dressed after a morning practice and see two wide receivers shouting at each other. One is a third-year player named David Kircus, a small-college star who played sparingly for Detroit in 2003 and 2004 but was out of football in 2005. The other is David Terrell, a University of Michigan All-American who was the eighth pick of the 2001 draft by Chicago but whose career hasn't taken off. Kircus, who lockers to my immediate right, is white, the only white wide receiver in camp, and is known around the locker room for the media's infatuation with the fact that he worked at a Subway after he was cut by the Lions, for a cockiness that borders on arrogance, and for his metrosexuality. Terrell, who is black, is known for his motor mouth and the reputation that followed him from Chicago, where he boasted incessantly about his talent, raised both middle fingers to home fans, and, after his infrequent touchdowns, punted the ball into the stands and pantomimed counting money or driving a car.

The Broncos are typical of most NFL teams. Two-thirds of the players in training camp are African American. The coaching staff is typical, too. Seven of Shanahan's twenty-one assistants (including the strength coaches) are black. The highest-ranking minorities are position coaches: Ronnie Bradford on the special teams, Bobby Turner with the running backs, Andre Patterson with the defensive tackles, and Jacob Burney with the defensive ends. None of the football front-office executives are black.

In 1946, while Jackie Robinson was still apprenticing in baseball's minor leagues, the NFL integrated—reintegrated, actually, as a few black men had played for teams in the league's early years. The transformation from an all-white to a black-dominated league was slow, but it was aided by Vince Lombardi and Paul Brown, who cared more about winning than about skin color or ethnicity. "If I ever hear nigger or dago or kike or anything like that around here, regardless of who you are, you're through with me," Lombardi told the Packers in 1959, his first season. "You can't play for me if you have any kind of prejudice."

By the early 1960s, most NFL teams had six or seven African American players. (One team had none: the Redskins, whose owner, George Preston Marshall, famously said, "We'll start signing Negroes when the Harlem Globetrotters start signing whites.") The hipper and culturally more progressive AFL was integrated more heavily than the NFL. In 1968, the Broncos became the first modern pro team to start a black quarterback, Marlin Briscoe. Briscoe set a record for touchdown passes by a rookie. The next year he was told that he was too short to play quarterback. Briscoe believed he was too black, and asked for his release.

In today's NFL, there are clear racial divisions by position: all four Broncos quarterbacks are white, as are all of the tight ends and most of the offensive linemen. Apart from veteran safety John Lynch and defensive end John Engelberger, the defense is entirely black. The kickers are white, though both of our full-time coaches, R.B. and T-Mac, are black. Apart from one eye-rolling complaint by a white player about hip-hop music dominating the locker room because the stereo is located near the defensive linemen, I hear no comments about race. One day, defensive back Nick Ferguson shows me his iTunes playlist, which includes LL Cool J, Cam'ron, Lil Bow Wow, and Jay-Z, but also The Cure, Tom Jones's "What's New, Pussycat?" and "(Don't Fear) the Reaper" by Blue Öyster Cult. "You cannot stereotype," Nick says.

The desert-island environment of the locker room—the players isolated against the forces of the coaching staff and management—and the largely postrace environment of American team sports minimize the potential for conflict. Coaches like Shanahan are long past needing to remind players that prejudice is intolerable. So it's easy to forget that the subtext of race persists. When it reveals itself, it's jarring.

Whether the spat between Kircus and Terrell is fueled by personal animus or end-of-camp nerves—with a glut of receivers, neither player is guaranteed a roster spot—the two go at it at high volume in front of Terrell's locker. The dispute centers on who's better, and it apparently was triggered in a practice huddle when both insisted on being the primary receiver on a particular route. "If I stopped playing right now," Terrell shouts, "more people will remember me than will ever know you." Then he drops a W-bomb. Kircus, Terrell says, is "getting the white privilege" in practice, meaning that more balls are being thrown to him because he's white. It's an explosive remark, implicating the coaches and quarterbacks in a racist passing conspiracy. "Yeah, like I got the white privilege in Detroit," Kircus responds. "I got five balls." (Actually, he caught six passes in twelve games over two seasons.)

The locker room falls silent. This isn't just unusual; it's comet-passing-near-the-earth rare. After the pissing match ends—badly, with Terrell refusing to shake Kircus's outstretched hand—Kyle Johnson explains to me that personal attacks violate an unwritten locker-room code. In private, with friends on the team, players constantly compare themselves to each other. But to disparage a player's ability to his face? Not only is it uncool, it's karmically perilous. The clash exposes the fault lines—racial, personal, competitive—lying just below the locker-room carpet.

As with any large group of employees forced to work in the same office, cliques form. Considering how much time football players spend clustered on the field and in meeting rooms, groups are determined as much by position as by race or alma mater or hometown. Players instinctively defend their peers. This becomes clear a couple of practices later, when Kircus is involved in a second fight. He lines up for a play and begins trash-talking the two defensive backs covering him, Domonique Foxworth and Curome Cox. "All right, all right," Kircus says aggressively. Translation: Here I come, get ready, bring it on.

"He said, 'All right'!" barks a safety named Hamza Abdullah, who is standing on the sideline nearby with the other defensive backs and me.

"I'd like salami on this one!" John Lynch shouts at the former sandwich maker.

After hundreds of drills during camp, it's clear the defensive backs don't like Kircus. Foxworth and Cox shove him to the ground and he shoves back. On the ensuing play, as soon as the ball is snapped, Cox and Kircus tangle. Kircus thrusts his hands under Cox's facemask, and the defender's helmet flies off. Foxworth head-butts Kircus, plastic on plastic. The players swing at each other before whistles blow and they are separated.

The receivers come to Kircus's defense. "He swung on your bitch ass!" one of them, Todd Devoe, shouts at Cox. "Knocked your helmet off!" Cox replies: "Guess you didn't see the first one!" On the next play, Kircus lines up on the far side of the field. "Sent you to Quiznos for this one!" Lynch shouts with a smile.

The only person unamused by the altercation is Shanahan. "I've never seen a guy get hurt in pads," he tells us after practice. But it's not about injury, he says. "Nobody is bigger than the team." Shanahan singles out Foxworth, saying that in a game his actions would have merited a 15-yard penalty, dumb and against the interests of the collective. "We're doing what's best for the team," Shanahan says. "The teams that can't keep their composure can't win in this league."

When Shanahan finishes, Nick Ferguson grabs me by the jersey and tugs me close. "See, it's mental," he says entirely seriously, linking this episode to my own kicks. "Keep your composure. It's all mental."

Ferguson, aka Niko, is a garrulous thirty-one-year-old safety with saucers for eyes and a smile as wide as Cheshire cat's. The third of eleven children, he grew up in the Scott Projects in Miami's rough Liberty City neighborhood, which his teammates have dubbed Beirut. His father is a longshoreman. Niko earned admission to Morris Brown, a small, predominantly black college in Atlanta, on his own—not because of football—and transferred, on his own again, to Georgia Tech, where he walked on to the team. Whatever expenses financial aid didn't cover, Niko did. He wasn't drafted by the NFL. He played three seasons in Saskatchewan and Winnipeg. He went back to Georgia Tech and received his bachelor's degree in management last year.

Foxworth, aka Foxy, is a twenty-three-year-old cornerback whose path was more privileged than his teammate's. He grew up in a middle-class suburb of Baltimore. His parents own a consulting business. He was a top high-school prospect who produced his own brochure for recruiters and received scholarship offers from more than a dozen Division I schools. He chose the University of Maryland, excelled on the field and in the classroom, and was drafted by the Broncos in the third round in 2005. As a rookie, he wrote a weekly journal for the *Denver Post,* then collected the articles in a short book, *On the Island.* In the off-season, he completed an NFL-sponsored program at Harvard Business School.

To most fans, a defensive back is a defensive back: The cornerback covers the wide receivers, and the safety helps him out. Foxy's job meets that description. But Niko's portfolio is much broader. He calls the safety a cross between a cornerback and a linebacker. His assignment depends on what a tight end does, what a running back does, what a wide receiver does—and then he has to process their movements and make a decision about where to run, all in the three seconds or so the typical play takes. Ultimately, he winds up hitting someone with or near the ball. "My position is like a car wreck every play," Niko says.

Despite their differences, Niko and Foxy have similar goals: to be decent people, set positive examples, take as much as they can from the sport, and change or correct the media's depiction—and the public's perception—of football players and of black athletes. That's what we talk about one afternoon. Niko is wearing a color-coordinated light-blue-and-white outfit: oversize Roca Wear cap, Nike T-shirt, and Nike sneakers. Foxy has on a stylish bowling shirt. Niko is five foot eleven and 200 pounds, with a jutting jaw and a goatee. Foxy also is five foot eleven, but just 180 pounds, with a baby face and a narrow build. I start by asking them what the media don't understand. Foxy picks up my tape recorder.

"Everything," he says slowly. "They're quick to blame somebody. They want to say this play was his fault. But if you're not in our meetings and you don't know the scheme of our defense, it's almost laughable. You have no idea. It should be considered entertainment. They should put a disclaimer before any football-related show saying, 'This is just entertainment. This is not fact.' They're just saying whatever the hell they want."

"It's just all opinion," Niko adds.

Even when ex-NFL guys are talking? I ask.

"They're some of the worst!" Foxy says.

"They are the guys that actually know what goes into a daily routine," Niko observes. "To me, it's their transition to being the media. There's always a sense of good cop, bad cop—and I'm not a media basher."

The problem, though, they assert, is bigger than a blowhard ex–wide receiver assuming an unknowable about a particular play. By spending so much time discussing, in Niko's words, "guys who do ignorant things," the media perpetuate the portrait of the reckless, privileged athlete. And by spending so much time discussing sports period, society makes the careers more alluring than they should be. Foxy recalls visiting a public-housing complex in Washington during college. He asked a group of boys what they wanted to be. All but one answered basketball player, football player, or rapper.

"Those are the types of stereotypes I'm trying to buck," says Foxy, who works with a local group that helps underprivileged kids go to college and envisions running an inner-city nonprofit someday. "Whenever I do an interview, I go out of my way to try to use big words. It sounds stupid. But I'm educated and I want people to know that. And I want to come across as such: I'm not what you think." When the *Post* contacted him about keeping the journal, it offered to have a reporter interview him and write it. Foxy said he would write it himself.

During stretch, Niko sits as close as possible to the fans, and I hear him banter and laugh with the crowd every day. Growing up in Miami, Niko remembers seeing Dolphins quarterback legend Dan Marino turn away autograph seekers. He promised himself that if he was in a position where people wanted him to write his name on a piece of paper, he would happily comply.

Both players know their careers could end this afternoon. Foxy says he has about $300,000 in the bank, which he realizes won't last a lifetime. In his six NFL seasons, Niko has never made more than the minimum salary, which isn't minimum wage but still can find a way of disappearing fast. They know that they could wind up on easy street, or not.

"All you need is five million dollars and you could live your life forever," Foxy says, "as long as you put it in the right place, you don't buy a Bentley—a Bentley and four cribs."

"And a couple of baby mamas," Niko adds.

"And some baby mamas and you're broke," Foxy finishes.

"The mentality when you come from nothing is as soon as you get it you spend it," Niko says, turning serious. "For me, it's the opposite. My parents didn't teach me how to save money."

"No money to save in Beirut!" Foxy proclaims. "They were saving pinto beans! Curled up on the dirt floors! 'Get away from my beans!'"

Niko ignores Foxy's banter. "You only play this game for a short period of time," he says. "There's so much that goes into guys' salaries. People look at *USA Today* and see our salaries. They say, 'These guys are rich.' You've got taxes, you've got lawyer's fees, you've got agent's fees. There's life after football."

"A lot of it, I hope," Foxy says.

I tell them I'm not hearing the same frustration with and ambivalence about football that I've heard from other Broncos. They seem to be the antidote to Bradlee's overthinking anguish or Preston's disillusionment. The defensive backs recognize the reality of the game, the pressure and risk, and they still love it. They attribute that partly to the amiable style of their position coach, Bob Slowik, a preternaturally youthful fifty-two-year-old who's been coaching since 1978. At the same time, they believe they've figured out the secret to coping in the NFL: Accept your place and capitalize on it.

"We're just drones," Foxy says. "I'm not a decision maker. I try to always remember that in comparison to everything else that's going on in this huge company, we're at the bottom of it."

"Bottom of the food chain, baby," Niko adds.

"We are the janitors of the NFL," says Foxy.

"You are the most dispensable and replaceable people in this sport," I offer.

"We are," Foxy replies. "And they treat us that way."

"But in exchange for being expendable," I say, "we'll give you half a million dollars this year."

"You may not get it next year!" Foxy says.

"You have to milk it for whatever it's worth, man," Niko adds.

"Trying to get it all," Foxy says. "I'm trying to get it all."

"When it's done . . . ," Niko says.

"It's done," Foxy finishes. "I don't want to coach. I don't want to do player personnel. I don't want to sell tickets."

"Foxy, you could own your own team, bro."

"I'm not going to work my way to owning it. I'm just going to come in and buy the whole damn thing and tell everyone to get the hell out. We're wearing pink jerseys and everyone have fun. Who cares how many games we win or lose? Just have a good time."

Preston Parsons and Bradlee Van Pelt spend the week quarterbacking the "scout team," preparing the starting defense for the next preseason opponent, the Tennessee Titans. This gives Preston a few more live snaps than earlier in camp. With Cutler the lock backup, and Bradlee in his own emotional doghouse, Preston should be optimistic. But he can't help thinking that no matter how many scout-team reps he accumulates, he can't catch up, can't convince Shanahan he should be on the fifty-three-man. I watch Preston run a couple of plays before the double horn sounds ending a practice. He squats and stays there, as if he can't believe that, to quote *Madeline*, that's all there is, there isn't any more.

After Detroit, Preston was sure things would change. But as the week progresses, it becomes clear he won't play against Tennessee, either. Preston's father, a former staff sergeant in Vietnam, thinks he should walk into Shanahan's office and demand to play. Preston does consider taking the bold, for football, step of asking Shanahan about his status. "Sitting here having to listen to these guys dictate the rest of your career pisses me off even more," Preston says. "They hold my career and basically my life in the palm of their hands. Right now, they're not opening up that palm, not letting me do anything."

Preston realizes he may not like what he hears, but at least he would get some clarity. He runs the idea by Mike Heimerdinger. Dinger says that approaching Shanahan would send the message that Preston isn't here to help the team. But he tells him he shouldn't worry. "You're competing for the spot without even knowing it," he says. "You're in a better position than you know."

The coaches, Dinger volunteers, are growing annoyed with Bradlee's endless questions, his smart-ass comments in meetings, his lack of respect for quarterbacks coach Pat McPherson. "You guys don't think we notice that stuff, but we do," Dinger tells him. Bradlee's performance on the field isn't helping. The coaches, Dinger says, are considering keeping a third quarterback, either on the active roster or on the practice squad. Preston is eligible for the practice squad. Bradlee isn't.

Preston has the ability and the arm strength, Dinger tells him. The problem is that Preston has taken only twenty or so throws during team drills so far in camp. That's more than some number four quarterbacks get, but it doesn't leave the staff confident Preston can execute the playbook in an emergency. For instance, Dinger mentions a single mistake a week ago, when Preston made a read to the wrong side of the field. In any event, Dinger says, Preston should just keep showing up and playing well when asked to play.

"I've never felt like this. It's hurting my heart. It's giving me ulcers," Preston says. It's not like his rookie or second seasons, when he was playing for fun. And it's not as if he once enjoyed a life-altering payday like his drinking buddy Jay Cutler, who this week is closing on a nine-thousand-square-foot, $1.3 million house to go with his downtown condo. Preston needs a steady income, health insurance, confidence that he can start a family. "It's like, give me a job."

During warm-ups for FG—we're doing the Down by Two drill, in which the offense has to get into field-goal position in a minute or two—Jason grimaces after a kick and grabs his left calf. I have done my full preparatory routine and then some, biking with Jason in the weight room and subjecting myself to the groin-stretching machine. (I can now spread 'em to 110 degrees, closing in on Jason's 125.) Jason says the calf hurts when he pushes off to start his approach to the ball. "You can hear it when he kicks," Micah says. The sound of Jason's foot hitting the ball is weaker, softer, duller, less authoritative. And the ball itself doesn't travel as high as usual, about halfway up the goalposts rather than the usual three-quarters or more. The plant leg is important.

I'm hoping Jason will tell Shanahan that he can't kick today so I can step in. But he doesn't. Even though he has no competition in camp, even though his spot on the team is guaranteed, even though his leg hurts and he probably shouldn't risk even a few easy kicks, Jason plays. And, naturally, he goes three-for-three in the drill, the longest from 49 yards. The Broncos win in the closing seconds, no thanks to me.

I'm convinced that Shanahan is done with me, that in his eyes my experience is complete. I felt the low of failure and the high of success. And I provided a camp diversion. With the season closing in, the players don't need another thirty-minute break from meetings. They don't need amusement. They need another warning that few jobs are safe. "We're not really sure who our fifty-three are," Shanahan says at the end of a morning session. What separates players from having jobs and having to look for jobs are missed blocking assignments, hustle on special teams, running the correct routes. "Doing the little things right," Shanahan says reflexively.

I may be through in camp, but I'm not willing to concede kicking in a preseason game. I raise the subject casually with Shanahan when I join him, Dinger, Bob Slowik, and their wives around a cocktail table at a bowling alley during another team outing. Shanahan surprises me by saying he'd be fine with it. "Shit," he tells the group, "I can't believe they let him dress out," referring to the starched shirts at NFL headquarters who allowed me to stand in uniform on the sideline during the Detroit game. It's possible that Shanahan's answer is influenced by the gin and tonic or two that he's had at the Arapahoe Bowling Center. But I think not. I think he's recognized how hard I've tried in camp and how the players have accepted me. Maybe he's even seen me make a 40-yarder. Maybe not. But I think I've earned Shanahan's respect, as a reporter and a kicker.

Armed with the endorsement, I again call NFL PR guy Brian McCarthy. Brian says he spoke with Joel Bussert, the official who authorized me to dress in Detroit. Brian's more-detailed answer now concerns the apparent sanctity of preseason games. "People are paying seventy, ninety, a hundred twenty dollars, and then having someone from off the street come in—it could have the appearance of an exhibition, which we fight," he tells me. "I wouldn't use the word joke, but . . ."

I *would* use the word joke—not to describe me but the fraud the NFL perpetrates on fans who are forced to buy tickets to these games, in which winning is neither everything nor the only thing. My participation would be as serious as, and possibly more entertaining than, anything else that will happen during our home game against Tennessee the following Saturday night. I politely explain my thinking to Brian, but also know that I'm wasting breath.

Solidarnosc, I want to tell my teammates. The NFL is indeed The Man. Joke? You know what's a joke? The Vikings wide receiver who this week led cops on a hundred-mile-an-hour car chase—while legally drunk. That's a joke. The parade of Bengals in handcuffs, seven in the last two months. That's a joke with multiple laugh lines. The twenty-two arrests of NFL players so far this year for everything from spousal battery to firearms possession to grand theft to boating under the influence. Hysterical. Me kicking an extra point or a short field goal in an exhibition game after working assiduously for months to prepare for the moment? That wouldn't be a joke at all.

The rejection means that, like Bradlee and Preston and so many other players, I also get to experience the heartless reality of an uncaring business: I'm good enough, goddamn it, but the system won't let me show it. I have an impulse to shut it down for good, to pack my cleats and notebooks and go home to start writing, as Plimpton did a lifetime ago after the NFL rejected his pleas to face players modeling different helmet decals. Instead, I decide that I won't be an NFL player much longer, so I might as well kick as much as I can.

In the training room, Jason lies on his stomach, a laser attached to his calf to circulate blood, reading *The Copper Scroll,* a messianic thriller by conservative Republican and best-selling author Joel C. Rosenberg, one of Jason's favorite writers. I lube up, wrap my hip and thigh, and head outside early. Micah practices drops. Paul stretches. Before I see the ball boys cavorting on the far field, I hear their voices full of happy innocence. I kick, watch practice, and head to the far end of the offense field, where our cabal gathers. Everyone's work is done, so the final forty-five minutes of practice involve standing around bullshitting. I peel off from the group, pull a white holder and a bunch of balls from the K bag, and drop them in the center of the field around the 20-yard line.

The goalposts are less than 15 yards from a high stucco wall in front of the visitors' parking lot at the front of the complex. There's no net. Jason has spiderwebbed many a windshield here. No one has noticed me slip away. My first ball, from 30 yards, hits the base of the wall after easily clearing the crossbar. I move the holder back two yards and calmly set up another ball, tilting it ever so slightly forward and to the right. Good from 32. I back up two more yards. Boom. Another effortless kick. Still no one has noticed, and I feel no urgency to alert them. I hear R.B., T-Mac, Paul, Micah, and Jeff Hays talking about colleges. Jeff's daughter wants to go to Colorado State or a school in Texas.

"Go to a real school!" I call over jokingly.

"Who'd want to go to Penn?" Jeff says. "Is that in the Ivy League?"

I return to my kicking zone. But I have their attention now. I move back three more yards and set up, 37 yards from success. One, two, three smooth steps back. Stop, examine target. One, two smooth steps to the left. Exhale, exhale. Focus on a spot on the pebbled leather. Exhale. Explode like a sprinter from the starting blocks. Jab step, right, left, heel to butt, rotate hips, snap down, left arm over. Grunt. Finish tall and toward the target.

Good. Again. Comfortably.

"Whoa!" R.B. says.

"Where'd that come from?" T-Mac exclaims. "Move it back!"

I pace off three more yards. Forty yards has been my outer limit all summer—I've kicked a few from there that were certainly good from 45, but in games no one measures a kick's total distance, just how far it is from the spot of the ball to the back of the end zone. I set the ball down behind the white stripe of the 30-yard line. In a game, this would be recorded as a 40-yard field goal. To me, it's 40-plus.

If I had kicked like this all summer, no one would have mocked. If I had converted just one in front of the team as authoritatively as any of the last four, I might have persuaded Ted Sundquist to sign me to a real contract for a preseason game, obviating the need to seek permission from the rulebook drones on Park Avenue. If I'd had this much leg strength every day in camp—I feel nothing, no pain in my left hip flexor, no tautness in my right groin, no crunching or popping in my left knee—I wouldn't have had to search for confidence like a blind man groping for the corner of a round room.

I absolutely scorch the football. I spy it in midflight and, as it rotates end over end in a spectacular parabola, observe it with detached wonder. If I have created anything in physical space more beautiful, I'm not sure what it is. The ball seems to hang in the sky like . . . like . . . like one of Jason's kicks, scaled to match my accumulated kicking knowledge and ability. Perfect, for me. The ball descends sweetly and thumps the ground well beyond the crossbar, near the wall. It bounces a couple of times, rolls a little, and stops. It might not have been good from 50, but it traveled 50 on the fly.

"Whoo-*hoooo!*" I shout, high-fiving T-Mac, Paul, R.B., Micah, and Jeff in succession.

Todd and Jason walk over from the sideline.

"How far was that?" Todd asks. There's no sneer on his face. There's no edge to his voice. Todd sounds sincere, even impressed.

"Forty," I respond, casually but proudly.

I didn't want to let Todd get to me, but of course he did. Jason had described Todd as harmless. Harmless to him, maybe. It's easy to ignore the put-downs and the sarcasm and the disdain when you're so good that you're emotionally untouchable. As a vulnerable outsider, though, every barb stings. Now I've finally disarmed the bully. Against every instinct in his being, Todd has paid attention to me, has accorded me the respect I have craved. The only way that could have happened was for me to have done something on the field worthy of his notice. I *made* Todd notice.

I had come to Denver believing that my performance would be judged by how far I kicked a field goal and whether I played in an actual game—that is, by typical, journalistic, sportswriterly ideas of success. But it had nothing to do with that. Kicking in a preseason game would make the highlight reel of my life, to be sure. But it wouldn't define me as a real player. Real players don't care what sportswriters think. They don't care what fans think. They care what their teammates think. And I've managed to get the most cold-hearted guy in the locker room—the guy whose breathtaking talent and jackass jock behavior make him an embodiment of the NFL in all its glories and faults—to treat me for one unguarded second like a real player. That my ultimate validation comes not from Jason or R.B. or Micah but from Todd fucking Sauerbrun feels at first like a surprise, and then it makes perfect sense. *How far was that?*

I decide to stop right there at 40 yards and one foot. I've proven what I needed to prove. Kickers like to end with a make, and I've done that, too.

18

It's Part of a Sickness

From time to time, I visit the tent reserved for disabled fans and their families. They recognize every player by number, name, and face. They recognize the assistant coaches and the scouts and the equipment guys. "Even the low office people," one of the regulars tells me. They break camp rules by soliciting autographs— which are supposed to be procured only from the players required to sign after practice in, naturally, a makeshift souvenir store at the rear of the weight room—but no one stops them.

Atop the hierarchy of Broncos superfans is Barrel Man, a heavyset, retired airline mechanic named Tim McKernan. Since 1977, when the franchise reached its first Super Bowl, McKernan has attended games wearing an orange barrel supported by suspenders. (He has just put his 1997 Super Bowl barrel up for auction online. It will fetch $30,000.) But Barrel Man doesn't come to camp. The undisputed queen here is Bronco Betty, the woman who met the team bus after we returned from Detroit. Betty, a retired bookkeeper whose real name is Helen Henry, has been doing that since the late 1970s. She's had season tickets since 1963. She rarely misses a practice.

Why drive to a football team's offices at three in the morning in a blizzard to wave to a bunch of football players who just want to get in their cars and go home? "Because it's fun. Because I have the time to do it," Betty tells me. "I love the Broncos. I've loved 'em for years. I'll always love the Broncos. It's just a kick. They're my Broncos! What isn't there to like? They feel like my grandkids." The players treat Betty like a harmless, wacky aunt, soothed with a smile and a few kind words.

Fans make modern sports possible, of course. Television networks pay the NFL billions to show its games because advertisers are willing to pay the networks to reach the tens of millions of people who want to watch football. The fans, in turn, are willing to shell out their own collective billions for tickets and jerseys and parking and beer and satellite-TV subscriptions and the cars they see in the commercials on those telecasts. The smart teams recognize the primacy of fans. Mike Shanahan had spectators at camp moved to the berm from bleachers in the players' parking lot to improve their view. When he saw photographers blocking some fans, he shifted the media to another location.

All of that is comprehensible to the players. They know who fills the NFL's coffers, and their bank accounts. And they understand fanhood, because they love the games, too. What's inexplicable is the life-or-death rooting, the irrational response to games, in the media and around water coolers, the cultishness that makes Jake Plummer reluctant to circulate in public or turns John Elway into a Zeus bestriding the Rockies. No one wants to do well more than the players; their careers really do depend on it. But once the game is over and the final score recorded, the fans, perversely, are the ones who die a million deaths, and blame the players for their misery, as if losing were intentional.

"We feel this sport so deeply in our core that we fight over the orange and blue, we neglect obligations over the orange and blue, we bleed, we cry," Nate Jackson writes, taking a fan's perspective, in his weekly journal on the Broncos' Web site. "We care so much for the fate of this team that we lose our tempers, we criticize, we insult. Often as we sit in front of the television or in our seats at the game, we feel so helpless and grow so desperate that we forget the true formula for progress and success . . . love and support."

Nate counsels that football "relies as much on chance as on plans." He says that children do better when they are praised rather than criticized. With passive-voiced misdirection, he says that "it is often difficult to see" that "our actions may in fact be depriving our beloved team of the atmosphere it needs to thrive." He observes that players and fans "need each other more than we normally admit, and we are both affected by the opinions we have for each other." He says that "nothing hurts us more" than when the team plays poorly.

Nate has taken a writing class at the University of Denver, and he writes and performs hip-hop/rock music (stage name: Jack Nasty). He is funny, caring, sensitive, and eager to explore the world and his own inner consciousness. His football worldview is shaped in part by the fact that he attended tiny, Division III Menlo College in northern California, and not some Division I factory. His football journal is a way to convey what's good about the game—it is the team Web site, after all—by subtly pointing readers toward what's not. In this instance, Nate's real message to fans is this: Stop behaving like lunatics who see players and teams as abstractions. Start behaving like compassionate humans who are watching other, equally fallible humans play a sport in which both sides are trying to prevail. Enjoy the event, win or lose, and form opinions, but keep it in perspective.

On the final day of camp, I emerge from the locker room with the kickers a little before 8:30. Adam Meadows is testing a hamstring that he pulled four days and seven practices after arriving—just as his shoulder was starting to feel comfortable. Adam gets down in his stance, cuts one way, then another, then pivots to his left. He didn't play against Detroit but plans to against Tennessee. For the last practice to which they will be admitted, hundreds of fans already are staking vantages beneath the pines, cottonwoods, junipers, and viburnums that border the fields. Including today, attendance will average 1,412 per practice, a Broncos record. I ask rhetorically what motivates people to come to football practice before the football players come to football practice, and then sit in the sun, on a weekday, and watch the technical and the mundane.

"It's part of a sickness," Todd says, and as with most of Todd's blunt pronouncements, there is truth in it. We'd all agree that arriving at 7 a.m. for a summer practice that won't begin for another ninety minutes is bizarre. These languid affairs come to life only during the team drills that usually occupy the last half hour.

Every contracted player in camp has excelled at football and been around others who excel at football for so long that few things seem remarkable. But it doesn't look that way to fans. Seeing from a few feet away the hulking physiques, blinding speed, whizzing passes, sky-high kicks, and resounding thuds is an exceptional experience. It's also a humanizing one. Fans who witness Jake Plummer audibly displaying leadership and a sense of humor might be persuaded to hold their tongues before screaming "You suck, Jake!" the next time he throws a pass two inches off target. It's an odd paradox. The average ticket for an NFL game costs $60, but the most intimate and instructive view of the sport, training camp, is free.

Of the dozen or so diehards in the disabled tent, one of the younger regulars is Elmer Gonzales Jr. Elmer tells me he's missed just ten practices since the Broncos shifted camp from Greeley four years ago. He takes vacation from his job as a construction site inspector to attend. Elmer's father, a former roofer who was injured when a conveyor belt fell on him, has missed just four practices. The family's basement is a Broncos shrine once featured in *Mile High Sports Magazine,* a copy of which Elmer Jr. extracts from a backpack to show me. Father and son have collected seven thousand autographs of Broncos past and present (including one hundred or more from each of several players). Every summer they get every player to sign a banner. One day, the younger Elmer shows me a three-ring binder of Broncos photographs in clear sleeves. He turns the pages until stopping at . . . me. I sign the picture and the banner, which he calls "something nobody else has, that no one else can come close to having."

The regulars' devotion makes them less judgmental. Bronco Betty has cheered me all summer. Before my first, botched kicks, Elmer was the fan I heard from inside the Port-O-Let defending me. And he defended me after the kicks, too. "You could tell the pressure was on, because you did well in the practices," he tells me.

Watching from this close has allowed Elmer to appreciate the complexity of the sport and the nuances of the team. "If they put in that big tight end Chad Mustard," he says, "they're probably going to run his way." As important to Elmer, though, is that training camp exposes him to what the players endure. "They're under so much pressure," he says. "But they're having so much fun and they're spreading that fun around."

"You understand more what they go through. It's not just every Sunday," says Shelly Gomez, a friend of Elmer's who brings her five-year-old son to camp.

"The only thing you accomplish by booing is making them feel worse," Elmer says. "Players don't want to play for fans who don't appreciate them. They want the fans to back them up."

"They know when they've made a mistake," Shelly says.

When players ask Elmer why he's there every day, he has an answer so simple it's disarming. "To support you guys," he says. Elmer's is an enlightened approach to modern fandom. Enjoy what these incredible athletes do, view them as people, learn something about the sport, enjoy the successes, don't overvalue the failures. "I'm not one to pine too much about a loss," Elmer says. "It's just a game in the end."

This is officially the last day of camp," Al Wilson announces, and he is rewarded with a standing ovation, if only because we're standing. "You don't have to stay at that damn hotel anymore," he says, which prompts more cheers from the rookies and free agents. Then he begins the rhythmic clap that marks every prestretch breakdown.

"Wait, wait!" he suddenly says. "This is *the last day of camp*! Hit it, deejay!"

Over loudspeakers the Broncos use only rarely—other NFL teams frequently pipe in earsplitting crowd noise during drills—the hip-hop hit "It's Goin' Down" by Yung Joc booms. Everyone starts dancing, even the coaches, even Larry Coyer, the gimpy, gray-haired, pipe-smoking, hobbitlike defensive coordinator. The sight of an old white guy jumping around to a rapper's tale of guns and bitches and life in the 'hood draws hoots audible above the incongruous blare. And then recess ends and class resumes, a shot of caffeine in the woozy monotony of one more day.

Predictably, I don't kick in FG again. Bradlee throws a touchdown bomb on the final play of the final drill before the double horn sounds, ending camp. Shanahan doesn't commemorate the moment. ("We've had a heck of a camp," he'll say at team meeting later. "You guys have worked your asses off.") But the players celebrate. A few of the team's better golfers—Preston Parsons, Mike Leach, Stephen Alexander—lead an expedition to the turf field, where we spray balls at the O in "BRONCOS" painted in the end zone and at the white hoops we've used for kicking target practice and through the goalposts. It's the first permissible on-field levity of the summer.

With ten days, two games, and just five practices before the first cuts, Ted Sundquist and his staff compile and compare projected rosters like a bride and groom preparing seating charts for a wedding. One of the players who keeps falling off the list is wide receiver Charlie Adams. Charlie is handsome in the matter of Taye Diggs: streamlined and elegant, with an ear-to-ear smile exposing white-white teeth. He is pals with Nate Jackson and Kyle Johnson and, like them, should excel at something after football. In Charlie's case, it could be on Wall Street, where his brother, an investment banker at Goldman Sachs, makes twice as much as he does.

The day we talk, Charlie is wrapped in a blanket and sniffling with a cold. A few days earlier he had banged knees with cornerback Darrent Williams and could barely bend one of them. But the pain didn't rise to a level where he requested more treatment than ice. Charlie didn't want to have to show up for work at dawn, and his job wasn't secure enough to take a day off. He had played long enough—since he was seven years old, but, more to the point, the past four years with the Broncos—to know how to go at less than full strength. "Because it's not about how fast you run," he says.

Instead, practice is about competence, Charlie says. His goal is to show the coaches he understands the game and his assignments: that he knows how to run his routes with precision, that he knows how to receive the ball properly when it is thrown toward him, that he knows how to catch punts and kickoffs. Charlie considers this his strength. When a play is called in the huddle, he envisions the diagram on the overhead in the meeting room. "If I hear Double Wing Right Zebra Bingo Cross, I see Zebra running his basic cross, I see a post over the top, I see a deep circus backside, and I see the tight end running a shallow cross," he says, listing the receivers' routes. "That's kind of cool. I guess my brain is set up for Xs and Os." Consequently, Charlie doesn't have to process when he plays. "It's definitely a struggle for other guys," he says. "You can tell when someone's running and thinking."

If he hadn't torn his right ACL late in his senior year at Hofstra University, Charlie would have been drafted. But he did and he wasn't and he bounced on and off the Broncos' roster before playing in every game in 2005, catching twenty-one passes and returning twenty-six kicks. In terms of career progression, Charlie should be approaching stability. But he knows better. On the one hand, he says, Rod Smith is getting older, no-show Ashley Lelie will be traded, newcomer Javon Walker is coming off his own ACL tear, and a fourth-round rookie named Brandon Marshall has been hurt. On the other hand, "you never know what they're thinking upstairs, you never know what their plan is." So he plays through the knee bump and the head cold and hopes he's part of the plan. If not, there are other NFL teams, and if they don't want him, there are other careers.

"There are guys who don't have that option," Charlie says. "If they can't play here they need to play arena ball, and if they can't play arena ball they need to go to Canada, and if they can't go to Canada they need to coach because they don't know anything but football. We're fortunate. There is life outside of football or life after football that doesn't necessarily have to involve football. I think that allows you to play a little more relaxed and a little more carefree and a lot less stressed out. You know that it's not the end of the world. Ninety percent of the guys are going to have to work when they're done playing football anyway. It's not going to be a big deal for me."

Not that Charlie, at twenty-six, is eager to move on. The psychological environment might be brutal, but hanging out with close friends all day and playing on Sundays and then having a few months off helps make up for the misery. Charlie has bought a house and settled in Denver, and respects the organization. One year, he recalls, the Broncos scrimmaged in Houston before a preseason game. During practice, the Texans receivers caught the ball, ran five yards, and walked back to the huddle. The Broncos, by contrast, sprint thirty or forty yards after every whistle and then run back.

After the final practice of camp, Charlie stays behind to catch punts. He attends a meeting about NFL insurance and health benefits. Then Shanahan asks him to come upstairs. A year earlier, Shanahan had summoned Charlie to say he had won the job as the number three receiver. But it's too early for that sort of news, and for cuts. So Charlie has no idea what to expect. Shanahan tells him he's been traded to Dallas. The Broncos weren't sure they would have a place for him on the roster, the coach says. The trade will allow Charlie to join a team before the market is flooded with cut players.

Charlie is stunned. He walks downstairs to the wide receivers' meeting. His coach, Steve Watson, a star with the Broncos at the position in the 1980s, wasn't told about the trade. Charlie announces it to the receivers, and starts crying.

Dallas wants him at its camp in Oxnard, California, that night. The contents of his locker are emptied immediately and boxed and shipped. Charlie doesn't get to say good-bye in person to Nate or Kyle. He goes home, packs a few things, heads for the airport, and arrives in Burbank at ten o'clock. The Cowboys pick him up and take him straight to camp. At midnight, Charlie spends an hour getting MRIs on both knees. (He tore his left ACL during high school.) His cell phone rings until two.

The next morning, in Denver, Ronnie Bradford walks past Nate in the locker room and, with impeccable comic timing, asks, "You need to go see Betsy?" meaning Betsy Klein, the team psychologist. Nate laughs it off, but it is jarring and sad to see Charlie's empty locker, all evidence of him erased like a disgraced Politburo member from a May Day photograph. "Professionally, he'll be fine," Nate says. "It just sucks to be told you have to leave now. And you have no say in it, unless you want to quit football."

After practice—an hour-long final prep for the next day's game against Tennessee—I talk with Ted Sundquist about the roster. Teams have to "get down" to seventy-five players after the third preseason game, then to fifty-three plus the practice squad after the final one. Veterans are usually the first to get cut. For financial reasons, teams don't want to risk veterans getting injured later in the preseason, because it would cost more money to settle or to place them on the injured-reserve list. In the Tennessee game, "those are the guys we'll focus on."

Sundquist tells me he had left Charlie off of his latest projected fifty-three-man roster. The competition at wide receiver had made him a "bubble guy." So when Cowboys coach Bill Parcells called a couple days earlier inquiring after Charlie, Sundquist and Shanahan were interested. Dallas offered a seventh-round draft choice. Shanahan called Gary Kubiak, the former Broncos offensive coordinator who had just taken over as the head coach in Houston. Kubiak liked Charlie. He offered a sixth-round pick, but not until after the third preseason game. The Cowboys upped the offer to a sixth-rounder now and the Broncos accepted.

As we're talking about this, Steve Antonopoulos, the trainer, calls to say that Dallas has concerns about Charlie's knees. Sundquist's assistant interrupts. Jeff Ireland, the Cowboys' head of pro scouting, is on the line.

"I just got off the phone with our trainer," Sundquist tells him. "He's had no problems here. Uh-huh. Uh-huh. Okay. Okay. Okay. He'll probably play. All righty. Okay. Okay. Okay. All right. Yeah. Okay."

Sundquist hangs up. "They flunked him on his physical," he says. "So he's back with the Broncos."

Mike Bluem, the Broncos' young salary-cap whiz, walks into the office with arms spread wide. "What?" he says. He can't imagine why Dallas rejected Charlie.

"Buyer's remorse maybe," Ted says.

"For what?" Mike asks.

"His knees," Ted says.

"Get him back. Play him in the game and show 'em he can play."

Bluem wants the Broncos to play Adams against Tennessee so other teams can see that he's healthy.

Sundquist slumps back in his black leather chair. Dallas's rejection will make it virtually impossible to trade Charlie anywhere but Houston. He feels badly for Charlie, and badly for the Broncos. They could have used an extra draft choice.

Charlie flies back immediately. The Broncos spend the night before home games at the tony Inverness Hotel resort, and I find Charlie in his room. He's mystified. The MRI revealed bone on bone and torn meniscus in his left knee—the one he injured in high school. He told the Cowboys' orthopedist that he had never missed an NFL practice, that he didn't wear a brace or even a neoprene sleeve, and that he didn't take anti-inflammatories or steroid packs (corticosteroids, which reduce swelling and inflammation and are not to be confused with illegal, performance-enhancing anabolic steroids). Charlie told them he's not in pain. The Cowboys said they weren't worried about his health now but in the future. Charlie considered that odd because NFL teams don't normally care about the long-term health of backup wide receivers on one-year contracts. To Charlie, and to Broncos management, it sounded as if Dallas used the MRI results as an excuse to back out of the trade.

More troubling to Charlie is how the episode might affect his chances of playing this season. The Broncos have already told him he's not likely to make the team. He knows a failed physical, fairly or not, is more than a red flag, it's a slamming door. All Charlie can do is try to change the Broncos' opinion or persuade other teams that he's healthy. "I'm confused," he says. "I don't know anyone who's ever been in this position."

A few days before every game, the Broncos coaches deconstruct that weekend's playbook: every player's assignment on every play, including basics introduced on day one of camp. The meeting to review the 101 plays for the Tennessee game lasted two hours and one excruciating minute. "Brutal," Stephen Alexander says.

The excessive preparation, I have concluded, is as much for the

coaches as for the players. Coaches, Nate Jackson observes, are motivated by power and fear. "They all have that glimmer of hope that one
day they'll be the most powerful guy in the building," he says. "And they
fear that one day they're going to be fired." So they overprepare, to cover
every base and every inch of their respective asses. But they're also like
stage parents. They live through their children, insisting they do well,
worrying they will fail. The coaches like to say that the players are running around with their paychecks in their mouths. But the infatuation
with the Xs and Os isn't just about protecting their jobs. The coaches
love the process. And they can't control themselves.

In a hotel conference room, Mike Heimerdinger and offensive coordinator Rick Dennison breathlessly recount every detail of the scripted
first fifteen plays against Tennessee. I turn their words into a sort of
football Beat poetry, flaccid yet, to the speaker, deeply meaningful:

> *Faking the 18 slot.*
> *The stutter.*
> *On the numbers now,*
> *Not to the far corner.*
> *We're going back to the east side with this thing.*
> *With the disk on the back side.*
> *If you got bump, we're going slant.*
> *If it's two deep, we turn it into a go.*
> *If the Will gets on the edge,*
> *There's no motion.*
> *The basic stays on with the two check slows.*
> *You've got the big one now.*

If we all tiptoed out of the room, the coaches wouldn't even notice. They
would continue their exegesis on 3 Jet Nickel Navajo Stunt Slice Center
Pinch Flex Skinny Cross. Then they would detect, out of the corner of
one eye, the absence of an audience. And, before a room of empty chairs,
silent but for the hum of the whirring laptop motor and overhead projec-
tor, they would keep right on talking.

I ride to Invesco Field with Jason. Three hours before the 7 p.m. kick-off, fans stand two deep outside the players' parking lot. We walk past them like movie stars at the Oscars and down a ramp into the bowels of the stadium. The locker room is spacious and pristine. Five televisions are suspended from the ceiling. One table is packed with Myoplex bars, gum, and other snacks. Another is loaded with tape and extra socks. On the blue carpeting decorated with the Broncos logo, a padded chrome chair faces each of the meticulously arranged lockers. I have my own this time, my name and number in white sans serif lettering on a two-foot-long navy blue card slid into a slot above the top shelf.

Players stare into their lockers, watch ESPN, read the game program. Kyle Johnson looks somber. He gets "bubble guts" before every game, preseason, regular season, playoffs, whatever. "Imagine twenty-two weeks of this," he says. "It builds up. I was less nervous when I was nine. It was less consequential." Tom Nalen rides a stationary bike. Bradlee Van Pelt lies on his back in a yoga pose, breathing rhythmically; his teammates shake their heads. Preston Parsons whispers that Dinger told Jay Cutler he would play the rest of the game after Jake Plummer takes twenty or so snaps. "That's good for yours truly," Preston says. It indicates that the coaches aren't interested in seeing Bradlee play, which indicates that Preston could make the practice squad.

My hopes for a long pregame kicking session are dashed by the weather: a summer deluge. I procure a blue long-sleeved shirt from the equipment guys to wear under my pads. Micah finds a plastic bag in which to stash my notebook. But we're barred from going on the field at our appointed time, and when we finally are let out, the rain is falling heavily and the turf is slick and the kicking perilous. Still, since this might be my only chance to kick in Invesco, I ask R.B. to hold. He puts the ball down on the 27-yard line—a 37-yard field goal—facing the south stands, which are topped by Bucky Bronco, a white statue cast from the model of Roy Rogers's horse, Trigger, that reared its legs at the old Mile High Stadium.

I kick the waterlogged ball through the uprights.

"You ever think of how many guys get to do this?" Jeff Hays says. "How many do you think appreciate it? Probably most of them don't. It takes a person with a certain sense of mortality to appreciate it. On the other hand, it's just a football game."

I actually believe most of the Broncos do appreciate it, especially the ones for whom the season may end before it begins. The impermanence of life in the NFL conditions players to expect, and then accept, the worst. For all the legitimate complaint and depression and doubt, the vast majority of players on the soaked field would admit that they love what they are about to do. "It's electric," John Lynch tells me on the sideline. "The nerves make you feel like you're sick. But when you don't feel it, it's probably time to hang 'em up and watch football like a fan."

That's the bipolar nature of the sport. Even in the rain, the pregame is all amped-up energy. I run back into the locker room behind Plummer, who's singing "Dancing in the Street," and I high-five a fan leaning into the tunnel. Inside, though, the energy vanishes. Players listen to music through earbuds and study playbooks. Jason, his pads off and his game pants unbuckled, makes a kicking motion across the carpet, shaking his right leg.

The Broncos' chaplain, Bill Rader, leads players in prayer outside the showers. Rader is a wandering presence on the team. He eats lunch with the players and hosts a regular Bible session. A former college football player, Rader sometimes plays catch before games with Jason, with whom he is close. I didn't have the impression he was a powerful influence until I attended a pregame chapel service in Detroit and counted thirty-one players, coaches, and staff. Rader, in a flowered Hawaiian shirt, said then that this is "a new season for us, not new for You" (meaning God) and preached about Job's protestation against his sins. In the locker room now, the players kneel on the bathroom tiles. I'm scribbling notes until one of the giant linemen grabs my hand for a group prayer.

Shanahan sits on a countertop in the middle of the locker room, one leg swinging. At 6:48, in his pads now, Jason kicks across the carpet again. Rich Tuten stretches an offensive lineman. Tim Brewster parades around knocking fists with players. "Come on, big boy," he says to me. I sidle up to Shanahan and whisper how eerily solemn the room is. "It's always like this," he replies. At 6:51, Pat Bowlen enters. A minute later, Shanahan jumps off the table and shouts, "Bring it up!" clapping twice.

"We know what we have to get done," he says. "Let's go have fun. Our house!"

Everyone kneels for the Lord's Prayer. Shanahan grabs my right hand. Paul Ernster grabs my left. "Amen!" everyone says. And then, "Offense!"

We crowd through the doorway and into the stadium concourse. John Lynch slaps me on the shoulder pads as I pass. "Let's go, Stef!" he says. Then Plummer does too, hard. We gather under a dark gray inflatable tunnel. The offensive starters are introduced one by one over the PA system, and the rest of us pour through the tunnel to midfield. Eminem's "Lose Yourself" is blasting, reminding the players that they "only get one shot." Rain or no rain, preseason game or not, the crowd is thunderous, the adrenaline coursing. And then, as if to remind everyone that NFL stadiums are little more than Hollywood stage sets, everything stops. The game is being televised nationally, and we're in a commercial break.

Plummer marches the team to three touchdowns in three series. It would be the ideal situation for me to kick: a meaningless field goal or extra point in a blowout preseason victory. After Cutler engineers another score for a 28–3 lead, I say to Jason, "Maybe I should call the league at halftime."

"Please, please, please, please, please," he replies.

The final score is 35–10. Charlie Adams doesn't catch a pass or field a kick return. Cutler plays well again. Bradlee does get in the game, but Shanahan doesn't let him throw a pass. He hands the ball off seven times and then drops to a knee twice to run out the clock. Jason misses a 51-yard field goal. Paul Ernster punts just once, for 51 yards. Four of his five kickoffs reach the end zone.

The rain makes taking notes difficult, so I just enjoy my own little things, as Shanahan might say. The coach berating rookie running back Mike Bell for stepping out of bounds rather than lowering his shoulder into a defender at the end of a 34-yard run. "On this team you never run out of bounds!" Shanahan screams. "If you do, you will never be on the field again! Do you understand?" Plummer enjoying the aftermath of a play in which he rolled out left while Nate Jackson blocked to his right and then snuck out over the middle, where he was wide open for a catch and run into the end zone. "That's a nasty fucking play!" Jake says to Tim Brewster. Tony Scheffler showing me an equipment trick—slicing the leather in the front of the cleats to create extra room for the toes when they jam forward while running routes. Tony says he cut too much room in the pair he's wearing and a Titans player stepped right in the hole. Ouch.

The unparalleled highlight of the game for me is Tony returning to the sideline with eyes as big as poker chips after scoring his first NFL touchdown, a six-yard reception from Cutler. Tony has continued to struggle with the workload and the detail and the daily humiliation, to the point, he tells me, that he began asking himself whether it was worth it. "Is this healthy? Is there where you want to be?" he says. "You start evaluating your life and it's kind of scary at twenty-three years old. You've been spending your whole life for this one moment and you get there and you're like, this is it? This is what I busted my ass for since I was ten?" The touchdown was a brief relief—Tony's first glimpse of how the triumph of game day can alleviate the agony of the rest of the week.

Unconcerned about getting cut, I plan to go home for a few days before the final week of the preseason. I'm not sure I'll dress out again. Unless the NFL changes its mind about letting me kick in an actual game, I don't see the point. I remove the nameplate from above my locker and slide it into my messenger bag.

19

One from Here for Everything

It is one of the NFL's most enduring, and shopworn, scenes: the knock on the dorm-room door from the turk, the team staffer who lets a player know he's being cut without actually telling him he's being cut. The turk has been around since at least the 1960s, apparently named for the Ottoman Turks who wielded long, curved, and lethal scimitars. On the Broncos, no one actually says, as cliché would have it, "Coach wants to see you, and bring your playbook." Rather, a player-personnel underling calls the casualty and summons him to Ted Sundquist's office. Cuts usually occur on an off day. Some players are in the building receiving treatment. Some come in expecting the worst. Others turn off their cell phones to avoid the call as long as possible. When the unpleasantness is done, a staffer sitting outside Sundquist's office escorts the player to see Shanahan.

After we beat the Houston Texans in the third preseason game, 17–14, Shanahan announces in the Invesco Field locker room that "moves" will be made between noon and 4 p.m. the next day. Thirteen players will be released. At the witching hour, I see P. J. Alexander in the hallway.

"How's it going?" I ask.

"Not good, man," he replies.

"I know."

"It's a nasty business, man. Need to learn that right away."

P.J. has already seen Sundquist and Shanahan. Getting cut was no surprise. He hadn't played against Houston. He had been in steady pain for weeks. As the first cuts neared, no coach had clued P.J. in about his status. But he didn't need to be told. He watched the film. He could tell from the pivot of a foot or a single step backward that he wasn't right. When the team signed Adam Meadows, P.J. knew the challenge exceeded what his knee would let him achieve.

P.J. goes upstairs to return an exit form signed by the trainer and the equipment manager. I head into the locker room.

"They fuck with you, Bibs?" offensive tackle Cornell Green asks offensive guard Martin Bibla. Green, in his seventh year, is the most veteran of the first cuts. Sundquist told him he just didn't have a good camp. The Broncos are releasing him now rather than in a week because if he were hurt in the final preseason game the team would be responsible for his full $585,000 salary, and $735,000 against the salary cap.

"Yeah. I love this business," Bibla replies. "Better than Atlanta, though. Atlanta, they gave me a garbage bag and a handshake."

Each cut Bronco does get a gray industrial garbage bag for the contents of his locker, but Sundquist also thanks every released player for his contribution and levels with him about his talents and shortcomings. He also makes a courtesy call to the player's agent, which most teams don't do. Sundquist told P.J. what he already knew: that the team had a glut of interior linemen—guards and centers—which had forced him to play tackle, where his reduced quickness was exposed.

P.J. stuffs some sneakers and cleats into his bag. He adds two pairs of gloves, and throws three more in the trash. "I need my drugs," he says, grabbing a prescription bottle of painkillers from a shelf. He packs his GOOD MORNING DOUCHEBAG! coffee mug, too. When P.J. is done, the equipment guys will descend like the Grinch into Whoville. They will box and ship onward his leftover belongings and repossess his nameplate, jerseys, helmet, game pants, and other gear belonging to the team.

I follow P.J., Cornell, and a cut guard named Rob Hunt out of the locker room, through the cafeteria, and into the parking lot. Most of their teammates aren't around; everyone has the day off after the win over Houston. Plus, hanging around while others are getting cut is awkward and depressing.

"We'll go out holding hands and singing," Cornell Green says. "We can sing 'Kumbaya.'" And he does. "Kumbaya, my lord, kumbaya," Cornell croons while walking to the weight room to say good-bye to Rich Tuten and his assistants.

A clutch of reporters waits outside the lot. The Broncos won't officially name the downsized players until the next day, so the writers and cameramen watch through the wrought-iron gates to see who's carrying the telltale garbage bags. "I may run one of them bitches over," Cornell says. He tosses his bag into his black Cadillac Escalade. "Someone's dying, my lord," Cornell sings, "kumbaya."

Before I can say good-bye, P.J. is behind the wheel of his Lincoln Navigator. I knock on the tinted window. He rolls it down and I see him crying. P.J. tries to conceal it. "It's okay, man," he says. I grab P.J.'s shoulder, tell him that I'm sorry, and thank him. He nods, rolls up the window, and disappears.

Charlie Adams and Micah Knorr weren't among the thirteen cuts, which is surprising. It was obvious the team didn't want Charlie; they already had told him that and tried to trade him. He had hoped the Broncos would release him so he could find another job before teams set their final rosters. But management decided it needs Charlie's body on special teams for the fourth and final preseason game. Plus, they figure Houston will sign him whenever he's cut.

As for Micah, Shanahan had told Ronnie Bradford before the Houston game that Paul Ernster had the job as long as he didn't screw up. Paul landed two punts inside Houston's 20-yard line and boomed a 51-yarder. Ronnie let Micah punt in the second half—47 and 55 yards—fulfilling his request for some game film. On the morning of the cuts, Ronnie told me how sad he was that Micah was out, that he was a consummate professional who did whatever was asked and never complained. "I really feel sick about it," he said. (I did, too. I was glad for Paul but anguished about Micah, who's taught me not only to kick better but to focus better, to practice like a pro. He's been a good teammate and a good friend.) Then Ronnie went to see Shanahan to plan for the final preseason game, in just three days in Arizona. Ronnie asked whom he wanted to punt, meaning Paul or Todd. Shanahan replied, "Micah."

I ask R.B. and T-Mac what changed. They just shrug. "We don't make the rules," T-Mac says. "We just live in this world. It changes every day around here. Every minute."

Indeed, in this minute, the coaches are trying to figure out who will hold for placekicks against Arizona. Plummer, like all the other starters, won't even wear shoulder pads for the game, so he can't do it. Shanahan wants Cutler only to quarterback. Micah can't do it because, in addition to punting, he's going to kick off and placekick; Jason is taking the game off to nurse his calf.

"Number five," I say, hoping to get Preston Parsons some playing time.

"He's not going to be around," T-Mac says.

"Yes he is," I reply. Sundquist has told me that a decision on the third quarterback—Bradlee on the fifty-three, Preston on the practice squad, or no third QB at all—won't be made until after the Arizona game. I know more about the team than the special-teams coaches know about the team. Holder problem solved.

Preston splits the scout-team reps with Jake. The quarter-by-quarter depth chart for the Arizona game posted after practice reads: CUTLER CUTLER CUTLER VAN PELT. Preston sits at his locker reading a chin-up letter from his family. But he feels doomed again. He had figured he would get some playing time against Arizona, at least for the courtesy of appearing on film. Like a teenager calculating the optimal moment to ask a girl to the prom, Preston has waited all summer to confront Shanahan. It's finally time, he decides.

Preston walks upstairs. Shanahan waves him in. Preston says he thought he was going to play against Arizona and just wants to know where he stands. Shanahan says playing will be a game-time decision. But he tells Preston he's been impressed with how he has handled himself on the field. His status as a Denver Bronco, Shanahan says, will come down to whether the team keeps three quarterbacks or two on the active roster. If it's two, Preston will be on the practice squad. Preston thanks him, and says he'll do anything to help the team win, which he knows coaches like to hear.

"Turned my frown upside down," Preston tells me later on his cell phone from Cutler's new house, where the two quarterbacks are drinking beer and watching the sunset. "I've had a lot of coaches say BS things to me over the years and I think he was sincere." He's even hoping that the Broncos agree to pay him more than the $85,000 or so practice-squad salary, because a quarterback who knows the system is valuable. But after two years out of football, Preston says, "just give me a fucking job. How many people make eighty-five thousand? Playing a game."

I don't tell Preston, but I'm convinced he has a job locked up, regardless of whether he plays in Arizona. (The Broncos, like many teams, try not to expose players earmarked for the practice squad so other teams don't pilfer them.) On Ted Sundquist's current fifty-three-man roster projection, Bradlee is among the cuts, and Preston is in red ink on the practice squad.

In jeans and a linen shirt, a press pass dangling from a belt loop, I was met on the field before the Houston game with hugs and fist bumps and jokes about being out of uniform. Rod Smith told me I was sure to be cut after skipping town. Even the offensive linemen greeted me warmly. Todd shook my hand. *Todd!* Pat Bowlen laughingly told Texans owner Bob McNair about my kicking travails. Intellectually, I knew I was in the proper place again: reporter, chatting with team owners, comfortable in my soft-soled size-8 shoes. Physically, though, it was wrong. I should be in uniform! With my comrades! On the sideline! I felt as if I were letting them down, letting myself down. I had decided I was done with the kicking portion of my summer. Now I wasn't so sure. The pull of the locker room was strong.

I spent the game in a team suite on the stadium press level. Jeff Hays and I sat behind Ted Sundquist and three other front-office executives. Jeff alternated between watching the game and watching video on his laptop of other teams' kickers; at Ted's request, he is compiling a database of every kick in every preseason game so the Broncos can have a record of every kicker, in case. (Jeff recorded eighteen different pieces of information, from prekick line of scrimmage to a mark on the Broncos Pro Grading Scale, which ranges from "1.1 ELITE PLAYER—Top 5 at his position, rare abilities, Creates mismatches, Dominant," to "8.1 RE-JECT—Non NFL player.") The game itself was dull and desultory. The starters played into the third quarter, their longest stretch of the preseason, but were content to take care not to get hurt. Observing from above offered a better vantage, especially with live action and replays available on TV monitors on the walls and in the end zones, but it was a letdown after the Sensurround of the sideline. Being a player is more interesting than being a spectator.

The Houston game was Sunday night. Monday was the first cut day. Tuesday is the last full practice of the summer. We leave for Arizona on Wednesday, play the Cardinals on Thursday, and fly home afterward. Final cuts aren't due in the NFL office until Saturday evening, but the turk will descend again on Friday afternoon so the fifty-three is set before the annual team extravaganza at Shanahan's house on Saturday night. This year's theme is western.

"You enjoy your sabbatical?" Shanahan jokes when he pokes his head into Ronnie's office on Tuesday morning. He turns to R.B. and T-Mac. "I'm going to call him into my office. Wait till he hears the fine." I walk downstairs and observe Micah using a tiny blade to remove some decorative stitches, one by one, from around the left toe of an old Copa cleat, widening it ever so slightly. "Yeah, kickers aren't freaks," I say.

Anyone obsessed with sports as a child remembers the sensation. Autumn day, the "faintly soupy quarter of an hour," in J. D. Salinger's words, when daylight ebbs into dusk, the urgent need to finish a game in progress, the irresistible desire to start a new one. And the conscious knowledge of the absolute freedom of running around on grass and dirt and throwing, catching, kicking, or hitting a ball. I can smell those moments still, and have never felt more alive than when the memories of them surface, or, even better, when they are conjured by something real.

When I ignore the sheer absurdity of my weekend-warrior body in a locker room of sculpted and/or immense professional football players, that's what this summer has felt like. Rare, unrestricted access to the workaday routine of the modern NFL, the journalistic equivalent of landing on Free Parking. It's been a gift: manicured fields, expensive equipment, knowledgeable coaches, nothing at stake on the field but thirty minutes of meetings and my pride. Salinger's narrator, Buddy Glass, is describing playing marbles on a New York City street. "At that magic quarter hour," Buddy says, "if you lose marbles, you just lose marbles." For the last year, I've just been losing marbles.

But I realize now that a lot has been at stake, too. Paul Woodside defined "athlete" as someone who plays out of his comfort zone. He meant someone who conquers his doubts and insecurities and performs on command to the best of his ability. Whether I make a 50-yard field goal is beside the point. I have performed the physical and emotional acts demanded of me—trained for months, got in real shape, gained a dozen pounds, practiced with the pros, listened to the coaches, observed the experts, faced the pressure, tried, tried, tried. I can call myself an athlete. I probably won't get to kick for the Broncos, in practice again or in a game, but I feel like a Bronco. When I kick now, I look like a kicker. When I idle in the locker room, I don't ponder the improbability of my presence there. I exit one comfort zone and enter another.

So I return with Micah to our lockers, pull on my knee-high socks and my own Copas, stitches intact, and join the team outside. It's sunny, not too hot, a perfect day to luxuriate in the life of the indolent kicker, better still since we're not wearing shoulder pads. I stretch one final time to Rich Tuten's drill-sergeant commands, which now seem less threatening than theatrically absurd. Paul, Micah, and Todd punt during forty minutes of Specialist and Special Teams. As the rest of the team works on the offense field, closest to the locker room, we observe from the space between the two fields, all five kickers plus R.B. and

T-Mac, standing around the battery-powered coolers that dispense chilled water or Gatorade from thin hoses. Jason sits on one cooler, Todd on another, palms down, legs outstretched, head tilted back and pointed sunward. "Hey, Todd, pull 'em up," Jake Plummer shouts, lifting the hems of his shorts. "Get a little tan. Maybe pull your shirt up, too."

Even kickers, though, get restless. After we discuss which teams will be good this season—Todd predicts a Super Bowl pitting his two most recent employers, Denver and Carolina—the water-cooler conversation ends and we stroll over to the empty defense field.

"You want to hit some?" Jason asks me.

"Sure," I say casually.

"I'll hold."

"Thanks."

I take a few warm-up swings and realize that these will be my final kicks in an NFL training camp. I'll dress out for Arizona, but unless Bowlen, Shanahan, and Sundquist decide to flout their NFL overlords, I won't kick in the game. I tried one more time to persuade the league office. No change. I could be seen as "a gimmick." Other teams might try to auction off kicks to the highest bidder. I could get hurt. Blah, blah, blah. That I'm not some fan walking out of the stands, that the league regulates who can and cannot play, that I'd be no different from every other player on the field for the last exhibition game—anonymous— none of it mattered. The NFL shall remain the No Fatsis League.

Paul offers to snap and Jason sets the first ball down on the 25-yard line, a 35-yard field goal. Boom. Easy.

"He goes away for a week and comes back crushing them!"

It's Todd, my new best friend.

"Let's move it back," I say in mock seriousness, cracking everyone up. Jason makes a show of taking two mother-may-I steps backward. I make it from 38. Jason moves it back some more and I barely miss six in a row between 40 and 43, every one a well-struck ball, every one a few feet short. As Jeff Hays once said of me: too old, too slow, too weak.

"Okay," Jason says. "Seventeen-fourteen, eleven seconds left. Geronimo."

I have wanted all summer to run Geronimo, the Broncos' name for the last-second, no-time-outs, no-way-to-stop-the-clock field-goal play. I did it once at a camp with Paul Woodside, an end-of-the-day drill in which Paul called out us kickers one by one while counting down the seconds, last kicker standing wins. I rushed, kicked the dirt before the ball, and was eliminated from the contest on my first attempt.

"You want to do it from the sideline?" I ask Jason eagerly.

"No," he says, "I don't want to run."

I do, though, so I leave Jason squatting in the holder's place on the 30-yard line for my game-tying, 40-yard attempt. I feel like I'm nine again, pretending to be Pete Gogolak in the backyard, hearing the pregnant roar of seventy thousand fans in Yankee Stadium. Why wouldn't I? Under routine circumstances, the field goal is compelling for no reason other than being so different from the rest of the game, the rare moment when the stadium's full focus shifts to an individual. Assuming, as we do, that the snap and hold are precise, and that the blockers restrain the rushers, the field-goal kicker stands truly alone, just him and the goalposts. Make it a last-second field goal, and the isolation and tension are even more magnificent. Make it a last-second field goal with the clock ticking to zero like the timer on a bomb in a Bond movie, and the anxiety, exhilaration, chaos, and release are as great as anything we can ask from sports.

On my first Geronimo attempt, I stutter on Paul's snap, flub the kick, and blame the hold.

"Don't ever blame the holder!" Jason snaps, and then immediately blames Paul's snap. "Pass it on," he jokes. This leads to an exchange about the unseemliness of kickers blaming holders. Jason imitates Morten Andersen, who after a missed kick sometimes stared down at his holder just long enough to convince the crowd that someone else might be at fault. We take our positions again.

"Eleven! Ten! Nine! Eight!" Jason calls as I run onto the field. I get into position, my right toe demarcating the spot. I wait until Jason gets to six before beginning my backward steps.

"Five! Four! Three!"

At the count of two I nod at Jason, who nods at Paul, who snaps the ball. I absolutely crush the thing. It floats end over end on a glorious arc. Jason stands and stares along with me as it clears the crossbar comfortably—by two or three yards, maybe four. Jason emits a deep, breathy faux-crowd cheer. I throw up my arms in triumph, fists clenched. I hug Jason and we jump up and down in mock elation.

"Don't ever celebrate like that!" T-Mac says. The story of Bill Gramatica tearing his ACL during a post-field-goal paroxysm is immediately invoked. "And it was like a nineteen-yard field goal," says Todd, reliving his war of words with the Gramatica brothers—"fucking greaseballs," he reportedly called them—over their celebratory histrionics.

We all laugh. And then the airhorn sounds. I leave the ball bag behind and jog to one more curt, end-of-practice talk from Shanahan. The second- and third-teamers who will play the entire game against Arizona, he says, can't make any mistakes.

20

This Ain't Good-bye.
This Is Life.

Bradlee Van Pelt saunters through the locker room the next morning wearing nothing but Kelly green briefs, black socks, and a smile. "All right, Brad!" Todd remarks. "Got your Hulk underwear on! Your Underoos!"

The runway turn is about as carefree as I've seen Bradlee lately. His practice reps have dwindled as the season has approached. He didn't play at all against Houston. Bradlee is snippy with the coaches during quarterbacks meetings. He makes jokes about getting cut. "Be there or be square!" he says of the home opener of his alma mater, Colorado State, on Saturday, implying that he'll have nowhere else to be.

A few hours before the Arizona game, I meet Bradlee in a second-floor lounge at the Hyatt Regency Phoenix. In brown board shorts and a white V-neck undershirt, he's just come from the pool, where he was swimming, listening to music, and studying his playbook, alone. He hasn't shaved in days. I ask how he's feeling, not in a journalistic sense but a humanistic one. Bradlee pauses before answering that he's not losing control. He's frustrated about what has happened, and resigned about what is about to happen. He feels invisible. The coaches haven't talked to him and he hasn't approached the coaches. Why should he? They've poured their time and effort into him for more than two years. Shouldn't they care enough to communicate their intentions? It's as if Bradlee is stubbornly staying silent to out their poor management skills.

But he also knows that by doing so, he's rolling a snowball of bad thoughts.

"They know your brain," he says. "They could calm your fears or calm your anxiety and help you. But they don't choose to do it. It's all mind games. It's just gotten more intense."

Bradlee is excited about playing, but also wary. With Cutler under center, the Broncos have attacked, passing the ball continually. When Bradlee has been in the game, it's been handoff after handoff. The few pass plays have been three-step drops. To get into the flow of the game, to feel comfortable, to make a big play, a quarterback needs five-step drops and seven-step drops and rollouts, a few of them in a row. "Yeah, I missed a read and got sacked and everything was my fault," Bradlee says, recalling the Detroit game. "But then they just run and waste your time. You watch the minutes clicking down. It's an opportunity for you to perform. But they're not even coaching it like a game after a while."

Bradlee isn't sure whether he's being treated like a leper because Shanahan doesn't care about him anymore or because the coach wants to "hide" him from other teams. Under the latter theory, the Broncos aren't showcasing Bradlee so other teams won't sign him after he is cut. Shanahan may not want Bradlee on the roster, but he may want him available should Plummer or Cutler get hurt, because he knows the system. Either way, Bradlee isn't surprised. "I've read Shanahan's book," he says, and he means that literally. Bradlee keeps a copy of Shanahan's *Think Like a Champion* in his locker. "They don't approach you, they don't compliment you, they don't tell you what they want," he says.

Bradlee says he has tried to stay calm and conserve energy: no hikes in the mountains, no 6 a.m. yoga classes, no drinking. The problem is that what Bradlee probably needs more than ever is a walk in the Rockies or an hour of kripalu or a couple of beers. Instead, he dwells on what's happened. A season ago, he was the lone backup on a team one game from the Super Bowl. If Plummer had been injured against Pittsburgh, "I walk in, the only guy," Bradlee says. And he believes that he has improved, even during camp. The game is slowing down. He is getting smarter. "And all of a sudden I'm not good enough to make the team," he says.

"It's fucking weird, man. I told my mom today. She said, 'What's the ideal circumstance for you?' I go, 'Mom, the ideal circumstance is to get let go here and find someone that wants to communicate with me and sees a future.' Yeah, get me out. Let me go find a home. Let me go find someone who believes in me.

"Wanting to be wanted. That's all I want. To be wanted."

I leave Bradlee to his thoughts and his playbook and go see Shanahan in his top-floor suite. His packed wheelie bag stands by the door. We sit in comfy chairs positioned at a right angle. We talk about the summer and the roster and the season. I ask about Bradlee.

"This is not a hard decision," Shanahan says. When camp "broke" a couple of weeks earlier, he says, Jake, Jay, and Bradlee had amassed a total of about six hundred reps each in all drills in practice. (Preston had half as many, at most.) After just a few months as a professional, Shanahan says, Cutler had surpassed Bradlee in ability. Project him to Bradlee's two years of experience and "there's no comparison." Losing your job to a better player is excusable, he says. Reacting as Bradlee did isn't, and it affected Shanahan's opinion of the quarterback. Shanahan was testing Bradlee. Bradlee failed.

"He got a chip on his shoulder. The one thing I'll share with him is life is not always fair. Sometimes people make mistakes. Sometimes they're right, sometimes they're wrong. But whatever it is, you've got to be positive. You've got to be positive with the supporting cast. You can't have your lip down. If you go around saying woe is me, people don't like that.

"That's the thing I've been more disappointed with with Bradlee. He's kind of like a whipped boy. He's a different guy. He was the one all the players would laugh with and make fun with. All of a sudden, they don't make fun of him, they don't give him a hard time anymore, because he doesn't handle it the same way. That's not good."

Shanahan may not have communicated that directly with Bradlee, but he was watching. Bradlee knew that, but ignored it anyway.

In photos, the Cardinals' new, architecturally progressive stadium looks like a spaceship in the desert. On approach, it resembles a shiny silver sea urchin. The team's ownership has just accepted a pile of money to name it, absurdly, after a largely online university that fields no sports teams. In any case, it's a fine metaphor for the modern NFL: sleek, costly, grandiose, luminescent.

I'm excited for the game, my last as a pro, and I take advantage. In the early pregame, dressed in my game pants and a T-shirt, I kick ball after ball. The offensive line goofily kicks with me. Looking like a latter-day Lou Groza, center Tom Nalen toe-kicks, as he did in high school in Foxboro, Massachusetts, in the late 1980s. The football soars off his foot like a beach ball, occasionally passing through the uprights, more often waggling thirty feet one way or the other. But it goes far. Nalen makes one from 45 yards, and even though he's six foot three and weighs close to 290 pounds and used to kick, I can't help but feel demoralized. Nalen and the other linemen challenge me to kick one from 50 yards, and I accept, hoping for one miracle, one kick that would justify my hard work and win approval from the group that has been least willing to grant any. Naturally, the ball alights in the end zone, a few yards short of the crossbar, a fact one of the linemen records in my notebook.

Then Mike Leach offers his own challenge.

"Okay, Fatsis. One from here. For everything."

"Here" is the 25-yard line, a 35-yard field goal. "Everything" is not defined.

"You go first," I say.

The former college punter misses wide right and short.

I nail it, straight and true and good.

What I love even more than the sheer thrill of kicking on an NFL field while fans file in is the sense of superiority, of specialness, that every professional athlete enjoys: I'm talented enough to be on this field while you have to watch me from above. It's not arrogance but self-possession. It's as if I'm kicking not in a stadium but in a room affixed with a one-way mirror. The fans can see me. I can't see them. But sub-consciously I know they're there, which is empowering. If I were kicking in the game, of course, I might not be so cavalier. I shag for Micah Knorr in warm-ups, but he barely acknowledges me, even after he placekicks a 60-yarder. "The posts look smaller on game day," he finally says. "And as the game goes on they start getting narrower. By the fourth quarter, they're like a foot apart."

In a battle of first-round rookie quarterbacks, Matt Leinart of South-ern California leads Jay Cutler of Vanderbilt at halftime, 20–15. Micah kicks a 35-yard field goal but pushes an extra point wide left. After a second touchdown, Shanahan instead tries a two-point conversion, which fails, and which once again makes me ponder the perceived harm in allowing me to kick. Momentarily ticked off, I remove my shoulder pads at halftime and decide to join the starters in jerseys and caps. Preston Parsons sees me.

"You're not going to shut it down, are you?"

"I'm shutting it down."

"Your last half of professional football? Don't be a pussy."

I put the shoulder pads back on and run on the field with Preston and Jake, who's been heckled all evening by Cardinals fans still bitter about his leaving the team, and the state where he nearly won a colle-giate championship. "Hey, Jake! Your fiancée's still waiting at the altar!" one shouted in the first half, referring to Plummer's publicized breakup with a longtime girlfriend. As we emerge from the stadium tunnel for the second half, another shouts, "You suck, Jake!" Plummer turns, grabs his crotch, and dances backward onto the field. "You suck this!" he yells back, laughing.

Bradlee drives the backups to two fourth-quarter touchdowns and we win, 29–23. He hands the ball off or runs it himself a total of twenty times and passes, or tries to pass, eight times. Cutler's ratio is the op-posite: twenty-one passes against ten rushes. On the field afterward, quarterbacks coach Pat McPherson congratulates Bradlee. "You won this game for us," he says. Bradlee smiles sarcastically and doesn't say a word.

———

When football coaches and players talk about getting cut as "a numbers thing," they're not just being diplomatic. After five months of practice, some cuts are obvious. Others result from a game of musical chairs. Six wide receivers instead of five can mean nine defensive backs instead of ten. Nine offensive linemen instead of eight can mean eight defensive linemen instead of nine. On the plane and bus rides home from Phoenix, Shanahan, Sundquist, and their underlings hold final talks about the team, with Shanahan making the ultimate calls. As Shanahan promised before the postgame Lord's Prayer in Arizona, the cuts begin the next morning.

"Bradlee? This is Meghan from the Broncos," player personnel assistant Meghan Zobeck says into the phone in her cubicle. "Ted Sundquist would like to see you." She stumbles over her words, then hangs up and buries her face in her hands. Across the divider, fellow assistant Mike Mascenik sounds oddly upbeat, as if he were just calling to say hi. "Micah? It's Mike from the Broncos. Ted Sundquist asked me to give you a call. He wants you to head on in. He wants to chat with you."

Micah is already at his locker packing when his cell phone rings. His suitcase is in his car and he's ready to make the thirteen-hour trip home to Dallas to his pregnant wife and young son. He plans to drive straight through, sleeping in a rest stop in Oklahoma if necessary. "Why wait around?" he says. "What's keeping me here?" As for football, he's optimistic. Green Bay might need a punter. Washington has already called his agent. Dallas might be in the market for a punt-kickoff guy. Houston is a possibility, too.

In returning to Denver, Micah understood that, all things being equal, the team would keep Paul because of its investment in the younger draft choice. He understood that he was there to pressure Paul, and would make the team only if Paul struggled. Paul did well enough to earn a chance to start, and Micah accepts that. But when Sundquist tells him that Paul was more consistent in camp, Micah shoots him a look of disgust. "Anytime it was windy or raining, I kicked his ass," Micah says back in the locker room. "Tell me he's more consistent? Don't waste my time with bullshit." It's the first time I've heard Micah angry or critical.

Micah doesn't hold it against his immediate coaches, who he knows have supported him. He drops his playbook on Ronnie Bradford's desk. "You kicked the ball well," R.B. says. "I'm not worried about you, dude. You're going to get fifty million calls." Ronnie says Micah is a better punter now than during his first stint in Denver. He says he's already put in a word for him with the special-teams coaches at Baltimore, Houston, and Arizona. "You worked your ass off for me, man. Anything I can do, I'll do it."

"You've done enough," Micah says, and the two men shake hands.

"You're a true pro, man," R.B. says. "What you did for us, man, that's huge. I'm sorry it didn't work out here."

"You earned a lot of respect," T-Mac adds. "It was great working with you, man."

Micah asks if he can take a six-pack of new footballs from the equipment room, and Ronnie says of course. I carry those and a gym bag to Micah's gray Lexus SUV. Micah carries two large, neatly packed boxes containing the contents of his locker. I thank him for everything he did for *me*—more than anyone on the team in terms of coaching and practicing and thinking. "It was fun," he says, and I know he means it.

Bradlee, meanwhile, strolls into the locker room talking on his phone and then walks back out to get his exit paperwork signed. As expansive as he was all summer, he is taciturn now. For the first time around him, I feel like a nosy reporter and a voyeur—and a guilty survivor.

In a small box, Bradlee carefully packs his practice jersey, a Broncos media guide, Shanahan's book, a black Matchbox Porsche, two rookie cards—in one of them he wears my number 9—a tube of hair gel, a red-and-blue headband, and a Florida State visor that belonged to a former Broncos backup quarterback, Danny Kanell. He leaves the green tinsel hanging in his locker.

"We think I'll be heading to Houston," Bradlee finally says. "We" is he and his agent. I tell him I hope that happens and say good-bye. "This ain't good-bye," he replies. "This is life."

For the players who make the team and those who don't, cut day does offer a welcome finality: an end to the store-window scrutiny and round-the-clock pressure of camp. For the survivors, it's a momentary relief; for the departed, it's a temporary and possibly permanent one. "Here's to no stress, Stefan," an offensive lineman named Taylor Whitley said on the plane from Phoenix. "What's done is done." Whitley is one of the cuts, but he doesn't throw a temper tantrum in the locker room or curse Shanahan or bemoan his fate. No one does. If there are tears, they don't flow until the tinted windows roll up, as they did for P. J. Alexander, or at home alone or on a call to family.

Many of the cut players have experienced rejection before. Everyone understands the abrupt, transient nature of the football business. But for some, this is it, and that resonates. I'm certainly not the first to sniff pathos in the end of an athlete's career, but he is so young and has known so little else and it's so final.

"These guys are all men," Sundquist tells me after he's done swinging the scimitar. "But certainly professional football is something that you think about, you dream about, since you're a kid. A lot of people don't necessarily grow up thinking, 'Boy, I can't wait to be an architect.' It kind of grows on you as you get older. But sports is deeply ingrained. And in what profession do ten guys get summoned to the boss's office and get fired? It's not like in architecture one month there's ninety guys and the next month there's sixty."

The Broncos make only ten of the thirteen cuts on Friday, because Sundquist is still working on possible trades. The final moves take place on Saturday morning. Instead of calling the victims, two football-operations staffers intercept players as they emerge from the parking lot. Charlie Adams arrives, still assuming he will be cut. "Charlie," one of the staffers says with a smile, "keep going, keep going." Without an explanation given or requested, Charlie is on the fifty-three-man roster. I congratulate him in the locker room. "I guess," he replies, skeptical that he'll be around long.

The eight practice-squad members also are steered upstairs. Those players can't be sure whether they're being cut and then kept—the required process, since teams must expose players to the rest of the league before signing them to the practice squad—or just cut. "I've never felt like this," Preston says. "I have so much riding on it." Before he is ushered into Sundquist's office, one of the football-ops staffers pulls him aside with a message: "It's all good." Preston has made the practice squad. "I'm so fucking happy," he tells me.

Former Heisman Trophy winner Ron Dayne is released, costing the Broncos $750,000, which in the Monopoly-money economy of the NFL doesn't merit a thought. My Scrabble-playing pal Chad Mustard makes the active roster. Adam Meadows's shoulder still hurts, but he's in, too, completing his comeback. Tony Scheffler survives Tim Brewster, who tells me he has finished breaking down his protégé and begun building him back up. At day's end, Todd Sauerbrun's four-game suspension officially begins. The Broncos, Sundquist says, are deeper at offensive line, deeper at wide receiver, deeper at tight end, and deeper at quarterback than they were the previous season, which ended a game from the Super Bowl. In the first meeting of the official team, Shanahan says he feels as good about this group as any he's ever coached.

Becoming a Denver Bronco didn't erode my journalistic convictions. Unlike the players saluting the media camped outside the parking lot during cuts—as he drove by, Tom Nalen formed his index finger and thumb into an L, for Loser, and slapped it against his forehead—I appreciate that the reporters aren't vultures who want to exploit the misery of these young men, but are trying to inform fans who care about all things Bronco. That the team chooses to make the cuts before it has to deliver them to the NFL—and chooses not to inform the media—doesn't mean the reporters shouldn't try to find out what's already happened.

The team has created a mystery soluble in only one way: by observing. As I left the facility after the first cuts, I talked with Bill Williamson, a *Denver Post* reporter with whom I've become friendly. He was sheepish about being part of the death watch but made no apologies.

At the same time, I feel transformed. I recognize better how the NFL portrayed by the media beast reflects the internal functioning of a team only barely. Every morning, a Broncos PR intern left in my locker a stapled pack of the day's news clippings, twenty to thirty pages thick, printed on both sides. It was startling how the world I was experiencing bore so little resemblance to the one about which I was reading—not because the impressions necessarily were wrong but because they were so definitive, ascribing to training camp a narrative inconsistent with the amorphous, imprecise events on the field. "People don't know what they're seeing, reporters don't know what's happening in a game," Joe Namath once said. "I throw a pass that's intercepted and people blame me when it was the fault of someone who wasn't where he should have been. I throw a touchdown pass and I get the credit when it was underthrown and only a great catch made the play."

Every subculture has an us and a them: those who understand the world because they are part of it and those who don't because they aren't and therefore can't. That writing about football is like dancing about architecture is no revelation. I didn't walk into Broncos camp believing I would suddenly morph into an NFL-caliber kicker or be embraced by the players as an equal. But official imprimaturs are everything in the NFL. If the owner and coach tell you to do something, you do it. So the players had to welcome me, the first writer granted passage into the NFL's Forbidden Zone since 1963, or at least they couldn't haze me into quitting. During the second half of the Tennessee game, Nate Jackson and I talked about the weirdness of my masquerading as part of the team and part of the game. "We're conditioned not to accept you," he said.

The comment stung, because Nate is one of my closest friends on the Broncos, but he was right. A couple of coaches had no time or patience for me, because they viewed my presence as a distraction or because they simply distrust reporters. A few players saw nothing to gain from opening up about their jobs or their lives. I watched others, including some of the team's bigger names, supply "quotes" to the daily pack but put off talking to me until I lost interest in talking to them. I often didn't press the matter, because I sympathized; even if they liked me, they weren't obligated to talk to me. As we milled around in the hallway waiting for meetings to start one day, Tom Nalen pickpocketed my notebook and waved it tauntingly after we were seated. I hated being reminded that I was, in fact, the outsider.

The division between athletes on one side and reporters and fans on the other is as impassable as the black gate guarding the players' parking lot. I had been granted the pass code, figuratively and literally—it was Al Wilson's number followed by Rod Smith's number—but chose to park in the employee lot. The barrier of age, ability, and experience would never permit me complete acceptance, I knew, but Nate said he was surprised by how close I came. No one admitted that he was on a drug-test-defying steroids regimen or injecting human growth hormone, though logic and probability said at least a few players likely were. (A year later, after he was cut, defensive end Kenard Lang was suspended for six games for violating the league's steroids policy.) But a few of my teammates casually told me they smoke marijuana in the off-season, when the league doesn't test for it. Far more important, though, they confided their inner thoughts.

The modern NFL player craves what we all crave: to be understood. When I wrote about Scrabble, a top player said that winning the world championship validated his existence. None of the Broncos I've spent time with need to win a Super Bowl, or even to make the team, to consider their lives worthwhile. They are athletes, cocky and confident, at least outwardly. But the Broncos did want to be seen as more than the characters in the NFL video games they themselves play. They wanted me to understand that football is manic-depressive. The game itself is a fun, thrilling, scary, addictive turn-on: Sunday! The rest of the job is a largely joyless, stultifying, demoralizing, infantilizing, breakdown-inducing drag: Wednesday. "You're just seeing the worst part," Charlie Adams said to me during camp. "Although the season kind of sucks, too."

On Saturday afternoon, the summer survivors attend a casual, by two-a-day standards, no-helmets, no-contact practice. Troy Smith, the groundskeeper, has rotated the direction of the fields ninety degrees—east-west instead of north-south—to give his bedraggled bluegrass a break. He is thrilled that there are thirty fewer players tramping around, and that the fans are gone and the media are banished from practice and the scouts are back on the road. The units switch jersey colors, offense in blue, defense in white. The changes feel symbolic: Congratulations, you've made it, isn't the world different now?

In street clothes, my bags packed in my locker, I sit, notepad in hand, on a slatted metal bench just outside the orange double doors where this story began. For the first time in three months, I am unwelcome on an NFL field, which is unexpectedly sad. I haven't enjoyed being perceived as tiny and unathletic, where in the real world I'm neither. The routine often was dull, my life as a player workaday and unglamorous. The physical discomfort was, if a pinprick compared to what others suffered, enough to be frustrating. And I couldn't overcome age or genetics, couldn't make one from 50 yards, couldn't kick to my own satisfaction when it counted most. I guess this is what it means, finally, to be an NFL player. You don't necessarily want to be on the field, but you can't think of anyplace else you'd rather be.

Paul comes over to collect the orange K and P duffel bags, which the equipment guys have dropped near my bench. I instinctively perform my rookie chore and carry the bags toward him. On the way back, I spot a stray ball. I hold it aloft and shout Paul's name. Then I punt it to him softly.

"One last kick!" Paul says, and turns his back and jogs away.

No, I'm a Bronco

O n the way to Mike Shanahan's organization-wide end-of-camp party, I stop at a western-clothing store and pick up a brown, orange, and denim-blue shirt with black snaps and snazzy embroidery on the back and pockets. I'm underdressed. Boots and chaps and Stetsons abound. Jason Elam wears a long suede cowboy jacket. Todd Sauerbrun has on an American-flag-motif shirt. Ronnie Bradford dons an all-brown outfit complete with fake gapped buckteeth, one of them gold.

As a wail of relief over the end of camp, as a reward for making the fifty-three, and as a final respite before the season, the party at Shanahan's gated-community McMansion works. Food stations teem with ribs, steak, shrimp, mashed potatoes, grits, fries, and more. The bar is wide open. A group of western musicians plays. Real casino tables are staffed by real croupiers, and we play craps, Texas hold 'em, blackjack, and roulette all night long, though not for real money. Everyone has a terrific time. All the complaints about the coaches, the dislike of the game and the system, the angst over injuries and playing time and the future—for one night, all is forgotten.

Nate Jackson adopts a cowboy twang. Tony Scheffler was married earlier in the day but makes an appearance with his wife, who is in her wedding gown. Tom Nalen tries to pickpocket me again. I lift up the back of my cowboy shirt and show him that—hah!—for once I'm not taking notes. I bust out of a poker tournament but clean up at the blackjack tables. The party lingers until well past one in the morning.

Leaving, I stop to thank my host. I tell Shanahan how grateful I am that he allowed me into his sanctum and then trusted me once I was there. He in turn tells me that I earned my way in.

"The players respected you," Shanahan says. "That's the highest compliment I can give a guy."

From a beach house on Cape Cod, I watch the final minutes of the Broncos' first game of the 2006 season. I feel like I should be in St. Louis with them, like I'm missing opening night after rehearsing for months. I feel like I was cut.

It apparently hasn't been a good day. Jake has thrown two interceptions and totaled just 100-some-odd passing yards, and the Broncos have scored just ten points. The announcers wonder whether Jay Cutler will make his debut. But, needing a touchdown and two-point conversion to tie, Jake stays in and leads the offense downfield. Then he rolls out and tries to thread a pass to a heavily covered Rod Smith. It's deflected and intercepted. Game over. The camera cuts to the sidelines: It's Different Jake, a guy I never saw in camp, a cocksure athlete humbled.

Don't blame Jake, my teammates tell me, blame the coaches. "We didn't do one single fucking thing from our preseason offense," Preston Parsons says. "We had the hardest, longest game plan you could imagine. They changed everything." That plus the noise in St. Louis's domed stadium and a bunch of dropped passes created an offensive breakdown. But the team rebounds with a 9–6 home win over Kansas City, courtesy of three Jason field goals, including the winner in overtime. The following week I meet the team in New England. Before the game, Jason plays catch with team chaplain Bill Rader. "Hey, number one!" I shout from the sideline. Jason spots me, smiles, and gives the Todd rock-'n'-roll point.

Jake throws two touchdown passes in a 17–7 win. But the victory isn't smooth, I learn later. "There were a lot of F-bombs dropped," Preston reports. Jake clashed with Shanahan after the Broncos failed to score a touchdown from New England's 5-yard line. "Just call the plays," he snapped. "I'm going out there and playing fucking football." In the locker room, I congratulate Jake, saying that after the criticism of the first two weeks, the game must have been a relief. "I don't play for them," Jake says of the fans and media. There's no edge in his voice. He is being factual, not mean.

Outside the locker room, I'm chatting with a couple of players when Patriots owner Robert Kraft hurries by with his entourage. I've interviewed Kraft many times over the years. I shout a hello, we shake hands, and he continues on his way. Then he abruptly returns to me.

"So are you a Broncos fan now?" he asks.

"No," I reply, "I'm a Bronco."

After a 13–3 win over Baltimore, Shanahan cuts Todd. He tells him that Paul Ernster kicked well enough that the team couldn't risk Todd getting into trouble again. It wasn't a difficult decision, Shanahan tells me, because Paul is younger and cheaper. (The Broncos saved about $1 million in the exchange.) Shanahan says he didn't want to cut Todd, but Todd forced his hand, with both his suspension and his behavior in camp. But he leaves the door open to his return. "You never know. He could wind up being back here someday," he says.

The Broncos split the back-to-back games against Indianapolis and Pittsburgh that Shanahan had alluded to in our first training-camp team meeting, barely losing to the Colts and beating the Steelers. After a win over Oakland, the team is 7-2. But Jake is blamed for consecutive defeats and for the team's failure to score early in the season. Before the second loss, at Kansas City, someone leaks word that Jake is on notice. Even though the Broncos remain in good position for a wild-card playoff berth, Shanahan demotes him. Cutler, the coach says, gives the team "the best chance to win."

I fly to Denver for the rookie's debut, against Seattle. "You don't have to be a genius," Shanahan says outside the media room at the facility, justifying his decision. "How many points did we have in the last eleven games?" But there were other, obvious problems besides Jake. Left tackle Matt Lepsis tore an ACL. Starting running back Tatum Bell sprained both big toes. Rod Smith's hip was ailing. After a strong start, the defense had faltered. But none of that appeared to matter, nor did the fact that Jake was 40-18 as the Broncos' starting quarterback in the regular season and playoffs.

I watch the game with Ted Sundquist and his staff, and it's clear to me they don't agree with the change. A few weeks earlier, Sundquist had told me he didn't feel Jake was the sole reason for the offense's poor play. On Cutler's first series, the Broncos run three plays and punt. "Same result," someone says. When Cutler fumbles a snap, Sundquist remarks, "He did that about three times in practice." Someone else replies, "I heard six." Then, as he is hit by a defensive lineman, Cutler wings the ball blindly into the air. It's intercepted and returned for a touchdown. Pens and binoculars fly in our box high above the field.

Shortly before the end of the first half, Jason lines up for a 43-yard field goal. Mike Leach snaps. Jake Plummer catches—and flips the ball blindly over his right shoulder.

"Oh my God!" I shout. "They're doing it!"

It's Rainbow Right, the play we had practiced only once, because Shanahan never calls fake field goals. Jason catches the ball and runs to the right as if fleeing a tidal wave. He slides for the first down. Jeff Hays and I high-five. Then we realize from the replay that Jason has pulled a hamstring. Later, we learn that he had talked Shanahan into the trick play, with the idea of scoring a touchdown.

With Denver trailing 20–13, NBC flashes a graphic: Jake Plummer has led thirty game-tying or -winning drives in the fourth quarter or overtime, the most in the NFL during his career. A Cutler touchdown pass ties the game. But the defense collapses. Seattle drives downfield and kicks a game-winning 50-yard field goal with five seconds to play.

In the locker room afterward, Cutler tells Jake that the team would have won had he been playing.

At 8 a.m. three days after the game, I meet Jake in the lunchroom. "Bad enough I got benched," he cracks. "Now I got this fucking guy wanting to interview me."

Since he was replaced, Jake has politely refused to speak to the media. He tells me he doesn't want to stir controversy or draw attention from Cutler, and also that he needs to remain cool in case Cutler fails or is hurt. But he is furious. Jake acknowledges that yes, he threw some interceptions early in the season and yes, the offense hadn't performed especially well. But it wasn't exclusively his fault, he says. Key passing targets from last year were gone. There were the injuries. And the play calling was tentative, especially when the Broncos had a lead. Yet the team was still in position to achieve the initial goal of every NFL franchise every season: to make the playoffs. "We're seven and four and on the peak of a wild card and they made a move that"—Jake pauses—"was the wrong move to make."

Jake believes the coaches scapegoated him for the team's broader problems, and then fed or at least failed to head off rumors that his job was on the line. "That's not a way to live, that's not a way to play," he says. "But they created that." Jake tells me he learned from the media that he wouldn't start against Seattle.

At 8:30 I point to the clock. Meetings are starting. "Ah, fuck it," Jake says, and keeps talking. I ask whether he'll play next season. He says he isn't sure but talks about his career mostly in the past tense. He talks about his time in Denver entirely in the past tense. Jake thinks that people—inside and outside the organization—will appreciate that he won a lot of games and helped restore the franchise's pride and winning tradition. But he is bitter about how he was treated this season by fans, the media, and Shanahan, who told him again that missing voluntary off-season workouts indicated to him that Jake didn't care.

"Yeah, I missed some workouts. And you know what?" Jake lowers his head to the table and talks directly into my tape recorder. "Mike Shanahan, you can kiss my fucking ass for being pissed at that. You can quote that. I made eighty-five percent of my workouts and he's still mad about it. He still brought that up. Give me a break. That's the dumbest fucking thing on earth.

"He's got to have me to be his leader," Jake says sarcastically. "Well, listen. When I'm out there on a Thursday, when everyone's half-assing it and just going through the motions, I'm the one who was calling motherfuckers out saying, 'Let's go.' No one else. Eighty-five percent workouts? Mad about that? And he's still mad about it? Well, if that's the reason [I was benched], then I'm glad I didn't make those. Because I don't want to be here every fucking day in the off-season. You don't get any escape.

"But, hey, he felt like I crossed him in some way. Once you do that, he'll never let those things go. If you cross him in some way, he'll hold on to that more than the times you've done good by him."

With a season-ending victory over a weak San Francisco team, the Broncos can make the playoffs. I attend the game in Denver on New Year's Eve. Wearing a thrift-shop western shirt, Jake saunters into the locker room around noon for a 2:15 kickoff, a couple of hours later than he would have arrived had he been starting. He had told me that he was not, for obvious reasons, studying as much as he had but felt he had better command of the weekly game plans. He thought he knew why. "When you're weighed down with all kinds of expectations and pressure, you can't learn," Jake said.

It's around thirty degrees but in the sunshine on the field it feels ten degrees warmer. No gloves. Jake and Preston play football golf, punting at targets like a goalpost or a logo on a wall. "He doesn't have a care in the world," Preston tells me. "And you know what? If he had to play I bet he'd tear it up. No worries. Call whatever plays he wanted."

The pregame locker-room scene is much like during preseason: quiet tension. Jason kicks his way across the carpet. Cutler sits with a towel draped over his head. Jake listens to his iPod and sips coffee. Shanahan and Bowlen stand in the center of the clubhouse, their butts against the counter in front of the coffee machines and framed copies of NFL regulations on uniforms and drugs. At 2:00, Shanahan shouts, "Bring it up!" He doesn't mention the stakes or the season or the score of the ongoing Kansas City game, which could allow the Broncos to get into the postseason, win or lose.

"We know what we've got to get done," he says. "Sixty minutes. Everybody play their asses off. In our backyard!" The players drop, as usual, to their knees and join hands for the Lord's Prayer. "Defense on three!" Shanahan shouts, and everyone responds. "DEE-fense!" As the players race out, Shanahan stops in the coaches' lounge, where the Kansas City–Jacksonville game is on TV. Kansas City leads 35–30 and holds the ball with two minutes to play. If the score stands, Denver will have to win or tie to qualify. Shanahan walks out, winks at me, and disappears down a tunnel to the field.

In the second quarter, Cutler is sacked and lands on his head. Sundquist calls down to the sideline: mild concussion. Jake enters the game for Cutler. "Come on, Jake," I say. On his first play, he hands off to Mike Bell, who rushes for 46 yards to San Francisco's 3-yard line. Sack, incomplete pass, scramble, Jason field goal. After Champ Bailey returns an interception 70 yards for a touchdown, the Broncos lead, 13–3.

San Francisco opens the second half with a touchdown drive. Shanahan puts Cutler back in. On his first possession, about to be sacked, Cutler throws the ball away weakly. "Oh my God! Oh my God!" Ted Sundquist shouts. A 49ers defender returns it for a touchdown. Mike Bluem grabs his hair and screams, "You've GOT to be kidding me!" And just like that, the score is 17–13, San Francisco. I learn later that Cutler was woozy but told the team doctors and coaches he could play.

As time ticks away, the outcome feels inevitable, as it has for weeks. The Broncos manage to send the game into overtime at 23–23. After three punts, the front office roots for the fifteen-minute period to expire, for the game to end tied. But San Francisco moves the ball deep into Broncos territory. "We didn't deserve to win this game." Bluem says. A 36-yard field goal ends the season.

Sundquist slams his laptop shut. Bluem slams the suite window shut. "We are so stupid sometimes," he says. Sundquist leans back, his left hand on his left knee, one black cowboy boot on the counter. A promo for *The Simpsons* on TV is the only sound in the room. I leave the executives to their misery and head to the locker room. Shanahan offers no pep talk, no congratulations, no thanks. "We'll do whatever it takes to get better," he says.

The players are disappointed—the abruptness of the end is the simplest and yet most surprising feeling—but hardly morbid. As Jake had observed, there is a winner and a loser in every football game. Everyone will stick around for a couple of days to clean out lockers and have exit physicals and performance reviews. Some won't return. The cliques of players discuss New Year's plans. I join Nate, Preston, Chad, some team staffers, and assorted family and friends at a party at a downtown club called Hush. No one is depressed, but no one is dancing on tables, either. I leave after midnight and drive back to my hotel.

At 9 a.m., the room telephone rings. I'm still sleeping. It's Preston.

"Did you hear what happened?" he asks.

"No," I say.

"D-Will was shot and killed."

Preston relays what few details he knows. Darrent Williams, the cornerback no taller than I, had left a party at another downtown nightclub, and apparently someone fired into the limousine in which he was riding with Javon Walker and some other players and friends. I dress quickly and drive to the facility.

Several players are sitting in lockers, elbows on knees. Preston, Paul Ernster, Adam Meadows, Brandon Marshall. I wouldn't protest if they asked me to leave this private space at this most private time, a place where I'm technically no longer welcome. But they don't. Some of the Broncos were no closer to D-Will than I was; it's impossible to befriend all ninety of your coworkers. But they—we—shared the ineluctable bond of the team, made stronger by the ultimate bonding experience, the incomprehensible death of one of its members. We sit in a stunned silence broken by bits of banal small talk about D-Will, about his last game, about his terrific 34-yard punt return in the second quarter.

Brandon Marshall was at the club, Shelter, and has already told his teammates what happened. He said there was a disagreement between some Broncos players and friends—including some of D-Will's buddies from home in Fort Worth, Texas—and another group. The argument spilled onto the sidewalk. One guy punched Brandon, who was intercepted by bouncers. The other group ran off. The half dozen Broncos piled into limousines, D-Will into a white stretch Hummer, Brandon into another limo. Brandon didn't learn what happened until he got home. Later, I see him weeping as he retells the story to a group of linebackers clustered near D-Will's locker, at which players and staffers stop and stare for a moment. It contains a pile of Nike cleats and sneakers, sweatshirts and T-shirts on hangers, a bottle of Nivea lotion, video cuts of the 49ers' wide receivers.

I have lunch with Preston and Bill Rader. When we return, Javon is in the locker room. Hanging in his locker is the long-sleeved white T-shirt, left side drenched in blood, that he was wearing when D-Will died in his lap. Javon is standing in shorts near the showers. He appears to be in shock. He tells Preston and me that he drove around all night. Demetrin Veal, who was in the other limo, brought Javon to the facility. Demetrin is still in his New Year's Eve clothes, a black dress shirt, black slacks, and black Chuck Taylor sneakers. In his locker, he tells me he led the Broncos players out of the club after the initial altercation.

The Hummer in which D-Will was riding drove off. A few blocks away, D-Will removed a chain and asked Javon to hold it and not lose it; apparently someone had tried to snatch it from his neck. D-Will was sitting in the far back of the Hummer on the driver's side, facing forward. Javon put the chain in his pocket and told D-Will he could afford a new one if it was lost. They didn't notice a Chevrolet Tahoe pull up alongside them. D-Will slumped onto Javon. "Get up, dog," Javon said. He didn't realize D-Will had been shot. The sounds followed: *blam blam*

blam blam blam. Fourteen shots in all. Remarkably, no one else was killed.

Drained, Preston and I go to his house. We play Scrabble as a distraction. Chad Mustard comes over and we relay Javon's account of D-Will's final moments. Chad stands near a window, crying.

When I return to Englewood in July for minicamp—as a reporter only—Jason Elam greets me on the turf field. No other kickers are around and Jason wants to practice. So, in my shorts and sandals, I hold while he drills a few 50-yarders. If the team would let me, I'd race into the locker room and change into workout clothes, stuff paper into the toes of the smallest pair of cleats I could find, and kick—out-of-shape hip flexor be damned.

In short, I've missed being here. No matter how contented I am in my real life, no matter how contentious, disappointing, and ultimately tragic the 2006 season was for the Broncos, no matter how the players may dread another training camp, the sense of renewal is present, and I feel it.

Thirty-seven now, Jason tells me he feels great. He made 27 field goals in 29 attempts in 2006, a career-best 93 percent. I attribute his success to pressure from the rookie placekicker challenging him in camp. While I hold, Jason reports that in the off-season he taught Iranian Christian clerics in Istanbul and took a weeklong course in apologetics at Oxford. He also enrolled in a master's program in the subject at Jerry Falwell's Liberty University, where he told a theology class he wants to be prepared to convert any of the five billion followers of the world's twelve major religions. He finished writing *Monday Night Jihad* and began a sequel.

In 2007, Jason makes four last-second game-winning field goals, one in the fire drill known as Geronimo (now named Toro) that we practiced at summer's end. Overall, he goes 27 for 31, records another 100-plus-point season, and climbs to sixth in NFL career scoring and fifth in career field goals. But Jason is without a contract at season's end. He tells me he doesn't want to leave Denver, but if he has to he'll play somewhere else—preferably in warm weather or a dome, certainly not for a northern team like New England. "Too many Democrats up there," he half quipped to me once.

Jason watches the Super Bowl with troops in Iraq, makes another Holy Land tour, promotes his book on Bill O'Reilly's radio show, and waits. When the Broncos offer a three-year contract with only a small signing bonus and no promises beyond the coming season, Jason explores the free-agent market. When the Atlanta Falcons offer a four-year deal with $3.3 million guaranteed, and an earnest commitment beyond 2008, age be damned, the Broncos don't budge. So Jason leaves Denver for his childhood home, heart in hand, the longest-tenured player in franchise history. Fans and teammates alike are shocked.

At the 2007 minicamp bowling tournament, I sit down with one of the players who had eluded me the previous summer: Todd Sauerbrun.

Yes, Todd is back. He was jobless until New England signed him with two games remaining in 2006. A contractual error made Todd a free agent. Saying he had been humbled and had matured, Todd asked Shanahan for another chance. This time, he had more than his leg going for him. In the off-season, Shanahan shifted Ronnie Bradford from special-teams coach to assistant defensive-backs coach and hired Scott O'Brien, who had coached Todd with Carolina. O'Brien didn't keep Thomas McGaughey, who joined the New York Giants, and he declined the services of kicking consultant Jeff Hays. The Broncos gave Todd a one-year contract worth $820,000—the veteran minimum—with another $600,000 in incentives. "I'm not worried about what other people think," Shanahan tells me. "But I'm not blind going into this."

Todd apologizes, sort of, for how he treated me. "You caught me real bitter, man. And I feel real bad about that," he says over the clatter of pins. "I had nothing good to say. I was extremely upset. I didn't understand what was going to happen with my life." What especially angered him, and still does, is how his transgression was treated. "We have murderers in the league. We have repeat DUI offenders. Repeat drug offenders. And they're still playing like nothing's happened. It makes me so angry."

I ask why his past is any different from theirs. Todd says his drunk-driving conviction was a one-time offense and, without confirming or denying anything, that the steroids allegations were just that, allegations. And the ephedra? "I swear on my kid's life on this one," he says. "I took it twice. I don't even like it. I just felt like I needed it. And I knew it was going to be out of my system in a day, two days. I think they came to my house and tested me that day. I was like, 'This can't be happening.'" Todd says he didn't realize that because of his conviction, he faced an automatic suspension. "But I did it. What's done is done."

Once suspended, Todd says he had a gut feeling the Broncos would dump him, regardless of how Paul Ernster performed. He knew R.B. and T-Mac didn't like him, and that the team would save money. Now, though, with O'Brien as his coach, Todd says he is finally having fun. "I fucked it up, man," he says. "I'm mad at myself for that. I could have been set for the rest of my life. Now it's been put off."

As usual, Todd kicks the ball far, averaging 46.8 yards per kick in 2007, fifth in the NFL. But that doesn't mean he kicks well. His net average of 36.1 yards is twenty-fourth in the league—implying that his hang times were poor (and the Broncos' coverage was, too). The low point comes against his former team, Chicago. Before the game, Todd tells reporters the Broncos won't direct the ball away from the Bears' superb returner, Devin Hester. Hester returns a punt and a kickoff for touchdowns, and the Bears also block a punt.

Then, early one Saturday morning in December, Todd is cited by Denver police after allegedly slapping a taxi driver who ordered him out of his cab for acting belligerently. He spends the night in a city detox facility. Todd disputes the cabbie's version of events. "Never happened," he says. Shanahan cuts him anyway, saying police told the Broncos that Todd was abusive to officers.

———————

Paul Ernster winds up out of the league, too. After displacing Todd, Paul leads the NFL in kickoff distance and produces the third-most touchbacks. His punting numbers aren't as impressive. Of thirty-two punters with at least forty kicks, Paul finishes twenty-eighth with a gross average of 41.7 yards. R.B. tells me late in the 2006 season that Paul sometimes is "like a deer in the headlights." Against Seattle, he runs onto the field to punt still wearing a white Broncos ski cap. "Where's your fucking helmet?" a referee yells at him. Shanahan gives him an earful, too.

Still, in what amounts to a rookie season, Paul does well enough—and is still sufficiently young and strong-legged—that the Broncos could let him develop further. But when Shanahan hires Todd and his former mentor, Paul doesn't stand a chance. After the third preseason game, Paul gets cut. "All they told me was to not be like Todd," he says. "Who's the guy they keep bringing back every time?"

Just before opening day, Paul beats out a few other kickers, including Micah Knorr, to fill in for Cleveland's injured punter. Paul drops his first snap—in the end zone—and awkwardly manages a 15-yard punt. He does fine the rest of the game, but is released a week later. At another tryout, Paul reunites with Micah. Neither punter is hired.

Micah tells me he turned down a job as a middle-school history teacher and coach to attend Detroit's 2007 training camp. He had no illusions of making the team, he says. Instead, he went to learn more about coaching and to make contacts; he plans to look for entry-level positions at small colleges. Meantime, he takes a $15-an-hour job driving a forklift in a Wal-Mart warehouse. "My agent keeps saying, 'Hold on, hold on,'" Micah says. "Nah. It's over, dude."

Paul has a few more in-season auditions. Then, when Todd is released, the Broncos sign him for the final two games of 2007, and two more seasons, possibly, after that. "There is absolutely no pressure," Paul tells me. "No matter what I do, I'm still not Todd." Paul joins the team on a Tuesday. He says the special-teams coaches aren't told in advance. He says they force him to alter his punting mechanics. In his first game back, Paul kicks terribly—he shanks his first punt 17 yards—and the Broncos cut him two days later.

Jake Plummer sticks to his word to go out on his own terms and never look back. In March 2007, Jake announces his retirement. A day later, the Broncos trade him to Tampa Bay for a draft choice. The Buccaneers try to persuade Jake to play, sending a team official to track him down in Idaho. Jake holds firm. He is on the hook for about $7 million in pro-rated bonus money that Tampa Bay could attempt to reclaim, but he apparently doesn't care. Jake vacations in Belize, gets married, and vanishes into a quiet life in a small town in an outdoor recreational paradise in northern Idaho. He leaves grants of $50,000 apiece for the Alzheimer's disease and at-risk-youth organizations in Colorado that he had supported, and resurfaces to visit his alma mater, Arizona State, and to play in a couple of handball tournaments with his brother. At one of those events, in Denver, Jake tells reporters they won't see him in an NFL jersey unless Preston Parsons gets into a game and Jake dons his friend's number 5 in support.

Ted Sundquist tells Preston that while the team can't promise anything, he believes Preston can be the number two quarterback. He says Preston will have an advantage over a veteran signed for the 2007 training camp because he knows the system. "It would break my heart if they were blowing smoke up my ass," Preston says. "But I don't think they are."

In March, while at the movies, Preston gets a text message: The Broncos signed Patrick Ramsey, a former first-round pick and starter in Washington, to be the backup. Ramsey's contract is for $4.5 million over two years, including $1.5 million guaranteed—amounts that all but doom Preston's chances. In the first week of training camp, Preston develops the yips, inexplicably firing passes into the ground. He recovers, but as he jogs on to join the third string one morning, Mike Heimerdinger tells him that he's been demoted to number four. Preston throws four passes in the final preseason game. He says it's not even fun.

Quarterbacks topple like dominoes during the 2007 NFL season. Carolina even signs forty-three-year-old Vinny Testaverde. But Preston gets only one tryout, in Miami. He is frustrated again, and his family and friends, including me, don't help by pestering him whenever a quarterback gets hurt. He attends a tryout for an arena football team in San Jose, California, and pronounces it a joke. "The frustrating part is I know I can still play, I know I can be on a team," Preston says. "I bounce back and forth between being okay with it and going, 'I fucked up something really good.'"

As the season ends, Preston accepts that his career is in all likelihood over. He doesn't want to be a camp arm, doesn't want to just hang on. He makes contacts in real estate and other businesses. In January 2008, his wife gives birth to their first child, Cole Thomas Parsons. Then, on the same day in March, Preston files retirement papers with the NFL and accepts a job as a regional representative for a company that makes devices used in spinal surgery. The burden of football lifted, Preston feels instantly changed. "Honest to God, I have never been so happy in my life," he says. His wife tells him, "I'm prouder of you now than whenever you played football."

Bradlee Van Pelt's football story doesn't end well, either. Midway through the 2006 season, Houston signs him to replace its injured backup. But Bradlee gets cut at the end of the 2007 training camp and gets no feelers. He returns to his mother's house in Santa Barbara, California, stays in shape, and tries to figure out whether to keep playing.

Bradlee doesn't return messages from me for more than a year. Finally, in late 2007, he calls. He says he didn't want to relive his summer in Denver and didn't want to talk about what happened in Houston, either. The Texans never gave him a chance to compete for the number two job, he says, and he didn't get many throws as the number three, so naturally he stressed when he did. "The more I struggled with football, the more I struggled out of football," he says. "It collapsed on me."

Bradlee says he moped for a couple of months, then vowed to stop letting football control his emotions. He takes a two-day introductory sommelier seminar, with an eye toward working in the retail wine business. He says he'll consider playing in Canada—if the right NFL camp offer doesn't come. "I'm okay with it," Bradlee says. "I feel like I can get back to being that person I was before my shell started to crack."

A couple of months later, the Hamilton Tiger-Cats of the Canadian league offer Bradlee a contract. It would be a way, his agent tells him, to play in actual games, and play without the pressure of believing that every throw needs to be perfect. If he did well, the NFL could become possible again. Bradlee deliberates for a week and turns it down. He's taken a job managing a wine-tasting room and, given the comparatively low pay in Canada, doesn't want to fall behind in his new career. With his dream of playing quarterback in the NFL dead, Bradlee lets his agent tell teams that he is willing to do what he has refused for years to do: change positions.

During the 2006 season, I keep a close eye on NFL player transactions, rooting for my ex-teammates to find jobs. When in mid-October Atlanta signs offensive lineman P. J. Alexander, I smile and check the schedule. The Falcons visit Baltimore a few weeks later. I walk onto the field after the game.

"Fatsis!" P.J. says. He wraps me in a sweaty, three-hundred-pound hug.

"You got a job!" I say.

"I got a job. That's all that matters."

I ask about his knees.

"They're burning. Both of them."

"How's the bad one?"

"It's bad."

In the locker room, P.J. tells me that, after an injury to one lineman and the suspension of another, he got the first start of his NFL career. The Baltimore game was his fourth straight start. "Funny business, man," he says. "Funny business. There's nothing you can do to predict. I'm just riding it. Ride it as long as I can ride it." P.J. tells me that his girlfriend had a baby girl, Laiila. He asks me to say hello to some of his former teammates in Denver.

The following week, P.J. is out of the lineup and doesn't play again the rest of the season. Atlanta cuts him at the end of the 2007 training camp. But, after season-ending injuries to starters Tom Nalen (torn biceps) and Ben Hamilton (concussion), P.J. rejoins the Broncos in October and plays in ten games.

Months after the 9-7 season that follows my stay at camp, Ted Sundquist retraces the strategic upgrades and expensive re-signings that the front office believed would be enough to get the team to the Super Bowl. "And we failed," he says. The whys might be explicable—injuries, poor play on defense, the quarterback controversy, the fact that other teams are trying, too—but they don't make the failure any easier to accept. "I've forgotten a lot about last year," Pat Bowlen tells me, "except some of the more critical things, like what happened the night after the game we lost that kept us out of the playoffs."

Bowlen extends Mike Shanahan's contract through 2011. With a reported annual salary of at least $6 million, the new deal is less a reward for a job well done than a renewal of marriage vows. "He might as well know that I have the faith in him until he and I both agree it's probably the end of his coaching career," Bowlen says.

Shanahan and Sundquist uncharacteristically overhaul the coaching staff and the roster, signing several big-ticket free agents. But while Jay Cutler shows flashes of a solid career to come, the 2007 season is even worse than 2006. The offense stalls near the end zone, the defense is among the worst in the league, the special teams allow one big play after another. A raft of injuries and a stream of locker-room distractions don't help; when it comes to character, the 2007 team won't be one of Shanahan's best "group of guys." Shanahan and Sundquist sign and release an average of three players per week, twice as many as AFC champion New England, and the team enjoys little of the continuity or consistency necessary for success in the Rube Goldbergian NFL. At 7-9, Shanahan posts just his second losing season as head coach of the Broncos.

His response: a virtual staff overhaul, More coaches go, including Mike Heimerdinger, Shanahan's college roommate, who leaves to run the offense for Tennessee, and a defensive coordinator who lasted a single season. Then, late one afternoon in March, Shanahan calls Ted Sundquist into his office and, without warning, fires him.

It is, to me, a stunningly cold end to an effective if not close relationship. But when teams lose, contrasting management styles that once looked like useful checks become irritants—Sundquist opposing Jake Plummer's benching, for instance, or wanting to re-sign Jason Elam. Before the 2007 season, Shanahan had, without Sundquist's knowledge, brought in a front-office consultant. After Sundquist made some benign comments about the team to a reporter, Shanahan barred him from his weekly local TV show and from blogging on the Bronco's Web site. Then Shanahan promoted to assistant GM a young scout with a law degree but just two years with the team and ordered Sundquist to keep him in the loop on all decisions. Shanahan took responsibility for the team's on-field woes, but he also had the power to show everyone else the door.

Pat Bowlen says Sundquist's firing is the inevitable result of clashing personalities, and that he is the ultimate check on the coach. But Bowlen also is on the hook for Shanahan's costly contract extension. Before cleaning out his office, Sundquist meets with Bowlen for an hour. The owner tells him that his dismissal—after sixteen years with the team—wasn't related to performance. "I understand the game well enough to know that he had no other recourse but to support his head coach and vice president of football operations," Sundquist tells me a few weeks later when I ask about the firing. "It was very hard saying good-bye."

———

This bit of where-are-they-now about my Broncos is, I realize, kind of depressing, a recitation of recidivist bad behavior, failed performances, broken dreams, ruthless, sometimes misguided management, and even death. Almost every player I befriended suffers some ignominy: released once, released multiple times, benched, injured slightly, injured badly, injured and released, injured and benched and released, treated like a magnet on a whiteboard and little more. Of the more than one hundred men who spent time with the Broncos while I was in Denver, just half are in training camp in 2007, less than a third on the roster in September. Even by the league's revolving-door standards, the turnover is substantial.

Charlie Adams is released by the Broncos two weeks into the 2006 season and then by Houston after the 2007 training camp. Tyler Fredrickson is cut by Dallas in the 2006 training camp and by Washington in 2007. After a terrific 2007 camp, Nate Jackson earns his first-ever start—and promptly tears a groin muscle. Chad Mustard is released at the end of the 2007 camp, then re-signed and released, re-signed and released, and re-signed again during the season. Ian Gold is released after the season.

Against Seattle in 2006, Al Wilson is carted off the field on a backboard. The team diagnoses a neck sprain but says the symptoms subside and Al plays the following Sunday. In the off-season, Denver decides to part ways with its veteran captain. When another team, the Giants, declares Al unfit to play, his new agent files a collective-bargaining grievance against the Broncos, asserting that before allowing him back on the field, the team failed to inform him that his injury could worsen with further play. The Broncos maintain that a bulging disc and narrowing of the spinal column that showed up on X-rays and MRIs existed prior to the injury. An arbitrator hears Al's case in March 2008.

Adam Meadows plays in just three games in 2006, returns for 2007, gets overworked in camp, and tears a calf muscle. He ends his career with a contract grievance against the Broncos and a settlement. Adam tells me he has no regrets about attempting a comeback, but that his final summer left a bad taste. "The bottom line is if you don't take care of yourself," he says, "no one is going to take care of you."

Kyle Johnson's follow-up might be the most revealing about the NFL life I witnessed. He sits out the final preseason game of 2007 with the other starters. The next day, he gets cut. Everyone is stunned, Kyle most of all. Ted Sundquist doesn't know what to say and sends him to Shanahan, who offers that the team decided to "go in a different direction" and had other running backs who "can do what you do." Kyle doesn't challenge Shanahan or even ask for further explanation because he knows he could be back. Sure enough, the day before Thanksgiving, the Broncos ask him to play, possibly for just one game. Kyle reluctantly returns, arriving at the facility at 6:15 on Thanksgiving morning. Shanahan greets him as if nothing had happened.

"You're kidding, right?" Kyle tells me a couple of weeks later. "I think about it now, it's almost ridiculous. Regardless of how he makes decisions, regardless of how that may apply on the gridiron, I'm a human who feels emotion. They almost try to apply the same sort of surreality to you as an individual that they do to you as a pawn in the chess game of football. It ratifies the idea that after all this time, they don't know anything about you." Kyle plays that next Sunday and is released on Tuesday.

I don't consider Kyle and Preston and Todd and the rest to be tragic figures in some giant morality play. That would exaggerate the importance of what they do for a living. But their fates convince me more than ever that the NFL, with its conga line of talent, the short attention span of its front offices, and the disposability of its players, is the most unmeritocratic of our professional sports leagues. My experience didn't make me more cynical about the NFL. It just showed me what players endure to get there and what they experience once they arrive. And it revealed the deep disconnect between what fans see on game day and what happens the rest of the week. As Nick Ferguson (who is benched midway through 2007 and signs with Houston after the season) says, recalling my palpitating moments in the training-camp glare, "Every time you see a game and it's the last second on the clock, now you know."

Yes, now I know. I will never criticize an athlete for dropping a pass or clanging a jump shot or striking out—and certainly not for missing a field goal. But for everything I know about pressure and performance, almost two years later I still wonder why they bother. It's easy to see why Jason Elam keeps playing. But why does Tyler Fredrickson? Why does Al Wilson, who wants to get back on the field in 2008? Why are they willing to suffer in the name of this game?

In these pages, the players answered for themselves, some more convincingly than others. I don't think the complete answer is the money, or the camaraderie, or the women, or the adrenaline rush, or the avoidance of a comparatively humdrum workplace. I think they play because they *can* play. Like anyone lucky enough to possess some exceedingly rare skill, they want to use it until they lose it. If at age twenty I could have made one monster field goal after another, I would have kicked for as long as the system let me. I think they play because they're like addicts trying to recover the feeling of that first, blissful high. And I think they play because they are as irrationally hopeful as any of us.

Making it in the NFL—and by that I mean enduring beyond the statistically average three-point-something seasons, to where the money gets serious—is, as I witnessed, not a little bit arbitrary. Just about everyone in training camp was capable of playing in the league. Not everyone was deemed worthy of playing at that particular moment in time. The players tolerate the physical and emotional indignities of the NFL because their entire lives have led them there. But they do it also because they believe that playing football is like pulling the lever on a slot machine. Three pineapples will pop up eventually. Why not act like the Omega pledges getting paddled in *Animal House*? Thank you, sir! May I have another?

"Everyone wants to say they could walk away from football," Bradlee Van Pelt observed during our post-football conversation. "But if football calls, they come back. They almost have a stranglehold on you. They have you exactly where they want you."

Football wouldn't be calling me. So I ended my NFL career the way the self-aware—or lucky—player does: without clawing to stay in the game, without illusion, without bitterness, without regret. When I removed my pads in the visitors' locker room at University of Phoenix Stadium in Glendale, Arizona, I was a football player no more. I wouldn't join a weekend semipro team, wouldn't return to Paul Woodside's camps to hone my technique, wouldn't kick another football, period. But I'm damn proud of what I accomplished as an athlete. I will dine out on the 40-yarders I made—and the short kicks that I missed, too—as long as anyone will listen.

Among Giants

A few days before training camp, I spent an afternoon at the East Seventy-second Street town house where George Plimpton wrote *Paper Lion,* edited *The Paris Review,* and entertained the literary beau monde. My host, his more-than-twenty-years-younger widow, Sarah, wasn't around during *Paper Lion.* But she described to me how much the book meant to Plimpton. Not only because it established his literary and popular bona fides, but because it charted the course of his life. Plimpton already had written *Out of My League,* about pitching to baseball all-stars, which Ernest Hemingway had lauded. But life among the Lions was the clincher. "I think it all just came together for him," Sarah told me. "He found his audience."

Paper Lion, she said, convinced Plimpton that he wanted to be "among giants." In the early 1960s, that word still could be applied to athletes, and Plimpton sought to understand and explain what made them so magnificent. "I don't think we see them as people anymore," Sarah observed. "They're cardboard figures in a way. They're not heroes. 'Heroes' is something people of George's generation grew up with. I don't think ours did. Heroes are people with great values and substance in addition to whatever brilliance they brought to what they did. George was writing about being with heroes."

I am indebted to Plimpton, of course, for the idea of joining an NFL team, but also for a belief that what great athletes do is extraordinary and, despite today's ceaseless coverage, poorly understood. I didn't view the Broncos as heroes, though, because I agree with Sarah that contemporary culture allows little room for them. I just wanted to humanize them, to show them as more than the commodities they've become: bundles of stats in fantasy games, extras in a multibillion-dollar marketing enterprise. But I'd happily swap some of our cynicism about sports and sportspeople for Plimpton's romantic notion of the jock as hero.

Sarah recalled for me how the Lions honored Plimpton in 2003 with a fortieth reunion of his summer at Cranbrook, the boys' school where the team had trained. She said he was excited for months about seeing his old teammates. Forty players attended a banquet the night before a game against Minnesota at Ford Field. During a halftime ceremony, each of the 1963 Lions received a period helmet with Plimpton's number 0 on the back. Plimpton was an honorary team captain for the day. Sarah showed me a photo from the event. In it she senses completeness. "There's a look of absolute transcendence on his face," she said. "His life had come full circle." Four days later, Plimpton died at home in his sleep. He was seventy-six.

Even if the Broncos don't throw a party for me in 2046, I was privileged to have joined their world for a short time. I first owe heartfelt gratitude to Pat Bowlen, Mike Shanahan, and Ted Sundquist, who supplied me with a locker, a uniform, unrestricted access, and their trust. If I could kick as well as they do their jobs, I'd still be in the league.

To Ronnie Bradford, Thomas McGaughey, and Jeff Hays: thanks for the time, expertise, humor, and candor—and for treating me like just another kicker. The rest of the coaching staff welcomed me into meetings, answered my Football 101 questions, and ensured I didn't hurt myself. Special thanks to Tim Brewster, Mike Heimerdinger, Pat McPherson, Andre Patterson, Bob Slowik, Cedric Smith, Jimmy Spencer, Rich Tuten, and Steve Watson.

Kickers rule, especially Jason Elam, Paul Ernster, Tyler Fredrickson, Micah Knorr, and Todd Sauerbrun. They tolerated my weak leg and open notebook with near-total patience. Bottle it, guys.

A locker room is a sacred place. I'm grateful to all of the 2006 Broncos for sharing theirs with me. My friendships with Nate Jackson and Preston Parsons will extend beyond our football careers. Charlie Adams, P. J. Alexander, Stephen Alexander, Keith Burns, Nick Ferguson, Domonique Foxworth, Kyle Johnson, Mike Leach, Adam Meadows, Chad Mustard, Jake Plummer, Tony Scheffler, Bradlee Van Pelt, and Al Wilson were especially generous with their time—and especially good to me. The following players also sat for interviews or helped in other ways: Mike Bell, Cooper Carlisle, Javiar Collins, Jay Cutler, Ron Dayne, George Foster, Ian Gold, Amon Gordon, Cornell Green, Ben Hamilton, Rob Hunt, David Kircus, Matt Lepsis, John Lynch, Patrice Majondo-Mwamba, Brandon Marshall, Brandon Miree, Chris Myers, Tom Nalen, Erik Pears, Jeff Shoate, Rod Smith, Landon Trusty, Demetrin Veal, Javon Walker, Gerard Warren, Ray Wells, Darrent Williams, and Jeff Williams.

The Broncos' public relations, football operations, and business staffs were always accommodating but never intrusive. Thanks to Mike Bluem, Dave Bratten, Chip Conway, Kate Doll, Joe Ellis, Fred Fleming, Dave Gaylinn, Brad Gee, Jim Goodman, Aaron Kalina, Paul Kirk, Betsy Klein, Ed Lambert, Cindi Lowe, Mike Mascenik, Adam Newman, Pam Papsdorf, Denver Parler, Bill Rader, Jim Saccomano, Patrick Smyth, Chris Trulove, Rebecca Villanueva, Lisa Williams, and Meghan Zobeck. On the equipment, training, medical, turf, and video staffs, thanks to Steve Antonopoulos, Bob Carpenter, Kenny Chavez, Kent Erickson, Mike Harrington, Kirt Horiuchi, Rawley Klingsmith, Gary McCune, Corey Oshikoya, Greg Roskopf, Jason Schell, Ted Schlegel, Troy Smith, Scott Trulock, and Chris Valenti.

With intelligence, wit, and zero tolerance for my excuses, Steve Kostorowski of the Water Street Gym in Washington, D.C., turned me into something resembling an athlete. Thanks to Jeff Halpern for introducing us.

While I wish Paul Woodside had enjoyed a record-setting NFL career, for selfish reasons I'm glad he didn't. Paul is not only the most inspiring—and effective—coach I've known, he's one of the most inspiring people, too. For not laughing at the old guy, I'm grateful to his student kickers, especially Eric Bjonerud and Anthony Perlozzo.

Speaking of kickers, Ben Agajanian, Morten Andersen, Jess Atkinson, Jim Bakken, Doug Brien, Brad Daluiso, Hank Hartong, Mark Moseley, Peter Gogolak, and Jan Stenerud shared their knowledge and memories. So did Gil Brandt, Bill Curry, Marv Levy, Dan Reeves, Mark Schlereth, and Dick Vermeil.

I was almost a Baltimore Raven. Thanks to Dick Cass and Kevin Byrne for trying, Matt Stover for teaching, David McDuff for head-shrinking, and Jeff Friday for advising about weight lifting.

Brian McCarthy and Greg Aiello at the NFL could have stopped this project at the line of scrimmage. I'm grateful they didn't. Their colleague Dan Masonson patiently answered statistical queries. Dave Kelly at the Library of Congress and Joe Horrigan, Pete Fierle, and Ryan Rebholz at the Pro Football Hall of Fame provided research assistance. Doug West of Reebok pretended that I was an actual player, which was very cool. My orthopedic surgeon, Dr. Thomas Wickiewicz of the Hospital for Special Surgery in New York, took time for a consultation and pep talk.

For treating me like a player while reminding me that I was a reporter, among other courtesies, I'm grateful to Mike Klis and Bill Williamson of the *Denver Post* and Jeff Legwold of the *Rocky Mountain News*. Thanks also to Aaron Schatz of Football Outsiders, Adam Schefter of the NFL Network, Pat Graham of the Associated Press, Josh Levin of Slate, Will Leitch of Deadspin, Robert Lipsyte, Drew Magary, and John Thorn. For providing photographs, I'm extremely thankful to Ryan McKee and Trevor Brown of Rich Clarkson and Associates, John Leyba, and Andrew Mason and Kyle Sonneman of DenverBroncos.com. NFL Films generously granted permission for the use of league footage of me in photo form. Many thanks there to Jeanne Diblin and Chris Barlow, and to Phil Aromando of Hock Films.

Rich Turner of *The Wall Street Journal* graciously arranged a leave of absence. My friends Jonathan Hock, Steve McKee, S. L. Price, and Jon Weinbach read portions of this manuscript and offered excellent suggestions. Neenah Ellis took my picture, and she and Noah Adams supplied, as they always do, advice, support, and friendship. Chris Di-Manna provided computer help. Jonathan and Lynn Hock and Bob Rifkin and Jane Levin put me up during my travels. (Nate Jackson and Paul Ernster did, too.) Chuck Heaphy and CeCe Nie supplied a quiet place to write. My brother Lampros and my nephew Michael joined my first attempt at kicking a football.

This is where the author says how incredibly lucky he is to work with his agent and his editor. I mean it. I've known Robert Shepard, my agent, since the day I walked into our college newspaper more than a quarter century ago. I trust him on matters of business and words, and I cherish our friendship. This book began at another publishing house, but Eamon Dolan saw fit to take it, and me, with him to his new job. He is the rare editor whose judgments I (almost) never dispute, because they are indisputably right—and that's about as big a compliment as a stubborn writer can offer. At the Penguin Press, I'd also like to thank Ann Godoff for bringing me aboard (and for the hospitality), as well as Laura Stickney, Adam Goldberger, Darren Haggar, and Sarah Hutson.

A kicker is nothing without his snapper and holder. Mine—my wife, Melissa Block, and our daughter, Chloe—make my life easier than an extra point and more fulfilling than a 50-yarder ever could be.

Secrets of Kicking the Football

This book is based on my experiences, observations, and reporting in 2005 and 2006 as a kicker-in-training and a nonroster member of the Denver Broncos. Team owner Pat Bowlen, head coach Mike Shanahan, and general manager Ted Sundquist imposed no restrictions on me. They didn't ask to (and didn't) review the manuscript before publication. They also didn't compel players, coaches, or staff members to talk to me, but almost without exception everyone I asked for help provided it. I conducted more than one hundred interviews, all of which offered insight but not all of which I was able to include directly, and I relied on numerous newspaper and magazine stories. Below are some books and articles about football and kicking that were especially helpful, or were just fun to read.

Blount, Roy Jr. *About Three Bricks Shy of a Load.* Boston: Little, Brown and Company, 1974.

Carroll, Bob, Pete Palmer, and John Thorn. *The Hidden Game of Football: The Next Edition.* New York: Total Sports, 1998.

Denver Broncos 2006 Media Guide. Denver: Denver Broncos Football Club, 2006.

Erb, Charles. *The Lost Art of Kicking.* Los Angeles: Adohr Milk Farms, 1940.

Gay, Timothy. *Football Physics: The Science of the Game.* New York: Rodale, 2004.

Gillette, Gary, et al. *The ESPN Pro Football Encyclopedia.* New York: Sterling Publishing Co., 2006.

Gogolak, Pete. *Kicking the Football Soccer Style.* New York: Atheneum, 1972.

Gogolak, Peter, with Joseph Carter. *Nothing to Kick About.* New York: Dodd, Mead & Company, 1973.

Groza, Lou. *The Toe: The Lou Groza Story.* Cleveland: Gray & Company, 1996.

Herrigel, Eugen. *Zen in the Art of Archery.* New York: Vintage Books, 1989.

Kramer, Jerry, and Dick Schaap. *Instant Replay: The Green Bay Diary of Jerry Kramer.* New York: The New American Library Inc., 1968, and New York: Doubleday, 2006.

MacCambridge, Michael. *America's Game: The Epic Story of How Pro Football Captured a Nation.* New York: Random House, 2004.

Maraniss, David. *When Pride Still Mattered: A Life of Vince Lombardi.* New York: Simon & Schuster, 1999.

Meggyesy, Dave. *Out of Their League.* Berkeley, California: Ramparts Press, 1970, and Lincoln, Nebraska: University of Nebraska Press, 2005.

Mills, Leroy N. *Kicking the American Football.* New York: G.P. Putnam's Sons, 1932.

Official 2006 NFL Record & Fact Book. New York: National Football League, 2006.

Oriard, Michael. *The End of Autumn: Reflections on My Life in Football.* New York: Doubleday, 1982.

Plimpton, George. *Mad Ducks and Bears.* New York: Random House, 1973.

———. *One More July: A Football Dialogue with Bill Curry.* New York: Harper & Row, 1977.

———. *Paper Lion.* New York: Harper & Row, 1966, and Guilford, Connecticut: The Lyons Press, 1993.

Schatz, Aaron, et al. *Pro Football Prospectus 2005.* New York: Workman Publishing, 2005.

———. *Pro Football Prospectus 2006.* New York: Workman Publishing, 2006.

Shanahan, Mike, with Adam Schefter. *Think Like a Champion: Building Success One Victory at a Time.* New York: HarperBusiness, 1999.

Storey, Dr. Edward J. *Secrets of Kicking the Football.* New York: G.P. Putnam's Sons, 1971.

Sullivan, George. *Pro Football's Kicking Game.* New York: Dodd, Mead & Company, 1973.

Wind, Herbert Warren. "The Sporting Scene: Placekicking." *The New Yorker,* January 18, 1982.